AF334757

Society Women and
Enlightened Charity in Spain

NEW **HISPANISMS**

Cultural and Literary Studies

ANNE J. CRUZ, SERIES EDITOR

Society Women and Enlightened Charity in Spain

The Junta de Damas de Honor y Mérito, 1787–1823

EDITED BY Catherine M. Jaffe
AND Elisa Martín-Valdepeñas Yagüe

Louisiana State University Press | Baton Rouge

Published by Louisiana State University Press
lsupress.org

Manufactured in the United States of America
First printing

DESIGNER: Michelle A. Neustrom
TYPEFACE: Adobe Jenson Pro

COVER ILLUSTRATION: *Francisca María Dávila Carrillo de Albornoz, Countess of Truillas,* by Agustín Esteve, 1797. Collection of the Real e Ilustre Junta de Damas de Honor y Mérito, Madrid.

LIBRARY OF CONGRESS CATALOGING-IN-PUBLICATION DATA

Names: Jaffe, Catherine Marie, 1958– editor. | Martín-Valdepeñas Yagüe, Elisa, editor.
Title: Society women and enlightened charity in Spain : the Junta de Damas de Honor y Mérito, 1787–1823 / edited by Catherine M. Jaffe and Elisa Martín-Valdepeñas Yagüe.
Description: Baton Rouge : Louisiana State University Press, [2022] | Series: New Hispanisms: cultural and literary studies | Includes bibliographical references and index.
Identifiers: LCCN 2021034379 (print) | LCCN 2021034380 (ebook) | ISBN 978-0-8071-7680-1 (cloth) | ISBN 978-0-8071-7704-4 (adobe pdf) | ISBN 978-0-8071-7705-1 (epub)
Subjects: LCSH: Junta de Damas de Honor y Mérito. | Women in charitable work—Spain—History—18th century | Women in charitable work—Spain—History—19th century.
Classification: LCC HV342 .J86 2022 (print) | LCC HV342 (ebook) | DDC 361.30946/09033—dc23
LC record available at https://lccn.loc.gov/2021034379
LC ebook record available at https://lccn.loc.gov/2021034380

Contents

III. The Junta de Damas' Contributions to Enlightenment Projects

Acknowledgments

We would like to gratefully recognize the support and generosity of our colleagues whose help and advice made this international scholarly collaboration possible. Anne J. Cruz provided the initial impetus and vision for this project, and timely conversations we had with Mónica Bolufer, María Victoria López-Cordón, Elizabeth Franklin Lewis, Silvia Bermúdez, Roberta Johnson, David Gies, Pedro Álvarez de Miranda, María Jesús García Garrosa, and Jesusa Vega helped us to refine and shape our plans for the book. We are indebted to their insights and collegiality.

We are thankful for research funding that enabled this project. Initial research for the book was supported by travel grants from the International Studies Program and the Department of World Languages and Literatures at Texas State University and by a Hispanex grant from Spain's Ministerio de Cultura y Deporte. A National Endowment for the Humanities Summer Stipend funded research and travel at a crucial moment in 2019, and the François Chevalier Fellowship at the Madrid Institute for Advanced Study permitted us to meet with our collaborators and to coordinate the research, writing, editing, and translating of the essays.

We thank the archivists and librarians at the Real Sociedad Económica Matritense—especially archivist Fabiola Azanza—as well as the Archivo Regional de la Comunidad de Madrid, the Casa de Velázquez, the Biblioteca Nacional de España, the Real Academia de la Historia, the Universidad Autónoma de Madrid, and others centers that we visited, whose expertise greatly facilitated our work. The Archivo Histórico de la Nobleza, the Instituto del Patrimonio Cultural de España, the Museo de las Cortes de Cádiz, the Archivo Histórico de la Villa de Madrid, the Archivo Regional de la Comunidad de Madrid, the Biblioteca Regional de la Comunidad de Madrid, the Biblioteca Nacional de España, the Fine Arts Museums of San Francisco, the Hispanic Society of America, and the David Rumsey Map Collection have all granted us permission to reproduce images from their collections, for which we are very grateful. We are also indebted to the Junta de Damas for allowing us to reproduce their portrait of the Countess of Truillas, and to the owner of the portrait of the Marquise of Fuerte-Híjar for generously permitting its use in this book.

One of the goals of this book is to bring Spanish scholarship to an English-speaking audience. We had the great good fortune to work with excellent translators, and we thank Catherine Jagoe and Kathleen Fueger for the care, skill, and tact they dedicated to the translations. We gratefully acknowledge the translation funding provided by the Department of World Languages and Literatures at Texas State University and the Facultad de Geografía e Historia at the Universidad de Educación a Distancia (Spain). And finally, we thank our colleagues, friends, and family, who listened to us and encouraged us along the way.

Abbreviations

ADMS	Archivo Ducal de Medina Sidonia, Sanlúcar de Barrameda, Cádiz
AGP	Archivo General de Palacio, Madrid
AHDM	Archivo Histórico Diocesano de Madrid
AHMC	Archivo Histórico Municipal de Cádiz
AHN	Archivo Histórico Nacional, Madrid
AHNSG	Archivo del Hospital de Nuestra Señora de Gracia, Zaragoza
AHPM	Archivo Histórico de Protocolos de Madrid
AHVM	Archivo Histórico de la Villa de Madrid
ARABSF	Archivo de la Real Academia de Bellas Artes de San Fernando, Madrid
ARCM	Archivo Regional de la Comunidad de Madrid
ARSEA	Archivo de la Real Sociedad Económica Aragonesa, Zaragoza
ARSEM	Archivo de la Real Sociedad Económica Matritense de Amigos del País, Madrid
BNE	Biblioteca Nacional de España, Madrid
MNP	Museo Nacional del Prado, Madrid

Society Women and
Enlightened Charity in Spain

Introduction

The Junta de Damas, Charity, and Feminism

CATHERINE M. JAFFE AND
ELISA MARTÍN-VALDEPEÑAS YAGÜE

... in the history of great expanses of time, the memorials to women's names are no more in evidence than the traces left by a ship crossing the ocean.
—ANNA MARIA VAN SCHURMAN, 1637

... men ... have robbed women of even the satisfaction that comes with having an enlightened mind.
—JOSEFA AMAR Y BORBÓN, "Discurso en defensa del talento de las mujeres," 1786

... if [woman] be not prepared by education to become the companion of man, she will stop the progress of knowledge and virtue; for truth must be common to all.
—MARY WOLLSTONECRAFT, *A Vindication of the Rights of Woman*, 1792

Women and the Enlightenment in Spain

In the twenty-first century, we do not question, in many parts of the world, women's right to study and to work outside the home, forgetting that only a little over two hundred years ago it was daring and subversive to claim such rights. The history of debates over women's abilities sheds light on why we still argue today about women's "natural" role in society. During the eighteenth century, women like Josefa Amar and Mary Wollstonecraft, although reasoning from different principles and traditions, drew on Enlightenment ideals of equality, social utility, a belief in progress, and the pursuit of happiness to assert women's right to an education and to contribute to society. Throughout Europe and America, in salons or in the mixed social gatherings in private homes called "tertulias" in Spain, literate women—a growing but unevenly distributed class—discussed new ideas they read about in books and in the new medium of the periodical press, and they formed associations dedicated to science, politics, and charity.

Among the feminine associations that sprang up in the late eighteenth century in response to Enlightenment ideals are the Naturkundig Genootschap der Dames (Women's Society for Natural Knowledge), established in the Netherlands in 1785; the Parisian women's association Société de Charité Maternelle, founded in 1788; the Female Association of Philadelphia for the Relief of Women and Children in Distressed Circumstances, the Newark Female Charitable Society, and the Boston Female Society, founded following the American Revolution; and in France the Society of Revolutionary Republican Women. These societies had interests ranging from political to patriotic, to charitable, to scientific but were similar in that they were formed by women eager to participate in the Enlightenment ideal of public utility by contributing to the improvement of their societies.[1] Women writers like Mary Wollstonecraft and Josefa Amar pressed to further women's education so they could better fulfill their maternal role and also contribute as useful citizens to the betterment of society and "to the progress of knowledge and virtue," as Wollstonecraft wrote.

During the eighteenth century, economic or patriotic societies were founded in many countries in Europe as a way for men of different backgrounds to meet to discuss scientific, technological, and industrial advances as well as new political theories.[2] Inspired by the Enlightenment's emphasis on public utility and by the founding of economic societies around Spain, the secular women's association known as the Junta de Damas de Honor y Mérito de la Real Sociedad Económica Matritense (Council of Women of Honor and Merit of the Royal Madrid Economic Society) was founded in 1787 despite vehement opposition from some of the society's male members. Its goal was to work with the Real Sociedad Económica to promote enlightened reform in Spain for poor women and children. As the Junta de Damas' *Statutes* state, "Its purpose is to establish and spread good education, improve manners through its example and enlightenment, introduce the love of work, and foment industry" (I, ii).[3] The *Statutes* established their membership ("Members must have a good education and good conduct, with proven instruction in the objectives of the Junta" [I, iii]), set out orderly procedures for presenting proposals and reports, for discussion, for voting, for the assignment of tasks, and described the duties of each officer. While the president and other officers would sit at the head of the table, other members would be seated in the order in which they arrived, thereby dispensing to a certain degree with hierarchies of rank. While the history of this remarkable women's association has not been completely forgotten, knowledge of these women's work has dissipated, as Anna Maria van Schurman had foretold long before its creation.[4] This has occurred for various reasons, including, perhaps, because of what Antonio Calvo Maturana called the "clearly prebourgeois and preliberal connotations (in the most patriarchal sense of both words) regarding its underlying message."[5]

Our premise is that the junta's work and its significance to women's history, to the history of Spanish feminism, and to the Enlightenment in Spain have not been adequately recognized. The book's title, *Society Women and Enlightened Charity in Spain*, reflects the elite status of the women of the Junta de Damas and the fact that they formed a feminine society to work toward Enlightenment goals.

This book provides an English-speaking audience with a comprehensive, documented history and analysis of the Junta de Damas, its work, and its members—something that has never been done before even in Spanish—that will allow it to be considered alongside other women's associations in studies of women's and gender history and the social history of the Enlightenment. Scholars' understanding of "the" Enlightenment—traditionally defined as a philosophical and intellectual movement originating in France and northern Europe—has broadened to include regional movements outside those cultural centers. These movements are sometimes called "peripheral" Enlightenments, but more often now they are acknowledged as centers of diverse Enlightenments that included practical reforms and programs of social and economic innovations. Today scholars discuss the social basis of the Enlightenment in terms of the transnational circulation of ideas and texts, mediations, cultural transfers, flows, and interactions that produced social change, as well as practical programs for social, political, and economic reforms. The Enlightenment and how it was experienced, in this more complex view, is considered to have manifested itself within diverse regional and national parameters, rather than exclusively in universalist terms.[6]

The Spanish Enlightenment was not mainly a theoretical movement but rather was characterized by more practical reforms: "The Spanish Enlightenment was essentially pragmatic, utilitarian and applied," claims Jesús Astigarraga. He concludes that the Enlightenment in Spain consisted of an interlocking body of projects of social and economic reforms intended to "address the problem of the country's backwardness."[7] The Enlightenment in Spain is usually described in terms that seem to contradict Enlightenment values, acknowledges María Victoria López-Cordón: "limited in both time and social impact; directed, because of the Monarchy's prominent role; pragmatic, because of the nature of its reforms; confessional, despite criticisms of religion and the advance of secularization; inadequate." She contends, nevertheless, that those men and women who engaged in Enlightenment debates and projects in Spain "contributed to creating the public opinion that was necessary for new ideas to take root."[8] Enlightenment studies must consider both the wide context and more local concerns, according to Brian Hamnett. He points out that, while the practical reforms in political economy, education, and government characteristic of the Iberian Enlightenment "represented specific aspects of a generalized European shift in thinking," it is also true that "the Enlightenment in Iberia and Ibero-America derived more from indigenous needs and traditions than from external influences."[9] Furthermore, Mónica Bolufer has recently asserted that setting the Hispanic Enlightenment into the context of the traditional (northern) European Enlightenment will "revitalize" the study of both.[10]

The economic societies, essential vehicles of Enlightenment thought and reform in Spain, were closely connected to the government. But by involving men (and a very few women) from different ranks, fostering debates, publishing translations and reports, and sponsoring reform projects, Spain's economic societies were crucial to the diffusion of Enlightenment ideas and values and were pioneers of the changes that led to the Spanish Constitutional Cortes de Cádiz (1810–12), which cannot be understood without them.[11] The Junta de Damas of the Real Sociedad Económica Matritense shared the economic societies' Enlightenment zeal to improve society. They chose as their object the reform and management of secular charitable institutions in Madrid that served poor women and children, implicitly aligning themselves with acceptable feminine and maternal roles. But in the process, by claiming and exercising a public role running these institutions, they became a significant example of women's active participation in the public sphere only a few decades before Spain's first liberal constitution would deny their capacity for independent citizenship and relegate them to a dependent role in the domestic realm of the home.[12]

Women and Enlightened Charity in Spain

This book studies the discourses, activities, and members of the Junta de Damas in the context of theories of charity that were being debated in late-eighteenth-century Europe, when the Christian ideal of *caritas* was transformed by utilitarian principles of social control and the psychology of welfare and work.[13] In relation to other Enlightenment women's associations within and outside Spain, the Junta de Damas is exceptional as a model to study women's empowerment during the Enlightenment because of its long trajectory, the breadth of its fields of action (education, charity, literature, science, and others), and its persistence in continuing its work. As will be seen in the following essays, the women of the junta studied the economics of training poor women to spin or to sew; they considered the unintended effects of direct charity; they tested new inventions for spinning silk; they considered a proposal to establish a school for maids and adopted educational innovations such as the Lancasterian system; and they experimented with new infant-feeding methods, the smallpox vaccine, and the benefits of ventilation in women's prisons.[14]

The Junta de Damas arose toward the end of a period that saw an evolution in social ideas regarding charity. Throughout the early modern era and continuing throughout most of the eighteenth century in Spain, explains William Callahan, there existed a type of social contract, preached in sermons and spiritual guides widely published throughout the century, in which the poor and needy were viewed within a religious framework that accepted unchanging social hierarchies but held that the rich had an obligation to help the poor, for all were the children of God. By practicing charity toward the poor and suffering, a Christian would not change the world, but could win salvation and maintain social equilibrium. In Spain, the Catholic Church and its related confraternities were expected to aid the poor. But during the reign of King Carlos III and toward the end of the century, the state's regalist policies and the Enlightenment belief in progress and perfectibility influenced social reformers in the economic societies, who emphasized self-help for the deserving poor and social utility over almsgiving. The poor were now no longer supposed to remain poor for life; they should be "worthy" and be taught to be useful citizens. The repeated economic and agricultural crises Spain suffered at the end of the eighteenth century put pressure on the authorities to deal with the problem of the poor and tore at the social contract. Undoubtedly the social and political upheavals in neighboring France and around Europe also informed the desire of the Spanish elite to defend their own status by showing their concern for the poor masses.[15]

The terminological evolution from Christian charity or caritas to public beneficence reveals the shifting ideologies upon which the Junta de Damas was founded.[16] For this reason, although "charity," "philanthropy," and "beneficence" are used somewhat interchangeably throughout this volume, the Spanish term "beneficencia" that took hold during the early decades of the nineteenth century refers to activities promoting social welfare, without the religious connotations of the Christian caritas, but also without the overtones of strategic philanthropy of wealthy elites who sought to gain social status.[17]

For many reasons, including religious observance and cultural expectations, women have traditionally been associated with charitable work. Scholars show that the gendered aspects of charity and social welfare in the eighteenth century blurred the sharp divisions between public and private spheres of action, between religious or voluntary associations and the state.[18] Sandra Cavallo points out that conflicts between elite groups determine which social group is involved in charity work at particular times, and that the changing conception of the worthy poor was related to "the discourses and sets of values which those controlling charity endorsed."[19] Relations and conflicts between different elite groups, and between elite groups and the poor, were expressed through ideologies of charity that determined how its objects were to be treated.[20] As Jonathan Barry and Colin Jones point out, borrowing Sandra Cavallo's term, "[t]he 'language of desert' is endlessly mobile."[21]

Lacking personal accounts of their motivations, we can only assume that women joined the Junta de Damas and other feminine charitable associations for mixed reasons. Linda Kerber suggests that "the deflection of women's patriotism into benevolence" may have made patriotism acceptable to early American women already burdened with domestic responsibilities.[22] According to David Garrioch, philanthropy was connected to the evolution of class identities in the eighteenth century, as the elite classes worked to differentiate themselves from the masses.[23] It is possible that aristocratic and other elite women in Spain at the end of the century saw an opening in the charitable activity of the Junta de Damas to exercise a measure of patriotic social protagonism that would transcend, to a certain extent, differences in rank and wealth among them, to prove their equal competence with men and even to assert their superiority for the work because of their unique feminine experience. These motivations do not necessarily negate their belief that they were complying with deeply-felt obligations to help the poor. Adopting the rhetoric of the enlightened monarchy, they chose poor women and children as the natural object of their compassion and improving spirit.

Studying the discourses of charity in Spain in the eighteenth century, Elizabeth Lewis claims that the charitable work of elite women in the Junta de Damas was "more than mere collusion" with the enlightened regime; it was also a means of "political activism." Mónica Bolufer and Theresa Ann Smith discuss the Junta's adoption of "civic motherhood" as a means of access to the public sphere.[24] The Junta de Damas resembles, in some ways, other voluntary feminine charitable associations founded during the last decades of the eighteenth century that were dedicated to women and children, such as the Société de Charité Maternelle (Society for Maternal Charity), founded in Paris in 1788. "Childbirth bridged the public and private spheres," observes Stuart Woolf: "Morals, law, power and authority were inextricably involved in the debates on child abandonment and infanticide, population and national strength, midwifery and the female anatomy."[25] All of these issues prevalent in the discourses surrounding women's role in charity in the eighteenth century can be traced—although not without difficulty, given chronological gaps, missing documents, and the transfer of records among different institutions— in the records of the Junta de Damas' activities that are mostly held in the archives of the Real Sociedad Económica Matritense and other archives throughout Spain.

Scholars are not in agreement that women's charitable activities in the eighteenth century necessarily established affective bonds between the elite women who practiced it and the poor women who were their objects, nor that late-Enlightenment women's charity represented an incipient "feminist" consciousness. Silvia Pinches concludes somewhat pessimistically that, in eighteenth-century Birmingham, "bourgeois women, circumscribed by law and convention, often treated as objects by their men folk, could only express agency in relation to objects more powerless than themselves."[26] Nevertheless, in her study of the Junta de Damas of Cádiz in the early decades of the nineteenth century, Fátima Salaverri claims that the members benefited from the experience of the Madrid Junta de Damas, which modeled new ways of occupying public space, allowing them to form a collective identity and to react to masculine power.[27] More granular research on the women of the Junta de Damas might shed light on their attitudes toward their work; however, the lives of many of these women remain unstudied, and the lack of archival resources limits what historians can uncover.

The Junta de Damas, Gender, and Feminism

Previous scholarship on the Junta de Damas has focused on specific aspects of its work, such as the care of abandoned infants, the reformation of poor children's and women's education, and the idea of women as enlightened citizens.[28] Other scholars have written biographies of its most famous members, like the erudite Josefa Amar, two noble women founders, the Countess of Montijo and the Countess-Duchess of Benavente, and one of its most active members, the Marquise of Fuerte-Híjar.[29] We chronicle here the history of this important project of Spain's Enlightenment and recount the lives of its most significant members—both famous and lesser known—during the first decades of its existence, from its polemical creation in 1787 during the reign of King Carlos III, through the upheavals of the Guerra de la Independencia (Peninsular War, 1808–14), to 1823, which saw the second return of absolutism during the reign of King Fernando VII. And we propose new ways of evaluating the contribution that the Junta de Damas as a body made to women's education; to the Republic of Letters as a collective authorial network; to the understanding of how the spaces of women's charity bridged the public and private spheres; and to the image of the enlightened woman through visual representation and portraiture.

This book also provides original contributions to the study of women's self-fashioning during the late Enlightenment. The 1794 *Statutes* of the Junta de Damas, translated here for the first time, is a fascinating document of Enlightenment women's public declaration of a civic role. In the *Statutes* they set out how they will conduct themselves in an orderly process so as to collaboratively carry out their joint mission with the male Sociedad Económica Matritense: "socorrer enseñando" (helping by teaching). The portraits reproduced throughout this volume (analyzed by Álvaro Molina in his essay) have until now never been presented as a collection. Together they represent a gallery of members of the Junta de Damas intentionally fashioning themselves as Enlightened women before the Romantic gender ideology of "the angel in the house" (*el ángel del hogar*) began to impose itself on the cultural imaginary and effect a change in representational strategies.

Despite the consideration given to the Junta de Damas and its members in groundbreaking work in the field of gender and women's history in Spain by scholars such as Paula de Demerson, Carmen Martín Gaite, Mónica Bolufer, Paloma Fernández Quintanilla, Sally-Ann Kitts, Elizabeth Franklin Lewis, Theresa Ann Smith, and María Victoria López-Cordón, among others, the work of the Junta de Damas and the history of women are still sometimes overlooked in the field of Spanish Enlightenment studies. Due in part to Spanish historiography's ambivalence toward the eighteenth century, the Hispanic world has been relatively neglected in transnational Enlightenment studies.[30] Scholars of gender and the Enlightenment have perhaps shown the most interest in the Spanish context.[31] Far from being peripheral and derivative, the Junta de Damas made a compelling contribution to the Spanish Enlightenment, to the evolution of gender roles in Spain, and to women's history. Because of its secular, enlightened reform of institutions such as the Inclusa, the Madrid foundling home, and the Escuelas Patrióticas (trade schools for poor women), the Junta de Damas is a pioneer in the history of modern women's networks of sociability and philanthropy.

By claiming a space for public action and pioneering work in women's professional education and the care of infants, the Junta de Damas is significant to the history of gender in the Enlightenment and to the history of feminism. The women of the Junta de Damas challenged traditional gender roles by asserting their capacity to manage civic charitable institutions. Mónica Bolufer cautions that "proto-feminism" or "rational feminism" are more appropriate terms for early modern discourses defending women, such as those studied here, than the modern concept of feminism, understood, in the words of the historian Karen Offen, as "a system of ideas and a movement for sociopolitical change" that opposes male privilege.[32] Theoretically, we also heed historian Joan W. Scott's description of the "fantasy" of feminist history—an imaginary projection of our own feminist convictions onto women of the past—to avoid using modern criteria when evaluating the activities and ideology of this historic association of women. They were enlightened but not revolutionary, defenders of women but respectful of the state, the church, and social hierarchy, and perhaps because of this traditionalism they have been overlooked in histories of Spanish feminism.[33]

In the book's first section we analyze the history and discourses surrounding the founding and evolution of the Junta de Damas, from its inception to the early decades of the nineteenth century. Mónica Bolufer analyzes the polemic surrounding the admission of women to the Real Sociedad Económica Matritense in the context of the founding of patriotic or economic societies around Europe during the eighteenth century. She shows that the Spanish discourses in favor of and against women's admission reflected a wider European debate over women's nature, talents, and abilities, and they reverberated in the press and intellectual circles outside Spain. The most significant voice defending women in this widely publicized polemic was that of Josefa Amar, who is considered, along with Benito Jerónimo Feijoo earlier in the century, as the preeminent forerunner of modern feminism in Spain. María Victoria López-Cordón discusses Amar's intellectual biography and shows how this remarkable woman author intervened strategically in the debate over women's admission and eloquently defended women's aptitude and right to form part of the Real Sociedad Económica itself. Amar did not favor the establishment of a separate association for women. Her essay is a touchstone for the history of the Junta de Damas, and its influence echoes throughout this book. Amar's example for the history of feminism during the Enlightenment is important, according to López-Cordón, because "[s]he was an enlightened woman [. . .] not only for her erudition, her pedagogical concerns and her presence in such representative institutions as the Economic Societies, but also because, rejecting culturalist explanations, she defended in the name of reason the principle of consubstantial equality between men and women."[34]

Elisa Martín-Valdepeñas Yagüe recounts the history of the delicate balance between independence of action and subordination to the male society's control that the women members negotiated throughout the junta's crucial first decades. As the Junta de Damas gradually assumed the management of popular schools for poor women and children, the Inclusa, and the women's prison known as the Galera, the women operated strategically and pragmatically to improve these institutions within the limits imposed by their economic realities. Elites themselves, many with noble titles, the members depended on royal patronage and publicly represented the power of the enlightened monarchs. The Enlightenment legacy of the Junta de Damas to the history of Spanish feminism has not been well understood, perhaps because of shifting political ideologies during the decades after the end of the Peninsular War.[35] Mónica

Burguera discusses the evolution of the Junta de Damas in the nineteenth century and what happened to its most critical and transgressive legacy regarding the gender debate that marked its founding. Burguera analyzes the process of politicization of social reform and feminine charity or beneficence in the context of postrevolutionary liberalisms (1833–68) and shows how the Junta de Damas, under the leadership of the Dowager Duchess of Gor and her circle—women close to the monarchy and reticently liberal—reelaborated the enlightened inheritance of the institution to project a model of conservative, elite, feminine beneficence opposed to the new middle-class models of the political imaginaries that would coalesce in the Revolution of 1868. This evolution can help to explain why someone so interesting as Josefa Amar was later dropped from the discourses critical of the situation of women that were elaborated in the 1840s and were crucial to later feminist debates and writers.

In order to portray the confluence of unique personalities and talents that gave rise to the Junta de Damas, the book's second section presents biographies of the socially and culturally privileged founders of the junta and their innovative work. Exceptional personalities from powerful aristocratic families—the Countess-Duchess of Benavente, studied by Paloma Fernández Quintanilla, and the Countess of Montijo, studied by Gloria Franco—directed the Junta de Damas throughout its first two decades. Their protagonism as leaders cannot be underestimated, and they were aided by women from different backgrounds, such as the Marquise of Fuerte-Híjar, an heiress who purchased a noble title for her second husband, studied by Catherine Jaffe. Gloria Espigado recounts the life of the Countess of Montijo's daughter, the Marquise of Villafranca, who played a leading role in the Junta de Damas and other women's patriotic associations throughout the Peninsular War and during the reestablishment of the Bourbon monarchy. Elisa Martín-Valdepeñas Yagüe has attempted to reconstruct the life trajectory of some of the lesser-known women who were integral members of the junta throughout this period, keeping in mind the difficulty of writing a biography based on very few records dispersed throughout the archives. By studying these women together in the context of the junta's work, we can appreciate the social range of the junta's members and the unique combination of talents and motivations that enabled its accomplishments. This essay attempts to restore protagonism to these lesser-known women by bringing to light personalities that have remained obscure, although their contributions to the collective efforts of the Junta de Damas are no less important than those of the more socially prominent members analyzed in the preceding essays. Their stories are crucial to the history of the institution of the Junta de Damas, its protagonists, and its works.

The third section turns to the significance of the collective identity of the Junta de Damas. The women's pragmatism, tact, and modern sensibility brought about social innovations in popular education, as Josefina Méndez shows. The women of the Junta de Damas participated in public debates and administered social welfare institutions, and Elizabeth Lewis maps how this charitable work allowed them to literally and figuratively cross over the supposed dividing line between public and private spheres. Catherine Jaffe traces the literary networks constituted by its members' writing, including formulaic institutional texts, paratexts of publications, and jointly authored institutional reports, to show how they fashioned a corporate identity as authors. By analyzing their self-fashioning in portraits intended to circulate publicly, Álvaro Molina considers the different contexts of the production and reception of images of the members of the Junta de Damas as enlightened women. He finds that representational strategies emphasizing their enlightened activities diminished after the end of the Peninsular War and the return of absolutism.

Women from varied backgrounds, with diverse motivations, talents, and possibilities, carried out the work and activities of the Junta de Damas. In many of the institutions of social welfare they managed, they struggled for success against immense and at times insuperable obstacles. The Junta de Damas was formed at the end of a period of enlightened monarchy, based on a foundation of social hierarchies that would soon be put under pressure; its social welfare work was practically obliterated by the vicissitudes of war; and new ideologies of liberalism began to redefine the social contract of beneficence. It may have been fashionable, at certain moments, for elite women to join the Junta de Damas. But the humanitarian commitment of those who carried on the junta's work during the war and then struggled to take it up again afterwards cannot be denied, whether their motivations sprang from Christian charity, feminine sympathy, or enlightened and patriotic enthusiasm. However history has judged, or will judge, the legacy of the Junta de Damas and their work, there is no doubt that for many of these women their experience was not just a passing fashion but a defining aspect of their identity.[36] As the essays in this book show, the example of the Junta de Damas stands at the beginning of modern Spanish feminism because its members carved out for themselves a space of public action and proved their intellectual capacity and practical ability to carry out their goals.

NOTES

1. Jacob and Sturkenboom describe the Naturkundig Genootschap der Dames, "A Woman's Scientific Society"; Woolf studies the *Société de Charité Maternelle*; Kerber describes the Philadelphia and New Jersey women's fundraising petition of 1780 and the women's service and reform societies that arose after the American Revolution, *Women of the Republic*, 99–105, 111–13; Levy, Applewhite, and Johnson discuss the Society of Revolutionary Republican Women in France, *Women in Revolutionary Paris*, 5.

2. See Stapelbroek and Marjanen, *The Rise of Economic Societies*, and the first essay in this volume.

3. See the translation of the *Statutes* in the appendix.

4. The epigraph is from Anna Maria van Schurman to André Rivet, November 6, 1637, quoted in Pal, *Republic of Women*, 266. See also the translation by Joyce Irwin in van Schurman, *Whether a Christian Woman*, 41–48.

5. Unless otherwise indicated, all translations are our own. Calvo Maturana, *Cuando manden los que obedecen*, 145–46.

6. Among the many recent studies of the Enlightenment as the interaction, exchange, circulation, and transfer of ideas, as a global movement with different manifestations in national traditions, cultures, and geographic locales, and as mediation, are Astigarraga Goenaga, ed., *The Spanish Enlightenment Revisited*; Astigarraga Goenaga, López-Cordón Cortezo, and Urkia Etxabe, eds., *Ilustración, Ilustraciones*; Butterwick, ed., *Peripheries of the Enlightenment*; Lewis, Bolufer Peruga, and Jaffe, eds., *The Routledge Companion to the Hispanic Enlightenment*; Fitzpatrick, Jones, Knellworth, and McCalman, eds., *The Enlightenment World*; Hamnett, *The Enlightenment in Iberia*; Kontler, "What Is the (Historians') Enlightenment Today?"; Lehner, ed., *The Catholic Enlightenment*; Gies and Wall, eds., *The Eighteenth Centuries*; Siskin and Warner, eds., *This Is Enlightenment*; Pagden, *The Enlightenment*; Nussbaum, *The Global Enlightenment*; and Outram, *The Enlightenment*.

7. Astigarraga Goenaga, *The Spanish Enlightenment Revisited*, 9 and 15. Philip Deacon also sets the moderate Spanish Enlightenment within the European context in "Notes on Spain and Enlightenment."

8. López-Cordón Cortezo, "The Enlightenment and Its Interpreters," 203–4.

9. Hamnett, *The Enlightenment in Iberia and in Ibero-America*, 271–72.

10. Bolufer Peruga, "The Enlightenment in Spain," 13.

11. Astigarraga Goenaga, "Connecting with the Enlightenment," 101–2; Franco Rubio, "El ejercicio del poder en la España del Siglo XVIII." About women and economic societies in Spain, see Arias de Saavedra Alías, "Las Sociedades Económicas de Amigos del País y la mujer"; Calderón España, "Presencia de la mujer en las Reales Sociedades Económicas."

12. Among the numerous studies of the Junta de Damas and their civic, maternal role, see Bolufer Peruga, *Mujeres e Ilustración*; Smith, *The Emerging Female Citizen*; Demerson, *María Francisca de Sales Portocarrero*; Martín-Valdepeñas Yagüe, "Afrancesadas y patriotas," "Beneficencia y mujeres en tiempos de guerra," and "El eco del saber."

13. Williams, *Keywords*, 54–55.

14. See Demerson, *María Francisca de Sales Portocarrero*. On the scientific activities of the Junta de Damas, see Serrano Jerez, "Chemistry in the City" and "Science for Women"; Martín-Valdepeñas Yagüe, "El eco del saber," 104–6.

15. Callahan, "Caridad, sociedad y economía"; see also Fuente Galán, "Aportación al estudio," 19–26.

16. Maceiras Rey, "Las niñas abandonadas," 25–40.

17. "Scientific charity" and "the new philanthropy" also became the culturally dominant paradigm in the early American republic, according to Jeremy Beer, *The Philanthropic Revolution*, 58.

18. Adams studies the maternal societies of nineteenth-century France in *Poverty, Charity, and Motherhood*, 29–57. Lindenmeyr asserts that charitable works "enabled women to play a major and long overlooked role in the development of a civil society in autocratic Russia," "Public Life, Private Virtues," 563. Garrioch points out that male role models in the eighteenth-century periodical press were philanthropic, "in the new enlightened sense of actively changing the world," while female role models were charitable, "Making a Better World," 495–97.

19. Cavallo, *Charity and Power*, 4–5.

20. Cavallo, "The Motivations of Benefactors," 38.

21. Barry and Jones, "Introduction," 11.

22. Kerber, *Women of the Republic*, 111.

23. Garrioch, "Making a Better World," 494–96.

24. Lewis, "Actos de caridad," 274; Bolufer Peruga, *Mujeres e Ilustración*, 378; Smith, *The Emerging Female Citizen*, 161.

25. Woolf, "The *Société de Charité Maternelle, 1788–1815*," 63.

26. Pinches, "Women as Object," 85.

27. Salaverri Baro, "La Junta de Damas como modelo," 638; see also Pérez Moreda, "Las Juntas de Damas."

28. See Sherwood, *Poverty in Eighteenth-Century Spain*; Vidal Galache and Vidal Galache, *Bordes y bastados*; Méndez Vázquez, *Formación profesional de las mujeres*.

29. López-Cordón Cortezo, *Condición femenina*; Demerson, *María Francisca de Sales Portocarrero*; Yebes, *La condesa-duquesa de Benavente*; Fernández Quintanilla, *La IX Duquesa de Osuna*; Martín-Valdepeñas Yagüe and Jaffe, *María Lorenza de los Ríos*.

30. Among the important studies of women, gender, and the Enlightenment in Spain are Demerson, *María Francisca de Sales Portocarrero*; Martín Gaite, *Usos amorosos*; Kitts, *The Debate on the Nature*; Fernández Quintanilla, *La mujer ilustrada*; Bolufer Peruga, *Mujeres e Ilustración*; Lewis, *Women Writers*; Smith, *The Emerging Female Citizen*; López-Cordón Cortezo, *Condición femenina*, Vicente, *Debating Sex and Gender*; and Molina, *Mujeres y hombres*. Recent general studies of the Spanish Enlightenment that, although otherwise excellent, do not consider gender, are Astigarraga Goenaga, ed., *The Spanish Enlightenment Revisited*, and Hamnett, *The En-

lightenment in Iberia. Global studies of the Enlightenment that overlook Spain include Kontler, "What Is the (Historians') Enlightenment," and Fitzpatrick, Jones, Knellwolf, and McCalman, eds., *The Enlightenment World.* For a historiographical study of the Hispanic Enlightenment that takes gender into account, see Bolufer Peruga, "The Enlightenment in Spain."

31. Knott and Taylor, eds., *Women, Gender*; Lehner, ed., *Women, Enlightenment.*

32. Bolufer Peruga, "Neither Male, nor Female," 396–400; Offen, *European Feminisms,* 20; see also the section on the eighteenth century in Bermúdez and Johnson, eds., *A New History of Iberian Feminisms.*

33. Scott, *Gender and the Politics of History* and *The Fantasy of Feminist History.*

34. López-Cordón Cortezo, *Condición femenina,* 10.

35. See Bolufer Peruga, "The Enlightenment in Spain," 11–12.

36. The Junta de Damas today is the oldest nonreligious, philanthropic, feminine association in Spain, with over 230 years of history. See juntadedamas.org.

I

Feminine Philanthropy in Spain

Women in Patriotic Societies

A Spanish Debate in a European Context

MÓNICA BOLUFER PERUGA

A "Political Revolution"? Discussing Women's Access to Economic Societies

From its foundation in 1775 until 1786, the Royal Madrid Economic Society of Friends of the Country (Real Sociedad Económica Matritense de Amigos del País) discussed the subject of the admission of women to its ranks. This institution belonged to a wider movement that extended throughout virtually the whole of Europe and some parts of North and South America: voluntary associations that took the name of "economic," "patriotic," or "improving" societies, the first ones being the Honourable Society of Improvers in Scotland (1723) and the Dublin Society of Improvement (1731).[1] Although their specific aims, their composition (a varied mixture of nobles, clergymen, lawyers, landowners, and middle class), and their organization differed, they shared a common engagement in improving production, technological development, education, and charity as well as fostering practical knowledge in the regions where they emerged.

Economic (also called patriotic) societies in the Spanish empire—puzzlingly absent from general overviews of these institutions—mushroomed from a relatively early date, starting with the Basque Society of Friends of the Country (Real Sociedad Bascongada de los Amigos del País), which developed in 1765 from an informal discussion group (*tertulia*) of nobles that had been meeting regularly since 1748.[2] The governments of King Carlos III (1759–88) encouraged them and considered them indispensable organs of collaboration and channels of transmission for official reforms, which stimulated their multiplication in the last quarter of the century in most major peninsular cities (Madrid, 1775; Valencia, 1776) and many smaller towns, but also across the Spanish territories of the Atlantic and the Pacific (in Manila, 1781; Santiago de Cuba, 1787; followed in the 1790s by Lima, Havana, Quito, Mexico, among others). These societies participated in networks that connected European and American enlightened institutions (including also scientific, artistic, and literary academies) through the exchange of correspondence, printed reports and other publications, and occasionally elected members affiliated to their foreign counterparts. Through all these channels, they created and cultivated a cosmopolitan sense of common purpose and emulation.

The Spanish economic societies displayed a considerable reformist activity, although not always at the level of their ambitions and varying widely from one to another.[3] In the field of education, they created modern establishments for the elite (like the Royal Patriotic Seminar of Bergara [Real Seminario Patriótico de Bergara]), promoted university chairs in botany, chemistry, mineralogy, and political economy, and founded and maintained popular schools. They struggled to improve agricultural and manufacturing production by debating reports, offering prizes for studies and practical experiments on crops, materials, farming, or industrial techniques, and translating foreign works.[4] They also promoted modern philanthropic ideas and initiatives against traditional notions and practices of Christian charity. Finally, at the government's request, they gathered statistical information about the regions where they operated.

All these activities draw a wide field of "patriotic" or "improving" activity which, in the language of eighteenth-century reformism, defined how the members of these institutions imagined themselves and their role in the reform and modernization of society. Conceived by the president of the *Consejo de Castilla* (Council of Castile) Pedro Rodríguez Campomanes as "political associations" that had to diffuse "love for King and Country" and collaborate with enlightened absolutism's own projects of control and development, some of these societies, however, came to understand their own nature as representative bodies with some political agency. In particular, the Basque Society portrayed itself, in its writings and its motto ("three make one") as a "body of a nation" that represented the three Basque provinces.[5] Some members of the economic societies considered their institutions as bodies representative of public opinion, understanding by that the voice of an elite legitimated by their "merit," their education, and their advocacy of "the general interest" and "public utility."[6] They viewed their own activity as a selfless mission through which they could carry out their condition as "citizens," a term often used in their writings, with the same sense as that of "friends of the country" or "patriots."

That is, they were individuals (implicitly, those educated and possessing a certain economic affluence) concerned with the "public good," who deemed themselves conscious of their social responsibilities and civic duties inherent to their good fortune, their position, and their education while at the same time respectful subjects of an enlightened monarch. In his funeral eulogy upon the death of King Carlos III in 1788, Gaspar Melchor de Jovellanos (1744–1811) credited among the king's successes his encouragement of the "patriotic bodies, models of political institutions," charged with overseeing "all objects of common profit," and praised the societies' members as "friends of the public good."[7]

These economic societies, like many other institutions engaging in enlightened sociability, set themselves up as examples of rationality and conviviality, not only by virtue of their aims, but also by their rules and modes of operation. Their criteria of admission were officially based on merit (although rank, influence, and personal connections played a key role), and their working principles invoked open discussion, disinterested collaboration, and equality of relations among members, thus defining an enlightened public sphere (open in theory, yet implicitly selective and elitist) as the legitimate framework for the expression and formation of opinion. Nowhere was it explicitly declared in their statutes that their membership should be restricted to men, although that was an implicit understanding. In fact, the question of women's participation was never posed in other European patriotic societies.

This symbolic imaginary is crucial to understanding why the debate over the admission of women to the Economic Society of Madrid assumed such a resonance and was seen by contemporaries as a turning point, opening up no less than a "political revolution," in Jovellanos's words. The debate began right after the creation of the society in 1775. Manuel José Marín, one of the founding members and a courtier (*ayuda de cámara*) at the service of King Carlos III, delivered at the meeting of October 28, 1775, a speech defending women's admission; Pedro José Rodríguez Campomanes and Luis de Imbille would follow. The discussion was then interrupted for unknown reasons in 1776. It seems that the society—with the possible support of the government and perhaps the king himself—was inclined to open its doors to women, but public opinion did not endorse this view. The opportunity to reopen the question came in 1786, after the young noblewoman María Isidra Quintina de Guzmán, daughter of the count and countess of Oñate, a courtier of King Carlos III and a lady-in-waiting of the Princess of Asturias, María Luisa de Parma, was awarded on the king's initiative a doctorate and an honorary chair at the University of Alcalá, and subsequently admitted to the Real Academia Española (Spanish Royal Academy) in 1785 and to the Basque and the Madrid Societies of Friends of the Country in 1786. She would be shortly followed in the latter by the Countess-Duchess of Benavente, a powerful and cultivated aristocrat, patron of artists and intellectuals. They had been preceded in 1782 by two women who accessed two provincial societies: Josefa Amar, admitted into the Aragonese Society, and María Manuela de Moctezuma y Carvajal, Marquise of Cerralbo y Almarza, who joined that of Ciudad Rodrigo.[8]

All this fit into a general European trend to admit a few "exceptional" women to literary, scientific, and artistic institutions from which they were generally excluded. Italian literary academies of the Arcadia opened their doors to a certain number of female members: in the case of the Roman academy, a total of 74 women (among them, a few foreign queens and aristocrats) out of 2,419 designations from its foundation in 1690 to 1728.[9] Artistic academies incorporated a few: the Paris Academy, only Rosalba Carriera, Elizabeth Vigée-Lebrun (official painter to Queen Marie Antoinette), and Adélaïde Labille-Guiard; the British Royal Academy, Mary Moser and Angelica Kauffmann; the Spanish Real Academia de Bellas Artes de San Fernando (Royal Academy of Fine Arts of San Fernando) admitted 34 women (about 8 percent of admissions) from 1752 to 1808.[10] Also, French provincial academies admitted into their ranks a small number of female writers and intellectuals, a number which rose in the 1780s.[11] Scientific academies—with the exception of the Accademia delle scienze dell'Istituto di Bologna (Academy of Sciences of the Institute of Bologna), of which Laura Bassi and Maria Gaetana Agnesi became members in 1732 and 1748 respectively—were a much less welcoming space: the Académie des Sciences (French Academy of Sciences) did not admit any women during the eighteenth century, and Émilie du Châtelet, in spite of having become the first foreign woman invited to the Bologna Istituto, had to maneuver her relations with the Paris academy as an outsider, using the resources due to her rank.[12] The case of Princess Ekaterina Dashkova, a close friend to Empress Catherine II, president from 1783 of the Imperial Academy of Sciences of Saint Petersburg and the Imperial Academy of the Russian language, admitted to the Economic Society of St. Petersburg, founded in 1765, and first female member of the American Philosophical Society in 1789, was absolutely exceptional in Europe and was frequently cited as such.[13] However, while the first female admissions to the Madrid Economic Society followed the logic often adopted by scientific, artistic, and literary academies, which accepted women as exceptions in the implicitly male domains of art, sciences, and letters, what was peculiar in this case is that the question was posed in more general terms, as the discourse of reform and improvement opened up wider—although certainly restricted—options for women's social and intellectual activism.

Those members of the Madrid Society who expressed their opinion on women's admission during the second stage of the discussion in 1786 included prestigious and well-connected names: the enlightened jurist Gaspar Melchor de Jovellanos, the professor Ignacio López de Ayala, the businessman Francisco de Cabarrús, and the erudite Josefa Amar (*Discurso en defensa del talento de las mujeres, y de su aptitud para el gobierno, y otros cargos en que se emplean los hombres* [Discourse in Defence of the Talents of Women, and Their Aptitude for Government and Other Positions in Which Men Are Employed]). The debate went far beyond the circle of the Madrid Society to reach Spanish, and to a certain extent European, public opinion: three of the essays were published in the *Memorial literario, instructivo y curioso de la Corte de Madrid*[14] and further advertised in the *Mercurio histórico-político*, periodicals that had subscribers not only in peninsular Spain but also in the Canary Islands, North Africa, Spanish America, and the United States.[15] Moreover, Cabarrús's essay was translated into French in the *Mercure de France* on March 24, 1787, and Amar's twice into Italian, in Rome (1789) and Bologna (1810).[16]

The real question under discussion was not only whether a limited number of ladies should form part of the institution and participate in its activities, but, more generally, what were the social roles and responsibilities to be undertaken by women within Enlightenment reformist projects and imaginary, and what were, ultimately, the intellectual and moral capacities of their sex. The latter issue had been passionately discussed decades earlier, starting with the publication of the *Defense of Women* (Defensa de las mujeres) by the enlightened Benedictine monk Benito Jerónimo Feijoo in 1726.[17] Feijoo, drawing on the long tradition of the European *querelle des femmes* and on rationalist feminism of the seventeenth century, affirmed the intellectual and moral equality between the sexes ("the Soul is neither male nor female") and women's capacity for arms, letters, and government. His text set off a polemical exchange that would explicitly last until 1750, but whose reverberations outreached that date, not only in peninsular Spain, but also across the Atlantic, in Spanish America, where Feijoo was a revered author (most particularly in New Spain but also in Peru), and in other countries, where his essay became known through translations into French, English, Italian, and Portuguese.

During the second half of the century, explicit vindications of men's natural superiority over women, of the type Feijoo's antagonists had brandished, became unfashionable in enlightened public discourse and were gradually replaced by a subtler notion of "complementarity" between the sexes, emphasizing their "naturally" differing qualities that suited a division of social spaces and functions: men were assigned a particular responsibility in the public sphere, while to women fell the duty to care for the well-being of the family and the moral education of their children.[18] However, the notion that reason, a quality distinctive to the human species, belonged to both sexes did not completely fade away but continued to nourish throughout the century a discourse of intellectual equality. Thus, the debate over women's admission to the Economic Society did not oppose enlightened reformers versus traditional misogynists, but more interestingly represents a fissure among the enlightened spirits themselves. Close friends with strong intellectual affinities, like Cabarrús and Jovellanos—who shared the values and rhetoric of reformism in terms of "reason," "utility," and "progress"—sharply diverged regarding the role that women should play in an enlightened society.

This debate therefore embodied the tension between two opposing positions, both rooted in the values and pragmatic concerns of enlightened reformism. On one side was the "Rousseauist" discourse that attributed to women, in the name of Enlightenment, a social and civic responsibility defined exclusively by the function of their domestic role (presented in turn as the consequence of their particular physical, moral, and sentimental nature), and that envisioned with suspicion other forms of female participation in social spaces.[19] On the other side were the different arguments that legitimated for women other forms of participation in reformist enterprises and thus presented their access to the Economic Society as an unavoidable requirement of the Enlightenment, while setting diverging limits for their participation. These disagreements do not mirror a division between reformers and representatives of a nascent liberalism that would question in later years the bases of political absolutism and the society of orders, but cut across established notions of what are "moderate" and "radical" Enlightenments. Bold affirmations of gender equality are found between female (and some male) writers who were in other aspects representatives of moderate positions in social and political issues, while other authors with more daring ideas about the social contract shared Rousseauist notions of male and female separate spheres. In this sense, the pragmatic, reforming spirit usually attributed to the Spanish Enlightenment (although in fact characteristic too of the Enlightenment in other territories, from Naples to Austria, from Scotland to Peru) can be seen not as a shortcoming, but as an opportunity for women to engage in improvement activities that expanded in practice what could be understood as female domains.

A Space for Women as Reformers

Brandishing the rationalist motto that several male and female authors had used before in Spain and the rest of Europe and that Feijoo had popularized, Manuel José Marín affirmed that "the understanding has no sex and the soul is not differentiated like the body" (los entendimientos no tienen sexo, ni las almas se diferencian como los cuerpos).[20] He and other members of the society were in favor of women's admission but differed regarding the specific formulas they proposed for it: some asked for their financial contribution, which others like Marín considered inappropriate; a few envisaged their normal integration into the society, while others suggested that they be organized into a separate body or that they just be listed as honorific members. For Marín, who mentioned as a precedent individual admissions of women to the Real Academia de Bellas Artes de San Fernando—where they never took part in regular meetings—the mere idea that women would attend the sessions, together with men or even on their own, was "ridiculous or extravagant."[21] However, he—like other members and, more generally, Enlightened reformers—shared a utilitarian perspective stressing the benefits that would derive from the participation of women and sought to promote their influence outside the strictly domestic circle, in the wider arena of reformist activities. By taking part in the endeavors and concerns of the patriotic societies, they argued, ladies would set an example for women of their class to abandon "frivolous" feminine pursuits and adopt instructive, useful, and morally worthy habits, such as formative reading, the education of children, and rational household management, virtues they would spread to less affluent women through their educational and charitable activities.

In this line, Campomanes underlined the prospective utility of the ladies becoming involved in the running of the Escuelas Patrióticas (popular schools for working-class girls) and suggested that female teachers of those schools be admitted, just as selected male members of the guilds, in a special class that would not be charged membership fees.[22] He concluded that women's admission was "not only fair, but convenient and necessary." In April 1776, Luis de Imbille agreed with him about incorporating ladies who would seek the honor of distinguishing as public benefactors, but also—seeking further involvement of public opinion—women who proved to have made practical contributions to technical improvement from their homes.[23]

Ten years later, in his speech delivered on March 27, 1786, Jovellanos also defended women's admission and rejected making it merely honorary and denying them access to the common meetings.[24] He was not shocked by the improbable circumstance that they might attend occasionally, in which case—he argued—the desire to please them would stimulate male members of the society in their patriotic efforts, but he clearly expected that decorum would deter them from frequenting the sessions.

According to these speeches and what they suggest about the opinions of other members of the society who did not express their position publicly, most of them seemed to not only tolerate, but actively require the participation of educated and respectable ladies in their shared social—and implicitly, political— mission. This was considered as a right that they should be accorded as rational beings, and at the same time legitimized on the grounds of their potential contribution to the general interest; more specifically, in different types of activities oriented toward social "improvement," including popular education, philanthropy, and promotion of technical advances in textile production. The idea that women could contribute to the betterment of society through specific actions was, indeed, embedded in the pragmatic spirit of the Enlightenment.[25] As Elena Serrano has shown, this notion that they should participate in the production and circulation of practical, "useful knowledge" helped to justify a wide variety of empiric and intellectual, including scientific, endeavours.[26] It facilitated the activities of the future Ladies Section of the Madrid Economic Society and also, in other European and American contexts, it fostered female participation in initiatives concerning agronomic experiments, economic discussions, and patriotic activism, from French physiocratic debates to philanthropic societies with an implicit political agenda in the early American republic. Thus, a notion of female citizenship not restricted to the domestic circle was defined within the boundaries of enlightened discourses and reformist practices. The shared reluctance to admit the mixing of the sexes shows that this notion was generally based on the idea of their complementary but distinctive roles and social spaces; however, these did not correspond in practice to a clean-cut division between a "public" and a "private" sphere, but constituted more flexible, overlapping areas of activity.

Reformulating Women's Exclusion

Although those who publicly expressed their view on this issue seem to have accepted that women's admission was necessary or even desirable, for others the only way that women should be "citizens" and collaborate with the objectives of enlightened reformism was through their domestic duties as wives and mothers, redefined in this period all over Europe as more demanding and politically charged. In the same year of 1786, the famous physician Jaime Bonells reminded women of the civic implications of those duties by accusing those who did not breastfeed their babies of being "in league against the public good."[27]

The fact that liberal and even progressive views on economic, social, and religious issues could go hand-in-hand with a strict gendered division of "public" and "private" spheres is illustrated by the arguments of Francisco de Cabarrús (1752–1810), a financier of French origin established in Spain, whose works and biographical trajectory are full of paradoxes. He represents in some respects the most liberal and anticlerical facet of the late Enlightenment in Spain, profoundly influenced by Rousseau, even as he served the financial institutions of Bourbon absolutism and obtained a noble title.[28] The only member of the Madrid Economic Society to raise his voice publicly against the admission of women, he might represent an opinion shared by a number of others.[29] In his speech delivered on February 18, 1786, Cabarrús emphasized the exceptional character of the new admissions, which did not justify opening the door to their sex: "let us close the door forever to their sex and not allow the advantages of such an example to conceal its drawbacks by making it a precedent" (cerremos para siempre la puerta a todo su sexo y no nos dejemos ocultar por las ventajas de un ejemplo los inconvenientes de una ley).[30] He invoked "the order as old as the world, that throughout all time and in all places has excluded women from public deliberations" (el orden, tan antiguo como el mundo, que siempre y en todas partes las ha excluido de las deliberaciones públicas), and insisted on the incompatibility between women's public activities and their family duties: sustaining the sentimental and moral foundations of the home, full of political resonances.[31]

His arguments, strongly indebted to Rousseau, are similar to those that would be deployed years later by French revolutionaries opposed to granting the new right of citizenship to women. Among others, André Amar, Pierre-Gaspar Chaumette, and Louis-Marie Prudhomme exhorted women to renounce political activity and devote themselves to domestic life, understood as a civil obligation.[32] A few years before the revolution, in 1787, Maximilien de Robespierre, then a young lawyer, might have read Cabarrús's essay in the French translation while he was preparing his reply to Louise de Kéralio's *discours de reception* to the Arras Academy, which would be read in the public session of April 18.[33] However, although he shared Cabarrús's idea of women's complementary qualities and roles in relation to men, he strongly argued for their right to develop their intellect as rational beings and against the "prejudice" of denying them admission to the academies.

Equality as the Cornerstone of Progress

Other participants in the debate, most notably Josefa Amar and Ignacio López de Ayala, rather than relying on the pragmatic criterion of utility, called on a theoretical concept of "reason" and a moral sentiment of "justice." For them, the admission of women to the society was the only possible result of admitting that women, just like men, were rational beings with civic duties toward the public good. Opposing Cabarrús, who had invoked in his favor immemorial tradition and the immutable laws of nature, the defenders of the admission of women admitted that this action, if it were accepted, would constitute a significant novelty and an important rupture with the past.

"It's about nothing less than making women the equals of men, about giving them a place in their [the male] assemblies and conferring with them on important topics, something that seems outside the established order and in itself extravagant" (no se trata de menos que de igualar a las mujeres con los hombres, de darles asiento en sus juntas y de conferir con ellas materias de gravedad, cosa que parece fuera del orden, y aun disparatada), wrote Josefa

Amar, supported by her friend Juan Antonio Hernández de Larrea, censor of the Aragonese Economic Society, who added his own comment: "opposing the membership of women in 'Economic Societies,' in my view, is to seek to strip them of their right of citizenship" (oponerse a que [las mujeres] sean Individuos de las Sociedades económicas, que a mi ver es lo mismo que quererlas despojar del derecho de ciudadano).[34] Her essay—the longest and most exhaustive by far—sent from Zaragoza and read during the meeting of June 24, 1786, adds a different perspective to the others: that of being the only one written by a woman, acutely self-conscious of her direct and specific implication in the question under debate.[35] She was the first Spanish woman to have been admitted to one of the patriotic societies, that of Aragón (Real Sociedad Económica Aragonesa de Amigos del País), in 1782, the same year that Mme de Bourdieu had been elected to the Nîmes academy and Fanny Beauharnais to that of Lyon, and that Mme de Genlis had been approached by d'Alembert with a proposal to become the first woman in the French Academy (Académie française).[36] On the grounds of her already established reputation as an erudite translator and member of an economic society, Amar assumed the voice of her sex in a debate whose theoretical and practical extent she foresaw. She used to her advantage the discourse of Enlightenment which, unlike traditional misogynist discourse, rejected the idea of women's inferiority, but fell short of assuming the consequences of admitting their intellectual equality.

For Josefa Amar, gender equality is not a purely rhetorical idea. The fact that it was not fully recognized in a century of Enlightenment is for her morally inexcusable and painful. She denies that women have their proper role in "civilized" societies, opposed to the "oppression" and "brutality" they suffered, according to common Enlightenment discourse, in primitive societies of the past and in non-European societies of the present. On the contrary, she characterizes their state as one of "dependence," a subtler but equally unacceptable form of inequality. Conscious that women "were banned from prizes and rewards," denied "the majesty of the scepter, the gravity of the toga, and military trophies" ([l]a majestad del cetro, la gravedad de la toga, y los trofeos militares) which were reserved to men, and having herself experienced those limitations, Josefa Amar stressed that economic societies themselves were an innovation, based on the effort to modernize Spain and a model of what a modern and enlightened society should be. Therefore, they should not become, as were other more traditional institutions such as the church and the universities, a "new sanctuary" or a "wall of separation," but should open their doors to women as a sign of progress.[37]

Ignacio López de Ayala, professor of the newly established Reales Estudios de San Isidro (Royal School of San Isidro), was the last member of the Madrid Society to deliver his speech, on September 2, 1786. He framed it as a philosophical dissertation on the natural equality of the sexes, taking as a point of departure the unity of the human species founded on the common attribute of reason. His arguments are close to the points of view that would be developed several years later by Antoine-Nicolas Caritat de Condorcet in several discourses: *On the Admission of Women to the Rights of Citizenship* (1790, *Sur l'admission des femmes au droit de cité*), and *Sketch for a Historical Picture of the Progress of the Human Mind* (1795, *Esquisse d'un tableau historique des progrès de l'esprit humain*), among others. But they also bear resemblance to the disagreement expressed decades earlier by d'Alembert in his *Letter from Mr. D'Alembert to Mr. J. J. Rousseau* (1759, *Lettre de M. d'Alembert à M. J. J. Rousseau*), where he accused Rousseau of disguising the oppression of women as nature's law in Rousseau's response to d'Alembert's article on theater in Geneva published in the *Encyclopédie*.

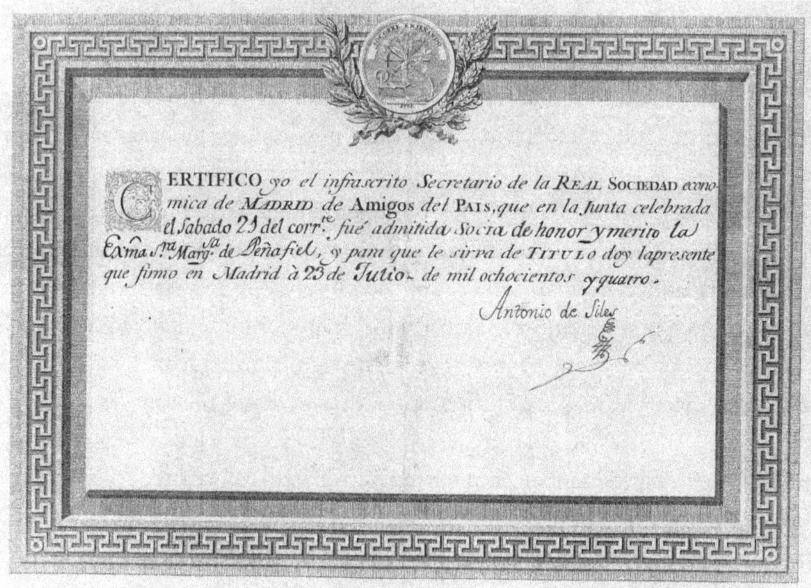

FIG. 1. Certificate of Admission of Francisca de Beaufort, Marquise of Peñafiel, 1804. Ministerio de Cultura y Deporte. Archivo Histórico de la Nobleza.

According to López de Ayala, gender equality cannot be questioned in an "enlightened century" and even less so within an institution that pretends to be representative and favorable to the Enlightenment. Recognizing women's equality and putting it into practice in the social order constitute a necessary sign of progress: "In this century, and especially in this place, it cannot be disputed that women are capable of all the learning and almost all the work of men" (En este siglo, y mucho menos en este sitio, no debe disputarse que la mujer es capaz de toda instrucción y de casi todos los trabajos de los hombres).[38] He argued: "Let us give this example of reason to the nations of Europe. All over the continent, philosophy is fermenting and its time has come. The world is new" (Demos este ejemplo de razón a las naciones de Europa. En toda ella fermenta la filosofía y ha llegado su tiempo. El mundo es nuevo).[39]

The Enlightenment Legacy

On August 27, 1787, a royal order (real orden) sanctioned women's admission to the Madrid Economic Society, stipulating that it should take the form of a Ladies' Section (Junta de Honor y Mérito or Junta de Damas), annexed to the Economic Society and in charge of works "proper to their sex," defined as education and the reform of luxury. The junta was composed initially of sixteen ladies of the highest nobility designated by a commission of male members of the Economic Society. Once they started their activities in October of that year, the ladies proposed to incorporate other associates: the first of them, Josefa Amar, in recognition for her reputation and her brilliant intervention in the debate. In her thank-you speech, she remarked that King Carlos III's decision would serve as an example in Europe, a comment that could not help but flatter the king of Spain and former king of Naples, who aspired to appear as an enlightened ruler and a friend of progress.[40]

Over the course of the following years, the Junta de Damas assumed, upon the request of the Madrid Economic Society or on its own initiative, other areas of competence in matters of education and charity: it took over the management of the four professional schools for poor girls that were operating in Madrid (Escuelas Patrióticas); the welfare of women in prison (Galera); the foundling hospital (Inclusa); and an institution charged with furnishing the raw materials for textile workers (Montepío de Hilazas). Elena Serrano and Elisa Martín-Valdepeñas Yagüe have convincingly shown that in all these tasks they also carried out an often underestimated scientific and technological activity in the form of practical experiments (about dyeing textiles, ventilation systems, and attempts at artificial feeding for babies) and translation and dissemination of technical novelties.[41] They justified their claims by appealing to the interests of reform (reducing mortality, promoting useful knowledge and productive labor) shared by male members of the Economic Society, while stressing that their condition as women and mothers gave them a particular responsibility to undertake these specific tasks.

The relations between the Junta de Damas and the Madrid Economic Society were never easy. The royal order specified that the junta should be affiliated to the latter as a subordinate organization. In this spirit, the statutes elaborated by a commission of male members of the society and approved by the king in 1794 established that the society should supervise the junta's activities, approve their annual report and proposals for new admissions, intervene in their dealings with exterior organizations, have a censor examine the essays and reports written by the members, and finally ensure a protocol of precedence in official ceremonies. However, in practice the junta functioned autonomously and continuously pushed back against the interference of the society in their activities and defended their character as an independent body, certainly affiliated, but not subordinated to the Madrid Economic Society; its first president, the Duchess of Osuna, and secretary, the Countess of Montijo, together with some of its most prominent members, like the Marquise of Fuerte-Híjar, who were particularly articulate and outspoken in this respect, frequently clashed with the representatives of the Economic Society.[42]

While most economic societies never admitted women or limited them to individual and honorific admissions, a number of them created their own women's sections at the end of the eighteenth century or throughout the nineteenth century (Murcia, Granada, Jaén, Cádiz, León, Las Palmas). As in Madrid, they were assigned functions regarded as a prolongation into the social sphere of women's domestic duties: responsibilities related to education and charity, especially those that implied other women (prisoners and poor) or children (abandoned infants). Although they were in theory submitted to the supervision and control of the masculine societies, they jealously preserved what they considered their own sphere of activity and responsibility. In Cádiz, like in Madrid, their conflicts with the economic societies or with local governments regarding questions of competences and protocol reveal the independence with which they assumed a space of power that they considered their own.[43]

Through their integration into the patriotic societies, elite enlightened women obtained social recognition and represented themselves as active subjects in the country's reform, exercising a particular type of "public representation," as the Countess of Montijo, secretary of the junta, wrote in a letter to King Carlos IV.[44] The ladies thus adopted reformist rhetoric that assigned to the elites the right and privilege to act as "friends of the country" by taking part in enlightened public opinion and spurring reforms that set in motion the reformist ideal: an ordered, productive society, aligned with the more advanced countries in Europe and presided over by an enlightened monarch and a benevolent and cultivated ruling class. In the symbolic and practical realization of their social engagements, elite women defended their status as "citizens," justified either on the grounds of their intellectual equality in relation to men, or, more often, by interpreting in their favor the discourse that extolled their different and complementary qualities.

The Spanish debate on women's admission to the patriotic societies was connected, to a larger extent than has been acknowledged up to now, to European discussions about the nature of gender difference, women's education, and their access to public spaces. Taking place in a period when the country was vindicating its place in European modernity, the participants in this polemic were aware that these were passionately discussed issues internationally. They used arguments taken from—either unconsciously or deliberately—a common pool of Enlightenment discourses and brandished the examples of women admitted into literary, scientific, and artistic societies in other countries to call for emulation. But they also—as the examples of Josefa Amar and Ignacio López de Ayala make clear—claimed that Spain could set an even more advanced example and become the model to be imitated, by making women's admission to enlightened institutions the rule instead of the exception.

The economic societies and their women's sections prolonged their existence beyond the Napoleonic invasion and the Peninsular War (Guerra de la Independencia), and into the liberal regime consolidated in the 1830s, after the failed experiments of the Cortes de Cádiz (Constitutional Convention, 1810–14) and the Trienio Liberal (Liberal Triennium, 1820–23). The Enlightenment's complex and paradoxical legacy thus lived on in the political cultures of liberalism, whose new definition of citizenship as the full possession of civil and political rights implicitly excluded women, while including them in their wider projects for the moral and sentimental foundation of the new social order.[45] In the transformed political context, one can discern, reshaped, the conflicting strands of Enlightenment thought that emerged during the debate on women's admission to the patriotic societies: its stress on reason as the key common denominator of humanity, but also its emphasis on the different, complementary natures and functions of the sexes; and its idea of progress as inextricably linked to improvement in the condition of women, albeit understood in widely differing ways—from equal access to education and public spaces, to empire over the family as the moral cornerstone of the public order.[46]

NOTES

Essay translated by Catherine M. Jaffe.

The research for this essay has received funding from the European Research Council under the European Union's Horizon 2020 research and innovation program (Project CIRGEN, ERC Grant Agreement No 787015).

1. Stapelbroek and Marjanen, eds., *The Rise of Economic Societies.*

2. Trojani, *L'écriture de l'amitié*; Astigarraga Goenaga, *Los ilustrados vascos.*

3. Franco Rubio, "Captar súbditos."

4. Astigarraga Goenaga, "Economic Societies" and "Connecting with the Enlightenment."

5. See Astigarraga Goenaga, *Los ilustrados vascos*, 49; Elorza Domínguez, *La ideología liberal*; Portillo Valdés, *Revolución de nación.*

6. For public opinion in eighteenth-century Europe, see Habermas, *The Structural Transformation*; Chartier, *Les origines culturelles*; and Melton, *The Rise of the Public.* Recent revisions of the validity of Habermas's theories in the Hispanic context include Guerra et al., eds., *Los espacios públicos*; Calvo Maturana, *Cuando manden los que obedecen*; and Kitts, "Spain and Habermas."

7. Jovellanos, "Elogio a Carlos III," 164 and 176.

8. Demerson, Demerson, and Aguilar Piñal, *Las Sociedades Económicas*, 44.

9. Graziosi, "Arcadia femminile"; Dixon, "Women in Arcadia," 372.

10. Chadwick, *Women, Art, and Society*; Sheriff, *The Exceptional Woman*; Smith, *The Emerging Female Citizen*, 50–73. The Academia de San Carlos in Valencia admitted ten women during the eighteenth century.

11. Including Antoniette Deshoulières (Académie d'Arles, 1680), Anne-Marie du Boccage (Rouen, 1756, and Lyon, 1758), Mme de Bourdieu (Nîmes, 1782), Fanny de Beauharnais and

Victoire Lallié (Lyon, 1782 and 1788), Marie Le Masson Le Golft, Louise Kéralio, and Mlle de Chatellier (Arras, 1787 and 1789), Nicole Lepaute (Béziers, 1788). See also Iverson and Pieretti, "Toutes personnes," about women's participation in prizes.

12. Cavazza, "Between Modesty and Spectacle"; Findlen, "Translating the New Science"; Petrovich, "Women and the Paris Academy"; Terral, "Gendered Spaces."

13. Leckey, "Patriotism, Agronomy," 236–37. Josefa Amar cites her as a precedent, in Negrín Fajardo, *Ilustración y Educación*, 168.

14. Hereafter, *Memorial literario*.

15. *Mercurio histórico-político*, June 1786: 188–89; July 1786: 282–83; September 1786: 87–88. The *Mercurio* sold slightly short of two thousand copies in America from 1780 to March 1781, with nine distribution points, the most important Havana, followed by Guatemala, Lima, Cartagena, and Panamá. Due to the high price overseas, the *Memorial literario* had only eight subscriptions outside peninsular Spain (including one each in New York, Havana, Veracruz, and Mexico). Larriba, *Le public de la presse*, 191 and 193.

16. *Mercure de France*, March 24, 1787: 176–86; Bolufer Peruga, "New Inflections"; Kitts, *The Debate*, chapter 5; Smith, *The Emerging Female Citizen*, chapter 3.

17. Bolufer Peruga, "Neither Male, nor Female."

18. Bolufer Peruga, "New Inflections."

19. Steinbrügge, *The Moral Sex*.

20. Negrín Fajardo, *Ilustración y educación*, 133–43 (quote on 139).

21. Negrín Fajardo, *Ilustración y educación*, 134 and 136.

22. Negrín Fajardo, *Ilustración y educación*, 143–47.

23. Negrín Fajardo, *Ilustración y educación*, 147–50.

24. Negrín Fajardo, *Ilustración y educación*, 157–61.

25. Koerner, "Women and Utility."

26. Serrano Jerez, *Ladies of Honor and Merit.*

27. Bonells, *Perjuicios que acarrean*, 358.

28. Elorza Domínguez, *La ideología liberal*, chapter 7.

29. Negrín Fajardo, *Ilustración y educación*, 150–56.

30. Negrín Fajardo, *Ilustración y Educación*, 151.

31. Negrín Fajardo, *Ilustración y Educación*, 152.

32. Badinter, *Paroles d'hommes*.

33. Sepinwall, "Robespierre, Old Regime Feminist?"; *Mercure de France*, March 24, 1787: 176–86.

34. *Memorial literario*, T. VIII, XXXII, August 1786: 430–38 (quote on 430).

35. There is more about Amar's contribution in López-Cordón's essay in this volume.

36. Schroeder, "Going Public," 377.

37. Negrín Fajardo, *Ilustración y educación*, 169 and 170. Amar would later become the first woman admitted to a Royal Academy of Medicine, that of Barcelona, in November 22, 1790.

38. Negrín Fajardo, *Ilustración y Educación*, 176–83 (quote on 176).

39. Negrín Fajardo, *Ilustración y Educación*, 178.

40. *Diario de Madrid*, January 26, 1788: 102.

41. Serrano Jerez, "Chemistry in the City," and *Ladies of Honor and Merit*; Martín-Valdepeñas Yagüe, "El eco del saber."

42. Martín-Valdepeñas Yagüe and Jaffe, *María Lorenza de los Ríos*.

43. Espigado Tocino, "La Junta de Damas" and "La marquesa de Villafranca"; Martín-Valdepeñas Yagüe, "Afrancesadas y patriotas."

44. Fernández Quintanilla, *La mujer ilustrada*, 151; Demerson, *María Francisca de Sales*.

45. Espigado Tocino, "Las mujeres en el nuevo orden"; Romeo Mateo, "Destinos de mujer"; Bolufer Peruga and Burguera López, "Género y modernidad."

46. See Burguera López, *Las damas del liberalismo respetable*, "Mujeres y revolución liberal," and her essay in this volume.

The Decisive Intervention of Josefa Amar y Borbón

Defending Women's Talent and Education during the Enlightenment

MARÍA VICTORIA LÓPEZ-CORDÓN CORTEZO

"Let Us Bring the Ladies on Board, Since We Cannot Dispute Their Worthiness"

On February 25, 1786, María Isidra Quintina de Guzmán y de la Cerda gave a speech to mark her induction as an honorary member of the Sociedad Económica Matritense.[1] She was the daughter of Diego Guzmán, the sixteenth Count of Oñate and seventh Marquis of Montealegre, and of María Isidra de la Cruz de la Cerda, the fourteenth Countess of Paredes de Navas. She was eighteen years old but was already known as a scholar, having been granted honorary membership by the Real Academia Española (Spanish Royal Academy) and a doctorate by the University of Alcalá.[2] Some months later, she was followed by María Josefa Alfonso-Pimentel y Téllez-Girón, the twelfth Duchess of Benavente, who gave her induction speech on July 22, 1786. She had married the Marquis of Peñafiel, who later became the Duke of Osuna, in 1771, and her entry into the Matritense was based on her noble rank as heiress to a great estate, and her well-earned reputation as an enlightened woman who was indisputably one of the leading lights of Madrid cultural life.[3] Both women were appointed to the society by royal order on January 22, 1786.

The entry of two such different and unusual women did not resolve the question of whether the Matritense should become open to female members, nor how this was to be done. Both women entered as equals of the male members and joined the Industry Commission, which ran the Patriotic Schools. But the debate continued and became unusually public with the publication of speeches in the *Memorial literario*, an Enlightenment periodical with a wide readership.[4]

The two Madrid aristocrats were not the first to enter such institutions. In 1782, the Real Sociedad Económica Aragonesa de Amigos del País (Royal

Society of Friends of the Country of Aragon) had admitted Josefa Amar y Borbón thanks to qualities "so unusual in her sex," which had earned her nomination. This was a high honor, underlined by her unanimous nomination and the society's willingness to incorporate her into ongoing projects. As noted in the minutes of November 15, 1782, she gave a speech in which she spoke of her gratitude for the nomination and her intent to carry out whatever tasks the society entrusted her with. This new female member had just published volume one of a translation from the Italian of the *Saggio storico-apologetico della Letteratura Spagnola* (Historical essay and apology for Spanish Literature), by the expelled Jesuit Javier Lampillas, a critique of the dismissive comments about Spanish literature that were common in Italy.[5] Josefa Amar was so convinced of the work's interest that she immediately sent the volume to the director of the Sociedad Económica Aragonesa, since Lampillas was an Aragonese author. It is clear that the translation led to her nomination and that she entered on equal terms with her male colleagues.[6]

The occasion was not wasted on the longtime advocates of opening the Matritense to female members. Thus, in 1786, they asked Josefa Amar to join the debate and sent her a pair of *memorias* (essays) on the topic by Jovellanos and Cabarrús, which encapsulated the two positions. She accepted right away, and within a couple of months she had written her own discourse (*Discurso en defensa del talento de las mujeres, y de su aptitud para el gobierno, y otros cargos en que se emplean los hombres*), dated Zaragoza, June 5, 1786, and mailed it immediately. Her personal involvement in the topic did not make her forget that she would be competing in a masculine forum. Perhaps because of this, she sent a draft to her friend José Antonio Hernández de Larrea, censor for the Aragonese Society. He gave his approval and agreed to publish his report on it, along with the discourse, in the *Memorial literario*, in August 1786. Larrea's arguments were as solid as Amar's; he wrote that denying women admission to the society meant "intending to rob them of the right to citizenship" (quererlas despojar del derecho de ciudadano).[7]

Josefa Amar referred directly to the essays by Cabarrús and Jovellanos. She pointed out that Cabarrús's refusal to admit women was grounded in generalities, since no one was proposing that all women should enter the society, "just as not all men are fit for it" (como tampoco son del caso para ella todos los hombres). She also critiqued his lack of practical common sense, since if women could be useful, there was "no reason to keep them out of it" (no hay razón para separarlas de ella). She saw Jovellanos's arguments very differently, calling him worthy of "perpetual recognition on the part of women" (perpetuo reconocimiento de parte de las mujeres) for having dared to come to their defense. She then focused on "the qualities" of the two ladies already admitted, and the incongruence of having to bypass the law in order to do so. Thus, other women should be allowed in, given "women's greater intelligence compared to men on various topics that come up every day and that must be promoted as important to the common good" (la mayor inteligencia que tienen las mujeres respecto a los hombres en varias materias, que se le presentan cada día y que deben promover, como importantes al bien general).[8]

Her essay, divided into thirty-four points, denounced the injustice of marginalizing women, calling it inappropriate for a civilized society, and advocated for parity with men based on four arguments: equality of origin, the role of willpower in forging the individual, the social nature of intellectual qualities, and the value of knowledge for self-esteem. Her piece, well written and skillfully structured, led to her nomination as member of the Junta de Damas at the Matritense by the governing board, shortly after the junta was founded by royal order on August 27, 1787. She was pleased with the nomination, but not with the way the issue had been resolved in Madrid, since female members of the society were not granted a "seat and a vote," as in her case, but a "separate chamber." She wrote an *Oración gratulatoria* (acknowledgment speech) in which she stated that it was appropriate to make the most of "the insights that women can provide, just like the men, because nature lends itself without distinction to all who wish to observe it" (las luces que pueden suministrar las mujeres, igualmente que los hombres; porque la naturaleza se presta sin distinción a cuántos quieren observarla).[9]

From that point on, she maintained intermittent, but ongoing, contact with the Matritense. In 1790, she sent a copy of her book *Discurso sobre la educación física y moral de las mujeres* (Discourse on the physical and moral education of women), not to the Junta de Damas, but to her colleagues in the Sociedad Matritense, who thanked and praised her for sending it.[10] In August of 1795, at the request of the Junta de Damas, she mailed another *Memoria*, in response to questions raised by different commissions about the education of women. Hers was one of the seven presented in June of 1796 by the secretary, the Countess of Montijo, to the censor for the Sociedad Económica Matritense, so he could write the report required for publication.[11] Each dealt with a different issue, and all received a favorable report, saying they were "in accordance with recent writings by the best physicians and doctors." The censor also recommended publishing the pieces together, but with the name of each author, because "they give the public an idea that upper-class people of the highest rank are not frivolous, they possess uncommon education and knowledge, and reading them may prove useful to many mothers and others charged with the education of young people of the opposite sex and, beyond this nation, they will give an idea not just of the zeal of Spanish ladies, but of the injustice of describing Spanish women as poorly educated" (dan una idea al público de que las personas de alta clase y primera jerarquía no están libres de preocupaciones, tienen una instrucción y conocimiento nada vulgares y su lectura puede aprovechar a muchas madres y personas encargadas en la educación de la juventud del otro sexo y, extendida fuera de la nación, darán una idea no solo del

FIG. 2. María Isidra Quintina de Guzmán y de la Cerda (engraved by José Giraldo), 1785. Ministerio de Cultura y Deporte. Biblioteca Nacional de España.

celo de las damas españolas, sino de la injusticia con que califican a las españolas de poco cultas).[12]

What Josefa Amar sent from Zaragoza focused on the "moral education that should be given to young women of marriageable age" (educación moral que se debe dar a las jóvenes que se hallan en edad de tomar estado). It was a commissioned text, with a different approach than she had taken in her *Discurso en defensa del talento de las mujeres*. In this new text she advised uniting "with agreeable examples, the general rules and maxims about moderation in habits" (con la amenidad de los ejemplos, las reglas y máximas generales de la moderación de costumbres) that should be inculcated in young women, whether they were inclined toward matrimony or the convent. The writer, who at the time was going through a difficult personal situation, had witnessed up close the tensions that had arisen in the Aragonese Economic Society between the more reformist members and the more aristocratically oriented group, and she was also aware that her exceptional presence among the other male members of the Aragonese Society did not please the Court nor the Madrid Economic Society.[13] Nevertheless, the censor of that institution observed in his report on her *Discurso* that it showed "great judgment, prudence and discretion"[14]—positive terms, but less warm than those he bestowed on other essayists, all of them titled noblewomen. Prefaced with the standard courtesy title of "Doña," this was Josefa Amar's last collaboration with the Sociedad Económica Matritense and the last piece signed with her name. One year later, her fears were confirmed. Floridablanca sent a letter dated August 27, 1797, suggesting that in Zaragoza they should also create a "separate Junta de damas" (Junta de damas separada). He even presented a plan to form it, but the intervention of Hernández Pérez de Larrea, among others, delayed the decision, which never took place.[15]

An Intellectual Biography

In much of Europe, the intellectual openness of the eighteenth century created conditions that favored the emergence into the public sphere of certain women who, thanks to their social position, actions, or talent, are nowadays obligatory historiographical referents. Thanks to a more fluid relationship between the sexes, the categorization in the way such women were represented relaxed, not because deep-seated misogyny had disappeared, but because certain assumptions were becoming incompatible with advances in thought. Spatially and socially, it was a limited change that was not free of contradictions, because acknowledging that some women possessed good minds and an education, or maintaining a certain degree of intellectual friendship with them, did not mean that masculine spaces, whether real or immaterial, were open to a presence that men found uncomfortable both in the public and the domestic sphere.

Little is known about many of these women, as in the case of Josefa Amar y Borbón. While she is not unknown, her biography has major gaps in it, so it is easier to follow her intellectual trajectory than her personal life. Both rested on four pillars: an excellent education; a realistic assessment of her abilities and the environment in which she functioned; an inclination toward topics and a literary genre rarely practiced by women—namely, the essay—and a public presence that was limited to just over twenty years, out of the eighty-four she lived.

She was born in 1749 in Zaragoza to a family with strong ties to the medical profession. Soon after she turned five, she moved to Madrid, where her father, José, and her grandfather Miguel Borbón y Berné were physicians for the royal family. They were interested in new methods of pedagogy, as was another relative, Andrés Piquer, also a royal physician. Her insertion in a network of medical and professional relations was important for her formation, as were the cordial relationships of the Amar and Borbón families with the Aragonese, and under King Carlos III they included politicians close to the Count of Aranda, who advocated reforms and the monarch's agenda.

As a little girl, Josefa was home-schooled, along with her siblings, by two excellent tutors: Rafael Casalbón and Antonio Berdejo, both Aragonese men with ties to Court circles and the Royal Library. From them she received excellent training in the humanities, as well as geography, history and religion, Spanish grammar and modern languages. For religious instruction, she used Fleury's catechism and was not exposed to pious extremism. Her scientific training was less extensive, but even so, she ventured to compose a volume titled *Aritmética* (Arithmetic), which is now lost. Was she hoping to follow in the footsteps of her Aragonese predecessor María Andrea Casamayor's *Tyrocinio aritmético* (Apprenticeship in Arithmetic), even though she makes no mention of it?[16]

She did not try to evade her destiny. When she came of age, she married a family friend twice her age, Joaquín Fuertes Piquer, the nephew of Andrés Piquer. That same year, 1772, they moved back to Zaragoza, where her husband had obtained a position as alcalde del crimen (criminal judge) for the Real Audiencia (Aragonese Apellate Court).[17] He was a cultured man, a founding member of the Sociedad Económica Aragonesa, and aware of his wife's intellectual tendencies, which he did not curtail. We will never know whether Josefa Amar was happy. Apart from the age difference, her marriage fit the model she recommended: a union of equals, "as befits reason," far from "the vicissitudes of amorous passion," which gave her the necessary autonomy for personal development.[18]

In Zaragoza, shortly after her son was born in 1775, Josefa Amar began gearing up. An avid reader, she became an assiduous client of the recently opened San Ildefonso public library, thanks to a special permit.[19] She also flourished in the intellectual climate of a city where the Sociedad Económica was gaining ground and notable figures—with whom she was in contact—came to visit.[20] Whether it was her own initiative or someone else's, translating Lampillas's work, the *Saggio storico-apologetico della Letteratura Spagnuloa*, represented an obvious opportunity,[21] thanks to the outcry created by the entry for "Espagne" by Nicolas Masson de Morvilliers in the *Encyclopédie méthodique*.[22] She foresaw the attention the work could generate and publicized it by sending it to the Marquis of Ayerbe, director of the Sociedad Económica Aragonesa.[23] It was unusual for a woman, even acting as a translator, to participate in a debate that included major names like Antonio José Cavanilles, Juan Pablo Forner, or the Italian Carlo Denina.[24]

Translation was starting to be a widely accepted activity for women. It was being practiced by high-society ladies and a few others who sought to earn money for their work and published under a pseudonym, or anonymously. They usually translated didactic or sentimental tales, often written by women, seeking to make the text relatable to its female readers. This was not the path taken by Josefa Amar, who chose a topic that was literary and "political," and thus male terrain. It was also a massive undertaking, since the six initial volumes were followed by a seventh, with a response from the author and an alphabetical index of authors and subjects, prepared by the translator.[25] In the prologue, she authoritatively explained the reasons for her choice: opportunity, a solvent author, and the measured tone of the work, "infrequent in apologies." And she laid out a theory of translation, which she summarized in one short sentence: "Those who do not forget they are translating will certainly not translate elegantly" (No traducirá con gala ciertamente el que no se olvide de que está traduciendo). Her closing words are no less significant: "We women also have some interest in its publication, because in the second part of the second volume there is a review of the famous female figures that the climate of Spain has produced in various branches of literature. Thus it has a claim both to please and to be welcomed by those of my sex. If I achieve acceptance from both, I can wish for nothing more."[26] Dedicated to María Luisa de Parma, the publication was well received and went through a second edition.[27]

She also translated the *Respuesta del Señor Abate Don Xavier Lampillas a los cargos recopilados por el Señor Abate Tiraboschi* (Reply to Señor Abate Don Xavier Lampillas to the charges brought by Señor Abate Tiraboschi), which she also dedicated to the Princess of Asturias.[28] Seeking the patronage of a member of the royal family or of a distinguished aristocrat to give prestige to a new work was a relatively frequent practice. In the case of a female author, it was also common to choose a woman to whom to dedicate her work, thereby establishing a relationship of complicity between both. In all cases, the dedication would have to be endorsed by someone of a certain standing because the work could only be published after it had been accepted. Josefa Amar was not only very familiar with these practices, but she also counted on good intermediaries. It should also be noted, though, that this patronage perfectly suited María Luisa who, from the moment of her arrival at the Spanish Court, made a great effort to promote her image as an enlightened princess, protector of the arts and letters, and of those dedicated to them. "Another reason," writes Amar in her dedication, "is that it is enough that Your Highness is the most illustrious, the highest, in a word, the head of all women, and the translator being a woman" (Otra [razón] es, baste ser V. M. la más ilustre, la más elevada; en una palabra, la cabeza de las mujeres, y ser una mujer la traductora).[29] The Junta de Damas and the *Elogios*, the feminine royal order of Noble Ladies that bore María Luisa's name, her patronage, are all aspects of the effective campaign to affirm the queen's image that eventually became a true propaganda machine.[30]

Since it was the cause of Amar's acceptance into the Sociedad Económica Aragonesa,[31] it is no surprise that she was immediately asked to do another translation, the *Discurso sobre si corresponde a los párrocos y curas de aldea instruir a los labradores en los buenos elementos de la economía campestre* (Discourse on whether rural parish priests should instruct farm laborers on the basic elements of rural economy), by Abbot Griselini, who also asked her to handle printing the work. Published in 1784, the book included an enthusiastic prologue by Juan Antonio Hernández y Pérez de Larrea, in which he stressed the importance of translations and compared Josefa Amar not just to "the Spanish Olivas" but also to Sevigné, Dacier, Beaumont, and other erudite women of her time.[32]

She soon became involved in the activities the society ran, such as the textile schools for girls or the Junta de Caridad (Charity Board), of which her husband was also a member.[33] There is no doubt that her presence in the society and her writings made her a well-known figure in Enlightenment circles both in Zaragoza and Madrid.

In 1790, she published her most extensive work, the *Discurso sobre la educación física y moral de las mujeres* (Discourse on the physical and moral education of women).[34] It was a text full of key topics, in which the pedagogical thought of the times is well represented. It was an erudite treatise, with many bibliographical citations, aimed once again at a male readership, which she wished to convert to her cause.[35] In it, she referred to two earlier works, the *Ramillete de escogidos consejos a la mujer que debe tener presente en la vida del matrimonio* (Bouquet of select advice to women on marital life) and the *Instrucción que conviene dar a las mujeres* (Education suitable for women), published in Zaragoza in 1784, both of which are now lost.[36] Subsequently she completed other unpublished translations: a travel narrative by Captain Henry Boyde, *Several Voyages to Barbary*, with descriptions of Mequinez and Alcazar (Meknes and Ksar el-Kebir—Morocco) and Oran (Algeria), and an educational text by Vicesimus Knox.[37] There is also an *Aritmética española* (Spanish Arithmetic)[38] attributed to her, and some other works referenced but never found.

In 1798, after a long illness, her husband died. After that, she devoted herself to charity work for the Sociedad Económica and other groups, and her literary activity declined. In 1808, as the senior sister of a community of laywomen at the Hospital de Nuestra Señora de Gracia in Zaragoza, the so-called Hermandad de la Sopa (Sisterhood of the Soup), she became very active, and her efforts multiplied during the first siege of the city by the French troops in 1808, since she did everything possible to safeguard the life and health of the refugees and deal with difficulties in accommodating them. It is difficult to prove whether she was involved in any other type of collaboration.[39] In 1809 she wrote a *Relación del bombardeo y ruinas del Hospital de Nuestra Señora de Gracia por las bombas francesas* (Account of the shelling and destruction of the Hospital de Nuestra Señora de Gracia by French artillery), in which she recounts what she herself witnessed.[40] The experience must have affected her intensely since, in 1811, the director of the congregation, Francisco Javier Landa, gave a brief outline of the institution's history in which, after praising Josefa Amar and other sisters, he stated that it had moved to a neighboring town, Cortes de Navarra, near Tudela, where she had relatives on her mother's side.[41] It was there, in 1810, that she must have received news of the death of her only child, Felipe, who was an *oidor* (judge) at the Real Audiencia (appellate court) in Quito (viceroyalty of Nueva Granada), and fell victim to the independence conflicts in the territories of Spain in America.[42]

After peace was declared, the Peninsular War ended, and she returned in 1816 to Zaragoza, where her brothers lived: Antonio, a military officer who had been deposed from his position as viceroy of Nueva Granada in America and returned to his home city, where he died in 1819,[43] and Francisco, a clergyman who was a canon. She went back to her congregation and must have taken up her former duties there. Perhaps she took up the pen, but sporadically, maybe the odd patriotic poem, a new translation project, but there is no firm evidence, nothing that helps dissipate the mystery surrounding her later years until her death in 1833.

Enlightenment Tropes and Controversial Topics

Josefa Amar's works speak for her. In them she projects the language and ideas of her generation, a body of concepts that was defined and coherent but not exempt from contradictions. She was a true Enlightenment figure, who had accepted most of those ideas, not uncritically, but from her position as a woman, a Catholic, and the heir to a cultural tradition she defended. In her texts, Enlightenment tropes recur: civility, public and private happiness, the common good, and of course, reason—ancient words whose meanings had by that time lost their transcendental nature. Civility, in her educational project, was hardwon; happiness came from fulfilling one's obligations and dealing kindly with others; a kind of *aurea mediocritas*, like the classics, or the humanists, which had nothing to do with the utopia of natural life advocated by some of her contemporaries. The common good took on a utilitarian meaning, as prosperity or well-being, which it had not possessed before. And reason, or understanding, was the most specific attribute of human beings, both men and women, so that to admit a difference between them was to deny the unity of the species. Amar was more reticent about feelings. Her distrust of them opened a gulf between her and the following generation.

Her reflections were not a demonstration of the wit of an autodidact, but rather the consequence of a context of intellectual opening with a constant flow of ideas that she, like other enlightened writers, would choose and adapt as best suited her purposes. Philosophically, although she did not read Descartes, nor his disciple Poulain de la Barre, her text is not far from the affirmations made especially by the latter, whose unequivocal "the soul has no sex" (l'esprit est de tout sexe) is also present in her texts.[44] The same is true of her explicit denunciation of the tyranny of opinion.[45] However, given the difference in their respective contexts and in the philosophical systems of their works, it is difficult to insist further in this comparison. Comparing the best-known work of Poulain de la Barre, *De l'éducation des dames* (On Women's Education), written as a dialogue, with Josefa Amar's *Discurso*, it is clear the former was able to play with different characters and use more agile and emphatic reasoning, while in her work Amar preferred to adopt a more doctrinal and erudite tone, full of clarifications and notes that supported her argument. Poulain says what he thinks; Amar has to justify her thoughts, so that the irony that pervades *De l'excellence des hommes contre l'égalité des sexes* (On the excellence of men against the equality of the sexes), would have been unthinkable for Doña Josefa. Even in her most daring text, *Discurso en defensa del talento de las mujeres*, she managed to smooth over the sharp edges of her thought. But her objective is clear: to use reason to dismantle the inequality between men and women and put an end to an age-old prejudice. It did not escape her that this could lead to social changes, among other things, by undermining the prohibition of certain activities to women. This was a question that tested many of her arguments.

Contradictory, restrained, there is no doubt of her curiosity, nor of her dedication when trying to satisfy it. And if she didn't receive the direct influence of the great masters, she was influenced by their heirs and opponents, Leibniz, Locke, and Condillac, whose scientific interests especially attracted her. The first served to demonstrate that Latin continued to be useful, and she praised his proposal for a universal language;[46] the others she read in French and appreciated their pedagogical aspects. Several special intermediaries helped her greatly: exiled Jesuits such as Juan Andrés and Antonio Eximeno, among others, who were closer to sensualist tendencies than to the Cartesian method.[47] Josefa Amar is a clear example of the influence that Italian Enlightenment (Iluminismo) had on Spanish culture and thought in the eighteenth century, and of its greatest interpreters, Genovesi, Filangieri, Beccaria, whose influence was also evident in the economic societies. And from this current, also, came her admiration for Gaetana Agnesi,[48] a follower of Newton and author of *Instituzioni analitiche ad uso della gioventú italiana* (1748), whose life trajectory, from student to chair (cátedra) in mathematics at the University of Bologna, from a public role to the silent exercise of charity and care of the sick, recalls Amar's own.[49]

Amar criticized men's selfishness and how it pervaded the nations that were called civilized, all determined to administer the critical instruments of the Enlightenment to suit their own interests.[50] She also blamed history for masking humanity as a nonexistent generic man that subsumed women in a masculine canon that ignored them.[51]

But no less significant are her pronouncements on more controversial topics like religion, societal dysfunctions, or marriage. Regarding the first, she never questioned the founding tenets of official religion, but that did not prevent her from criticizing certain practices of the church as a temporal power, or being less than enthusiastic about monastic life, especially for nuns. Knowing god and religion were "a Christian's first and most essential duty," she writes in her *Discurso*. In it, she argues for a religious practice free of external, formulaic devotional practices that she considered "less than reasonable," following the Spanish Jansenists. Like them, she argued that the clergy should collaborate with the state in spreading useful knowledge.[52] But she goes further, invoking the egalitarianism of the gospels to defend parity between the sexes.[53] She was of course not unaware that many arguments against the equality of the sexes were based on religion and, in the case of Christian denominations, on the sacred scriptures. It was not easy to contradict them, because of the lack of opportunity and censorship, but it was possible to turn them around with daring affirmations, in the context in which they were published. Thus, when she speaks of the original equality between Adam and Eve, she denies that any punishment ended up altering it and that, if there were subjection, it was relative.[54] And she warmly praises, in relation to these passages, Eve's sin as the driving force of knowledge and intellectual life.[55]

Amar saw the world as the natural setting for individual lives to develop, and society as the environment that men and women could fruitfully take action to improve. Her treatise, which was divided into various categories, but tended toward dichotomous polarization, did not criticize the foundations of the social system, but rather the dysfunctions that led to bad behaviors. Regarding social relations, she distinguished between those where one is superior, in which case one should be affable but maintain one's distance, and those between equals, ruled by respect and courtesy.[56] She says nothing of hereditary nobility, but castigates sloth and ostentation. She describes luxury as "apparent wealth," and contrasts it with "the poverty and decadence of the majority of individuals."[57] She argues that it is not use but rather abuse that should be corrected, since the difference between what is necessary and what is superfluous depends "on class and the circumstances of those concerned."[58] The same occurs with fashion, a recurrent topic in sermons and the press. She was irritated that people talked about it only in relation to women and protests that some argued that "we should dress nowadays the same way our grandmothers did" (haya de vestir ahora como vestían nuestras abuelas). Following fashion was a social imperative, but one should avoid falling into "ridiculous affectations."[59]

But none of these questions was as important, in her eyes, as matrimony, because of its implications for society in general and for women in particular. This was one of her recurring themes, closely linked to her critique of customs. Disunity in families, scandals, the disparity between future spouses, were all part of daily life, and not just in the theaters. Increasingly, there were recommendations to take the wishes of both into consideration, based on a greater consideration of women. And there were political actions aimed at improving marriage's bad image with something more positive, in the hope of augmenting the population.[60] In the process of transition from the old-style patriarchal family to the new, "sentimental" one, Josefa Amar drew attention to the dangers inherent in the change, convinced that women were going to be subject to more subtle but no less harmful limitations. Thus, her voice was a dissonant one, since she was going against the flow in always advocating for a marriage based on reason rather than passion. From her position as an Enlightenment writer, and not a Romantic, the ideal of a voluntary, mutual pact between equals seemed more suitable to her. "If you want a good marriage, marry an equal" (Si quieres casar bien, casa igual), she recommends, following the classics. She recommends taking into consideration the educational level of the spouses. As to age, she says one should marry at the time of "most robustness of nature," although she favors "the man being a few years older than the woman, since she ages earlier and would be subject to her husband's coldness" (el hombre tenga algunos años más que la mujer, respecto a que esta envejece antes y está expuesta a sufrir la frialdad de su marido). She also argues that it is a good idea for would-be spouses to get to know one another before the wedding, but prudently, "given the fragility of a young woman's reputation" (por lo delicado de la opinión de una soltera). On these bases, one could achieve reasonable happiness, based on "esteem," "mutual appreciation," and "trust," and husband and wife could live "in peace and harmony." Because she mistrusted feelings, she recommends that mothers be sure to teach their daughters to avoid the danger of passion and of marrying "without knowing anything about the state into which they are entering" (sin tener noticia del estado que van a contraer). She does not question the differential role assigned to the two sexes within the family, and repeatedly warns of the "inadvisability" of jealousy or shrewishness, traditional stances, whose limits lay in the development of personal autonomy, which she linked to intellectual exercise.[61] Thus, her "perfect wife" is virtuous and diligent, but also takes time to "broaden her understanding."[62] She was not, of course, unaware of the "obstacles" that women had to overcome to do this, but she was an optimist because she trusted in the inherent abilities of her sex.

Education for Life

Education is a central theme in Josefa Amar's writings. With the pedagogical optimism characteristic of the Enlightenment, she sees it not as an end in itself, but as an instrument of collective transformation, achieved through improving individuals. "Thus, the better the educational system, the greater the number of contented people and the greater [...] the advantages to the Republic" (Así, cuando mejor fuera la educación, será mayor el número de personas felices y más grandes [...] las ventajas de la República).[63]

This was a principle that few disputed, but that, in her case, was intrinsically united to her defense of reason and the equality of talent between the sexes, because only through them could one obtain the satisfactions of interior life and the reconciliation of women with themselves that Amar proposes. Very far from this, however, is the "universal neglect" they found themselves in, since "men promote it to keep them in ignorance so as to dominate them more freely" (lo fomentan los hombres para mantenerlas en la ignorancia y dominar así más libremente). This "vulgar" and wrong-headed behavior, she says, prevents "intimate and perfect society with the husband" (la íntima y perfecta sociedad con el marido), and has implications for household management and the upbringing of children, neither of which could be conducted from a position of ignorance. She buttresses these arguments by pointing to misogynist clichés such as women's curiosity or the claim that they "dominate and govern men at their whim" (dominan y gobiernan a los hombres a su antojo), to make her point and to emphasize the little benefit that their ignorance had for everyone.[64]

But the problem, as she saw it, was not only male selfishness, but also that women did not appreciate the advantages of being educated. She aimed to draw them out of their indifference by presenting intellectual training as an antidote to the fragility of beauty and the passage of time. Training the mind provided a "fund of philosophy" to counter the world's falsehoods, and acceptance of the inevitable. Thus, given the arbitrariness with which nature bestows her graces, she claims there is nothing better than "to acquire others that are more solid and permanent" (adquirir otras más sólidas y permanentes) such as those "of the mind, which never withers or ages" (del entendimiento que no se marchita ni envejece). There were many reasons for women's lack of interest in education. Of all of them, "lack of incentive" was what sharpened the differences between the sexes, because while males "study with the certainty of gaining employment, honors, interests" (estudian con la seguridad de lograr los empleos, los honores y los intereses), women had to do so "for their own good," with no stimulus. Since their destiny did not depend on how hard they studied, those who did so were heroines.[65]

Besides these principles, in her *Discurso*, she also developed the two sides of education, physical and moral, citing a veritable multitude of authors and references. From Fénelon and Locke to Rollin and De Puy, many contemporary writers appear on her pages, some recently translated and others she is proposing to translate, such as Blanchard or Knox.[66] There is only one indirect citation from Rousseau.[67] We should mention her praise for a very controversial Italian work that was almost included on the *Índice romano* of censored books, the *Trattato degli studi delle donne* (Treatise on women's education) by Nicolás Bandiera, dedicated to a Venetian lady, Isabel Cornara Foscarini, that "proves the equality of attitude and talent of that sex" (prueba la igualdad de actitud y talento de aquel sexo) and that she considers "the only one that purposefully deals with women's literary education" (la única que trata de propósito de la educación literaria de las mujeres).[68] In it, Bandieri assumes, like Poulain de la Barre, that women's intellectual capacities equal men's, and he advocates for in-depth literary instruction as compatible with women's traditional functions. He suggested a broad curriculum that Josefa Amar described as "highly advisable."[69] Among the many foreign authors she cites, the only Spaniard is Lorenzo Hervás y Panduro, whose first volume of the *Historia de la vida del hombre* (History of the life of mankind) had just come out in Spanish.[70]

Especially interesting are the sources Josefa Amar used on physical education and children's health, since she refers to Alphonse Le Roy, Jean-Louis Fourcroy, and Samuel Auguste Tissot, whose works were being translated at that time, or would be some years later. She also cites Joseph Raulin and Jacques Ballexserd, obligatory references among physicians and "hygienists" of the period. Amar also followed closely contemporary polemics about breastfeeding and physical education. She defended breastfeeding as a "natural right" for infants and saw physical education as a way of correcting in women that "faintheartedness and timidity" that makes them "useless for everything." Following Plato, she called for them to be taught "the same way as the men," as the Spartans had done.[71]

She deliberately cited many of the women authors who had written on the subject, such as Madame Le Prince de Beaumont, whose *Magasin ou instruction pour les jeunes dames* (Magazine or instruction for young ladies) she cites in the original French, even though there were already two translations into Spanish.[72] Likewise, for the Countess of Genlis, she mentions *Les Veilées du Château ou cours de morale* (Evenings at the Chateau or Course on Morality) translated by Fernando Gilleman as *Las veladas de la quinta* (Soirées at the Country House), although she preferred the French edition.[73] But she was most closely aligned with Madame de Lambert, whose works had been translated by the Countess of Lalaing, although Amar quotes them in the original.[74] While not her contemporary, Lalaing was the writer whose views most closely matched her own, and she repeats with approval maxims from Lalaing's *Réflexions nouvelles sur les femmes* (New Reflections on Women).[75]

There was no lack of references in her work to classical authors; from the accuracy of the quotes it is clear that she was consulting them directly, and at times she even gives the library where they could be found.[76] She was also familiar with medieval and modern works on the education of women, from the *Llibre de les Dones* (Book of Women) by Francesc Eiximenis,[77] to Vives or Erasmus; and medical treatises, citing the *Arte de las comadres* (Art of Midwifery) by Damián Carbón[78] or the works of Septalius.[79] She highlights *Nobleza virtuosa* (Virtuous Nobility),[80] a work by Luisa de Padilla, Countess of Aranda, referring to her on several occasions as "virtuous and discreet" and also from Zaragoza. The arguments she gives to support her points of view demonstrate the erudite nature of her essay.[81]

Agreeing with Locke and Madame Le Prince de Beaumont, and contradicting Helvetius, Condorcet, and Jovellanos, Amar defended homeschooling. A cultured and educated mother was, in her opinion, the best teacher, and if this was not possible she recommended seeking "an educated woman with good judgment as a governess to take care of her daughters' education" (una mujer instruida y juiciosa, que con título de aya, cuidase de la enseñanza de sus hijas). Or male teachers might be employed if they were "of good judgment and seemly behavior," but always under the mother's oversight to monitor progress and avoid any excessive familiarity. She was not in favor of school education, a "highly disputed point" in which the *Encyclopédie* itself had issued an opinion which she repeats, saying that young women's training should not be entrusted to nuns who have withdrawn from the world.[82] The same opinion was held by authors as diverse as Pedro de Montengón or Mary Wollstonecraft.[83]

Her educational proposals were aimed at promoting "good use of the rational faculties so as to act with good sense and discretion" (el buen uso de las facultades racionales para obrar con cordura y discreción).[84] They consisted of reading and writing, grammar and spelling, history and arithmetic, using texts by Plutarch and Cicero, Juan Luis Vives, Fray Luis de León, and Miguel de Cervantes, Jerónimo Zurita, and Florián de Ocampo, Father Flórez's *Reinas de España* (Queens of Spain),[85] and, of course, Charles Rollin. Only for girls with "superior" intellects, she proposes studying Latin, Greek, and modern languages: French, English, and Italian. As for geography, she recommends the works of Manuel de Aguirre, Juan Manuel Girón, Tomás López or Antonio Ponz, Nicolle de La Croix or Anton Friedrich Büsching. Among the essential "skills" she lists drawing, music or dance, preferably French and not Spanish, "because it does not call for so many suggestive movements." Her reading list was dry: there were few entertaining works and many classics.[86] She includes lessons in "feminine needlework," which involved "characteristic accomplishments for women," compatible with their studies. She also mentions "household economy and management," which consisted of "continual vigilance and care for the possessions and interests and good order of the family" (una continua vigilancia y cuidado de los muebles e intereses y en el buen orden de la familia), which prepared one for running a household.[87]

But Josefa Amar does not limit herself to demonstrating her authority on the matter of education or testifying to her knowledge of medical and hygienic works, but rather she conceives of education as a way to correct certain social disfunctions. So also did her contemporary, Mary Wollstonecraft, whose biography runs parallel to Amar's years of public activity. Amar would have been very interested in Wollstonecraft's *Thoughts on the Education of Daughters* (1787) and her *Vindication of the Rights of Woman* (1792), but it is almost impossible that Amar could have known of these works. Amar was more conventional, Wollstonecraft more daring, but this does not prevent them from coinciding in format, the choice of the articulated essay, and in subject, critiquing girls' education, accusing men of egotistical selfishness, calling for women to take upon themselves the development of their intellectual abilities to achieve greater autonomy that, in the case of Wollstonecraft, included economic independence. Both coincided in their concern for single women, for whom Josefa Amar defended the right to "make use of their liberty," like men in the same circumstances, to access "useful occupations."[88] For her part, Wollstonecraft, with her sights set on women of the emerging middle class, proposed a more all-inclusive system from the social point of view.[89] The Spanish writer voluntarily renounces this consideration and addresses the highest and, above all, more imprecise ranks of society, belonging to a traditional social structure in which the petty nobility and the professional groups had not yet cohered to form an intermediate social body. Despite her defense of the aptitude of women for the highest roles, Amar's recommendation of autonomy is limited for married women, to avoid the "disorder" that this might provoke in the exercise of family functions.[90]

From the traces of a life trajectory abruptly interrupted by silence and with the indispensable support of her writing, the identity of Josefa Amar eludes a complete characterization. She was an erudite woman proud of being so, who always avoided risking herself too much regarding certain issues. She pieced together a large part of her arguments with the thoughts of others, but always included some trace of her own. Her two great themes, the defense of the equality of reason between men and women and the education of the latter, were intimately connected and manifestly present in enlightened debates of her time. She knew this, and she used the themes to make herself known. But as a woman, with full consciousness of being so, she committed herself when it came time to state her convictions. She also wanted to render a well-deserved homage to her female predecessors who had fought in favor of their causes, weaving together a network of arguments, readings, and examples that recognized them. It is undoubtable that, in relation to her contemporaries, Mary Wollstonecraft and Olympe de Gouges, her proposals are more moderate, and she never took up, for obvious reasons, the theme of political rights. She also never had the intellectual rigor nor the expressive force of Madame de Staël. But more revealing than making comparisons between people of different qualities inserted in very distinct contexts is to ask ourselves how an average woman, who grew to adulthood in Spain between the reigns of Kings Carlos III and Fernando VII, came to formulate her own original thoughts, what was her affirmation with respect to tradition or the intellectual environment in which she lived, and what happened to her legacy.[91]

It is not necessary to turn to her most assertive work, the *Discurso en defensa del talento de las mujeres*, nor to the framework of the polemic in the Sociedad Económica Matritense to realize that Josefa Amar y Borbón used the debate about the sexes as her starting point and that it gave her work a public dimension that only Feijoo's had had until then. She did not aim to subvert male-female relations, but "to rectify as far as possible" the balance between them, pointing out that it was the result of a series of social conventions, accepted but mutable, and not a natural or divine imperative. She was not seeking to rally other women around her, but to convince them to apply themselves for their own benefit, since "wisdom is its own prize" (la misma sabiduría lleva consigo el premio competente).[92]

She was a gradualist, convinced of the difficulty of even gaining women for her side, and of the necessity of not closing off the channels of dissemination that she had managed to open. In her case, the past supplied female models with which to identify, but she interpreted their "celebrity" differently than most:[93] she saw them not as an exception, but as evidence that ability is manifested only when prejudices break down and circumstances allow women to exercise their will. She harbored no doubt that men and women enjoy the same intelligence and similar abilities, but, conscious that her readers were male, she was cautious about saying so. Only certain phrases allow us to glimpse that this accommodation exacted a major personal toll.[94]

Her premise is clear: human nature is not split, but shaped by bodily and spiritual aspects; the mind, the specific feature of our species, has no sex and even "manly fortitude" could be achieved with adequate physical education.[95] But at the same time she was eager to emphasize that true education and instruction did not merely consist of the acquisition of knowledge, but also in the exercise of the will and mental discipline. This is why in her texts the equality of the sexes is always linked to education, just as it is for her contemporaries, Condorcet, Mary Wollstonecraft, or even James and J. S. Mill, understanding, as they did, that it would suffice to educate men and women in the same way, that is, to provide a similar intellectual development, for them to achieve it.

The education she proposes is physical and moral, and she insists on the first, because "our machine is so organized in all its parts, that when one suffers, the others cannot freely exercise their functions (nuestra máquina está de tal suerte organizada en todas partes, que cuando alguna padece, las otras no pueden ejercer libremente sus funciones).[96] This benefits both sexes, and it is not surprising that Amar defends it, since without a doubt she knew well the *Praxis médica* (Medical Practice) of her relative Andrés Piquer. But even as she reveals herself to be "mechanistic" in these expressions, her proposal for women's moral education differs from manuals in use at the time, since it is not only directed at the regulation and correction of manners, but also meant to facilitate "the correct use of the rational faculties" so that each woman could be "happy in her rank and circumstance."[97] This is the "proper prize" that she desires her students to reach, and their ultimate goal, self-esteem.

Does this mean the renunciation of other aspirations? The adaptation to the possible in the face of the impossibility of many aspirations? Josefa Amar appears as willful as she is realistic, and her optimism and her purpose are clear: she does not want to promote "a fantastic plan" but rather to rectify as far as possible the established norm.[98]

And in case these arguments were not enough, Josefa Amar turned to two authorities always used in the polemic: the holy scriptures and history, pointing out the "perfect society" of the lost paradise;[99] and evoking wise women from the past and present but defending their abilities not with the misogynistic argument of exceptionality, but as specifically female and not anomalies of nature. On this basis, Josefa Amar is a clear representative of what has been called Enlightenment feminism or equality feminism, which points to the overall unity of the human race and attributes differences between the sexes to the influence of society, especially education. An observant woman, she had not failed to perceive that it was hard to determine whether some of the characteristic features of each sex should be attributed to nature or to culture.[100] Also, many of these differences tipped the scales in women's favor, since in her opinion they were the more imaginative and flexible of the two sexes. Thus, her model woman was as far from the masculine prototype as it was from the sentimental one, because she did not want women to have "manly minds" and because being "extreme in all their emotions" would put them beyond reason.

Reading Josefa Amar y Borbón's texts and her incomplete biography, we can reflect on the conditioning that shaped the creative process of this late-eighteenth-century scholar and her striking differences from her Enlightenment contemporaries—a minority made up of aristocrats, scholars, jurists, and scientists, all men of letters who combined literary creation and professional writing with barely any hitches, even sometimes putting their knowledge to political ends. It was an efficient system that matched Enlightenment ideology, but it failed when the author taking up the pen was a woman who lacked channels for disseminating her work, private resources enabling her to publish, or any "prize" or incentive for doing so. The idea that "they have so many more agreeable occupations to attend to that are more suited to their nature and customs" (ellas tienen tantas ocupaciones que atender más agradables y más análogas a su naturaleza y costumbres) was so widespread that such men little thought that someday they would have to share with women "the empire of literary reputation."[101]

This set of formative social and ideological circumstances constrained women's literary production and explains why, in general, it was limited to a short period of time. The case of Josefa Amar is very clear in this respect, since her life and work fell into obscurity. What would have happened if this scholar, at the peak of her powers, had carried on writing? What topics would she have covered, and how would the passage of time and experience have affected her? Since history never trades in suppositions, in Josefa Amar's life and in her work, silence is a crucial part of her legacy. I think that breaking this silence, recuperating her legacy, and inserting her into her proper place in the Spanish Enlightenment are not disproportionate.

NOTES

Essay translated by Catherine Jagoe.

1. The title of the epigraph refers to "Hagámoslas de nuestro partido, ya que no las podamos disputar el mérito." José Antonio Hernández y Pérez de Larrea wrote this sentence in the letter that accompanied Josefa Amar's "Discourse in defence of women's talent," *Memorial literario,* T. VIII, XXXII, August 1786: 437; Guzmán y de la Cerda, *Oración gratulatoria.* The discourse was also published in the *Memorial literario,* T. VII, XXVII, March 1786: 357–61.

2. Vázquez Madruga, *María Isidra Quintina de Guzmán.*

3. ARSEM, Expediente 93/10; Fernández Quintanilla, *La IX Duquesa de Osuna.*

4. See *Memorial literario,* T. VII and VIII, 1786; Larriba, *El público de la prensa,* 85–88; Negrín Fajardo, *Ilustración y Educación,* 33–38. This last work reproduces all the discourses of the polemic over the admission of women to the Real Sociedad Económica Matritense from 1776 to 1786.

5. Lampillas, *Ensayo-apologético.*

6. See also Lewis, "Women as Public Intellectuals."

7. *Memorial literario,* T. VIII, XXXII, August 1786: 430.

8. *Memorial literario,* T. VIII, XXXII, August 1786: 400–430 (quotes on 418–20 and 427–28); ARSEM, Expediente 81/10.

9. Amar y Borbón, *Oración Gratulatoria.* The discourse was also published in the *Diario de Madrid,* January 26, 1788: 101–3.

10. ARSEM, Expediente 115/1.

11. See Jaffe, "Networks of Enlightenment: Women Writers and the Republic of Letters," in this volume.

12. ARSEM, Expediente 146/11.

13. Pérez Sarrión, "Casual poverty"; Deacon, "Juan Meléndez Valdés en la Real Sociedad Económica Aragonesa."

14. ARSEM, Expediente 146/11.

15. Sullivan, "Josefa Amar y Borbón."

16. Casamayor y de la Coma, *Tyrocinio arithmético.*

17. See her biography in López-Cordón Cortezo, *Condición femenina,* 40–51.

18. Amar y Borbón, *Discurso sobre la educación física,* 229. All quotations are from the 1994 López-Cordón edition. López-Cordón Cortezo, *Condición femenina,* 129–35.

19. Amar y Borbón, *Discurso sobre la educación física,* 259.

20. Some were connected to the judiciary, like Arias Antonio Món or Juan Meléndez Valdés; others came and went, like Ignacio de Asso or Lorenzo Normante.

21. Lampillas, *Ensayo histórico-apologético.*

22. Masson de Morvilliers, "Espagne," 565.

23. Minutes of meeting. November 8, 1782, ARSEA, Actas; Sullivan, "Josefa Amar y Borbón," 118; López-Cordón Cortezo, *Condición femenina,* 55–56.

24. Cavanilles, *Observaciones;* Forner, *Oración apologética;* Denina, *Respuesta a la pregunta.*

25. Lampillas, *Respuesta del Señor Abate Don Xavier Lampillas.*

26. "También tenemos las mujeres algún interés en su publicación, porque en el tomo segundo de la parte segunda se hace memoria de las insignes, que ha producido este clima de España en varios ramos de literatura. Por esta razón pudiera pretender igualmente el agrado y buena acogida entre las de mi sexo. Si consigo la aceptación de ambos no me queda que desear." Amar y Borbón, "Prólogo de la traductora."

27. Lampillas, *Ensayo Histórico Apologético . . . Segunda edición.* The authorization of the dedication, AHN, Estado, Legajo 3234, Expediente 30.

28. Lampillas, *Respuesta del Señor Abate Don Xavier Lampillas.*

29. Lampillas, *Ensayo Histórico Apologético . . . Segunda edición,* T. I, 2–3.

30. Calvo Maturana, *María Luisa de Parma,* 77–83; López-Cordón Cortezo, *Condición femenina,* 82–83.

31. Minutes of meeting, October 11, 1782, f. 169–70, ARSEA, Actas.

32. Oliva Sabuco (1562–1622) was an erudite Spanish author who wrote a book on philosophy. Hernández y Pérez de Larrea, "Prólogo."

33. Forniés Casals, *La política social,* 343–50.

34. Amar y Borbón, *Discurso sobre la educación física,* 1790.

35. López-Cordón Cortezo, "Josefa Amar y Borbón."

36. Palau y Dulcet, *Manual del librero hispanoamericano,* refs. 10720 and 10726; Aguilar Piñal, *Bibliografía de Autores españoles del siglo XVIII,* vol. 1: 228–29.

37. Boyde, *Several voyages to Barbary;* Knox, *Liberal Education.* The references are in Latassa y Ortín, "Doña Josefa Amar, y Borbón," 231.

38. Latassa y Ortín, "Doña Josefa Amar y Borbón," 234.

39. Corona Marzol, "La voz de las mujeres."

40. Gil Novales, *Diccionario bibliográfico de la Guerra de la Independencia,* vol. 1: 25; AHNSG, Libro IV de Acuerdos.

41. Casamayor, *Años políticos e históricos,* 301; Salas Valdés, *Obelisco Histórico,* 330–36.

42. López-Cordón Cortezo, *Condición femenina,* 53–56.

43. Pumar Martínez, *Don Antonio Amar y Borbón.*

44. Stuurman, *François Poulain de la Barre; Memorial literario,* T. VIII, XXXII, August 1786: sections 7 and 9.

45. Fraisse, "Poullain de la Barre ou le procés des prejugés."

46. Amar y Borbón, *Discurso sobre la educación física,* 191.

47. Juan Andrés y Morell (1740–1817), after his expulsion from Spain, was received in Mantua by the Marquis of Bianchi, and remained there until the Napoleonic invasion. He was the author of various works, such as *Origen, progresos, y estado actual de toda la literatura* (Madrid, 1784–1805); Antonio Eximeno (1729–1809), a Valencian professor of mathematics at the Royal College of Artillery, was also expelled in 1767. He wrote *Instituciones filosófico-matemáticas,* inspired by Locke and Condillac, and a eulogy of Machiavelli. He was called "the Newton of music" for having established a new musical system. See Picó Pascual, *El padre Antonio Eximeno Pujades.*

48. María Gaetana Agnesi (Milan, May 16, 1718–Milan, January 9, 1799).

49. Amar y Borbón, *Discurso sobre la educación física,* 261–262.

50. *Memorial literario*, T. VIII, XXXII, August 1786: section 6.

51. Amar y Borbón, *Discurso sobre la educación física*, 81–84 and 209.

52. Amar y Borbón, *Discurso sobre la educación física*, 147–52.

53. Tomsich, *El jansenismo en España*, 26–65; Saugnieux, *Le jansénisme espagnol*, 20 and following pages.

54. *Memorial literario*, T. VIII, XXXII, August 1786: section 9.

55. *Memorial literario*, T. VIII, XXXII, August 1786: section 8.

56. Amar y Borbón, *Discurso sobre la educación física*, 162–63.

57. Amar y Borbón, *Discurso sobre la educación física*, 202–4.

58. Amar y Borbón, *Discurso sobre la educación física*, 127.

59. Amar y Borbón, *Discurso sobre la educación física*, 199–202. In *El Pensador* by José Clavijo y Fajardo there are several criticisms. See Pensamiento LIII, LIV (T. V, 1767: 1–22 and 1–15) and LXIX (T. VI, 1767: 1–15).

60. Seixo, *Discurso filosófico*, 35; Bolufer Peruga, *Mujeres e Ilustración*, 359 and following pages.

61. Amar y Borbón, *Discurso sobre la educación física*, 232 and 234–36.

62. Amar y Borbón, *Discurso sobre la educación física*, 195.

63. Amar y Borbón, *Discurso sobre la educación física*, 57.

64. Amar y Borbón, *Discurso sobre la educación física*, 61–63.

65. Amar y Borbón, *Discurso sobre la educación física*, 61–67.

66. The first, a defrocked Jesuit, author of *L'École des Moeurs*, translated by Ignacio García Malo en 1786. Of the second, she recommends *Liberal education*, that she qualifies as a "method of classical studies" (método de estudios clásicos). Amar y Borbón, *Discurso sobre la educación física*, 264.

67. Speaking of *Émile Chrétien ou De l'éducation de C. de Leveson*, a pseudonym, she says "it is the opposite of Rousseau's *Emile*" (el opuesto del de Emilio de Rousseau). Amar y Borbón, *Discurso sobre la educación física*, 263.

68. *Trattato degli studi delle Donne* was published anonymously in Venice in 1740; Amar y Borbón, *Discurso sobre la educación física*, 261–262.

69. Amar y Borbón, *Discurso sobre la educación física*, 262.

70. Hervás y Panduro, *Historia de la vida del hombre*.

71. Amar y Borbón, *Discurso sobre la educación física*, 83 and III.

72. Le Prince Beaumont, *Conversaciones familiares*, trans. Miguel Ramón y Linacero; *Almacén y biblioteca completa de los niños*, trans. Mathias Guitet; *Biblioteca completa de educación para señoras y jóvenes*, trans. Joseph de la Fresa; *Almacén de las señoritas adolescentes*, in the version by P. Barco López and different editions.

73. Genlis, *Las veladas de la quinta*. The second edition was published in 1791.

74. Lambert, *Obras*.

75. Amar y Borbón, *Discurso sobre la educación física*, 195.

76. Thus, of the *Económico* by Jenofonte, she mentions four editions, the last, translated by Ambrosio Rui Bamba in 1786, which "is in San Ildefonso de Zaragoza." Amar y Borbón, *Discurso sobre la educación física*, 252.

77. Eiximenis, *Llibre de les dones*. There is a Spanish adaptation from 1545 entitled *Carro de las donas*, to which Amar refers.

78. She notes that "don Nicolás Antonio did not know of it, for he does not cite it in his *Bibliotheca Hispana Nova*," published in 1541. Amar y Borbón, *Discurso sobre la educación física*, 257.

79. The work by Ludovico Settala, *De ratione instituendae et gubernandae familiae*, published in 1626, was in the Biblioteca de San Ildefonso. Amar y Borbón, *Discurso sobre la educación física*, 257.

80. Aranda, *Nobleza virtuosa*.

81. Amar y Borbón, *Discurso sobre la educación física*, 267.

82. Amar y Borbón, *Discurso sobre la educación física*, 244–46, and 248–51. The article by Desmahis, "Reflexiones imparciales sobre las mujeres," was published in *Miscelánea instructiva, curiosa y agradable*, T. II, 4, 1796: 58–77 (see p. 63); *Espíritu de los mejores diarios literarios que se publican en Europa*, 48, October 20, 1787: 474–75; Bolufer Peruga, *Mujeres e Ilustración*, 140.

83. Montengón, *Eudoxia*; Wollstonecraft, *Thoughts on the Education of Daughters*.

84. Amar y Borbón, *Discurso sobre la educación física*, 135.

85. Flórez, *Memorias de las Reinas Católicas*.

86. Amar y Borbón, *Discurso sobre la educación física*, 181–84 and 193.

87. Amar y Borbón, *Discurso sobre la educación física*, 160, 169, and 187.

88. Amar y Borbón, *Discurso sobre la educación física*, 226.

89. Wollstonecraft, *Vindicación*: 101; Taylor, *Mary Wollstonecraft and the Feminist Imagination*.

90. Amar y Borbón, *Discurso sobre la educación física*, 72–73; *Memorial literario*, T. VIII, XXXII, August 1786: section 6.

91. Diggins, "The Oyster and the Pearl"; Dosse, *Le pari biographique*; López-Cordón Cortezo, "La vida intelectual de las mujeres."

92. Amar y Borbón, *Discurso sobre la educación física*, 66.

93. Thomas, *Historia, ó Pintura del carácter*.

94. Amar y Borbón, *Discurso sobre la educación física*, 72–73.

95. Amar y Borbón, *Discurso sobre la educación física*, 80–81.

96. Amar y Borbón, *Discurso sobre la educación física*, 79–80.

97. Amar y Borbón, *Discurso sobre la educación física*, 135.

98. Amar y Borbón, *Discurso sobre la educación física*, 72.

99. *Memorial literario*, T. VIII, XXXII, August 1786: sections 7, 8, 9, 11, 15, and 18.

100. Amar y Borbón, *Discurso sobre la educación física*, 205.

101. Review by Manuel José Quintana of *Obras poéticas* by María Rosa de Gálvez, in *Variedades de ciencias, literatura y artes* 3 (1805): 159–64.

Women's Associationism and the Pursuit of Public Happiness, 1787–1823

ELISA MARTÍN-VALDEPEÑAS YAGÜE

The admission on an exceptional basis of two women to the Real Sociedad Económica Matritense in 1786 provoked heated debates about the regular collaboration of women in the institution. Overwhelmed by the controversy, which had been made public when the speeches were reproduced in the press, and in order to avoid harsher criticism, the institution agreed to consult with King Carlos III and await his decision. By royal order on August 27, 1787, the monarch clearly expressed his intention to promote the Junta de Damas, establishing the guidelines for its organization in a separate forum and with its own juntas (assemblies), in which the women associates would "proceed with and address together the means by which to promote good education, improve customs with their example and their writings, introduce the love of work, reduce extravagance, which [. . .] destroys the fortunes of private individuals [. . .] to the detriment of the State, and replace foreign adornments or those merely whimsical with domestic kinds" (procedan y traten unidas los medios de fomentar la buena educación, mejorar las costumbres con su ejemplo y sus escritos, introducir el amor al trabajo, cortar el lujo, que [. . .] destruye las fortunas de los particulares [. . .] con perjuicio del Estado, y sustituir para sus adornos los géneros nacionales a los Extranjeros, y de puro capricho). The objective of the women's meeting consisted of analyzing "the best means of promoting virtue, determination, and industry in their sex" (los mejores medios de promover la virtud, la aplicación, y la industria en su sexo).[1]

Throughout its first thirty years of history, the Junta de Damas accomplished the objectives indicated by the king upon its foundation. The junta utilized strategies such as royal protection, especially by the queen, to carry out its activities; it exercised power; and it defended equality—union did not mean subordination—with the Sociedad Económica Matritense, under whose protection the junta had been created. Through the members' dedication to education, charity, and writing, they collaborated in projects of general utility advocated by enlightened men. By turning their attention to the most unfortunate, they helped to ease social tensions and preserve social order; with their moralizing attitude they assured a certain stability during the conflictive years of the end of the old regime in Spain. They also took on an exemplary function, because they acted as "a mirror of virtues for women of the lower ranks of society."[2]

The Establishment of the Junta de Honor y Mérito

Following the authorization, a supervisory committee composed of members of the sociedad worked painstakingly to establish the new women's section. From the content of the royal order they deduced that the Junta de Damas would remain "at all times dependent on the Sociedad, as a part of this body" (en todo tiempo dependiente de la Sociedad, como parte de este Cuerpo), and that to form it they should choose "those women who, because of their circumstances, are deserving of this honorable distinction" (aquellas Señoras, que por sus circunstancias sean acreedoras a este honrosa distinción).[3]

The inaugural session of the women's section took place on October 5, 1787, in the hall of the Casas Consistoriales (Town Hall) of Madrid, where the Matritense had held its meetings since its foundation. The event was fittingly reviewed in great detail in several of the capital's daily newspapers—*Gaceta de Madrid*; *Diario curioso, erudito, económico y comercial*; *Memorial literario*; and *Mercurio de España*—which distributed the review throughout the country. The newspaper articles included the king's consent, the development of the act of establishment, the catalog of the founding damas, the objectives of the association, and the male associates' explicit support of the women's group. From the content of these articles, readers were able to easily conclude that the women "came together as one board, where there was no objective but patriotism" (concurrían a una Junta, donde no había otro objeto que el patriotismo) and that they took very seriously the opportunity that had arisen when they gathered.[4] Of the sixteen founding members, ten attended the meeting and were received by the members of the supervisory committee.[5]

The Countess-Duchess of Benavente, who had been previously designated president by the sociedad, delivered an eloquent speech. Then, the order of seniority of the members, including those not in attendance, was decided by raffle, "in order to avoid any complaint and etiquette thereafter" (para evitar toda queja y etiqueta en lo sucesivo), while respecting that the Countess-Duchess of Benavente herself and María Isidra Quintina de Guzmán, admitted prior to the formation of the junta, would be at the head of the list of members. Afterwards, the attendees elected the secretary, the Countess of Montijo, and appointed the guardians of the Escuelas Patrióticas, whose supervision had been entrusted to the women by the sociedad.[6] These centers had been founded in 1776 by the sociedad to seek career opportunities for the poor youth of the city.

The president, following the recommendation of the supervisory committee, proposed admitting Josefa Amar y Borbón, "because it was just that this gesture of recognition be given to her for the paper she published in support of women when the issue was raised whether it was advisable or not that women be admitted to the Sociedad" (por ser justo se le diese esta señal de reconocimiento, por el papel que publicó en favor de las mujeres, cuando se ventilaba el punto, de si convenía o no que fuésemos admitidas en la Sociedad).[7] A month later, the writer replied from Zaragoza, expressing her thanks for the honor that she had been accorded and accompanying her letter with a congratulatory statement that was later printed.[8] She offered her collaboration as well: "The distance at which I find myself does not allow me to offer my personal services; but if perhaps absent members can contribute in some way, I ask that Your Excellency assure the Junta [de Damas] that I of course will always be swift to employ myself in its service in whatever way my person and talents can be useful" (La distancia en que me hallo no me permite ofrecer mis servicios personales: pero si acaso pueden contribuir de alguna manera las socias ausentes, pido a V. E. asegure desde luego a la Junta [de Damas], que estaré siempre pronta a emplearme en su obsequio para cuanto guste disponer de mi persona, y talentos).[9]

Finally, at the suggestion of the members' committee, the junta decided that the Matritense would inform the King Carlos III of their desire to place themselves under the auspices and protection of the Princess of Asturias, María Luisa de Parma, wife of the heir to the throne, the future King Carlos IV, repeating the request that the Countess-Duchess of Benavente and María Isidra de Guzmán had made earlier through Count Floridablanca, the secretary of state.

The secretary of state's reply on October 11 announced that the king had consented to their wishes. The Princess of Asturias and the Infantas (Princesses) María Josefa de Borbón and María Ana Victoria de Braganza joined the women's forum. These admissions constituted the clear indication of the monarchy's explicit support of the recently created women's institution and, at the same time, the involvement of several of its members in its activities.[10]

First Steps

After the inauguration, in order to begin working, it was essential to recruit new members so that the "patriotic ideas that the Junta has conceived and is beginning to carry out be disseminated in the Court [city of Madrid]" (que se difundan en la Corte las ideas Patrióticas, que la Junta ha concebido, y empieza a poner en ejecución),[11] as well as to formulate operational procedures.

The committee of sociedad members entrusted with supervising the Junta de Damas drafted the articles after debating them and sent them to the women with the considerations they considered pertinent. The women discussed them, gave their opinions, and with the agreement of both groups, proceeded to the final version. The women accepted the majority of their associates' proposals but incorporated some amendments.

These provisional statutes governed the Junta de Honor y Mérito until the definitive ones were approved by royal order on April 10, 1794.[12] In line with the statutory modifications that the sociedad itself had made during this time, they varied considerably and staunchly subordinated the Junta de Damas to the Matritense, which on occasion strained the relationship between both institutions because of the male associates' excessive eagerness to subordinate the women.[13] These statutes were in effect until 1851, although there was a thwarted attempt to modify them in 1821.[14]

In the statutes of 1794, the objective to strive against luxury, which had been one of the reasons for the establishment of the junta according to the royal order that approved its formation, disappeared. The purposes of the Junta de Damas were limited to "establish and spread good education, improve manners through its example and enlightenment, introduce the love of work, and foment industry" (establecer y radicar la buena educación, mejorar las costumbres con su ejemplo y sus luces, introducir el amor al trabajo, y fomentar la industria).[15]

The leadership positions, which in the provisional statutes of 1788 were limited to the president, elected every three years, and the secretary, a lifelong position, along with their alternates, were expanded in 1794 by the incorpo-

FIG. 3. Cover page of statutes of the Junta de Socias de Honor y Mérito, 1794. Comunidad Autónoma de Madrid. Biblioteca Regional de la Comunidad de Madrid.

ration of the position of censor and her alternate, the vice-censor. The statutes more clearly established their roles. The president, whose position now became annual, would be a member of all the committees, would maintain control and order in the meetings, avoiding that "the Junta's harmoniousness be disturbed by talkative personalities in the meetings but rather she will impose silence which will be observed as inviolable" (se turbe la buena armonía de la Junta con personalidades en las conferencias, sino que impondrá silencio, el que se observará inviolablemente).[16] At the meeting prior to the elections, she was to present a report about her administration. In the event of absence or illness, the vice-president would substitute for the president. The censor would be responsible for the observance of the statutes, the agreements, and the members' fulfillment of their duties. This position was also an annual one.

Regarding the secretary, the statutes listed all of her responsibilities, among which were the preparation of an annual report to be read at the public or general meetings when awards were distributed (juntas públicas de distribución de premios) of the Matritense and in which the names of the deceased members would be mentioned. The secretary would be elected every three years.

The novelty of the formation of the Junta de Damas resulted in a respectable number of applications for admittance, but subsequently the admissions stagnated to two or three a year, surpassing one hundred members around 1823. Although the 1794 statutes proclaimed equality without discrimination, contrary to what occurred in the provisional statutes of 1788, which established different classes of members with varying rights, the section remained limited to women of the elite class with a preponderance of aristocrats, a group that had most strongly assimilated the reformist ideas of enlightened despotism.[17] The majority came from families whose male members held high positions in the Court, in the politico-administrative network, and in the army. The women's practical stance, focused on popular education, contrasted with the excessively theoretical, arbitrary nature that their male companions displayed, which became easily entangled in useless theoretical arguments in any given situation.[18]

María Luisa de Parma, Protector of the Junta de Damas

The founding members of the women's council considered the incorporation of María Luisa de Parma in 1787, then the Princess of Asturias, as a fundamental asset for their success. A year later, the ascent of King Carlos IV to the throne provided a new opportunity to strengthen contacts with the monarchs. On December 20, 1788, the Countess of Montijo wrote to the secretary of the Real Sociedad Matritense informing him of the members' desire to have an audience with the new queen to pay her their respects, and at the same time to petition her, "since the Junta has had the honor of having her [Queen María Luisa] as a member, that it might have the honor of her being its Protector" (ya que la Junta ha tenido el honor de tenerla por socia, tenga el de que sea su Protectora).[19] The damas needed the queen's active protection because of the ongoing occasions in which they resorted to her influence with the king, especially to try to alleviate the chronic economic problems that the educational and charitable establishments in their care suffered. The queen repeatedly demonstrated her willingness to support the women's institution that, in turn, publicly expressed its appreciation through the *elogios*.

The collection, printed between 1794 and 1801, contained a certain formal symbolism, customary in these kinds of works and intended as propaganda of the monarchy as it was envisioned in the ancien régime. All this gave the pieces a forced, monotonous character even though their authors tried to endow them with originality and modernity by exalting the qualities that Queen María Luisa embodied as the personification of the archetypal queen and woman according to the prevailing model in Enlightenment Spain. The attributes of an absolute enlightened monarchy, in this case, were personified in the female subject of the monarchy. María Luisa appeared in the works embodying ideal values, both public and private, that her status as queen encompassed. Her protection of the feminine association, which constituted the first conquest of public space on behalf of women in the eighteenth century, highlighted her exemplary role. She served as a model for the junta and for women in general, representing a meaningful femininity symbolically constructed and publicly expressed through charity and philanthropy.[20]

The establishments dependent upon the Junta de Damas had to overcome immense obstacles, which were happily resolved thanks to the constancy of the members, but also thanks to the queen's direct support, a recognition which the damas constantly acknowledged in the *elogios* (eulogies). The king and queen's economic contributions to the Junta de Damas, which originated from the government as well as from their personal funds, were substantial, thanks to the ability of those ladies who performed roles in the Court to influence the monarchs, especially Queen María Luisa. The educational centers in the women's care benefited by receiving numerous commissions for dresses and accessories for palace servants.[21]

The Consolidation of the Junta de Damas: Educational and Charitable Activities

The polemic surrounding the use of fabrics manufactured in Spain constituted one of the first chapters in the conflicts between the Junta de Damas and the Sociedad Económica Matritense. The women, after "many discussions about the means of reducing the excessive luxury of garments and feminine adornments" (muchas conferencias que había tenido sobre los medios de disminuir el excesivo lujo de los trajes, y adornos mujeriles), felt that the junta had not been able to implement any effective measures.[22] On May 2, 1788, they decided unanimously to refrain from buying any silk that was not manufactured in the kingdom. The women were aware that it was a small, almost imperceptible, gesture that nevertheless could have results in the future. The sociedad applauded the proposal and quickly sent the news to the Count of Floridablanca. King Carlos III praised the women's "public testimony of patriotic love" (testimonio público del amor patriótico).[23]

The women learned through the newspapers that the king was pleased, and it seemed to them that it could be perceived as a slight that the Princess of Asturias, a member of the Junta de Damas, had not been informed first as "was proper," and they tried to mitigate the discourtesy. María Luisa de Parma restricted herself to thanking the damas for their initiative, since she found it "agreeable to use fabrics from these Kingdoms" (agradable servirse de telas de estos Reinos).[24] The Junta de Honor y Mérito felt offended because the male board had moved ahead without asking their opinion beforehand.

Satisfied with the step taken by the women, on June 16, 1788, the Count of Floridablanca sent the Countess of Montijo the anonymous pamphlet entitled *Discurso sobre el lujo de las señoras y proyecto de un traje nacional* (Discourse on Women's Luxury and Project for a National Dress).[25] He intended that, "as an appropriate matter for the Real Junta" (como materia propia del instituto de la Real Junta), this would offer an award of 1,000 *reales* to whoever "proposed a model of a National Uniform for Ladies composed of domestic fabrics" (propusiera un modelo de un Traje Nacional para las Damas compuesto de géneros del país). The contestants had to present a prototype and a report that would explain the advantages of the outfit that should bring together "integrity and decency with grace and agility" (la honestidad y la decencia con la gracia y agilidad). The Count of Floridablanca believed that the damas, after taking the first step by committing themselves to use domestic fabrics for their dressmaking, would support the project of standardizing the female wardrobe, everyone dressing the same way, and differentiating themselves only according to their social category.[26]

At a meeting on July 4, 1788, the women considered the response that should be given to the minister, the composition of which was entrusted to the Countess of Montijo.[27] The junta was emphatically opposed to the idea due to the impossibility of putting this proposal into practice. The reform of customs would have to be a consequence of a broader education, not the promulgation of prohibitive laws. On this occasion, the Real Sociedad shared the decision of the women's council. The controversy still continued for a time, although the Count of Floridablanca avoided a direct confrontation with the women.[28] The Madrid press conducted an intense campaign in favor of the project with articles signed by purported women who supported the idea. Without a doubt, through the public response, the women understood what the official opinion of their refusal was: the all-powerful secretary of state had not accepted well at all the women's criticism of his project.

After the establishment of the women's council, the damas directed their attention to the girls from Madrid's most disadvantaged populations. The Matritense tasked them with the supervision of the Escuelas Patrióticas which were languishing despite efforts to provide for them during more than ten years of arduous work. The male associates did not hide the lamentable state of the schools from the women.[29] The Junta de Damas carried out all kinds of improvements, diversifying and complementing the curriculum with new subjects such as sewing, embroidery, knitting, and upholstery, the most useful specialties for the inclusion of the schools' pupils into the workforce.[30]

During the following years, the junta opened new, specialized professional schools such as the Escuela de Bordados (Embroidery School), inaugurated in July of 1789, the Escuela de Flores Artificiales (Artificial Flower School, protected by the queen), created in December of 1796, and the so-named Colegio de Educación de la Sociedad (Society Education School) or Escuela de Modas (School of Fashion), founded in July of 1790.[31] This experience was the most ambitious from a pedagogical point of view, with two specialties, sewing and adornments. The Countess of Torrepalma, president of the Junta de Damas between 1790 and 1801, was in charge of preparing the definitive organizational plan and the center's guidelines for operation, in which she gave special importance to hygiene, moral formation, and recreational activities.[32]

These educational centers were conceived as free workshop schools for the girls of Madrid's poor neighborhoods, who were intended to be trained as skilled workers for incorporation into the labor market. Instruction was complemented with reading, writing, and the rudiments of mathematics and religion. The basic purpose of this type of education was the preparation of women for the roles of Christians, wives, and homemakers. While the results that the damas obtained were modest due to the chronic shortage of means and to the sociedad's misguided initial design that aspired to self-finance with the products of the students' work, these centers constituted a pioneering experience in women's professional training.[33] Nevertheless, in the enlightened project of working-class textile schools, moral indoctrination of the girls was as important as their contribution to the increase of national wealth through labor development.[34]

The Junta de Damas occasionally also focused on the theoretical aspect of education. According to the statutes approved in 1794, the institution was obliged to create two permanent commissions of physical and moral education, to which the members were immediately appointed.[35] Theoretical reflections on matters such as pediatrics, childcare, and pedagogy combined with practical experience acquired in the management of the Escuelas Patrióticas, in a productive debate of scientific interest.

In the physical education commission, the damas debated issues related to the upbringing of children, echoing the newest medical literature, such as the recommendations for children's care of the doctor Santiago García who, years later, was employed by the Junta de Damas as the physician of the Inclusa o Casa de Expósitos de la Corte (Royal Madrid Foundling Hospital).[36] In the moral education commission, the tone of the debate was more disappointing, for the women could not cast off their enlightened, but elitist, mindset. While they tolerated the inclusion of women into the public sphere—always in areas that were considered to be appropriate and acceptable for their sensibility—they restricted their conduct to a model of femininity that limited their training to "a utilitarian education that would instill in women the values of domesticity and of work." As a result, they were excluded from knowledge of certain fields because they were not suitable to their nature. Even so, the damas demonstrated themselves to be in favor of women's education and the view that the state should be actively involved in making it more widespread; however, they did not support equal education.[37]

In 1799, after obtaining the authorization of King Carlos IV, the Junta de Damas took charge of the management of the Real Inclusa de Madrid.[38] Faced with such an undertaking, the women hesitated at the complexity of the task: "After seeing itself tasked with such a difficult responsibility, the Junta wavered at its seriousness, and the women doubted their skills" (La Junta luego que vio sobre sí tan delicado ministerio tembló por su gravedad y dudó de sus aciertos). Nevertheless, they quickly got to work. The damas introduced basic

FIG. 4. Francisca María Dávila Carrillo de Albornoz, Countess of Truillas (Agustín Esteve), 1797. Collection of the Real e Ilustre Junta de Damas de Honor y Mérito. Photography by Ana María Fernández Piquer.

reforms in the orphanage with the objective of reducing the elevated mortality rates and improving the children's quality of life. They reorganized the establishment, separating the healthy children from the ill ones, setting up a space as an infirmary and arranging the children by age.[39] In addition, they prohibited wet nurses from caring for more than two children and from sharing a bed with them, a cause of frequent accidents. The hiring of permanent wet nurses, who were paid a salary and provided lodging and living expenses, improved conditions for the abandoned children. According to Joan Sherwood, "The Inclusa of Madrid is an example of the evolution of a foundling hospital into a pediatric institution."[40]

The women collaborated with the Real Academia de Medicina (Royal Academy of Medicine) and other orphanages throughout the country, gathering all kinds of news about domestic and foreign scientific advances in order to test new methods of lactation and childhood-disease prevention. From the introduction of the smallpox vaccination to artificial lactation, the women spared no effort for the orphans' preservation. They also cooperated with prestigious physicians, like Santiago García and Ignacio Ruiz de Luzuriaga, knowledgeable experts on the scientific literature about foundlings.[41] Occasionally these relationships were problematic: "there were complicated back and forth negotiations between the influential ladies of the Junta and the doctors, in which both groups lost and gained and in which gender played a crucial role in the establishing of scientific authority."[42]

In 1807, the Junta de Damas added a new center dedicated to orphaned and defenseless girls when they took charge of the management of the Colegio de Nuestra Señora de la Paz, or Colegio de Niñas de la Paz (School of Our Lady of Peace, or Girls' School of Peace), founded in 1679 thanks to the testamentary bequest of Ana María Fernández de Córdoba-Figueroa, Duchess of Feria. In this colegio, the girls received a basic education and learned a trade. From there they left to find employment, to marry, and to be taken in by a family, although the institution always reserved legal authority over the orphans since it did not allow full adoptions. However, it was always possible for the girls to return to the center because they were not obliged to leave it when they reached a certain age. They could remain in the institution throughout their entire lives or temporarily when they found themselves unemployed or ill. The junta joined the center with the Inclusa in a building belonging to the colegio, where both establishments remained until the beginning of the twentieth century. (See fig. 5.)[43]

Finally, in 1790, the Matritense entrusted the Junta de Damas with the management of the Montepío de Hilazas—"literally, an assistance fund for yarn"[44]—an institution for the development of industry for the poor and working classes inspired in the "poor policy" measures of the Consejo de Castilla. This social service establishment's objective was that the lower classes of Madrid's population might supplement their incomes.[45] It was founded by the Sociedad Económica in 1778 to procure women's inclusion in the workforce by providing them the necessary resources to manufacture thread at home. The Montepío paid the women for the yarn they delivered and took charge of their subsequent sale. While the experience was successful initially, thanks to the support of a considerable amount of money from the Consejo de Castilla so that it could collect the raw materials necessary to begin working, the establishment showed dangerous signs of decline when its management was entrusted to the women, due to the inability to self-finance.[46] Sales of the manufactured products accumulated in warehouses, without an easy way to get them on the market.[47] "In the day-to-day operations of the Montepío, the Junta de Damas drew on its experience gained in administering the Society's schools. For example, the group adopted for its new venture a governing structure identical to that found in the schools, as well as used the same system for reporting the status of the Montepío to the women's council. The damas also adopted familiar mechanisms to encourage workers at the Montepío, such as sponsoring prize competitions with monetary awards for exceptional producers."[48] Despite the energy expended by the women to reverse the declining situation of the Montepío de Hilazas, the task was too complex, and in the end, the experience failed. The establishment was closed in 1805 as a result of its significant losses.[49]

The Peninsular War (1808–1814)

The outbreak of the war against the French in 1808 presented a difficult challenge for the women of the Junta de Damas. Despite the difficulties that they would have to face throughout the war, the women did not want to end their involvement with the establishments in their care and continued their work with an enviable dedication in terribly adverse conditions.[50]

When on November 4, 1808, the president of the junta, the Dowager Duchess of Osuna, read, like every year, the annual report, it emphatically revealed the sentiments of the people of Madrid in the face of the magnitude of the events suffered in the previous months.[51] The president was convinced that the unrest and violence had very negatively affected the charitable and educational entities, especially the Inclusa, in spite of the dedication of her colleagues in the junta: "But who can possibly calculate the dire effects that the horrors and frights of the second of May, the constant anxiety of that entire month and the two following, might cause the nursemaids both inside and outside the house? [. . .] How many diseases and deaths of adults know no other origin? And what else can credibly explain so much loss when the care of the supervisors has been greater every day?" (¿Pero quién es posible que calcule los funestos efectos que causarían en las nodrizas de dentro y de fuera de la casa los horrores y sustos del día 2 de Mayo, la continua zozobra de todo aquel mes y los dos siguientes? [. . .] ¿A cuántas enfermedades y muertes de adultos no se les ha conocido otro origen? ¿Y cuál otro podemos inferir más verosímil de tanta pérdida cuando el cuidado de parte de las Señoras Curadoras ha sido cada día mayor?).[52]

After the occupation of Madrid by the Napoleonic armies in December of 1808, the Junta de Damas was reduced to a few women who remained in the capital after the majority of members fled together with their relatives, following the Junta Central (Patriotic Council), the government institution that gathered those opposed to Napoleon Bonaparte in the territories not occupied by the French. The vice president, the Dowager Marquise of Sonora, assumed command of the institution until her death in April of 1811. Following the elections held in November of the same year, it was the Marquise of Fuerte-Híjar, elected president, who was faced with the arduous challenge of preserving the educational and charitable institutions in the care of the women's council.[53]

The damas did not cease in their efforts to petition the French authorities to provide resources so that the establishments would suffer as little as possible, but the lack of financial means forced them to limit some of their activities. The educational institutions were reorganized during French rule in order not to scatter the few available resources.[54] Early in 1811 the junta considered closing the institutions.[55] They requested a temporary suspension from the Sociedad Económica Matritense, since they could not meet the rent of the premises where they were located nor the salaries of the teachers. However, the sociedad preferred to keep them open, trusting that the problems would be resolved if they were to appeal to the government.[56] In June of 1812, lacking a definitive response from the French administration, the schools' situation became unsustainable. Finally, the Embroidery School and the Artificial Flower School (Queen's Flower School), as well as two of the Escuelas Patrióticas, were closed.[57] The other two and the Colegio de Educación survived until May of 1813, when they were definitively closed, all resources exhausted and with astronomical debt.[58]

In the Inclusa and the Colegio de Niñas de la Paz, the war was lived in a particularly dramatic way. King Joseph Bonaparte himself, who visited the Inclusa in early 1809, promised to provide them with independent financing so that they might suffer as little as possible the vicissitudes of the war. Nevertheless, the aid provided by the government was scarce, and the junta had to resort to the generosity of the residents of Madrid.[59]

In mid-1813, the Marquise of Fuerte-Híjar lamented deeply the terrible state in which the orphanage had fallen during the difficult ordeal of the years

1812 and 1813 when Madrid was subjected to the continuous bustle of the coming and going of the French, English, and Spanish armies. María Lorenza de los Ríos, helpless against the orphanage's dire situation, turned to the authorities once again for urgent aid in order to "avoid the slow and desperate death that threatened the residents of these refuges of desperation" (evitar la muerte lenta y desesperada que amenaza a los habitantes de estos albergues de la desesperación).[60] The document achieved the desired result: the political chief of Madrid, the city's highest authority at the time, ordered that the orphanage be helped urgently.

In early 1816, the president, the Dowager Duchess of Osuna, newly returned from Cádiz after the Peninsular War, summarized with sadness the time that had just passed and thanked the members for their dedication during such a terrible juncture: "Your Excellencies [the damas] in the middle of so much conflict, did not abandon these sanctuaries of innocence and of misery, for whose benefit you did not cease to carry out all those tasks dictated by their anguished heart, which only momentarily delayed some of the evils" (V. E. en medio de tanto conflicto, no abandonaron estos asilos de la inocencia y la miseria, en cuyo favor no dejaron de practicar cuantos oficios las dictaba su angustiado corazón, que solo retardaban momentáneamente algunos de los males).[61]

The Reactivation of the Junta de Damas (1814–1823)

After the end of the war in 1814, the Junta de Damas gradually returned to normal. Some members had participated in women's patriotic associations established in the provinces not occupied by the enemy during the war, with the objective of raising money for the army, sewing uniforms, and carrying out humanitarian work.

King Fernando VII himself tried to redirect the women of the élite toward charitable work and encouraged them to join together so that their selfless work to benefit the disadvantaged might contribute to making the kingdom more prosperous. These "heroines of charity" (heroínas de la caridad), moved by their "tender sensibility" (tierna sensibilidad), would help "with the laudable exercise of their fervent charity, so that the effects of their beneficent intentions would be propagated throughout all the provincial capitals, where the influential nobility resides, and with their impetus similar establishments would be built" (con el laudable ejercicio de su caridad fervorosa, para que se propaguen los efectos de mis benéficas intenciones en todas las capitales de provincia, en donde reside la nobleza pudiente, y a su impulso se erijan en ellas establecimientos semejantes).[62] As had occurred in the period prior to the Peninsular War, the Junta de Damas took advantage of their influence with the royal family, including Queen María Isabel de Braganza and the Infantas María Francisca de Asís de Braganza and Luisa Carlota de Borbón as protectors.

In these years, the Junta de Damas concentrated its efforts on improving the conditions of the Inclusa and the Colegio de Niñas de la Paz, resuming the trials and medical experiments that had been suspended during the war, such as preventive vaccination plans and experiments in artificial lactation.[63]

After the liberal government's approval of the Ley General de Beneficencia (General Law of Beneficence) in 1822, during the Trienio Liberal (1820–23), the public establishments of Madrid that were destined for this purpose transferred to the jurisdiction of the Junta Municipal de Beneficencia (Municipal Council of Beneficence). However, in recognition of its many years of work, the Junta de Damas was approved to continue managing the Inclusa and the Colegio de Niñas de la Paz, which it continued following the fall of the constitutional regime in 1823.[64]

In 1819, the Junta de Damas, led by the Marquise of Villafranca, became involved in a new girls' educational institution, the Escuela de Enseñanza Mutua, or Escuela Lancasteriana (Mutual Teaching School, or Lancasterian School), based on the Bell-Lancaster Method and encouraged by the success of the same technique at the boys' school that the Real Sociedad Económica had opened the year before. The educational system of mutual instruction, a technical and pedagogical revolution at the time, was based on the use of outstanding students as teaching assistants and the grouping of students according to subjects in order for monitors to instruct them.[65]

With the restoration of the constitutional regime in 1820, the Junta de Damas took the opportunity to send a plan to the liberal government to establish an Escuela Normal de Maestras (Normal School for Woman Teachers), according to which girls, in addition to the "needlework tasks typical of their sex" (labores de aguja propias de su sexo), would learn writing, reading, arithmetic, and Christian doctrine, "along with the Constitution of the Monarchy and a touch of political catechism" (juntamente con la Constitución de la monarquía y un pequeño catecismo político), that is, the same subjects that the boys studied. An educational program truly advanced for its day, and which would have included for the first time political education for women, it was never implemented because of political instability.[66]

The fall of the constitutional regime in 1823 did not signify an interruption in the work of the Junta de Damas, in contrast to what happened with the Real Sociedad Económica Matritense, which had to suspend its sessions for ten years. The women, who had always been reluctant to become involved in political matters, were able to continue their charitable work undisturbed.

Through feminine associationism centered on social welfare work during the Enlightenment, Spanish women from the ranks of the elite demonstrated their commitment to society. In this way they were able to manage their own cultural and social activism that was disseminated thanks to their efficient propaganda echoed in the press. Nevertheless, the Junta de Honor y Mérito did not survive merely because of the dedication of its socias. Royal protection favored its success. The feminine forum took full advantage of the resources within its reach to develop a strategy that connected the damas and the queen. The ladies were able to project their influence publicly through their eulogies that highlighted the symbolic archetype of the enlightened queen and through the annual submission of the account of their labors to the monarchs to win royal economic support for their initiatives. In the popular feminine schools, the ladies surpassed the initial objectives set for them by the Economic Society that conceived these centers of feminine professional formation or workshop-schools as units of production with cheap labor. The junta believed that girls' education should be aimed at learning a trade. The successive reforms of the education plan introduced mandatory literacy, the rudiments of arithmetic, and other subjects that were more useful for professional development. If this instruction directed and relegated women toward certain labor considered "feminine" and could not avoid the scale of values of a hierarchical society, it was nevertheless a praiseworthy attempt in a desolate educational panorama to educate specialized professionals with a guarantee of success and to avoid as far as possible their exploitation. However, this education was also destined to model conduct. The discourses of the damas are riddled with references to "domesticity," but also to the "domestication" that attempted what is defined rhetorically as the education of "mothers of families." With their charity they imposed on the lower ranks of society an elite model of femininity by teaching aesthetic, cultural, and moral patterns of conduct, to which were added those of hardworking, honest, and disciplined laborers.

The activism of the Junta de Damas was the practical manifestation of the Enlightenment ideal of the pursuit of public happiness. The goal of utility connects this feminine association with other European women's associations that had similar objectives, such as those that dedicated themselves to the protection of abandoned infants. In her *Oración gratulatoria*, Josefa Amar demonstrated that Spanish women were not unaware of the European debate over women's inclusion in the public sphere through the means of enlightened associationism: "At the same time that in Germany they are debating whether women should, or not, be admitted to the Societies, Carlos III, [. . .] cuts [. . .] this knot, discretely showing the affairs respective to each sex. [. . .] The women already know they must promote good education and love of work, with other points certainly more useful to the general good. [. . .] With this example, the doubts of those in Germany will be resolved, and other nations can also follow them."[67]

Years later, the prestige of the Junta de Damas due to its successes in the field of welfare had even reached Russia. The Marquise of Villafranca informed the assembly of socias that the mother of the czar, Sophia Dorothea of Württemberg, had written to the Junta de Damas to ask about the management, organization, and improvements implemented in the Madrid orphanage.[68] With their successful management, the socias had demonstrated that they could also contribute to the enlightened ideal of "the pursuit of public happiness."

NOTES

Essay translated by Kathleen Fueger.

Research for this essay was carried out within the project I+D: "Espacios de conocimiento, cultura y agencia femeninas en el mundo Moderno y Contemporáneo (siglos XV–XX)" (PGC2018-097445-B-C21), part of the collective project: "Género, cultura y subjetividad: más allá de las políticas del conocimiento (siglos XV–XX)," financed by Spain's Ministerio de Ciencia, Innovación y Universidades (MICINN).

1. The consultation with the king took place on March 23, 1787. Six months later the answer arrived, communicated by the Count of Floridablanca, secretary of state. Minutes of meeting. September 12, 1787. ARSEM, Libro A/55.

2. Bolufer Peruga, *Mujeres e Ilustración*, 382; Pérez Cantó and Mó Romero, "Las mujeres en los espacios ilustrados madrileños," 63.

3. Minutes of meeting. September 12, 1787, ARSEM, Libro A/55. This commission met between September 12, 1787, and October 22, 1788. Rosa María Capel has speculated about the possibility of a change in plans regarding the organization of the Junta de Damas between August and October of 1787, because the recommendation made to the king and what the king authorized was a "junta de socias de mérito y honor" (council of [female] members of merit and honor), but suddenly the terms were inverted, becoming a "junta de damas de honor y mérito" (council of ladies of honor and merit), reflecting an aristocratic composition. Capel Martínez, "Las mujeres de la Matritense," 25.

4. *Diario curioso, erudito, económico y comercial*, 467, October 10, 1787, 411.

5. Those attending were the Duchess of Osuna, the Countess of Montijo, the Marquise of Villa-López, the Marquise of la Torrecilla, the Marquise of Palacios, the Countess of Benalúa, María del Rosario Cepeda, Teresa Losada, the Marquise of Ayerbe, and the Countess of Santa Eufemia.

6. *Memorial literario*, T. XII, XLVII, October 1787, Part I: 208. The supervisors elected for the Escuelas Patrióticas were: for the parish of San Martín, the Marquise of Palacios and the Countess of Benalúa; for the parish of San Ginés, María del Rosario Cepeda and Teresa Losada; for the parish of San Sebastián, the Marquise of Villa-López and the Marquise of la Torrecilla; and for the parish of San Andrés, the Countess of Santa Eufemia and the Marquise of Ayerbe, "suspending that of the Embroidery School since it was not yet founded." Minutes of meeting, October 5, 1787, ARSEM, Libro A/55.

7. Minutes of meeting, October 5, 1787, ARSEM, Libro A/55.

8. Amar y Borbón, *Oración Gratulatoria*. The discourse was also published in the *Memorial literario*, T. XII, LI, December 1787, Part I: 588–92.

9. ARCM, Instituciones Antecesoras, Fondo Junta de Damas de Honor y Mérito, Expediente 8482/7.

10. Sempere y Guarinos, "Sociedad Económica de Madrid," 217.

11. Minutes of meeting, October 10, 1787, ARSEM, Libro A/55.

12. ARSEM, Expediente 93/8. The statutes of 1794 were published; see appendix.

13. Demerson, *María Francisca de Sales Portocarrero*, 140.

14. Ríos Izquierdo and Rueda Roncal, "Análisis de las normas jurídicas," 152.

15. Article II of Title I of the statutes of 1794.

16. Article V of Title IV of the statutes of 1794.

17. Ríos Izquierdo and Rueda Roncal, "Análisis de las normas jurídicas," 155.

18. Fernández Quintanilla, "La Junta de Damas de Honor y Mérito," 68–69.

19. ARCM, Instituciones Antecesoras, Fondo Junta de Damas de Honor y Mérito, Expediente 8482/7.

20. Calvo Maturana, *María Luisa de Parma*, 64; Bolufer Peruga, *Mujeres e Ilustración*, 375.

21. Among the account records of the queen's secret purse are different receipts for payments to the Marquise of Ariza, lady-in-waiting to the queen, and, above all, to the Countess of Torrepalma, governess of the Infantes (Princes), to name only two well-known members of the Junta de Damas, as payment for items ordered from the schools, such as "blonde lace, wreaths, gauzes, lace, ribbons, braiding, flowers, and hats" (blondas, guirnaldas, gasas, encajes, cintas, redecillas, flores y sombreros). Martín-Valdepeñas Yagüe, "La reina María Luisa de Parma," 752–53.

22. The initiative came from the second secretary, María del Rosario Cepeda. ARSEM, Expediente 98/9.

23. *Gaceta de Madrid*, 40, May 16, 1788, 319.

24. ARSEM, Expediente 98/9.

25. For years the pamphlet was attributed to Martín Fernández de Navarrete, but recently it has been revealed that its true originator was José Espinosa y Brun. The Count of Floridablanca received it anonymously in February 1788 and ordered its printing. The author, disguised under the initials M.O., attempted to propose a uniform for all Spanish women with three types of dresses, called "la española," "la carolina," and "la borbonesa," which would be differentiated by type of fabric, color, or other details of adornments and accessories. Álvarez Barrientos, "Eutrapelia y control," 465; about this controversy, see Molina and Vega, *Vestir la identidad, construir la apariencia*, chapter 7.

26. ARSEM, Expediente 98/16.

27. Demerson, *María Francisca de Sales Portocarrero*, 157.

28. Rueda Roncal, Ríos Izquierdo, and Zábalo Rojas, "Carlos III y la Junta de Damas," 123. On October 18, 1788, the author of the *Discurso*, José Espinosa, sent to the secretary of state his reply to the damas, whom he explicitly cited. The Count of Floridablanca ordered the printing of another anonymous discourse also opposing the women's reply, with the title *Respuesta a las objeciones*. Álvarez Barrientos, "Eutrapelia y control de la distinción," 467–68.

29. Minutes of meeting, October 19, 1787, ARSEM, Libro A/55. The censor, Guevara Vasconcelos, made a report in October 1787 that, after being approved by the sociedad, was delivered to the Junta de Damas. It raised the question of whether the centers had accomplished their objectives or whether they had ended up being harmful. Palma García, "Las Escuelas Patrióticas," 46.

30. Demerson, "Las Escuelas Patrióticas entre 1787 y 1808," 197.

31. *Diario de Madrid* 201 (July 20, 1789): 803; 355 (December 21, 1797): 1452; 206 (July 25, 1790): 826.

32. Negrín Fajardo, *Ilustración y educación*, 113–19.

33. Méndez Vázquez, "La Junta de Damas y las Escuelas Femeninas," 114; Negrín Fajardo, *Educación popular*, 217, 247.

34. López Barahona, *Las trabajadoras*, 273.

35. Articles I and II of Title VIII of the statutes of 1794.

36. ARSEM, Expediente 146/11; Vidal Galache and Vidal Galache, *Bordes y bastardos*, 57; García, *Breve instrucción*.

37. Bolufer Peruga, *Mujeres e Ilustración*, 151; Capel Martínez, "Las mujeres de la Matritense," 35.

38. Demerson, "La Real Inclusa de Madrid a finales del siglo XVIII," 263.

39. ARCM, Instituciones Antecesoras, Fondo Junta de Damas de Honor y Mérito, Expediente 8880/17/5 and 4.

40. Vidal Galache and Vidal Galache, *Bordes y bastardos*, 64; Sherwood, *Poverty in Eighteenth-Century Spain*, 152.

41. Martín-Valdepeñas Yagüe, "El eco del saber," 102–6; Pérez Moreda, "La Junta de Damas y las inclusas españolas," 18–19.

42. Serrano Jerez, "Science for women," 54.

43. Vidal Galache and Vidal Galache, *Bordes y bastardos*, 159, and 162–63.

44. Smith, *The Emerging Female Citizen*, 170.

45. Castro Monsalve, "Orden público, política social y manufactura," 18–25.

46. Martín-Valdepeñas Yagüe, "Ilustrados, afrancesados y liberales," 116–17.

47. ARSEM, Expediente 117/17.

48. Smith, *The Emerging Female Citizen*, 171.

49. Martín-Valdepeñas Yagüe, "Ilustrados, afrancesados y liberales," 321.

50. Martín-Valdepeñas Yagüe, "Afrancesadas y patriotas," 359–60.

51. Minutes of meeting, November 4, 1808, ARSEM, Libro A/56/9.

52. ARSEM, Expediente 205/9.

53. Minutes of meeting, November 11, 1811, ARSEM, Libro A/56/10.

54. Minutes of meeting, January 30, 1809, ARSEM, Libro A/56/10.

55. Minutes of meeting, January 14, 1811, ARSEM, Libro A/56/10.

56. Minutes of meeting, May 13, 1811, ARSEM, Libro A/56/10.

57. Minutes of meeting, June 6, 1812, f. 110v, AHVM, Sección Secretaría, Libro 242.

58. Minutes of meeting, August 14, 1813, ARSEM, Libro A/110/38.

59. *Gaceta de Madrid* 61 (March 2, 1809): 332; *Diario de Madrid* 337 (December 3, 1812): 663–64.

60. AHVM, Sección Secretaría, Expediente 2–371–13.

61. ARCM, Instituciones Antecesoras, Fondo Junta de Damas de Honor y Mérito, Expediente 8880/17/16.

62. *Gaceta de Madrid* 28 (March 7, 1815): 240.

63. Serrano Jerez, "Chemistry in the City," 149–52.

64. The first General Law of Beneficence placed all charitable institutions under state control. Vidal Galache, "El impacto de la Ley General de Beneficencia," 55.

65. Villafranca, *Memoria instructiva*, 1820, 9–10; Martín-Valdepeñas Yagüe, "El eco del saber," 102.

66. "There was a scandalous argument in the French National Assembly, about the system of education called Lancasterian" (Escandalosa discusión en la cámara de diputados de Francia, sobre el sistema de enseñanza llamado de Lancaster), *El Censor* 51 (July 21, 1821): 224–25.

67. "Al mismo tiempo que en Alemania se está disputando si las mujeres deben, o no, ser admitidas en las Sociedades, Carlos III, [...] corta [...] este nudo, señalado con discreción los asuntos respectivos a cada sexo. [...] Las mujeres saben ya que han de fomentar la buena educación, y el amor al trabajo, con otros puntos ciertamente más útiles al bien general. [...] Con este ejemplo, resolverá sus dudas la Alemania, y podrán también seguirlo las demás naciones." Amar y Borbón, *Oración Gratulatoria*, 7–9.

68. Marquesa of Villafranca, *Memoria instructiva*, 1820, 14.

Women and Charity between the Spaces of Enlightened Reformism and the *Moderado* Liberal State, Madrid, 1833–1868

MÓNICA BURGUERA LÓPEZ

The Junta de Damas in the Scenarios of (Post)Revolutionary Liberal Philanthropy

Throughout the middle decades of the nineteenth century, the Junta de Damas de Honor y Mérito, united to the Madrid Economic Society, became the dominant example of charitable feminine associationism in Madrid and of the social welfare framework developed by the liberal state of Queen Isabel II. The women surrounding the Dowager Duchess of Gor, president of the Junta de Damas for three decades beginning in 1828, actively participated in the configuration of a new space for charity in the capital as debates over philanthropy and social reform permeated the new scientific, literary, and beneficent societies at the end of the 1830s. These spaces that arose to celebrate the foundations of the new respectable, liberal, postrevolutionary society from the late 1830s through the 1840s were soon politicized, polarizing the different readings of an ambivalent social discourse that was potentially inclusive but also profoundly repressive. Throughout these decades, the damas of the junta mobilized their symbolic capital associated with enlightened reform, adapting themselves to the new public spaces of social welfare opened by the liberal rupture. But during this transition they lost the most critical aspects relating to the debate over the rational nature of women and the importance of their education and civic role. In the years immediately following the liberal revolution, we see the public projection of distinct models of respectable middle-class femininity. The ideological resituating of the women in charge of the resources and initiatives in the Junta de Damas placed them at the most conservative extreme of the liberal debates over the woman question.

After the death of King Fernando VII (1833), the war against Carlist absolutism and the popular radicalization of the revolutionary process (1835–36) had forced the Crown to support the liberal cause.[1] The Constitution of 1837 had laid the foundations of a new liberal political system around different political discourses, moderate and progressive, which shared the constitution's rejection of the egalitarian ideal of national sovereignty, but which differed, among other things, on the degree of participation of civil society and the potential autonomy of a dynamic public sphere. The following years, 1838–43, were crucial for the consolidation of a new political elite called to imagine the moral and political foundations of the new society within a central, renewed, and lively public sphere.[2] The debates over social reform and the woman question that reached Spain from Europe circulated in the new spaces of postrevolutionary sociability, ordering the visions of class and gender of a liberal society that desired stability.

In mid-July of 1838, the Sociedad Económica Matritense de Amigos del País circulated an invitation among all the "charitable people" of the capital to "form an association devoted to promote and improve the education of the people" (formar una asociación destinada a propagar y mejorar la educación del pueblo) at the request of the government of Her Majesty, the Queen Regent María Cristina de Borbón, widow of King Fernando VII. It had already done something similar in 1835 when the Madrid Athenaeum (Ateneo de Madrid) was reopened following the death of the absolutist King Fernando VII, and it would do the same a few months later when the Madrid Savings Bank (Caja de Ahorros de Madrid) was created. The invitation was published in the city's most important newspapers and was extended, in this case, "to all people of both sexes who, sincerely interested in the welfare and advancement of their homeland, are disposed to take part in this charitable work" (a todas las personas de ambos sexos, que interesadas sinceramente en el bien y adelantamientos de su patria, estén dispuestas a concurrir a esta obra de beneficencia).[3] As the *Semanario pintoresco español* (Picturesque Spanish Weekly) stated, the "spectacle" of philanthropy was returning in the midst of a "heated battle of passions and parties that divided the country" (enconada lucha de pasiones y partidos que dividían al país), certainly, but hand in hand with an association whose only hallmark was its "patriotism" and its dedication to the "public good."[4]

On the one hand, the proposal implicitly mobilized the enlightened symbolic capital of the Sociedad Económica, alluding to the enlightened foundations of the new liberal framework and its limits which were central to the public construction of the image of the ideal citizen associated with the new political elite, which the modern *catedrático* or *sabio* (learned man) embodied. A revitalized romantic and respectable public sphere projected foundational values such as talent, knowledge, patriotism, rationality, and the liberty of the free, conscientious, and capable citizen. Modern philanthropy was the ideal terrain for the projection of this collection of foundational values exhibited by the members of the Athenaeum, the Lyceum, the Savings Bank, or the Society for the Advancement and Improvement of Public Education (Sociedad para propagar y mejorar la educación del pueblo). On the other hand, in the midst of the reorganization of liberal political discourses and interests, the debates regarding female nature, women's education, their intellectual abilities, and their public visibility were also reactivated in terms very similar to those that had been expounded upon in the Junta de Damas united with the sociedad since 1787.[5] Fifty years later the Junta de Damas was called upon to play a leading role in the new scenarios of liberal sociability and social reform, and to spearhead the rearrangement of women's philanthropic associations of enlightened origin to the new frameworks of action that social reformism proposed, at the rise of philanthropic associationism beginning in 1838.[6]

Charity of the "Principal (*moderadas* and *cristinas*) Ladies"

In the mid-1830s, the Junta de Damas enjoyed even greater recognition and social brilliance than the Sociedad Económica itself, to which it remained "united," but to which in practice it was scarcely linked but in name.[7] The Sociedad Económica Matritense had sharply decried the exile of many of its principal members following the Liberal Triennium (1820–23), to the point that, between 1823 and 1833 when King Fernando VII died, "the public considered [it] dissolved." The Junta de Damas, however, despite the difficulties had remained active and visible at the head of emblematic institutions such as the Inclusa and the Colegio de Niñas de la Paz, from 1799 and 1806, respectively, under the shelter of monarchical patronage and of the Court itself.[8] María del Carmen Chacón Carrillo de Albornoz, the Dowager Duchess of Gor, was president of the junta from 1828 until her death in 1860. She had joined the Spanish nobility in 1803, during the reign of Fenando VII's father, King Carlos IV. She became a member of the Junta de Damas in 1816, shortly after her arrival to Madrid from Granada, and she led the institution's passage across the changing political landscapes that preceded the liberal rupture. During her long presidency she managed the problematic readjustment to the constitutional system of an institution closely bound to a reluctantly liberal court environment, as were she and the Junta de Señoras itself.[9] She had been present during the absolutist reign of King Fernando VII, when, for example, in 1819, "a free school for the daughters of military personnel and civil employees of distinguished classes" (una escuela gratuita para las niñas de militares y empleados civiles de las clases distinguidas) had been created. And she had already begun to serve as president of the Junta de Damas in the years of the regency of King Fernando's widow, María Cristina de Borbón, who had come to this ladies' institution in 1835 in order to "provide a conscientious education to the orphans of national militiamen and soldiers who had died in the defense of the national cause, and of the legitimate throne of [her daughter] Doña Isabel II" (proporcionar una educación esmerada a las huérfanas de Milicianos nacionales y militares que han muerto en defensa de la causa nacional, y del trono legítimo de Doña Isabel II).[10] Years later, *El Amigo del País*, a publication of the Sociedad Económica Matritense, praised this ability to readjust to diverse political scenarios, since not even in the moments in which "the constitutional system had been abolished and the Sociedad Económica Matritense [suspended]" had the Junta de Damas ceased "in the exclusive government of these establishments" (en el gobierno exclusivo de dichos establecimientos).[11]

The model of the Junta de Damas represented the ideal of the "principal" woman, whose social prestige enabled her to mobilize economic resources, both her own and those of others—through raffles, dances, or donations— and whose natural sensitivity, above all, permitted her to exercise that typically enlightened "social motherhood" with which she presented herself in public space. In 1821, during the debates that preceded the passing of the General Law of Beneficence (Ley General de Beneficencia), the suitability of including women in the liberal legislation about public welfare had been discussed for the first time in the National Assembly (Cortes). The senior member, Manuel Luis González Allende, explicitly referred to the Junta de Damas of Madrid and to its management of the Inclusa: "I have seen that Society, composed of principal ladies, shed tears over the unfortunate children" (compuesta de señoras principales [a las que] yo he visto verter lágrimas sobre las criaturas infelices). The nascent liberal administration, he argued, should rely on this type of exclusively female associations that had carried out their activities within the framework of enlightened reformism, because "their sensibility should be counted upon," since this was "the sex that had been born for caregiving [. . .] they are women, they are mothers, and this is sufficient" (el sexo que había nacido para este cuidado [. . .] son mujeres, son madres, y esto basta).[12] When in 1836 the General Law of Beneficence of 1822 came into effect again, for these same reasons that González Allende had stated, the Junta Municipal de Beneficencia kept the Junta de Damas in charge of the Inclusa and the Colegio de Niñas de la Paz, as well as of the Escuela Lancasteriana and the Colegio Nacional de Huérfanas de Patriotas (National School for Orphans of Patriots). Both parties tacitly and naturally assumed the legitimacy of its management at the head of all these institutions.

Without ceasing to project their social brilliance and the celebration of the new scientific and moral reformist presuppositions common to the set of respectable liberalisms, the Junta de Damas along with the rest of the new associations protected by the Sociedad Matritense emerged tinged with the implicitly moderate tones that overlapped with the tepidly liberal courtesan circles closest to the Queen Mother, María Cristina. These tones were especially evident when the women were convened for the first time to participate in an educational activity related to childhood and women's education, with which the junta had involved itself since its foundation. Thus, in 1838, it was significantly the same tight-knit nuclear family around the Dowager Duchess of Gor who took over the positions of the brand new women's section that was emerging within the new Society for Popular Education (Sociedad para la educación del pueblo), presided over, furthermore, by her own son, the Duke of Gor, a gentleman of the Royal Chamber in the court of Queen Isabel II.[13] The same Dowager Duchess of Gor and her daughter-in-law, the Duchess of Gor, a lady-in-waiting of María Cristina, together with her sister María Patrocinio Chacón, herself the guardian (curadora) of the Colegio de Niñas de la Paz, joined the new women's section. Moreover, its vice president, the Marquise of Malpica, was the daughter of the Dowager Duchess of Gor.[14] The ladies of the palace circle—followers of María Cristina de Borbón and moderates, and practically family members of the Junta de Damas—were the ones who capitalized on the junta's incorporation into the spaces of liberal sociability. As the principal representatives of enlightened women's charity, they were willing to deploy all the mechanisms of public and political representation that they were able to mobilize.

Women's Reason and Social Reform

The reform of the social body was articulated thanks to modern *sabios* (learned men) and social scientists returned from exile, like Ramón de la Sagra, Pablo Montesino, or Mateo Seoane, and began with the creation of a liberal and respectable dynamic associative fabric. At the request of the Duke of Gor himself, as president of the recently founded Society for Popular Education, Montesino wrote his celebrated *Manual para maestros de las escuelas de párvulos* (Manuel for Teachers in Primary Schools), published in 1840. More than a methodological explanation for the teachers of the centers that the society was going to open, it was a reflection on the role of philanthropic associationism as a precursor to social change, tied to the idea of a moral order managed through the family. To begin with, it was a project designed for "all classes of both sexes"[15] and largely revolved around the centrality of women's education and the organization of their participation in the societies as a symbol of modernity and civility. Hand in hand with social reform came, therefore, the echoes of the so-called "feminine question" and the terms in which women's "social mission" was to be understood as well as the need to give women "their rightful place in society" (en la sociedad el lugar que le corresponde).[16] From the heart of a broad consensus about the reassessment of women and the importance of their education, the new social and political order, which was to rest on a supposedly deeper sexual order, was being forged.

Within the same enlightened framework of sexual complementarity, the profound and paradoxical contradiction regarding the concept of the individual and of woman reopened diverse positions and arguments. The voices that most clearly defended the incorporation of women into the Sociedad Económica Matritense at the end of the eighteenth century, from Campomanes to Josefa Amar, resounded in Montesino's *Manual*. Half a century after their defense of women's right to join the Sociedad Económica Matritense, the physician from Zamora appealed to the necessity not only of improving women's education but also of, effectively, considering women, like men, rational beings by nature who needed an education in accordance with their abilities. He wrote: "This fatal error, the atrocious injustice that we do to half of the human race, considering it scarcely susceptible to intellectual progress or hardly in need of reason, is an offense done to the Creator who endowed her with this faculty [just] as he did to man" (este funesto error, la atroz injusticia que hacemos a la mitad del género humano considerándolo poco susceptible de progresos intelectuales o poco necesitada de razón, [es] una ofensa hecha al Criador que la dotó de esta facultad como al hombre).[17] Montesino argued against those who thought that women's education "should be applied to only the heart."[18] He advocated a rational female education capable of shaping the behaviors, intellectual abilities, and the moral expectations of women in order to reinforce precisely that social and sexual order on which the ideally harmonious complementary liberal society and its political stability were conceived.

There were also echoes of the debates surrounding the creation of the Junta de Damas when Montesino outlined in the statutes the terms under which the ladies would become a part of the Society for Popular Education and of its women's section. As subscribing and contributing members, they were considered "individuals voluntarily associated for a specific purpose" (individuos voluntariamente asociados para un fin determinado).[19] It was, therefore, simultaneously an equal and an exclusive status. However, the ladies' roles were clearly restricted by their gender. From among all the members, the society's board of directors elected the Junta de Señoras, whose activities remained basically oriented toward the inspection of women's education, but kept them away from managerial and administrative positions.

In sum, women invaded men's spaces with their own unique attributes. Modern reformism could thus reconstruct a beneficent public space around both sexes. The modernity of social reform lay in its ability to integrate "the heart" and "the head" in a single philanthropic system articulated around what we could call a "public" complementarity of the sexes. The man's companion was to be so both within and outside the domestic home.

Legitimate Owners

Liberal social reformism, therefore, incorporated women into a central, although restricted, public sphere of action in collaboration with men. It demanded the education of their understanding and reason, and it afforded them a public and civic projection that avowedly transcended the limits of domesticity although it did not question the complementary sexual order. But, for the women of the Junta de Damas, the approach of this social reform meant, in practice, relinquishing their previously acquired independence and visibility. It dissolved, as a matter of principle, the internal structure of women's beneficence (spared from men's) that they represented and that the liberal legislation was struggling to incorporate into the public welfare system. In this context of institutional change, in March 1839, a minor procedural conflict had arisen between the Junta de Damas and the Junta Municipal de Beneficencia. Following the death of the director (rector) of the Inclusa and of the Colegio de Niñas de la Paz, the inspector (visitador) of the Junta Municipal de Beneficencia accepted the candidate proposed by the Junta de Damas, Cándido Antonio Heras, but he insisted that, by law, it was the City Council that had to choose from among a list of three candidates proposed by the Junta de Damas. The (political) unease between the two juntas increased with the first progressive electoral victory in the Madrid City Council in December 1839—and within the context of growing tension, too, between moderantism and progressivism at the state level following the approval of the Constitution of 1837. Two days after the change of government, in that same month of December 1839, the Junta Municipal de Beneficencia informed the ladies that the law did not allow them to make decisions about appointments or dismissals of Inclusa personnel and that it rejected their candidate in favor of another of those proposed on the list, Mariano José Fontana.[20]

Significantly, a few days later, the recently elected progressive mayor, Salustiano de Olózaga, together with a team of experts led by Ramón de la Sagra, laid the cornerstone of the Society for the Improvement of the Prison, Correctional and Penal System (Sociedad para mejorar el sistema carcelario, correccional y penal). Despite his appeal to the communion of the great liberal family, to "characters of all political hues" (personajes de todos los matices políticos), the foundation of this society began to reveal the political undercurrent of an open struggle to appropriate the symbolic and foundational capital around liberal philanthropy.[21]

The pages of the moderate newspaper, *El Correo Nacional*, denounced the "manifest intrusion into a field cultivated by legitimate owners" (intrusión manifiesta en un campo cultivado por legítimos poseedores).[22] The newspaper alluded especially to the Real Asociación de Caridad de Señoras para alivio de las presas (Royal Ladies' Association to relieve female inmates), created in 1788 under the auspices of the recently founded Junta de Damas de Honor y Mérito to take charge of attending to the Galera, the main women's prison in the capital, and the Good Shepherd Association (Asociación del Buen Pastor), a men's association created in 1799 to complement the Ladies' Association and

FIG. 5. Inclusa of Madrid at Embajadores Street, ca. 1900. Comunidad Autónoma de Madrid. Archivo Regional de la Comunidad de Madrid. Fondo Fotográfico Martín Santos Yubero.

which in 1840 was still in operation. Olózaga's society, it read, came to "dispute the primacy" of these associations and, implicitly, of the historical and quasi-patrimonial relationship that legitimized the appropriation, by the preexisting associationism, of which the Junta de Damas was a leading example, of an entire field of charitable action related to prisoners, prison, and penitentiary reform.[23]

The political confrontation over an entire symbolic capital forged in the shadow of the monarchy became explicit when the government of María Cristina de Borbón itself, regarding the decision of the Junta Municipal de Beneficencia, sanctioned the independence of the Junta de Damas and its management of the Inclusa from interference by the Junta Municipal. The ladies were recognized "in the administration and management of the house of foundlings with absolute independence from the Junta Municipal, being null and void the appointment of the rector Fontana and [...] approving the Damas' proposal in support of the vice-rector Heras" (en la administración y dirección de la casa de expósitos con absoluta independencia de la Junta Municipal, quedando nulo y sin efecto el nombramiento del rector Fontana y [...] aprobando el propuesto por las Damas a favor del vice-rector Heras).[24] But, immediately after María Cristina's departure from the country in October of 1840, the arrival of General Baldomero Espartero to the regency, and the consequent transfer of political power from the influence of moderate liberalism to that of progressive liberalism, the initial decision of the Junta Municipal was quickly reactivated, and the recently created Council of the Provisional Provincial Government (Junta de Gobierno Provisional de la Provincia) reinstated Fontana at the head of the Inclusa, despite the protests of the Junta de Damas. In the midst of the reverberations that this entire process had stirred in the city's press, on October 9, 1840, the ladies relinquished their post and, throughout the entire decade that followed, the rector appointed by the Junta Municipal de Beneficencia remained in charge of the Inclusa and of the Colegio de Niñas de la Paz.[25]

The years of Espartero's Regency (1840–43) were not very favorable for the Junta de Damas, whose only associative platform was the Ladies' Association for the Aid of Religious Women in Madrid (Asociación de Señoras para el Socorro de las Religiosas de Madrid). The "bello pensamiento" (beautiful idea) for this association was due to the Marquise of Malpica, and the presidency fell, also on this occasion, to her mother, the Dowager Duchess of Gor. The new association was dedicated to addressing the excesses of the government's confiscation of ecclesiastical property carried out between 1836 and 1837, one of the milestones of the liberal revolutionary process. In this manner, the leading women of the Junta de Damas were displaying once again the same reluctantly liberal tones of the pro–María Cristina court, which fit in with a strictly elitist and religious model of women's charity, increasingly distant from the reformist projection of enlightened thought. These ladies, however, saw their charitable "patrimony" in the capital drastically reduced.

New (Progressive) Scenarios for the Middle-Class Woman

Founded in April of 1839, some months after the inauguration of the Society for Popular Education, the Instituto Español sprang up in the shadow of the Athenaeum, the Lyceum, and the rest of the philanthropic initiatives sponsored by the Sociedad Económica Matritense. With the slogan "instruction and charity" (instrucción y beneficencia), the Instituto Español was raised from its creation to be a bastion of the principles that should guide the *revolución social* forged from a recreational, educational, and philanthropic associationism designed for *familias de clase media*, but focused on its teachers, boys' and girls' schools, adult Sunday schools, and above all, on its most celebrated initiatives, its schools for artisans and for mothers. The school for artisans was managed, yet again, by Sagra and the school for mothers by Antonio García Blanco. Among the Instituto Español's founding members were almost all those renowned intellectuals who were openly progressive and anti–María Cristina de Borbón, and who had disappeared from the membership lists of the first associations, the Athenaeum and the Lyceum, such as Eugenio de Hartzenbusch or Modesto Lafuente, among many others.[26] Just as the earlier associations had gradually been cast as moderate and pro–María Cristina de Borbón, the instituto became openly aligned with Espartero, especially since the end of 1841, when he periodically began to publish his *Boletín* and enjoyed greater social and political impact. Espartero, the "undefeated warrior" (invicto guerrero) who had won many battles against the Carlists, exercised in this case, as was seen with María Cristina, the traditional monarchical protection of the beneficent and charitable societies as an authority figure representing an explicitly liberal and revolutionary political project.[27]

The articles of García Blanco in the *Boletín del Instituto Español* reinforced the association's intention to lead the debates about women's education and their incorporation into the public sphere, occupying a space for reflection on the matter opened by Montesino's *Manual* and social reformism in general. One of the keys to this education was the need to incorporate "judgment" into feeling. It was not a matter only of "a mother loving her daughter, but of her loving her daughter intelligently" (una madre ame a su hija, sino de que la ame con talento).[28] From their classrooms, magazine, and women's section, they began to project the ideal of a "middle-class" femininity based on motherhood, morality, and patriotism but also on modernity, civility, and social progress. Likewise, the women's section of the instituto also began to play a prominent role as soon as it was founded. "Supervised" by his secretary, Basilio Sebastián Castellanos, just as Montesino had intended for the Society for Popular Education, the women's section embodied, from its inception, that public complementarity of the sexes, equal and exclusive at the same time. The women's section of the instituto mobilized politically by fashioning itself as the negation of everything that the Junta de Damas represented.

The appointment in July 1842 of the Countess of Espoz y Mina, the so-called *dama del progresismo* (lady of progressivism), as president, and the invitation to the Duchess of la Victoria, Espartero's wife, to become part of the ladies' section, illustrate the importance of the political struggle for spaces of representation of beneficence and public femininity.[29] Juana de Vega, the Countess of Espoz y Mina, was the governess of Queen Isabel II beginning in August 1841 and lady-in-waiting (camarera de palacio) beginning in 1842. She was the feminine figure whom Agustín Argüelles and Salustiano de Olózaga had hoped would make Isabel II into "another Queen Victoria [of Great Britain]." The Countess of Espoz y Mina represented the confrontation from within the court to the anti-liberalism of Isabel's mother, María Cristina de Borbón, and the profoundly patrimonial conception of the crown into which Isabel II had been born and in which she had been educated until then.[30] In her memoirs, written after leaving office in 1843, the countess expressed her criticism of the suffocating atmosphere among the ladies-in-waiting of a conspiratorial court loyal to María Cristina—from which the Junta de Damas itself was nourished; between the countess and the other ladies there was a distance that separated the "aristocracy" from a woman "of the class of the people."[31] Educated but modest, affectionate and restrained, equable, judicious, and reflective, austere, charitable, and reformist: this is how the countess represented herself, that difficult compendium of heart and head of which Montesino, Sagra, and García Blanco had so often spoken. In April 1842, García Blanco referred to the various "masked enemies" (enemigos enmascarados) of the instituto, frankly describing the nature of the political tension that had surreptitiously penetrated the emergence of liberal associationism and the celebrated communion of the great liberal family around the enlightened values of public interest and philanthropy. This tension placed the "middle class" and "the people" in opposition to the "aristocracy"; "philanthropy" and social science to political and personal interests; progressivism to moderantism; the Junta de Damas to the women's section of the Instituto Español.[32]

The Junta de Damas and the (Moderate) Institutionalization of Public Charity: Toward Control of the Social Body

Espartero's departure in July of 1843, the coming of age of Queen Isabel II in November, and the new political turn that definitively displaced progressivism and liberal radicalism from official policy also dislodged the openly progressive reformism that threatened the restrictive principles of moderate public order. The new Constitution of 1845 responded to a large extent to this necessity of limiting the autonomy of civil society and of narrowly controlling the public sphere. In this new political context, the initiatives of the celebrated philanthropic associationism weakened during the early years of the 1840s. The Society for Popular Education disappeared, its schools falling into the hands of the city government, as did the Society for the Improvement of the Prison System, by 1845. The Instituto Español survived with many difficulties by adopting a profile that was much less politicized and central. Throughout the 1840s, only the debates that arose about the prizes awarded by the Sociedad Económica Matritense, still presided over during many years by Mateo Seoane, showed the terms in which the moderate administration was thinking about the topics related to charity and modern society. More than open debates, the announcement of these awards and the texts that were published functioned merely as legitimizers of the different legislations that were being passed, such as the Vagrancy Law (Ley de Vagos) of 1845, the Beneficence Law (Ley de Beneficencia) of 1849, or the Penal Code (Código Penal) of 1850.

In general, the languages elaborated by social reform were maintained through a much more conservative reading of the liberal project found in social discourse. The ideal of a participatory civil society formed by free individuals who contributed selflessly to the common good by means of associationism gradually became the ideal of a society of individuals capable of internalizing a set of normative behaviors regarding their own physical and moral self-regulation. The emphasis that the emerging philanthropic associationism of the early 1840s had placed on the scientific "social revolution" had evolved, at the end of the same decade—and especially after 1848—into a powerful hygienist discourse as well as into a charitable legislation that was more repressive than integrative.

The women of the Junta de Damas openly expressed their pleasure about the change of sensibility enabled by political turnaround in their annual summary (*Memorias*) of the Association for the Relief of Religious Women of Madrid.[33] They were not mistaken. In 1845, immediately after the return of María Cristina de Borbón and through her explicit request, the Duchess of Gor herself and her family entourage began the Royal Association for Domestic Charity (Real Asociación de Beneficencia Domiciliaria), which throughout the following decades expanded and dominated the landscape of women's public beneficence. Right away, in 1844, the question of the leadership of the Inclusa was also reopened in the pages of the newly created *El Amigo del País*, which tried to present the exclusion of the Junta de Damas as the (liberal) municipal administration's questioning of the women's ability in general for charitable administration. It pointed out the difficulty of replacing "the maternal solicitude of the ladies [because] their experience has demonstrated that [it is] singularly reserved for people who, because of their sex, virtues, and social position, can dedicate themselves to the free exercise of such philanthropic acts" (la solicitud materna de las Damas [porque] la experiencia ha demostrado que está únicamente reservada a las personas que por su sexo, virtudes y posición social puedan dedicarse al libre ejercicio de actos tan filantrópicos).[34] But the Junta Municipal de Beneficencia replied harshly and made *El Amigo del País* publicly retract each and every argument with which it had justified the petition to return the administration of the foundlings home to the women of the junta, emphasizing that the Junta Municipal had already begun to create a women's commission to take charge of the Inclusa.[35]

The new Beneficence Law of 1849 continued without sanctioning women's participation in public charity. That same year, however, the Junta de Damas regained the management of the Inclusa, which they had always considered theirs because, probably, as could be read in one of the prize-winning essays of the Sociedad Económica Matritense, it was "indispensable [to the ladies] to let them sometimes work at their discretion" (indispensable dejarlas obrar algunas veces discrecionalmente).[36] The women of the Junta de Damas had been definitely linked to an elitist and conservative associationism based exclusively on the supposedly essentially charitable and religious nature of women. They had gradually appropriated an enlightened tradition redirected toward the reticently liberal and profoundly exclusionary moderantism of ex-Regent María Cristina de Borbón, and later, of Queen Isabel II herself.

The Enlightened Legacy beyond the Junta de Damas

The evaluation of the influence of enlightened debates about women's nature, their education, and their public projection surpasses the history of the Junta de Damas de Honor y Mérito itself. Both in historiography and from feminist literary studies about Spain, it has been difficult to resituate the foundational influence of the enlightened epistemological legacy in the liberal conceptual frameworks about femininity and modern feminism. Studies of the nineteenth century had traditionally minimized this Enlightenment influence, emphasizing the weight of prior Catholic traditionalism in the construction and validation of feminine cultural models, exemplified frequently in *La perfecta casada* (The Perfect Wife, 1583) of Fray Luis de León. At this juncture, however, it is difficult not to acknowledge both the centrality of the paradoxical enlightened conceptual framework around sexual difference as well as the depth of the process of liberal rupture and the need to reevaluate the rhythm and character of the gender transformations to which the emerging society gave rise.[37] The debates about the incorporation of women into the Sociedad Económica Matritense de Amigos del País at the end of the eighteenth century disseminated the terms in which modern femininity had begun to be reconsidered within the framework of the complementarity of the sexes.

The emergence of public opinion and of liberal associations, following the opening of different liberal frameworks of the first half of the nineteenth century, 1808–14 and 1820–23, and until the middle of the 1830s, definitively demonstrated that the debates remained open, including for women themselves. Throughout the experience of the Peninsular War (Guerra de la Independencia), the very idea of "social motherhood" was mobilized in distinct ways by female patriotism, depending on whether it was absolutist—in which case models of domestic and essentially charitable femininity were reproduced—or liberal, from whose spaces new forms of civic and citizen participation for women were conceived. At the same time, various women's associative traditions were forged, whether charitable, following first the example of the Junta de Damas in Madrid through different provincial capitals where they emerged in the heat of the rearguard and the experience of war, or later of the patriotic societies and the socialization of liberalism.[38] In general terms, liberalism maintained, at least since the Liberal Triennium (1820–23), a profound contradiction by considering the presence of women in its political project to be distinctive and indispensable while excluding them from the public realm of full citizenship. It thus settled on an irresolvable tension: between the need to broaden the scope of women's action, giving them greater civic responsibility as rational individuals in charge of the formation of conscientious citizens, and the fear that, as such, women would overstep the boundaries of their natural femininity, essential for the reproduction of the familial social order. Or, in other words, liberalism was based on the mobile foundations of a sexual order considered within the framework of the complementarity between the sexes and the consequent contradiction between being at once an individual and a woman.

From this perspective, the study of the evolution of the Junta de Damas and of its political projection in the midst of the formation of postrevolutionary liberal political cultures helps us to understand the ambivalence and breadth of the legacy of the Enlightenment in the formation of modern feminine subjectivity and in the public projection of diverse models of women. The nucleus of women surrounding the Dowager Duchess of Gor, who led the association's entry into the spaces of sociability and liberal institutions, shared the same anti-liberal and patrimonial reluctance of María Cristina herself—and of her daughter shortly thereafter—to whose palace circle she belonged. In the face of this charitable, religious, and elitist femininity, progressivism—and in general the entirety of respectable demo-republican liberalisms—appropriated a reformist project (and its enlightened legacy), the civic and political projection of which the Countess of Espoz y Mina embodied during the beginning of the 1840s in Madrid. This model of a middle-class woman—patriotic, judicious, intelligent, charitable, and anti-aristocratic—circulated throughout the provinces during the 1850s and 1860s, reincarnating itself in the following decades in the powerfully influential figures of Carolina Coronado or Concepción Arenal.[39]

Furthermore, we should not underestimate the penetration and influence of the social reformism and of the possibilities opened for women by this associative impulse that came out of a political universe prone to that "public complementarity of the sexes" (complementariedad pública de los sexos). Actually, the opening of new spaces and circles of literary (and political) discussion in Romantic Madrid throughout the 1840s amplified the debates—rooted in the Enlightenment—concerning the place of women in liberal society.[40] The writers Gertrudis Gómez de Avellaneda and Carolina Coronado appeared on the literary scene of the capital as true celebrities, projecting alternative critical discourses with the situation of "slavery" to which women were subjected: the first regarding intellectual equality between men and women as individuals, the second regarding a collective conception of femininity with a public and civic vocation. Between these two writers, from within the principal spaces of respectable Madrid sociability, the fundamental terms of feminist imagination in Spain were constructed. These terms, which contained an explicit critique of the liberal revolution and the way it excluded women, undoubtedly were inspired by the dilemmas that Josefa Amar herself had expressed fifty years before regarding the inclusion of women in the Royal Madrid Economic Society: the defense of the rationality and the intellectual ability of women, the importance of their education and public role, and the potential equality between the sexes. Nevertheless, during the 1840s, neither the Junta de Damas nor all the cultural capital that it had accumulated over the years would form part of the models upon which the new traditions of modern women's writing would be based, nor of the wider feminist imaginaries from then on. In sum, the political trajectory of the Junta de Damas can also explain why, after the liberal rupture, the traces of the institution that arose among the same debates and in the same framework of the complementarity of the sexes upon which the liberal state was being constructed seem to be erased. The later history of the Junta de Damas (1833–68) would have eclipsed an enlightened legacy that had been changing in meaning, becoming the banner of a feminine philanthropy whose pedagogical, civic, and reformist role had gradually been stripped away.

NOTES

Essay translated by Kathleen Fueger.

This work forms part of the research project PGC2018-097445-A-C22 financed by Spain's Ministry of Science, Innovation, and Universities.

1. The Carlists were traditionalists who supported King Fernando VII's brother Don Carlos's pretension to the throne and opposed the accession of Fernando's daughter Isabel. The conservative Carlists carried out several civil wars throughout the nineteenth century and remained a political force in Spain through the first half of the twentieth century.

2. Burdiel Bueno, "Myths of Failure, Myths of Success"; Millán García-Varela and Romeo Mateo, "Was the Liberal Revolution Important to Modern Spain?"; recent and fundamental books about the period include: Burdiel Bueno, *Isabel II*; Andreu Miralles, *El descubrimiento de España*; Shubert, *Espartero*; and Romeo Mateo and Sierra Alonso, *Historia de las culturas políticas en España*.

3. "Sociedad para propagar y mejorar la educación del pueblo," *Semanario pintoresco español* 120 (July 15, 1838): 637.

4. "Noticia de los trabajos y adelantos hasta el día, de la Sociedad para propagar y mejorar la educación del pueblo," *Semanario Pintoresco Español* 128 (September 9, 1838): 699.

5. Bolufer Peruga, "New Inflections of a Long Polemic"; Jaffe and Lewis, eds., *Eve's Enlightenment*; López-Cordón Cortezo, *Condición femenina y razón ilustrada*; Martín-Valdepeñas Yagüe, "Ilustrados, afrancesados y liberales."

6. Burguera López, *Las damas del liberalismo respetable* and "Mujeres y revolución liberal en perspectiva."

7. "Cristinas" refers to the circles ideologically and personally close to María Cristina de Borbón, wife of the deceased King Fernando VII, regent of the kingdom of Spain between 1833 and 1840, and mother of Queen Isabel II. María Cristina opposed the absolutist groups who supported the coronation of the brother of her husband, Carlos María Isidro, and embraced, although reticently, the liberal cause supported by her regency and the reign of her daughter.

8. Bosch, *El centenario*, 116.

9. "Necrología: La duquesa de Gor," *Gaceta de Madrid* 78 (March 18, 1860). I thank Elisa Martín-Valdepeñas Yagüe for supplying me with this article. Burdiel Bueno, *Isabel II*; San Narciso Martín, "Políticas desde las cámaras de Palacio."

10. *Guía de forasteros en Madrid para el año 1841*, 226.

11. *El Amigo del País*, T. I, 3 (April 1, 1844): 68.

12. *Diario de Sesiones de las Cortes: Legislatura 1821–1822, Extraordinaria*, December 19, 1821, 1356–57.

13. On the Duke of Gor, see Pérez Núñez, "Del Ministerio del Interior al de la Gobernación."

14. "Sociedad para propagar y mejorar la educación del pueblo: Instalación de la junta de señoras," *Semanario pintoresco español* 134 (October 21, 1838): 747.

15. Sagra, *Discurso leído el día 2 de enero de 1842*, 8. The fundamental text is Sagra, *Lecciones de economía social*.

16. "De la mujer," *Semanario pintoresco español* 123 (August 5, 1838): 661.

17. Montesino, *Manual para los maestros*, 55.

18. "Estudios morales, 'Consejos a las madres de familia,'" *Semanario pintoresco español* 112 (May 20, 1838): 580.

19. Montesino, *Manual para los maestros*, 71 and 80.

20. Vidal Galache and Vidal Galache, *Bordes y Bastardos*, 79–84.

21. "Solemne instalación de la Sociedad para la mejora del sistema carcelario, correccional y penal de España," *El Corresponsal* 216 (January 2, 1840): 1.

22. "Cárceles," *El Correo Nacional* 796 (March 22, 1840): 3.

23. "Cárceles," *El Correo Nacional* 796 (March 22, 1840): 3.

24. Quoted in Vidal Galache and Vidal Galache, *Bordes y bastardos*, 81.

25. Madoz, *Diccionario geográfico-estadístico-histórico*, 876.

26. *Guía de forasteros en Madrid para el año de 1840*, 226–28.

27. *Boletín del Instituto Español* 8 (January 8, 1842).

28. García Blanco, "Educación moral: Consejos a las madres," *Boletín del Instituto Español* 42 (September 3, 1842).

29. "Secretaría: Sección de damas," *Boletín del Instituto Español* 34 (July 9, 1842). The Duchess of la Victoria had belonged to the governing council of the Junta de Damas precisely until 1841. *Guía de forasteros en Madrid para el año 1842*, 237.

30. Romeo Mateo, "Juana María de la Vega"; Veiga Alonso, "Modelos de feminidad: Juana de Vega."

31. Espoz y Mina, "Apuntes para la historia," 179.

32. García Blanco, "Enemigos con distintas máscaras," *Boletín del Instituto Español*, April 30, 1842.

33. Gor, *Memoria leída por la Presidenta de la Asociación*, 6.

34. *El Amigo del País*, T. I, 3 (April 1, 1844): 66–69.

35. *El Amigo del País*, T. I, 6 (May 15, 1844): 182.

36. Sáez Ordóñez, "De la supresión de la mendicidad," 69.

37. Espigado Tocino, "Las mujeres en el nuevo marco político"; Romeo Mateo, "Destinos de mujer"; Burguera López, *Las damas del liberalismo respetable* and "Mujeres y revolución liberal en perspectiva."

38. Pascua Sánchez and Espigado Tocino, *Frasquita Larrea y Aherán*; Castells Oliván, Espigado Tocino and Romeo Mateo, *Heroínas y patriotas*; Bolufer Peruga and Burguera López, eds., "Género y modernidad en España"; Yetano Laguna, ed., *Mujeres y culturas políticas en España*; Fuentes Aragonés and Garí Aguilera, *Amazonas de la libertad*; Burguera López, "Mujeres y revolución liberal en perspectiva."

39. Burguera López, "Coronado a la sombra de Avellaneda"; Romeo Mateo, "Concepción Arenal"; Caballé Masforroll, *Concepción Arenal*.

40. For this period, see especially Jagoe, Blanco, and Enríquez de Salamanca, eds., *La mujer en los discursos de género*; and Fernández Rodríguez and Ortega, eds., *La mujer de letras o la letraherida*.

II

Forgotten Foremothers of a Collective History

María Josefa Alfonso Pimentel, Countess-Duchess of Benavente, 1750–1834

An Aristocrat at the Service of the Enlightenment

PALOMA FERNÁNDEZ QUINTANILLA

"Más Vale Volando"

If María Josefa Alfonso Pimentel y Téllez-Girón, fifteenth Countess-Duchess of Benavente and ninth Duchess of Osuna, had been a man, today she would find herself in Spain's Parnassus of the most famous figures of the Enlightenment, all of whom shared her deep sense of obligation to reform the country's economy and the mentality of its people as a way of modernizing Spain and helping it move toward prosperity.[1] The Duchess of Osuna worked tirelessly in the Junta de Damas to improve the Inclusa and to reduce the infant mortality rate. However, until recently, María Josefa has barely occupied a few short lines in several little-known books.[2]

Studies of the life of María Josefa or Pepita, as she was known to her family and friends, will necessarily be multifaceted. Not only was she a highly educated, knowledgeable, and enlightened noblewoman who knew how to manage the Benavente patrimony with an iron fist, but she was also the driving force that brought Italian opera to Madrid. She raised bulls that fought in Hernani's ring next to the Puerta de Alcalá in Madrid; she was a patron of important artists such as Francisco de Goya (see fig. 6), Agustín Esteve, and Antonio Carnicero; she was the selfless president of the Junta de Damas de Honor y Mérito as well as the benefactress of the hospital that belonged to her family in Benavente.[3] Not least, she was also an excellent mother and the devoted companion of her husband, Pedro de Alcántara Téllez-Girón, ninth Duke of Osuna.

In the late eighteenth century, the Duchess of Osuna's *capilla musical* (chamber ensemble) was widely recognized abroad. The Osunas were great music lovers; they frequently commissioned compositions from Joseph Haydn and even hired Luigi Boccherini as their orchestra's conductor. She and her

FIG. 6. María Josefa Alfonso Pimentel Téllez-Girón, Countess-Duchess of Benavente (Francisco de Goya, engraved by Fernando Selma), 1794. Ministerio de Cultura y Deporte. Biblioteca Nacional de España.

husband also owned an important library that contained up to 25,000 volumes of extraordinary works, such as Arabic and Jewish manuscripts, magnificent bibles with fabulous bindings, and first editions of great works of Spanish literature. It included a collection of works by renowned French Enlightenment figures such as Voltaire, Rousseau, and Diderot, which Pedro de Alcántara was able to read with special permission from the Inquisition.

The Countess-Duchess of Benavente created within her salons in her Puerta de la Vega palace in Madrid and at her country estate, El Capricho at the Alameda de Osuna, authentic paradises of freedom where she shone as a brilliant hostess, mixing daringly in the same room renowned bullfighters, fashionable performers of *tonadillas* (musical skits), famous actors, and important artists whom she patronized.[4] All across Spain—from her castles at Puebla of Sanabria and at Benavente in Zamora, to El Capricho in Madrid, or to her grave at Osuna in the province of Sevilla—we can appreciate her aesthetic sense. Lady Holland remarked that she was "the most distinguished woman in Madrid from her talents, worth, and taste. She has acquired a relish for French luxuries, without diminishing her national magnificence and hospitality. She is very lively, and her natural wit covers her total want of refinement and acquirement. Her figure is very light and airy."[5] María Josefa's education was carefully planned.[6] Quite early on, she stood out from other women of the Spanish elite, some of whom barely knew how to read or write. Her exquisite handwriting indicated her fluency of expression, typical of a good reader. As Fernando Fernández de Córdova wrote, without being a beautiful lady, she was very attractive, due to her elegance and intelligent look.[7]

In 1770, María Josefa's mother, María Faustina Téllez-Girón, neglected her palace duties as a lady-in-waiting to devote herself to the crucial marriage of her daughter, the heiress of the family's entailed estate. The elder Countess Benavente desired a suitor worthy of the prestige of the Pimentel lineage, but whose titles would not overshadow those of her daughter. Consequently, she looked for a nobleman among *los segundones* (second-born sons) who would never inherit their families' titles.[8] This condition would therefore mean that María Josefa's five great titles of Spanish nobility would take precedence. Finally, María Faustina's choice was her nephew, Pedro de Alcántara Téllez-Girón, second heir to the House of Osuna. The young noble, still underage and even younger than his bride, seemed to accept the primacy of the House of Benavente. Nevertheless, María Faustina's plans to protect her daughter's future were thwarted when, three months prior to the wedding's celebration, Pedro's eldest brother passed away. The title of Osuna passed to María Josefa's fiancé, radically transforming his social position, and he became the Marquis of Peñafiel. Moreover, after his father's death in 1787, he would become the ninth Duke of Osuna.

Prior to their marriage in 1771, María Josefa and Pedro de Alcántara signed a detailed prenuptial agreement that reveals the circumstances to which marriages of convenience were submitted during the reign of King Carlos III.[9] The agreement reinforced María Josefa's economic position and preserved the well-being of her mother, María Faustina. Although these accords were drafted with no major problems and were authorized by the Vatican (the bride and groom were cousins), complications arose when it became known that the Benavente fortune was foreclosed at the time of the wedding. Only two days after the signing of the agreement, the wedding was celebrated. Some decades earlier, María Josefa's parents had married to unite the Benavente and the Téllez-Girón families, a strategy to maintain patrimonies that occasionally caused negative effects on the health and the vigor of the lineage. Thus, María Josefa and Pedro de Alcántara's marriage united the houses of Benavente and the Osuna, and they became the sole heirs of two important entailed estates.

Their first home was in their palace of Puerta de la Vega, a building decorated with Chinese motifs where they collected important works of art. To paintings by Van Dyck and Rubens, they added works by Francisco de Goya, particularly for the collection at El Capricho. Furthermore, at Puerta de la Vega, Pedro de Alcántara began building his majestic library for which he required up to four librarians. In the same manner, the Countess-Duchess of Benavente opened her popular salon, an essential social reference point for the Spanish capital.

Soon, María Josefa dedicated herself to the arduous role of motherhood. She knew the massive responsibility she had on her shoulders as the sole heiress of two families. Consequently, the couple firmly committed themselves to perpetuating their lineages. These were years of enormous suffering, of births and the days that followed them, and of continuous losses, most likely due to the consanguinity of the cousins. One after the other, four children died, causing the family deep pain. In 1783, when the Countess-Duchess of Benavente's health was restored, she bore her daughter Josefa Manuela. Two years later, her daughter Joaquina was born and only a year later, Francisco de Borja—who later became tenth Duke of Osuna—was born to continue the family's lineage. In 1787, their second son, Pedro de Alcántara, was born. After him came, in 1794, the youngest of the family, Manuela Isidra. Soon, she became her progenitor's favorite and a source of great tenderness. Achieving motherhood had been an extremely painful task for María Josefa. Consequently, she devoted her complete love and dedication to her children, something which was quite unusual at the time among female nobles whose social responsibilities took priority. To ensure the well-being of her children, María Josefa used the best and most modern educational and health systems in Europe and provided her children with music, art, and dance instructors.

The Dukes of Osuna carefully planned the marriages of their children. Thus Josefa Manuela became Marquise of Camarasa in 1800. Unfortunately, she passed away early in 1817.[10] This event traumatized the whole Benavente family, but it especially affected María Josefa, who would never recover from it. Joaquina, the duchess's most attractive daughter, who resembled her the most in her social qualities, was married in 1801 to José Gabriel de Silva Bazán, Marquis of Santa Cruz. She became a lady-in-waiting at Court until her retirement in 1847.

But it was without any doubt the dukes' eldest son's marriage that was their primary concern. In 1803, Francisco de Borja married Francisca de Beaufort-Spontin in Madrid. The union of the Benavente and Mendoza and Infantado families gave the Dukes of Osuna great satisfaction. However, this happiness did not last long due to Francisco de Borja's bad temper, difficult character, and limited intelligence, which at one point led to his estrangement from his mother. Nevertheless, his trajectory was limited because after his entrance to the court he was banned by King Fernando VII himself for his irregular behavior, and he died in 1820 at the age of thirty-four.[11] Upon the death of his widow ten years later, the Countess-Duchess of Benavente was obliged to care for her two grandsons, Pedro de Alcántara, eleventh Duke of Osuna, born in 1810, and his brother and heir, Mariano Téllez-Girón, who would later cause the House of Osuna's bankruptcy. María Josefa had great affection for Pedro, for he was much like her in his taste for literature and art. She hoped he would continue her work as patron and collector; however, he too died at an early age.

In 1811, María Josefa's second son, Pedro de Alcántara, Prince of Anglona, married María del Rosario Fernández de Santillán, daughter of the Marquis of Motilla.[12] Pedro was a cadet in the Royal Spanish Guard with a profound military vocation, like his father. He was undoubtedly far more courageous, intelligent, and brave than his brother Francisco de Borja. However, due to his liberal ideology, King Fernando VII sent him into exile until he was finally permitted to come back to Spain in 1831.[13] Because of his good taste and cultural activity he later become the director of the Museo Nacional del Prado, an academic historian, and a member of the Real Academia de Bellas Artes de San Fernando. In 1813, Manuela Isidra, the youngest of the Osuna family, married Ángel María de Carvajal, Duke of Abrantes and Linares. She loved singing and drawing, to which she devoted her time and energy.

A Little Versailles

An admirer of French and British authors such as Jean-Jacques Rousseau and Horace Walpole, and an avid horseback rider, in 1783 María Josefa and her husband purchased a country estate in the village of Barajas, east of Madrid. It rivaled other country houses or *folies* that began emerging near Madrid toward the end of the eighteenth century, such as La Florida, La Moncloa, La Zarzuela, La Quinta del Pardo, La Moraleja, and, in the nineteenth century, the property of the Montijos in the Carabancheles.[14] El Capricho was organized according to popular physiocratic concepts.[15] The Countess-Duchess of Benavente not only sought aesthetic beauty but also wanted to introduce different arboreal species such as the Lebanese cedar, the magnolia, and the ginkgo biloba. Spanish botany was experiencing a great moment, and important scientists such as Casimiro Gómez Ortega, José Quer, José Celestino Mutis, and Antonio José Cavanilles made daring expeditions to the Americas and Asia. Goethe's visit to the Botanical Garden in Palermo in 1786–88, recounted in his *Italienische Reise* (1816–18), inspired a deeper interest in the natural world, while the fashion for *vedutas* or "views," as described by Jacques-Henri Bernardin de Saint-Pierre, John Milton, and the Spaniard Pedro Montengón y Paret, became María Josefa's source of inspiration for her ideas about nature. This gave rise to the creation of a very personal, deeply eclectic garden of extraordinary good taste and exquisite sensitivity, an Enlightenment project.[16]

Using a preexisting building, the palace's refurbishment began in 1784. Its lower part was destined for guest rooms, the oratory, and the dining room, highlighted by a magnificent mosaic imitating one from Pompeii, opened to the oldest part of the garden, the Frog Pond. The upper part, considered the noble area, was decorated with marble copies of Roman sculptures that had been chosen by José Panuchi, including an Apollo and the group of Laocoön. The two towers on either side of the building allowed the dukes to preserve their individual spaces, given that the couple—like many members of the aristocracy in the eighteenth century—slept in different rooms.

The most spacious areas of the palace were reserved for the Countess-Duchess of Benavente, who gave them romantic names. They were decorated with six engravings illustrating Bernardin de Saint-Pierre's 1787 *Paul et Virginie*, a novel, set in the exotic island of Mauritius, that strongly defended individual freedom of choice and social equality. This theme captivated the palace's owner, who projected through it her particular vision of love and her defense of nature, even though in her final days she would shift sides to favor King Fernando VII's reactionary ideology. When visitors arrived at El Capricho they were always surprised by the beauty and magnificence of the French and English furniture, the impressive silver objects from the owner's trousseau, the

Buen Retiro or Sèvres porcelain, and the quality of Francisco de Goya's paintings hung on the palace's walls.[17]

The best part of El Capricho was undoubtedly the garden, where the Countess-Duchess of Benavente worked hard to achieve a small-scale Versailles, hiring the best gardeners of the time, such as Boutelou, who also worked in the royal gardens at La Granja and Aranjuez. Later, in 1797, she hired Jean-Baptiste Mulot, who had worked on *Le Petit Trianon* in Versailles for Marie Antoinette. The countess's fantasies started emerging in the garden: the Bacchus Temple, the Labyrinth, the Rustic House, and the Beekeeper's Hut. In the latter, visitors were able to experience an intimate view of nature while admiring the busy bees on the building's exterior. María Josefa could often be found inside, enjoying a cup of chocolate and contemplating the sculpture of Venus created by José Adán, which had been ordered especially for the interior of the Beekeeper's Hut. She also hired Ángel María Tadey, master stage-hand from Milan, who became her indispensable collaborator and produced the beautiful paintings inside la Casa de la Vieja (the Old Woman's House). However, his relationship with María Josefa (as well as those of other workers) soured due to her delays in payment and the lack of any form of gratitude on her part.[18]

In 1785 she contracted another French gardener, Pedro Provost, whose work ended in 1810 when the French military assassinated him while he tried to defend the countess's property that was left unprotected when she was forced to seek safety in Cádiz during the Peninsular War. In 1810, with General Belliard occupying the country house, musical instruments, crystal chandeliers, clocks, and furniture disappeared. Fortunately, a good family friend, the painter Carafa, was able, at great risk, to save the major paintings by hiding them in a secure location. Not only did El Capricho suffer pillaging by the French, but so too did the Puerta de la Vega palace, occupied by General Merlin. In 1808, the French destroyed the family's castle in the city of Benavente, burned the family's archive, and looted the lands of Arcos. After she returned from Cádiz, the Countess-Duchess of Benavente's administrators slowly started to recover some of the stolen objects, the glassware from El Capricho, and some of its furniture, but nothing was as it had been.

The Countess-Duchess of Benavente enjoyed receiving her friends at her palace at Alameda de Osuna, especially during Carnival time and during the long summers. They arrived from Madrid, which was nine kilometers away, in open carriages, their faces dusty from the road, and their hostess served them wine and imported champagne. She never hesitated to spend impressive figures on parties and banquets: incredible pastries, great casks of wine, luxurious chairs that she would rent exclusively for the event, musicians to enhance the evening, and a battalion of servants (many times reaching up to two hundred people) hired for those special occasions.[19] These same expenses were simultaneously being incurred in their Puerta de la Vega palace, their Osuna-Farinelli palace at Aranjuez, and in El Capricho.

Protocol, although more relaxed during Carnival dinners and gatherings, was strictly preserved. Lists were created so that guests received different treatment and distinction according to whether they held a noble title. Among them was María del Rosario Cepeda, María Josefa's ally in the Junta de Damas' tasks. Among those with noble titles we find the Marquises of Fuerte-Híjar, the Countess of Truillas, the Countess of Carpio, the Duchess of Alba, the Marquises of Malaspina, the widowed Marquise of Sonora, and Cecilia Sabatini.

Although some of her guests were in fact nobles, the hostess's deeply held intention should not be mistaken. Her objective was solely to create a social meeting point. Consequently, she would also invite actresses like Josefa Correa, along with playwrights like Ramón de la Cruz. In 1781, María Faustina, María Josefa's mother, was in charge of commissioning a *sainetero* (sketch writer) to write a short play called *El día de campo* (A Day in the Country) to be presented in their private theater at Segovia Street. This process was repeated in 1786 with *El Extranjero* (The Foreigner), produced in the small theater at El Capricho, and the roles were played solely by the female members of the family.[20]

Another interesting guest was Tomás de Iriarte, author of works such as *El don de gentes* (Good People Skills) and *Donde menos se piensa salta la liebre* (Where Least Expected), both played by family members on El Capricho's stage. His brother Bernardo, resident in Vienna, brought together Joseph Haydn and the Duke and Duchess of Osuna, who wanted to commission several compositions. The playwright Leandro Fernández de Moratín was a regular guest who depended on the protection and patronage of María Faustina. Moratín exchanged books and ideas with the Countess-Duchess of Benavente, for whom he wrote a *zarzuela* (Spanish operetta) called *El barón*, which was later performed at the Coliseo de la Cruz in Madrid.

Frequent guests at El Capricho were Lord and Lady Holland. She gave very interesting insights on the social gatherings organized by the Countess-

Duchess, whom she considered to be a woman of great intelligence and unusual talent, like her husband, the Duke of Osuna, "who is a very tolerably sensible man and of considerable knowledge."[21] Another great friend was Gaspar Melchor de Jovellanos, whose enlightened culture and dedicated political career were admired by both spouses, and who was also a friend of the Countess of Montijo, secretary of the Junta de Damas and a great collaborator of María Josefa.

The Marquises of Bondad Real were also regulars at the country tours, theatrical performances, dinners, and concerts. Manuel de La Peña, Marquis of Bondad Real, had been Pedro de Alcántara's fellow officer and was his longtime personal friend. It is difficult to define when he became the Countess-Duchess of Benavente's *cortejo*—a Spanish custom, related to the Italian *chichisveo*, in which a married woman had a constant male companion, sometimes but not necessarily in a sexual relationship, that was tolerated by her husband.[22] There are many early references to his presence in the family, such as when he attended their daughter's baptism in August 1783.[23] In his position as lieutenant colonel of one of the regiments of the infantry of the Spanish Royal Guard, he would spend his abundant free time accompanying María Josefa in her daily activities. Their relationship lasted until the countess's final days, when she chose him as the executor of her will. Undoubtedly, this loving friendship was one of her main moral supports when she faced the most difficult experiences of her life. However, being her *cortejo* did not stop the Marquis of Bondad Real from visiting El Capricho every summer with his wife and children.

Of particular interest is the relationship of patronage and friendship between the Dukes of Osuna and Francisco de Goya, who was also a habitual guest at the summer gatherings at El Capricho. It was probably Infante (Prince) Luis Antonio de Borbón, brother of King Carlos III, who introduced Goya to the Osuna family. When María Josefa met him, she was impressed with the artist's skill and offered him her friendship and protection. Goya painted the couple on three occasions, producing the last and most important portrait in 1788, *La familia de los duques de Osuna*.[24] On this dazzling canvas of shades of silver and gray, the artist portrays the duke and duchess with four of their five children.

For El Capricho, in 1788 Goya created a group of seven small paintings that represented typical country scenes, very fashionable toward the end of the eighteenth century, following the format and style he used for the cartoons for the Royal Tapestry Factory (Real Fábrica de Tapices). Ten years later, Goya would once again honor the couple with a series of six paintings destined for their palace at the Alameda de Osuna, though with much darker content: the main theme was witchcraft, an interest Goya shared with the duchess.[25] Genre paintings with more cheerful scenes were scattered around the palace. By 1785, Goya had also painted María Josefa's most attractive portrait,[26] where we find the countess dressed in the French style. The artist highlights the qualities of the fabrics, the embroidery of her gown, and her powdered wig. Goya captures the delicate spontaneity of the lady's face, as well as her deeply intelligent look. The dukes commissioned Goya to paint all of their children. The patronage that the Dukes of Osuna offered to Goya was so committed that in 1799 they even bought the eighty prints of *Los Caprichos* (Follies) that the Spanish painter dared to publish, openly challenging the Inquisition. Although the Countess knew the goal of *Los Caprichos* was, to a certain extent, to criticize the aristocracy to which she belonged, she bought them nevertheless, paying a total of 1,500 *reales* to help the painter.

A Woman Committed to the Enlightenment

Thanks to the royal order issued by King Carlos III at the Palacio de la Granja on August 27, 1787, the Real Sociedad Económica Matritense de Amigos del País became the first institution in Spain's history that admitted women. The monarch wanted to involve the Spanish female nobility in the process of necessary new reforms, and later, to set an example, the Princess of Asturias María Luisa de Parma and the Infantas María Victoria and María Josefa joined the Junta de Damas as honorary members. Before the polemic regarding the admission of women, recounted in the first and second essays of this volume, in January 1786 two women were admitted to the Madrid Society as honorary members. The first was María Isidra Quintina de Guzmán, who held a degree from the University of Alcalá de Henares, and the second was the Countess-Duchess of Benavente, admitted because her husband was the society's president. On July 22, 1786, she gave a speech to all of her colleagues thanking them for the opportunity.[27] The general consensus in the organization was that the next president of the Junta de Damas should be the Countess-Duchess of Benavente. María Josefa carried out her duties as president admirably during three periods: 1787–89, 1802–8, and 1815–17, working with enthusiasm and offering exemplary dedication. She never hesitated to give her money, time, and personal effort, which were also very necessary for managing her own rich heritage and taking care of her large family.

The meeting room of the Casas Consistoriales (Town Hall) was a silent witness to the ladies' weekly gatherings. These encounters were scheduled every Friday in the afternoon. As they did not have a private space for themselves, the female members had to store their material in a borrowed cabinet that was unceremoniously moved by the City Council. In it they kept a silver writing case, a gift from Pedro de Alcántara, and the black and white balls used for the voting process, as all decisions were voted upon democratically.[28]

Not all of the members proposed by the junta accepted the invitation to join, perhaps lacking the required enlightened spirit. But what is certain is that the ladies who did join never lacked the strength, enthusiasm, or creativity to save the charities from many of their economic troubles. Some posts, such as that of secretary, were carried out by the same person, the Countess of Montijo, for seventeen years.[29] Surprisingly, the women's membership fees—160 *reales*—were higher than those paid by their male counterparts. The Countess of Montijo promptly turned this money over to the members of the institution.

For the president's post, the candidates had to be well-educated women, learned, and with a rich command of languages; the Countess-Duchess of Benavente thoroughly surpassed these requirements. The president had the deciding vote and could be reelected, as happened to the Countess-Duchess of Benavente. In 1804, María Josefa brought into the Junta her daughter-in-law, Francisca de Beaufort-Spontin, Marquise of Peñafiel (see fig. 1), and in 1805 her daughters Joaquina and Josefa Manuela, who became the vice-censor in 1807. Later, in 1814, the youngest member of the family, Manuela Isidra, also joined, serving as vice president from 1835 to 1838.

The Osuna family was thus actively implicated in their mother's tasks. On several occasions, the president herself anonymously made very important donations. María Josefa was also in charge of directing the Colegio de Educación de la Sociedad or Escuela de Modas in 1806, after the previous director, the Countess of Truillas, was banished from the Court. This was one of the first tuition-based schools in Madrid for girls, where the Junta de Damas developed a valuable pedagogical project that expanded the number and depth of the subjects taught to the students. Unlike in other schools, reading, writing, history, and spelling were all part of the children's academic curricula.

The Countess-Duchess of Benavente's activity in the Inclusa was unceasing. She and her companions restructured unhealthy hygienic practices, disinfected the rooms, and built cribs.[30] Even when Pedro de Alcántara passed away in 1807 she did not stop her whirlwind activity, donating her lieutenant general widow's pension to the junta. She also knew how to defend the orphans whenever she mistrusted official state policies. For example, the government of King Carlos IV wanted to carry out inoculation trials of the smallpox vaccine in 1795 on the children of the Inclusa. However, the Junta de Damas discovered that they were not going to use the Jenner vaccine, so their president did not hesitate to present their objections to the secretary of state, Pedro Ceballos.

However, in 1805, María Josefa did promote a valuable experiment with infant nutrition in the Inclusa, since it was clear that the milk offered by their wet nurses was totally insufficient. A comparative test was carried out with twelve children: six were fed by goats and the other six by wet nurses. The goats were fed on barley, carob, and straw. These tests were not at all satisfactory, as the majority of the children died. Nevertheless, there was such an important need to solve this problem that the junta did not hesitate to become involved once again, in 1817, in finding another solution for the orphans. On this occasion they used as food a special flour from the Orinoco that the Countess of Casa Flores herself had imported, which unfortunately was also unsuccessful.[31]

At times the male members of the Madrid Society sought to confront the female members of the Junta de Damas as a way of forcing them into submission and asserting their jurisdiction over them. These confrontations gave María Josefa great satisfaction. The Countess of Montijo and the Countess-Duchess of Benavente always agreed on how to face these problems. They were enlightened, refined, highly educated women, and also shared the good fortune of having had liberal husbands who defended Enlightenment philosophy. Thus, the secretary of the junta did not hesitate to make it clear to her male colleagues that the damas would never work in submissive or humiliating conditions and that between two analogous bodies there was no room for dependence or superiority.

After her return from Cádiz in 1813, where she had taken refuge with her family after fleeing the violence unleashed in Madrid in 1808 by the French invasion, María Josefa was a changed woman. The suffering she had witnessed and endured had taken its toll. She had helped the patriots who were courageously defending Madrid in May 1808, collaborating with them when they set up an infirmary on Calle del Viento. However, toward the end of the war, her personal fortune was in a shambles due to Napoleon Bonaparte's persecution of her family. The atrocity of so many vanished lives and, in her view, so many betrayals of their homeland by some of her French-influenced friends (*afrancesados*) made her evolve from an enlightened attitude to a deep conservatism that supported King Fernando VII and the world and ideals he defended. Little by little, her most valuable qualities as a cultured woman—those that had led her to subscribe to the *Memorial literario*,[32] devour the press, or purchase hundreds of books in French in order to read the encyclopedists in their own language—began to disappear. That whole world was erased, while in its place arose her interests as a landowner who hoped to recover her rents and her family's fortune which now had been taken by Napoleon Bonaparte.

Nevertheless, her allegiance to the Junta de Damas endured. In her annual reports delivered to her companions, her voice expressed the pain and the fear she had suffered during the war. It was for her the end of an era, the disappearance of an aristocratic way of understanding society's organization, which was becoming extinct due to the wave of liberal thinkers from across Europe.

Abandoning the presidency at the end of 1817 due to her advanced age, María Josefa continued to collaborate with the Junta de Damas. Unfortunately, her health was quickly deteriorating, as can be observed from the hesitant handwriting used on the notes she wrote to justify her absences. Finally, still active and committed as she had always been, her life came to an end on October 5, 1834, at the age of eighty-two, in her Puerta de la Vega palace in Madrid.

NOTES

Essay translated by Pilar Arenas Merino.

1. The subtitle, "Más Vale Volando," comes from the saying "Más vale pájaro en mano que buitres volando" (a bird in the hand is worth two in the bush). This motto, "an affirmation of personal liberty in the face of pre-established norms" (masvalevolando.blogspot.com/p/que-es-mas -vale-volando.html), belongs to the House of Benavente and is the insignia on the Pimentel family's coat of arms at Santa María del Azogue in the town of Benavente. Atienza Hernández, *Aristocracia, poder.*

2. Basic bibliography until the current century about the Countess-Duchess of Benavente

was limited to the following titles: Yebes, *La condesa-duquesa de Benavente*; Ezquerra del Bayo, *Retratos de la familia Téllez-Girón*.

3. Amo Lobo, Barrio Prada and Regueras Grande, *El Hospital de la Piedad de Benavente*; Regueras Grande, *Pimentel*.

4. Pérez Hernández, *Correspondencia de la Duquesa de Osuna*.

5. Holland, *The Spanish Journal*, 195. Elizabeth Vassall Fox, Lady Holland (1771–1845) was a renowned English political hostess, the wife of Whig politician Henry Vassall-Fox, Lord Holland. With her husband, she held political and literary gatherings at their home, Holland House. Her husband was nephew of Charles James Fox, a prominent British Whig statesman. Lady Holland and her husband made several trips to Spain, where they mixed with intellectuals, politicians, and artists. They protected liberal Spanish politicians exiled in London during the first third of the nineteenth century. Distinguished guests to Holland House included Lord Byron, Charles Dickens, and Washington Irving, among others. Regarding the Hollands' relation with Spain, see Kitts, "The role of Holland House."

6. We do not know what kind of education she received, nor where. However, her mother's fondness for music and theater, together with the cultural patronage that she exercised, had a profound influence.

7. Mendigorría, *Mis memorias íntimas*, 50.

8. In Spanish, "los segundones" also expresses a pejorative sense of the second-borns' condition.

9. AHPM, Libro 19556.

10. Fernández Quintanilla, *La IX Duquesa de Osuna*, 450.

11. The scandals provoked by Francisco de Borja after divorcing his wife, and his uncontrolled violent scenes, led to King Fernando VII's decision to ban Francisco from Madrid.

12. Fernández Quintanilla, *La IX Duquesa de Osuna*, 126.

13. Fernando VII's dislike of the Prince of Anglona is well-documented. Pedro de Alcántara was very openly and actively in favor of the liberal ideas presented in the 1812 Constitution, to the king's displeasure.

14. Fernández Quintanilla, *La IX Duquesa de Osuna*, 73.

15. See Añón Feliú, *El Capricho de la Alameda de Osuna*.

16. Juan F. Remón Menéndez calls the Capricho a "Garden of Ideas" and notes that it was influenced by Edmund Burke's theories of the sublime, Thomas Whately's *Observations on Modern Gardening*, and William Chambers's theories on Chinese gardens. See Remón Menéndez, "The Alameda of the Duchess of Osuna," 224–25. For Adrián Fernández Almoguera, the Capricho is a remarkable Spanish example of the European culture of *"vivre à la mode"*: "The Osunas' Capricho is strong evidence of a connection between Spanish modern artistic culture and the latest European aesthetic ideas." See Fernández Almoguera, "From the Private Cabinet to the Suburban Villa," 238.

17. Fernández Quintanilla, *La IX Duquesa de Osuna*, 77.

18. Fernández Quintanilla, *La IX Duquesa de Osuna*, 80.

19. Fernández Quintanilla, *La IX Duquesa de Osuna*, 90.

20. Fernández Quintanilla, *La IX Duquesa de Osuna*, 95.

21. Holland, *The Spanish Journal*, 195.

22. See Martín Gaite, *Usos amorosos del dieciocho.*

23. In letters received by the Countess-Duchess of Benavente on behalf of their friends, she was frequently asked about her health and her life with her *cortejo*. In her responses, the learned lady preferred to talk about him rather than about her husband or children.

24. Prado Museum inventory no. MNP, P000739.

25. Fernández Quintanilla, *La IX Duquesa de Osuna,* 108.

26. Collection of Bartolomé March. Another portrait of the Countess-Duchess of Benavente, engraved by Fernando Selma, by Goya (BNE, IH/298/1).

27. Benavente, *Discurso.* The discourse was also published in *Memorial literario,* T. IX, XXXIII, September 1786: 3–5.

28. Fernández Quintanilla, *La IX Duquesa de Osuna,* 293.

29. Fernández Quintanilla, *La IX Duquesa de Osuna,* 299.

30. The Countess-Duchess of Benavente dedicated a great amount of time and money to the Inclusa. She struggled to find sources of funding for the institution, which had high expenses due to the large volume of abandoned children.

31. Serrano Jerez, "Chemistry in the City," 48–52.

32. Martín Valverde, *María del Rosario Fernández,* 291.

María Francisca de Sales Portocarrero, Countess of Montijo, 1754–1808

An Atypical Biography in the Age of Enlightenment

GLORIA FRANCO RUBIO

The sixth Countess of Montijo, María Francisca de Sales Portocarrero, was one of the most widely known women in Spanish society in the second half of the eighteenth century. Her importance is not due to her aristocratic lineage as one of the highest-ranking noblewomen in Spain, her presence in Court circles, or her dealings with the royal family, but to her brilliant personality, which led her into areas that virtually no other Spanish women had ventured into until that point. (See fig. 7.) In the field of ideas, her strong personality, firm convictions, and considerable independence of judgment led her to align with forms of spirituality and religious practice that were frowned upon by the official church, which kept her under constant surveillance throughout her life. She also hosted an important tertulia at her home in Madrid, which was especially critical of certain government measures, incurring the wrath of some politicians, who eventually punished her by banishing her from the Court. But it was no doubt her commitment to social causes and her awareness of certain problems in Spanish society that led her to become involved in the Junta de Damas de Honor y Mérito, a branch of the Real Sociedad Económica Matritense de Amigos del País, one of the most emblematic of King Carlos III's Enlightenment reformist projects. Like other such societies under the monarchy, it contributed to the development of a new political culture and became one of the most politicized spaces of the moment, fostering a change of status from subjects to citizens.

She lived during the final decades of the ancien régime, a historical crossroads in which two opposing models of womanhood clashed head-on: the model of an educated, cultured woman from the aristocratic or bourgeois elite, who moved in Enlightenment social settings, took an active part in the Republic of

Letters, was far from indifferent to the realities of her time, and figured to some degree in public life, versus the traditional archetype of woman in the home. This old model, permanently propagated by the moral texts and sermons of ecclesiastical figures, was undergoing a resurgence thanks to bourgeois ideology. Supported at this time by writers and politicians, it aimed to exclude from public spaces the (few) women who had dared to invade them, in order to confine them once and for all to the domestic sphere. The Countess of Montijo's life story shows the various facets of an exceptional woman who refused to be simply a passive witness to the challenges facing society at the time, even though that meant not following the typical norms for women of her rank. On the contrary, she wished to participate in the social dynamism of her time by becoming actively involved in public affairs, and she took a personal stance on the reform plans of the Enlightenment governments, almost always in solidarity with her own sex. Her behavior matched the new ways of thinking brought by the Enlightenment, but clashed with Spanish society, which was still rooted in tradition, and very loathe to embrace any type of change.

The biography of the Countess of Montijo shows an exceptional woman, transgressive and atypical, an undisputed protagonist in the society of her time, whose life surpassed the model of the feminine ideal. For Lady Holland, who met her in 1803 during her trip to Spain, "Mde. de Montijo has the reputation of being the cleverest and best informed woman in Spain. Her society is the best in Madrid, and was composed of the most remarkable men,"[1] among them Gaspar Melchor de Jovellanos, for whom she was "the best woman that I ever met in Spain, a friend of twenty years, [. . .] always active and constant in her good offices."[2]

Some Details of Her Biography

The countess was born in Madrid in June 1754, the daughter of Cristóbal Portocarrero (1704–1763), the sixth Marquis of Valderrábano, and María Josefa López de Zúñiga Girón, Countess of Miranda del Castañar. Both of her parents came from ancient and elevated noble families with extensive estates and wealth, and numerous aristocratic titles, two of which made them grandees of Spain. She was their sole heiress. Her birth placed her in a clearly privileged situation, but that did not prevent a series of hardships from striking her from a very early age, so that her life did not play out along traditional lines but quite

FIG. 7. The Countess of Montijo and her daughters (Agustín Esteve), between 1793 and 1796. Ministerio de Cultura y Deporte. Instituto del Patrimonio Cultural de España. Casa Moreno. Archivo de Arte Español (1893–1953).

the contrary. Her father's accidental death when she was four years old left her effectively an orphan, since her mother, devastated by his death, decided to abandon the world and enter the Convent of Las Maravillas in Madrid, to join an order of barefoot Carmelites, leaving the little girl in the care of her paternal grandfather.

The responsibility of rearing and educating a girl destined to be the inheritor of so many titles and estates seems to have proved overwhelming for a man of advancing old age, so he decided to send her to boarding school at the Visitación convent in Madrid, at that point the best boarding school in Spain. An institution for educating the daughters of noblemen, it had been created at the request of Queen Bárbara de Braganza some years earlier, and was run by nuns from the Order of the Visitation of Holy Mary, which was founded in France by Saint Jane Frances Frémiot de Chantal and Saint Francis de Sales. During her time there, she received a thorough education, which included reading, writing, grammar, spelling, arithmetic, religion, and French language, up to the age of fourteen, at which point she left the convent to marry.[3] The choice of a spouse, as stipulated by the marriage contract drawn up by her grandfather, with the acquiescence of her mother and in line with her family's interests, as was normal at the time, fell on an Aragonese nobleman, Felipe Palafox (1739–1790), the sixth Marquis of Ariza's son, who was twenty-nine years old. He had extensive military experience, and had reached the rank of lieutenant general. Even though they had never met, they had a good life together for twenty-two years. Theirs was a happy marriage, and they produced six children, who respected and loved their mother deeply.

In the mid-1790s, when she was forty-one years old, at the height of her powers, she decided to change direction in life by marrying for a second time. At that point she had been a widow for five years; she had married off most of her children; she was involved in interesting work as secretary of the Junta de Damas, she hosted a tertulia frequented by the *crème de la crème* of court intellectuals, and she had recently been awarded the sash of the Royal Order of Noble Ladies of Queen María Luisa, a great honor. The countess had a strong personality and a charismatic effect on those around her. While her first marriage, arranged by her family, had given her an amiable companion who proved a good husband and father to her children, this time she only took her own feelings into account and was completely free to choose her future spouse. The man she selected was her close friend and tertulia counterpart for many years, Estanislao de Lugo (1753–1833),[4] with whom she shared ideas and religious beliefs. He supported her through difficult times and accompanied her in her banishment to the various places she lived up until her death in Logroño in 1808.

In her decision, she prioritized her personal desires and expectations over social conventions, minimizing the fact that her fiancé was of a much lower social rank, which would mean an unequal marriage. She knew her decision could be interpreted as an embarrassment, as it contradicted the Pragmática (royal law) on marriage approved by King Carlos III in 1776 to counter the "social disorder" caused by unequal matches.[5] But that did not intimidate her, and she went ahead. According to the Pragmática, given her status as a grandee of Spain, she had to request royal assent, which was granted but only in the category of "secret" marriages.

The countess was a woman of great intelligence, very cultured, with deep convictions, noble ideals, and a strong personality. She always stuck to her beliefs despite the hardships they caused her, which made her a rather atypical figure among women of her rank. Her behavior over the years did not always fit the norms expected of women in her day; it was the product of a complex personality that can be seen on the different fronts on which she defied the system at the time. However, her public profile as an aristocrat committed to the reform policy of the Enlightenment governments gave her great authority among her contemporaries, to the point that she was awarded various honors throughout her life, including the prestigious sash of the Royal Order of Noble Ladies of Queen María Luisa in 1795.

Translator and Writer in the Republic of Letters

Her involvement in the literary field occurred very early, thanks to translation, a task she took on unwillingly; it was not her own initiative, but had been requested by Bishop Climent, one of her tertulia guests. She was initially reluctant because she was not confident of understanding a theological text. Neither of them foresaw the treacherous nature of the terrain she was entering, which would lead to a direct confrontation with the church. When she translated the *Instrucciones Christianas sobre el sacramento del matrimonio y sobre las ceremonias con que la iglesia lo administra* (Christian instructions on the sacrament of matrimony and the ceremonies whereby the church administers it), written by a French priest, Nicolás Le Tourneux,[6] who was under suspicion of having embraced Jansenism, she became a target of suspicion herself, accused of potentially professing religious ideas that contradicted Catholic orthodoxy. This sin was never forgiven, despite her indisputable devoutness, and it re-emerged at various points during her life, causing innumerable worries.

When the countess did the translation, she was only twenty years old; it is hard to believe that at such a young age, having spent almost all her life as a boarder at a convent school, she could have been an expert in Jansenist doctrine, rather than just a translator trying to fulfill a request from a person she respected and admired. However, Paula de Demerson states that the translation "caused her to be seen as a leader among the Spanish Jansenist group."[7]

If it had been an isolated episode, perhaps things might have turned out differently, but over time, her correspondence with various French clergymen fueled suspicions of heterodoxy on her part, since she wrote to people who were very critical of the official stance of the Spanish church. In her letters to Clément, she was responding to the priest's interest in learning about the situation of the Spanish church from people like herself, who were familiar with its role and social influence. A dim view was taken of her two letters to Bonnet, the editor of the Jansenist journal *Nouvelles ecclésiastiques*, which harshly criticized the strict censorship exercised by the Inquisition on Spanish culture, citing its negative consequences. Her letters gave her detractors an excuse to argue that the countess might have had a hand in the work of supplying first-hand information to the author. Lastly, she was also accused of having corresponded with the French Bishop Grégoire, who advocated religious tolerance and suppression of the Inquisition, which he described as "a continual calumny against the Catholic church" in an open letter to the new inquisitor general that was published in French and Spanish, and widely read.[8] It is clear that the countess, who believed in inner spirituality, was always very critical of unedifying displays of religious devotion that bordered on spectacle, which were so typical of Spanish religious life.

Other aspects of her thought can be seen in the numerous texts, short works, and reports she wrote throughout her life, such as the *Elogio de la Señora Doña Petra de Torres Feloaga, Marquesa de Valdeolmos* (Eulogy of the Lady Petra de Feloaga, Marquise of Valdeolmos). She used this funeral eulogy of a woman who had been a personal friend for years and companion-in-arms in the Junta de Damas to develop a series of ideas about the female sex and women's destiny in society. (See fig. 8.) On the one hand, she states that the ideal space for women is "the narrow and sacred space of our homes" (estrecho y sagrado recinto de nuestras casas) because women should be honored "only by the eyes of our parents, our husbands, our children, and families" (a los ojos de nuestros padres, de nuestros esposos, de nuestros hijos y familias) but, on the other hand, she is convinced of women's ability to act as good citizens. After dutifully praising the virtues, character, and conduct of the dead woman, she hones in on two aspects of her life. In the private sphere, she describes Feloaga as a "faithful wife and tender mother" (esposa fiel, a esta tierna madre), praising her constant devotion to her family and the care and effort she had gone to in raising her children; but when she turns to the public dimension, she enthusiastically applauds Feloaga's work for the Junta de Damas as head of the San Sebastián School and the Embroidery School. All of this led her to the following reflection: "What a vast field opened to her sensitive heart when our Enlightenment government decided to establish the Junta de Damas for the education of that part of the people that had been abandoned until now!" (¡Mas qué campo tan vasto se abrió a su sensible corazón cuando nuestro ilustrado gobierno pensó en establecer esta Junta de Señoras destinada a la educación de aquella clase del pueblo que hasta entonces estaba abandonada!) Lastly, to forestall doubts about women's ability to reconcile the twin aspects of public and domestic life, she ends by saying that, "in any case, she carried out the many challenging assignments the Junta entrusted her with, as if they were her only occupation, while, as we have seen, she never neglected in the slightest her obligations at home" (De tal modo desempeñaba las muchas y delicadas comisiones que la Junta ponía a su cargo, que parecían ser su única ocupación, al mismo tiempo que como hemos visto no descuidaba un punto las obligaciones de su casa).[9]

To date, no in-depth study has yet determined the true author of the *Discurso sobre la autoridad de los ricos hombres sobre el Rey y cómo la fueron perdiendo*

FIG. 8. Petra de Torres y Feloaga, Marquise of Valdeolmos (engraved by Blas Amatller), 1797. Ministerio de Cultura y Deporte. Biblioteca Nacional de España.

hasta llegar al punto de opresión en que se halla hoy (Discourse on rich men's authority over the King and how they have gradually lost it to arrive at the state of oppression seen today), published in 1794. This text, supposedly written by the Count of Teba, the countess's first-born son, caused an outcry by stating the nobility's opposition to the power garnered by the upstart Manuel Godoy, who had the count banished to the city of Ávila as a result.[10] However, some historians, based on testimony by people close to the countess, have speculated that, in fact, it was she who wrote the piece, even though her son subsequently received public punishment for it. If the countess was truly the author of the piece, it would attest to a facet of her personality that reflected her political ideas, capable not only of critiquing the direction of governmental policies at the time, but of examining and theorizing about the position and political role of the nobility in a monarchy.

The Countess's Tertulia: A Forum for Critique and Opinion

She took another step forward in fulfilling her wish to be actively involved in the public sphere when she followed Enlightenment social practices of the time and started hosting a tertulia in her home. It was attended by intellectuals, writers, clergymen, magistrates, and senior civil servants and became one of the most brilliant spots in Madrid society.[11] Her tertulia was known as a forum for Enlightenment ideas, and for being very critical of certain attitudes in Spanish society, to the point where some scholars have described it as the editorial powerhouse behind *El Censor*, one of the most influential newspapers of the era, and one which they see as the group's mouthpiece.[12] The tertulia brought together a circle of public figures from different socio-professional positions who were increasingly critical of Godoy, the royal favorite. These included some of the countess's own relatives, such as her son-in-law, the Marquis of Villafranca, and his brother, the Count of Miranda.

During the second phase of the Godoy administration (1801–8), all of them became a danger to the government, or at least that was the royal favorite's fear, judging by the events that took place. Opposition to Godoy arose because of a series of circumstances caused both by the economic crisis, which led to food shortages, and by the consequences of the international conflicts between France, Britain, and Portugal. There were also the rise of the Fernandist Party; the intrigues of the heir to the throne, the Prince of Asturias, Fernando; discontent among the nobility; and efficient propaganda against Godoy's policies, which intensified as he was given ever more power by the king and queen, culminating in the banishment of numerous aristocratic families.[13] In this context, the countess's enemies seized the occasion, and the old accusation of her Jansenism was revived, although it was really a pretext to deal her a political blow.[14]

In the summer of 1805, the countess remained in Madrid, since she had noticed a hostile atmosphere; the lack of an invitation to visit the *Sitios Reales* (royal residences) showed that she had fallen into disfavor, and this materialized in September with a royal order of banishment. She was ordered to abandon her residence, family, and friends, as well as her regular activities as secretary of the Junta de Damas. The loss or disappearance of the file on this means we cannot know the allegations made against her by the authorities to justify this punishment, which she accepted obediently, moving to her Montijo estates in Extremadura, where she spent several months. From there she moved to Logroño, where she met Urquijo, the ex–secretary of state, a friend and guest at her Madrid tertulia. The whole time, the government kept her under constant close surveillance, both her actions and her correspondence.

The Countess as Secretary of the Junta de Damas: Her Work on Social Causes

The prospect of women being allowed to join the patriotic societies generated enormous controversy. It was featured widely in the press and in various short published works, leading to a bitter polemic among the enlightened male elite that showed the misogyny of Spanish society. After ten long years of debate, a royal order by King Carlos III, dated August 27, 1787, recognized that women could form rule-based associations to adopt the best methods for "promoting virtue, application and industry in their sex" (promover la virtud, la aplicación y la industria en su sexo). The royal order advocated making a careful selection of women who, "due to their circumstances are most worthy of this honorable distinction and can work together to find the means of promoting good education, improving customs with their example and their writings, introducing a love for work, and discouraging luxury, which both destroys the fortunes of private individuals and dissuades many from matrimony, at the expense of that institution, and substituting the general for the foreign in their adornments" (por sus circunstancias más acreedoras de esta honrosa distinción y procedan y traten unidas los medios de fomentar la buena educación, mejorar las costumbres con su ejemplo y sus escritos, introducir el amor al trabajo, cortar el lujo que al paso que destruye las fortunas de los particulares, retrae a muchos del matrimonio, en perjuicio del estado y sustituir para sus adornos los generales a los extranjeros). This was explained in a communiqué from the Count of Floridablanca, secretary of state, to the secretary of the Matritense.[15]

When "fourteen ladies of great distinction" joined the Junta de Damas, the group was able to take over various projects that male Matritense members had handled with lackluster results, such as the administration, running, and management of the so-called Patriotic Schools in Madrid. These were strategically located in certain neighborhoods to provide free education to girls with no means, enabling them to learn how to prepare yarn and spin linen, hemp, silk, and wool.

The countess was one of those ladies; her acceptance and her subsequent work on the governing board of the Junta de Damas clearly demonstrate her commitment to social causes, as well as her awareness of the problems of the country in general, and the situation of women in particular. Her appointment as secretary put her in a position she held for eighteen years, until she had to resign due to the banishment order. She combined this position with her role on the Education Commission to promote the physical, moral, and intellectual education of women.

In these roles, she proved willing and able to perform important work on behalf of her sex, supporting women's autonomy by providing the conditions necessary for them to learn a trade with which they could earn their own living, and facilitating their moral rehabilitation, in the case of imprisoned female inmates.[16] She did so by competently performing the different aspects of her job, spearheading numerous initiatives, and coming up with novel proposals that revealed an energetic, brilliant personality, with reformist leanings and a clear social conscience. In fact, she was the true *alma mater* of the Junta de Damas throughout that long period.

As part of her work, she constantly had to write reports of all types, in addition to composing essays on women's education. In these, we can glimpse her thoughts on women's situation, which are indicated by her expressive titles: "Sobre la educación moral que se debe dar a las jóvenes que se hallan en edad de recibir estado" (On the moral education that should be given to young women of marriageable age), and "Sobre la educación que se debe dar a las mujeres acerca de la constitución civil y negocios políticos" (On the education that should be given to women about the civil constitution and political affairs). These refer to the two central topics in women's lives, one dealing with the most personal and private sphere and the other with women's role in the public sphere. In the latter, presented to the junta and approved by the rest of the members in June 1795, she recognizes nature as the exclusive source of legitimacy in the position of the sexes in society, while also endorsing and upholding the traditional patriarchal distribution of social space, which assigned the public sphere to men and the domestic one to women. This implied that women should be excluded "from political functions and public employment" (de las funciones políticas y empleos públicos). She not only disagrees with equality for the sexes in terms of social roles, but warns about the problems that might arise if women "were to neglect the obscure occupations of home and attempt to usurp men's empire" (se disgustasen de las ocupaciones oscuras de su casa y quisiesen usurpar a los hombres su imperio).[17] She closes by stating that the biggest benefit women can bestow on the state is to fulfill their role as wives and mothers. For this to be possible, the education young women receive would have to include certain subjects like reading, writing, arithmetic, and some notions of geography and history, although the most important topic would be their moral education. This stance reveals the major contradiction between her behavior and the discourse she defended with her words. It is pertinent to draw attention to this because at that time social space was being redesigned in terms of the theory of the two spheres, and the location of the sexes within them.

One of her most important initiatives was her attempt to improve the personal situation and daily life of female prison inmates by creating an association of ladies. It was a great success, and even became a model for the creation of similar associations in other Spanish provinces, in the cities of Oviedo, Valencia, or Zaragoza. Thus, we should recognize the importance of having been the first female prison reformer;[18] indeed, when she got news of the dire conditions at three Madrid prisons—La Galera, the Cárcel de Corte, and the Cárcel de Villa—for women inmates being held for crimes of passion, crimes against property or morality, or prostitution, she convinced the other members of the Junta de Damas of the need for reform. They requested the creation of the Real Asociación de Caridad de Señoras para alivio de las presas (Ladies' Charitable Association for the Relief of Women Prisoners), whose objective—

according to its statutes—was to make women "into useful beings for the State [. . .]; inspire a fear of God in them and love for honest work; console them in their prisons, and teach them a trade during their time behind bars, so that once their sentences are served, they can earn their living honorably" (en seres útiles para el Estado [. . .]; inspirarles el temor de Dios y el amor al trabajo honesto; consolarlas en sus prisiones, y enseñarlas un oficio durante su encarcelamiento a fin de que, una vez purgada su condena, puedan ganar dignamente su subsistencia).[19]

In order to do this, the countess designed a work plan to follow while the statutes were being approved. In it, she stipulated the teaching of reading, writing, and arithmetic and, above all, learning a trade. The association members committed to visit the jails on Sundays to read pious and edifying works to the inmates, and give catechism lessons. They paid the prisoners a small sum for their work, in addition to visiting the dormitories and inspecting the infirmary to make sure everything was in order and appropriately clean and tidy. In a short time, they received spectacular results. They continued their work for seventeen years, during which time they managed to carry out major reforms: adopting rational measures to improve food, hygiene, and sanitary conditions; separating inmates according to the crimes committed; moral rehabilitation and instilling personal dignity, by providing a way for inmates to earn a living honorably once they had served their sentences and returned to the outside world.[20]

The other field in which the countess showed her valor and did laudable work was in reforming the Hospital de la Inclusa, a home for foundlings in Madrid. She set out to improve the miserable situation of abandoned children and stem the high mortality rates, which were a result of poor economic management, abuse by the staff, deficient nutrition, and a complete lack of hygiene and sanitation. The Inclusa's high mortality rate was common knowledge. Children there rarely reached three years of age, thanks to the epidemics that regularly ran rampant among them and to the dreadful conditions caused by the neglect of the orphanage staff, who engaged in continual fraud and abuse. This translated into bad policy in hiring wet nurses, which led to deficient nutrition, and material conditions where the lack of hygiene and overcrowding contributed to exacerbating the children's weakened physical state.

It was not an easy task, and she had to exert all of her authority and tenacity to achieve it. But it proved worthwhile since, from 1799 on, after she was named the "foundlings' supervisor" (curadora de expósitos), she managed to instill order at the orphanage and improve the dire situation she encountered there. It all began ten years earlier, in July 1789. Hoping to raise awareness among her colleagues in the junta about an issue that had preoccupied her for some time, she presented a *Memoria* (essay) laying out the wretched conditions at the establishment, along with a proposal to take charge of the children's upbringing. Although the project was accepted by her colleagues, it was not approved by the Real Sociedad. Instead of giving up, she tried again in 1792, presenting a second project that also failed to obtain the desired objective. The promulgation of a *real cédula* (royal decree) by Carlos IV in January 1794, in which he called for rescuing the foundlings from the infamous and shameful conditions they had suffered until then, offered her a new opportunity to try again. However, despite her continual efforts, and the social publicity her proposals generated, it was not until December 1796 that the Junta de Damas was charged with inspecting the Inclusa. The inspection was done by the countess with the help of the Countess de Truillas, Francisca Raón, and her niece the Marquise of Ariza. In October 1799, the Junta of Damas took over the running of the Inclusa in all matters. From that point on until her banishment, the countess worked tirelessly as foundlings' supervisor and obtained excellent results; not only did the children's living conditions improve, but the changes introduced significantly reduced the death rate.[21]

The Countess of Montijo was an unconventional woman, not anchored in tradition, critical of prejudice, open to new things and willing to adopt them if she thought they were appropriate at both the individual and the collective level. She decided to be a woman with a life history that was very far from the conventional patterns of her time, choosing a path that was very different from the destiny predetermined for women, with an attitude and ways of life that she put into practice through activities that were far from usual for her sex. Without being strident or willfully iconoclastic, she became a true milestone for other women, in her own time and for future generations. In her closest circle, she was an especially important role model for her own daughters, who became accustomed to attending the tertulias held at her home and to value involvement in social causes through her activity at the heart of the Junta de Damas. María Tomasa, the Marquise of Villafranca, followed in her footsteps and became the junta's president from 1817 to 1823.

Thanks to her attitude, she was able to take advantage of the cracks in the political architecture of the ancien régime to operate as a proactive social agent and bequeath a legacy that would later be taken up by other women. Her female solidarity and her fight to improve conditions for women, especially the most vulnerable, make her worthy of inclusion in a lineage of women who helped lay the foundations for the construction of women's long and winding road toward equality.

NOTES

Essay translated by Catherine Jagoe.

This work forms part of the research project Proyecto de Investigación I+D+i RTI2018-095379-B-C31, "La vida cotidiana entre los discursos y las prácticas: aspectos materiales, sociales y culturales en la Monarquía española del Antiguo Régimen."

1. Holland, *The Spanish Journal*, 102–3. Also, Lady Holland wrote a brief sketch of the Countess of Montijo in her *Journal*, emphasizing that she "[h]as an uncommon share of wit and talent," 193–94.

2. Quoted by Demerson, *María Francisca de Sales Portocarrero*, 346.

3. Franco Rubio, "Patronato regio."

4. Lugo was a well-known scholar who had studied liberal arts, law, and canon law. He was the tutor of Prince Don Luis's first-born son, an official of the Secreteriats of Grace and Justice and State. In 1793 he was named director of the Reales Sitios (Royal Sites) of San Isidro, and he was awarded the Grand Cross of the Order of Carlos III. Demerson, "Un canarien eclairé."

5. *Novísima Recopilación de las Leyes de España*, Libro X, Título II, Ley IX.

6. Nicolás Le Tourneaux (1640–1686) was confessor in the Convent of Port-Royal and later prior of Villers. He was the author of numerous works, some of which were suspected as Jansenist and were the object of ecclesiastical censorship although, in the end, they could not be condemned. On Jansenism in Spain, see Miguélez, *Jansenismo y regalismo en España*; Appolis, *Les Jansénistes Espagnols*; Tomsich, *El jansenismo en España*.

7. Demerson, *María Francisca de Sales Portocarrero*, 262.

8. Herr, *España y la revolución*, 349.

9. Montijo, *Elogio de la Señora Doña Petra de Torres Feloaga*.

10. Egido López, *Carlos IV*; La Parra López, *Manuel Godoy*; Corona Batarech, *Revolución y reacción*.

11. Franco Rubio, "El salón parcialmente iluminado."

12. Caso González, "*El Censor*, ¿periódico de Carlos III?"

13. AHN, Consejos, Legajo 11907.

14. Sarrailh, *La España Ilustrada*, 701–2.

15. Sempere y Guarinos, "Sociedad Económica de Madrid," 215–16.

16. Franco Rubio, "María Francisca de Sales Portocarrero."

17. ARSEM, Expediente 146/11.

18. Demerson, *María Francisca de Sales Portocarrero*, 200.

19. Demerson, *María Francisca de Sales Portocarrero*, 185.

20. Demerson, *María Francisca de Sales Portocarrero*, 183–96.

21. Demerson, *María Francisca de Sales Portocarrero*, 215–42; Demerson, "La Real Inclusa de Madrid"; Sherwood, "El niño expósito."

María Lorenza de los Ríos, Marquise of Fuerte-Híjar, 1761–1821

Reformism and Culture

CATHERINE M. JAFFE

A Woman on the Margins of Enlightenment History

Recently widowed and remarried, twenty-seven-year-old María Lorenza de los Ríos, Marquise of Fuerte-Híjar, joined the Junta de Damas in 1788 and soon became deeply involved in its charitable and administrative activities. (See fig. 9.) She wrote *memorias* (essays) and reports, oversaw the Patriotic Schools, ran the Inclusa, and attempted to reform and administer the Montepío de Hilazas. Twenty years later she unexpectedly found herself faced with the overwhelming challenge of leading the junta and the Real Asociación de Caridad de Señoras and the institutions they supported—the Inclusa, the Patriotic Schools, and the unmarried pregnant women's shelter, the Sala de Reservadas—throughout the difficult years of the Peninsular War. Adding to the desperate circumstances she faced during those unsettled years of foreign occupation, shifting authority, and vacuums of power in Madrid, María Lorenza became a widow for the second time at the age of forty-eight when her husband was arrested and imprisoned in France, where he died in 1810. Nothing of what is known about her upbringing or earlier life would have prepared her for the role she would eventually be called upon to play for the Junta de Damas. María Lorenza de los Ríos transformed from a traditional feminine role as the wife of a government jurist to a public role as one of the most active members of the junta. Her life is evidence not only that women from aristocratic families participated in the economic societies' projects of reform to improve society, but that some women discovered Enlightenment values through circles of sociability and intellectual exchange rather than through family privilege. María Lorenza's adoption of the Enlightenment goals of public utility can not only be discerned in her literary works and in the cultural sociability

FIG. 9. María Lorenza de los Ríos y Loyo, Marquise of Fuerte-Híjar, 1774. Private collection. Photography by Eugenio Martínez Jorrín.

she fostered in her Madrid tertulia, but most importantly in her pragmatic Enlightenment projects as a member of the Junta de Damas, including the reform of the Escuelas Patrióticas, the Inclusa, and the Montepío de Hilazas, and her support of the Real Sociedad Económica's construction of soup kitchens for the poor, inspired by the works of Benjamin Thompson, Count Rumford.

María Lorenza de los Ríos has remained virtually unknown to scholars of the Spanish Enlightenment until relatively recently.[1] Her literary works—two manuscript plays, *El Eugenio* and *La sabia indiscreta*, a published translation of a French article about the life and works of the American-born British physicist and inventor Count Rumford, and a brief, published poem—appeared in bibliographies of women writers, often with erroneous details about her life.[2] Studies of her husbands, Luis de los Ríos and Germano de Salcedo, did not connect her to both men. Nevertheless, her biography as a figure of the Spanish Enlightenment clearly divides into two periods demarcated by her marriages.

In contrast to many of her close companions in the Junta de Damas, such as the Countess-Duchess of Benavente or the Marquise of Villafranca, María

Lorenza de los Ríos was not exiled from Madrid during the war years, nor was she born into an important aristocratic family. Rather, she rose to social prominence through the strategic deployment of her inheritance to purchase a title for her ambitious second husband, the untitled scion of an aristocratic family who thereafter became a member of the highest governing body of the monarchy, the Consejo de Castilla. Like the Countess of Montijo, the Countess of Torrepalma, and the Marquise of Villafranca, María Lorenza remarried after becoming a widow, and like them she chose a second husband more for personal inclination than for a family strategy of kinship and wealth preservation.

María Lorenza de los Ríos came from the wealthy class of bourgeois merchant families centered in the southern port city of Cádiz in Andalucía. She represents a different type of enlightened Spanish woman than noblewomen like the Countess-Duchess of Benavente or the Countess of Montijo, who enjoyed an exceptionally privileged education, were accustomed to administering great estates, and had always moved in the rarified atmosphere of court society. María Lorenza did not share the intellectual background of the erudite Josefa Amar, the daughter of a physician from a highly educated family associated with court society, or that of her fellow *gaditanas* (Cádiz natives) María del Rosario Cepeda, a child prodigy who passed a public academic examination in 1768 when she was twelve years old, and María Isidra Quintina de Guzmán, from a powerful family, who at seventeen was awarded a doctorate at the University of Alcalá, named to the Royal Spanish Academy, and admitted to the Real Sociedad Económica Matritense following her public academic examination in 1784.[3] María Lorenza most likely received a typical education for well-to-do girls at the time. In this she was like other future companions in the Junta de Damas from the merchant, military, and professional classes of Cádiz, such as Ana Rodríguez de Carasa, María del Rosario Cepeda and her sister Francisca Cepeda, and Loreto Figueroa.[4]

María Lorenza appears to have discovered and cultivated her interest in reform, her philanthropic zeal, and cultural ambitions first through contact with the professional class of legal and government officials in the provincial Castilian capital of Valladolid, where she lived with her first husband, a judge in the *Real Chancillería* (Royal Chancery Court), and later in Madrid with her second husband. Like her close collaborators, María Lorenza's dedication to the work of the Junta de Damas was unwavering. When war broke out in Spain with Napoleon's invasion, she met the challenge thrust upon her by historical events and fought to defend the junta's institutions devoted to poor women and children in Madrid throughout the chaos and hardship of the war.

Marriage as a Family Strategy

María Lorenza de los Ríos y Loyo was born August 10, 1761, in Cádiz, one of the most important port cities in Europe at the time, a center for trade between the Americas and Europe. She was the daughter of Francisco Javier de los Ríos y Mantilla, a prosperous merchant from an impoverished family of *hidalgos* or petty nobility from the town of Naveda, near Reinosa, in the mountainous region of Cantabria in the north of Spain, and Feliciana Joaquina de Loyo y Treviño, whose father, Andrés de Loyo, had also come to Cádiz from the northern town of Redecilla del Camino (Burgos) in La Rioja. María Lorenza became an orphan at five years old and inherited a fortune of nearly three million *reales*, which grew to four million after she inherited from her grandparents. Andrés de Loyo was her guardian until his death in 1772, after which her great aunt, Marquise of Casa Tabares, and other members of her mother's family helped to care for the young heiress.[5]

When she was twelve years old, in 1774, María Lorenza was married by proxy to her thirty-eight-year-old paternal cousin, Luis de los Ríos y Velasco, at the time a prosecutor in the *Real Audiencia* (Royal Tribunal) of Santa Fe of Bogotá in the Viceroyalty of New Granada. He belonged to a family of hidalgos who lived in constrained circumstances in Naveda. Luis received a degree in canon law at the University of Valladolid, studied law in Valladolid and at the University of Salamanca, and finally earned his degree at the University of Alcalá. Although he aspired to a government position in Spain, the lack of important family contacts meant that eventually he had to accept a position in Santo Domingo in the Viceroyalty of New Spain, a post that at least would offer crucial financial support for his family back in Naveda. In 1770, on his way to America, Luis de los Ríos passed through Cádiz, borrowed money from Andrés de Loyo, and met Loyo's granddaughter, María Lorenza, then nine years old.

Between 1771 and 1774, Luis worked in Santo Domingo and Caracas, and in 1774 took up his position in Santa Fe de Bogotá in the Viceroyalty of New Granada. During all this time, he was busy negotiating by letter his marriage to his cousin María Lorenza, with an eye to keeping her fortune in the family, well aware of the financial advantage the match would bring to his family.[6] By 1774, when María Lorenza was twelve years old, the cousins were married by proxy. She spent two years waiting for her husband in the Augustinian Convent of Nuestra Señora de la Candelaria in Cádiz, and in 1776 Luis de los Ríos returned to Cádiz with a leave of absence to finalize the marriage. María Lorenza was fourteen years old and had only briefly met her new husband five years earlier when he passed through Cádiz.[7]

Her marriage to Luis de los Ríos was resented by her mother's family, and her inheritance from her maternal grandfather was only settled years later, after her second marriage.[8] Arranged marriages at such an early age were not unusual among wealthy bourgeois and aristocratic families of her time, but upon writing her will in 1812, María Lorenza reflected on her youth and lack of agency during the negotiations for her first marriage: "I add, for greater clarity, that my aforesaid deceased husband [Luis de los Ríos] left me nothing; for he had only his position as judge in Valladolid, and when they married me to him, I was twelve years and three months old and had inherited several million [*reales*] from my parents and grandparents" (yo añado para mayor claridad que dicho mi difunto marido, nada pudo dejarme, pues solo tenía su empleo de oidor de Valladolid y yo era a la edad de doce años y tres meses en que me casaron con él, una muchacha de algunos millones y heredera ya de padres y abuelos).[9] Now in her fifties and widowed for a second time, María Lorenza seems to reflect critically upon the match negotiated for her by her family. We have no evidence, however, that the marriage itself was an unhappy one.

After arriving in Cádiz and finalizing his marriage, Luis de los Ríos immediately requested further leaves of absence from his post in Santa Fe de Bogotá and began to lobby politically to secure an appointment in Spain. These efforts meant frequent, protracted trips to Madrid over the next several years, beginning barely one month after their wedding. His young wife was left behind in Andalucía. María Lorenza endured two miscarriages during this time, and thereafter frequently suffered poor health. Despite Luis's often expressed hopes for an heir, María Lorenza never bore any children, perhaps a consequence of complications from these early miscarriages.[10] In 1779, Luis accepted an appointment as judge in the Real Audiencia of Galicia, in the northwestern port city of La Coruña; at least he would not have to return to his post overseas. The couple traveled north, stopping in Madrid and then passing through Naveda so that María Lorenza could meet her in-laws for the first time. After a difficult journey due to bad weather and terrible roads, they arrived in November 1779 in La Coruña, around the same time that John Adams, the future president of the new United States, visited there after landing in El Ferrol.[11] María Lorenza and Luis never adapted to the chilly, damp climate of Galicia. After spending about two years in La Coruña, Luis was finally appointed judge in the Real Chancillería of Valladolid, a busy, provincial capital in Castile, a destination much more to their liking.

From the beginning of his marriage, Luis de los Ríos sought to take control of the remainder of his wife's inheritance from her mother's family, although with limited success. He did employ her fortune to shore up his family's finances and stature in Cantabria. Luis began to renovate his family's home in Naveda, drawing up elaborate plans and following news of the construction eagerly from afar.[12] He invested more of María Lorenza's money by purchasing land around Reinosa and buying flocks of sheep. He also supported his unmarried sisters and paid for his nephews' education.

Perhaps his most grandiose scheme was to build a *palacio* or mansion in town in Reinosa along the lines of those of titled families there. Work on this grand house dragged on and was never finished during his lifetime. However, a legend grew up in Reinosa around the house, today called the *Casona* (great house) or the *Casa de la Niña de Oro* (House of the Golden Girl). It was said that, when the daughter of the man who built it became gravely ill, her father promised her weight in gold to the local church if she recovered. Thus the identity of Luis de los Ríos's young bride—who could easily have been his daughter—was elided, and she became his daughter in the legend. This is perhaps why the only portrait of María Lorenza known to exist, one half of a matching set of portraits of the couple made upon their marriage in 1774, was thought to be of Luis de los Ríos's daughter. In the portrait, held in a private collection today, the young girl is represented in a stiff, elaborately embroidered gown, like a small jewel to be traded as part of her family's strategy of alliances.[13] (See fig. 9.)

Airs of the Enlightenment in Valladolid

When María Lorenza and Luis de los Ríos arrived in 1782, Valladolid boasted a theater, several newspapers, an important university, and various Enlightenment associations, such as the Royal Academies of Geography and History, Mathematics and Noble Arts, Surgery, National Theoretical-Practical Jurisprudence, and so forth, as well as a Sociedad Económica de Amigos del País.[14] María Lorenza was now twenty years old and had been married for eight years. Although we have no personal records of hers from this time, we can surmise that she would have enjoyed the busy city immensely and that these were years of her coming of age, when she became aware of the reformist, modernizing energies generated by the academies, the tertulias, and the general currents of the Enlightenment driving the intellectual and political life of Spanish society.

The young María Lorenza had probably had the opportunity to read many books and the different newspapers to which her scholarly, jurist husband subscribed. In Valladolid she met men and women interested in reforming Spain's economy, arts, and institutions. However, Luis never joined any economic society or academy, and his letters to his family reflect a very traditional piety and religious observance. Four years after moving to Valladolid, in 1786, when María Lorenza had just turned twenty-five, Luis died suddenly of a brief illness. In less than four months, the young widow had remarried, much to the dismay of the de los Ríos family, for they sensed that their advantageous financial relationship with her would come to an end. María Lorenza married Luis's former colleague in the Real Chancillería of Valladolid, thirty-eight-year-old Germano de Salcedo y Somodevilla, from Santo Domingo de la Calzada in La Rioja, a nephew of the Marquis of Ensenada, who had been a minister of King Fernando VI.

Germano came to Valladolid after serving as judge in Mallorca. He was an ambitious, active man and a member of many different Enlightenment institutions. He helped to found the Sociedad Económica of that city, and later served as its director and promoted its reformist activities. He also belonged to Sociedades de Amigos del País in other parts of the country, such as Mallorca, La Rioja, Cantabria, the Basque Country, Valencia, and he joined the Real Sociedad Económica Matritense in 1793.[15] Certainly his activities encouraged his wife's interest in reform and modernization in Spain. After his marriage to María Lorenza, Germano was able to resolve the problems regarding the remainder of her inheritance. María Lorenza gradually ended her financial support of her ex-husband's family and the costly construction of the great house in Reinosa. In her will of 1788, María Lorenza left her entire estate to Germano, with no mention at all of the family of Luis de los Ríos.[16] Germano de Salcedo, the press reported, renounced all claims to his wife's fortune. María Lorenza would now be able to use her inheritance to petition for a title of nobility of Castile for Germano, a necessary step to promote his social and professional career.

Given his meritorious service to the state and his aristocratic family background, in 1788 Germano was granted the title of Marquis of Fuerte-Híjar, a name taken from a dam on one of María Lorenza's properties by the River Híjar. Although once again María Lorenza's inheritance was used to promote her husband's ambitions, this time it seems to have been a collaborative strategy between the spouses. Soon after receiving the title, the couple moved to Madrid. A year later, Germano was admitted to the elite Order of Carlos III (Real y Muy Distinguida Orden de Carlos III).[17] Finally, he was appointed to the Consejo de Castilla, where he held different appointments until 1808.

Society and Enlightened Charity in Madrid

Once in Madrid, Germano's involvement in Spain's economic societies and in reformist projects undoubtedly reflects the alacrity with which María Lorenza joined the Junta de Damas in August 1788, less than a year after its founding, joining a group of thirty-three members that had expanded from the original sixteen founders. She replied to the approval of her admission and acknowledged that she had received a copy of the statutes of the Junta de Damas: "I am informed of everything, and I am extremely obliged to the Real Sociedad, which with no merit on my part, has seen fit to bestow upon me such a significant honor" (Quedo enterada de todo y sumamente reconocida a la Real Sociedad que sin mérito alguno mío se ha servido dispensarme un honor tan apreciable).[18] María Lorenza may also have been motivated to join the Junta de Damas by the participation of friends such as María del Rosario Cepeda from Cádiz, or Rafaela de San Cristóbal and María Josefa de Cañas y Portocarrero, Viscountess of Valoria, from Valladolid, where María Lorenza later supported the establishment of a Junta de Damas.[19]

The couple participated in the vibrant sociability of the late Spanish Enlightenment, and they owned country estates south of the capital in Seseña y Ciempozuelos, near the Jarama River. They hosted a tertulia attended by writers such as Germano's friend, the poet Nicasio Álvarez de Cienfuegos, the actor Isidoro Máiquez, the singer Manuel García, poet Manuel José Quintana, and painter Francisco de Goya, among others. Most likely, María Lorenza's two plays were presented privately in her tertulia, as was Cienfuegos's play

Zorayda. Cienfuegos wrote two poems for his friends: "La escuela del sepulcro" (The School of the Tomb), in which he describes María Lorenza's grief upon the death of her friend from Valladolid, María de Quero y Valenzuela, Marquise of la Merced, and "Al señor marqués de Fuerte-Híjar, en los días de su esposa" (To Señor Marquis of Fuerte-Híjar, on his Wife's Birthday), in which he exalts their friendship. Cienfuegos dedicated his play *La Condesa de Castilla*, "in terms of passionate friendship," to his dear friend, the Marquise of Fuerte-Híjar.[20] "La escuela del sepulcro" was published in 1816, years after it was written and after both Cienfuegos and Germano had perished in detention in France. This may have inspired María Lorenza's only known poem, also published in 1816, *A la muerte del Excelentísimo Señor Don Francisco Álvarez de Palafox*, an ode upon the death of the son of the Marquise of Villafranca.[21]

Fuerte-Híjar's two known plays, *El Eugenio* and *La sabia indiscreta*, feature intelligent women protagonists facing the dilemma of ascertaining whether a relationship of equality and true friendship rather than subordination is possible in matrimony. Their conclusions are mixed: in *La sabia indiscreta*, an educated woman learns that an intellectual relationship with a man may confusingly lead to love, while in *El Eugenio* (loosely based on Beaumarchais's *L'Eugénie*) a strong female character rejects marriage with a man she does not respect, calling matrimony a "yoke" and "chains," and a virtual "slavery" for women.[22]

María Lorenza and her husband stayed up-to-date with all the latest publications that were inspired by Enlightenment interest in reform and facilitated by the translation and circulation of texts throughout Europe.[23] The marquise subscribed to translations of classical literature, such as *La Ilíada* and *Décadas de Tito Livio*, and of popular novels, such as Samuel Richardson's *Clara Harlowe* (*Clarissa*, 1748). María Lorenza also subscribed to Enlightenment periodicals such as the *Semanario erudito y curioso de Salamanca*, and to a 1792 book on education, the Chevalier de Brucourt's *Ensayo sobre la educación de la nobleza* (*Essai sur l'éducation de la noblesse*, 1747). In 1795, as part of a commission formed in the Junta de Damas to study issues regarding women's education, María Lorenza delivered two essays, now lost, the first on "how important women's education is to the success of politics and the State" (cuanto importa a política y al buen suceso del Estado la educación de las mujeres) and the second on "the most convenient rules [for women] to rid themselves of the ill effects of luxury and fashion, while remaining decent and not becoming the object of ridiculous criticism" (reglas más convenientes para librarse de los perjuicios del lujo y de la moda, sin faltar a la decencia, ni hacerse objeto de censuras ridículas).[24]

The Enlightenment projects of María Lorenza and Germano were often intertwined.[25] Just as Germano authored a "Eulogy for the King" in 1794, María Lorenza wrote a "Eulogy for the Queen," María Luisa de Parma, the royal patron of the Junta de Damas, which was presented in 1798 at a public awards ceremony attended by both the male Sociedad Económica and the Junta de Damas. She praises the queen as a model spouse and mother dedicated to her family and the nation, and she lauds the charitable kindness and generosity of the sovereign: "The picture of public miseries, [. . .] wounds her heart, and she resolves openly to sacrifice her own comforts, [. . .] dedicating half of her private purse and all the jewelry that she can decorously dispose of, to succor the nation" (El cuadro de las miserias públicas, [. . .] hiere su corazón, y resuelve abiertamente el sacrificio de sus mismas comodidades, [. . .] cediendo la mitad de su bolsillo secreto y todas las alhajas de que puede desprenderse con decoro, para ocurrir a las urgencias de la nación).[26] A total of seven of these formulaic works were presented and published yearly between 1794 and 1801. They mirrored similar eulogies for the king produced by the Sociedad Económica, with the purpose of publicly acknowledging (and encouraging) the patronage of the royal family.

As president of the Sociedad Matritense, Germano led an effort to construct fuel-efficient kitchens based on the plans of American inventor Benjamin Thompson, Count Rumford, to feed the poor who came flooding into Madrid between 1802 and 1804 due to economic hardship and famine. María Lorenza demonstrated her knowledge of French and her skill as a writer by publishing in 1802 a translation of an article from a French periodical about Count Rumford, his experiments in thermodynamics, and his modern theories of charity and rational poor relief.[27] María Lorenza's translation, published along with a fine engraving of Rumford, demonstrates her fluency with technical terms and reveals the Sociedad Económica's strategy to situate Spanish Enlightenment projects within the wider field of enlightened reform in Europe.[28] They proposed to care for the needy in a modern, progressive way, quite distinct from traditional alms-giving associated with religious observance, through economy and efficiency, and encouraging self-sufficiency for the worthy poor.[29]

María Lorenza de los Ríos was one of the most stalwart members of the

Junta de Damas for over twenty-five years, holding a variety of leadership positions. In 1796 and in 1802 she was censor, in charge of making sure the junta followed its statutes, and in 1804 and 1805 she was vice-censor. In 1797, 1803, and 1806, she was vice president, and in 1808 she was curadora of the Inclusa. She also served as supervisor of the Patriotic Schools and the Montepío de Hilazas. Finally, María Lorenza became president between 1811 and 1814, during the Peninsular War.[30]

María Lorenza authored many reports of the junta's activities. During her first year in the junta, in 1789, together with María Josefa de Veitia she evaluated a proposal to establish an asylum for maids.[31] They express admiration for the proposal's motivation—compassion for the often destitute young girls who arrive in Madrid from the provinces looking for work and are seduced into immoral practices—but they quite logically point out the many practical impediments and uncertainties attached to the project. They estimate the cost of running such an asylum and conclude that there is no sure way of financing it. This report is a good example of the teamwork and the pragmatic and scientific attitude the women of the Junta de Damas brought to their charitable work. With the Countess of Superunda, the Marquise of Espeja, and Ana Rodríguez de Carasa, Fuerte-Híjar wrote several reports on the Montepío de Hilazas in 1790 and 1791, and one on her own in 1792 answering the Sociedad Económica's criticism of the junta's administration of the Montepío.[32] In 1805, María Lorenza wrote another report with María del Rosario Cepeda explaining the "painful state" of the Montepío due to changing technology, market demands, and lack of funding. With the Marquise of Canillejas, Fuerte-Híjar wrote a report in 1795 about their testing of a new machine for spinning silk.[33] In 1806, María Lorenza directed a letter to the king stoutly defending the work of the Real Asociación de Caridad de Señoras and expounding upon the urgent need for funds to assist women prisoners.[34]

The Disasters of War

With the invasion of Spain by Napoleon's troops and the abdication of King Carlos IV, María Lorenza and Germano's optimistic world of enlightened reform and sociability crumbled. Germano was arrested in 1809 along with his friend Cienfuegos for refusing to swear an oath of allegiance to José Bonaparte. They were imprisoned in Orthes, France, where they both perished. María Lorenza was briefly held in a convent in Madrid, but later released. All this she recounts in her testament of 1812, where she states that she was completely ruined and her dowry lost following the French invasion. Most of her papers and personal effects were misplaced or stolen after their home was seized to house French soldiers. María Lorenza states that, although Germano left her as his heir in the will he signed before his death in Orthes, he had nothing left except his salary, and so the will only shows her "more and more the love and friendship that he had for me" (más y más el amor que me profesaba).[35]

María Lorenza's reports and letters written for the Junta de Damas and the Real Asociación de Caridad de Señoras during this time reflect desperation, destitution, and urgency. While personally trying to remain aloof from political entanglements with the French-imposed government, she employed all her persuasive, rhetorical skills in letters to Pablo Arribas, police minister, in 1810, and to the Marquis of Almenara, minister of the interior, in 1811, pleading for resources and housing for the Inclusa and the Sala de Reservadas, where unwed mothers could give birth in secret. "Come," she writes to Almenara, "give me some house quickly and even more . . . for I have fifteen letters from pregnant women who, if their parents found out, would slit their throats, without admitting that they might once have been in the same position" (Vamos, deme V. M. la casa y breve y algo más . . . pues 15 memoriales tengo de otras tantas preñadas que, si lo saben sus padres las degüellan, sin acordarse de que ellos, en sus tiempos, hicieron otro tanto).[36] In 1813, Fuerte-Híjar directs an urgent and passionate letter to Joaquín García Domenech, political chief of Madrid, laying out the Inclusa's desperate state and begging for help. All the wet nurses have left, she reports, and only five are left to care for fifty-two infants who cry unceasingly. If they knew what kind of death awaits them, she warns, they would give up trying to live.[37]

María Lorenza's last known writing as director of Real Asociación de Caridad de Señoras was jointly authored with the Countess of Castroterreño, its vice secretary. The report was addressed to King Fernando VII in 1815, and they recount at length the history of the Asociación. They urge the reestablishment of the Sala de Reservadas, "to avoid infanticides and disturbances between parents, children and families" (ya para evitar los infanticidios que se cometen y ya para evitar los disturbios que hay entre padres, hijos y familias). They assert that they are much more suited to run the sala than the men who run the "house of mortal sin" (una casa llamada *del pecado mortal*): "men whose talents and virtues may be very respectable, but, really, they are not the most appropriate for matters of this nature, because of the indecency and shame caused by someone of a different sex helping a woman give birth" (por hombres cuyos talentos y virtudes serán muy respetables, pero que, a la verdad, no son los más a propósito para asuntos de esta naturaleza, por la especie de indecencia y de vergüenza que ocasiona la asistencia de una mujer preñada y parida entre personas de diferente sexo).[38] Fuerte-Híjar's official letters and reports written for the Junta de Damas, like those of her fellow socias, are concrete evidence of their strategy to assert their role in the public sphere and to demonstrate their social utility by invoking their own feminine expertise and observations based on their pragmatism and organizational talents. They drew on any personal and political connections they could to defend and promote the junta's Enlightenment charitable projects to improve the lives of poor women and children.

The Final Years

As the war came to an end and her companions in the Junta de Damas returned from exile, María Lorenza, financially and emotionally exhausted by her protracted efforts, turned to setting her personal affairs in order. In addition to her activities with the Junta de Damas and the Asociación de Caridad de Señoras, in 1812 she had joined the recently created Asociación Patriótica de Señoras de Madrid, when the city was finally free of enemies, for the purpose of soliciting donations to produce military uniforms to outfit the Spanish troops. It is unclear exactly why she disappears from the activities of the junta after 1816. Possibly, since her presidency during the war was approved by José Bonaparte, her loyalty was questioned. María Lorenza was prosecuted by the reinstated Bourbon government because she had purchased a property confiscated by the French during the war. A heavy fine was imposed on her, which she had difficulty paying due to her poverty. She also had most likely made investments before the war that drained her of all her capital.[39]

María Lorenza made several trips to Valladolid during her final years, perhaps to attend to legal matters having to do with property there. In her final will, of 1816, she stipulates that she prefers a simple funeral, refusing even a headstone to mark her grave: "I wish to be mixed with my fellow Christians and neighbors, with whom I will dwell" (es mi voluntad confundirme con los hermanos y vecinos con quienes voy a habitar).[40] Her estate has dwindled, she claims, to a few small sheds to store wool in Reinosa, two orchards, several fields, and her farms at Quinta-Jarama and Ciempozuelos. She leaves her title and whatever is left of her estate after paying her debts to the girl she calls her niece, Anselma Josefa Roca, when she comes of age. If Anselma dies without descendants, her remaining estate should go to the Inclusa. In a previous will of 1812, María Lorenza had related how this girl, born in 1797, had been entrusted to her and Germano by her mother—a close friend of the marquis and the marquise—on her deathbed. The child's father died before they could marry, and so María Lorenza hastily had the baby baptized and admitted to the Inclusa, "a victim of prejudice and the barbarity of her grandfather" (víctima de la opinión y de la barbarie de un abuelo). The Marquise of Fuerte-Híjar paid for the child's wet nurse and her expenses until, after the death of the feared grandfather, María Lorenza was able to bring her home and adopt her. Germano had also charged María Lorenza with Anselma's care in his testament of 1810, evidence of the childless couple's loving relationship with this unfortunate girl. In the Inclusa's records, the child's name is covered over with a note that forbids giving information about the child to anyone without the express permission of the ladies of the junta. María Lorenza refers to this story in a veiled way in her play *El Eugenio*.[41]

María Lorenza de los Ríos died August 15, 1821, in Madrid, having just turned sixty years old. Although she was never able to bear her own children, her decades of working closely with the women and children of the Inclusa and in the Sala de Reservadas allowed her to empathize with the trials that women of all classes suffered during motherhood and the precarious existence of poor women and their children. The orphaned heiress from Cádiz rose from relative anonymity to become a leader of late Enlightenment women's civic activism in Madrid. Her cultural achievements, especially her two plays, almost lost to literary history, provide an intriguing glimpse into the preoccupations and ideals of enlightened women of her class around the turn of the century: skepticism regarding marriage's benefits for women, frustration at the limitations for educated women in society, and the value of friendship. María Lorenza's contributions as a writer and a dedicated, pragmatic reformer may have been obscured by Spain's tumultuous history, shifting political ideologies, and the blind eye historians turned to women's accomplishments, but today we recognize that she helped to lay the foundation for later women's advances in the public sphere.

NOTES

1. Martín-Valdepeñas Yagüe and Jaffe, *María Lorenza de los Ríos*, 14; Jaffe and Martín-Valdepeñas Yagüe, "Sociabilidad, filantropía"; see also Acereda Extremiana, *La marquesa de Fuerte-Híjar*; Díaz Saiz, "Las estrategias" and "D. Luis de los Ríos."

2. For an edition and study of these works and other writings by Fuerte-Híjar, see Martín-Valdepeñas Yagüe and Jaffe, *María Lorenza de los Ríos*.

3. Álvarez de Miranda, "¿Una niña en la academia?"; Bolufer Peruga, "Galerías de 'mujeres ilustres.'"

4. Martín-Valdepeñas Yagüe and Jaffe, *María Lorenza de los Ríos*, 38.

5. Martín-Valdepeñas Yagüe and Jaffe, *María Lorenza de los Ríos*, 26–39.

6. Over three hundred letters of the De los Ríos clan are held at the Archivo Histórico Provincial in Santander, Cantabria.

7. Martín-Valdepeñas Yagüe and Jaffe, *María Lorenza de los Ríos*, 38–46.

8. Martín-Valdepeñas Yagüe and Jaffe, *María Lorenza de los Ríos*, 41–46.

9. Martín-Valdepeñas Yagüe and Jaffe, *María Lorenza de los Ríos*, 406.

10. Martín-Valdepeñas Yagüe and Jaffe, *María Lorenza de los Ríos*, 48–49, 58–61.

11. Martín-Valdepeñas Yagüe and Jaffe, *María Lorenza de los Ríos*, 46–54.

12. Díaz Saiz, "D. Luis de los Ríos."

13. Martín-Valdepeñas Yagüe and Jaffe, *María Lorenza de los Ríos*, 62–67, 179–92.

14. Martín-Valdepeñas Yagüe and Jaffe, *María Lorenza de los Ríos*, 67–69; Bolufer Peruga, "Traducción, cultura y política," 302–6.

15. Martín-Valdepeñas Yagüe and Jaffe, *María Lorenza de los Ríos*, 77–83.

16. Martín-Valdepeñas Yagüe and Jaffe, *María Lorenza de los Ríos*, 85–86.

17. Martín-Valdepeñas Yagüe and Jaffe, *María Lorenza de los Ríos*, 88–89.

18. Martín-Valdepeñas Yagüe and Jaffe, *María Lorenza de los Ríos*, 366.

19. Martín-Valdepeñas Yagüe and Jaffe, *María Lorenza de los Ríos*, 111–12.

20. Martín-Valdepeñas Yagüe and Jaffe, *María Lorenza de los Ríos*, 96–99; see also Álvarez de Miranda, "Las inquietudes lingüísticas de Cienfuegos"; Sebold, "Hórrido yermo"; Froldi, "Lirismo, sensibilidad."

21. Martín-Valdepeñas Yagüe and Jaffe, *María Lorenza de los Ríos*, 227–33, 341–44.

22. Martín-Valdepeñas Yagüe and Jaffe, *María Lorenza de los Ríos*, 223–59, 302.

23. On translation in Spain during the Enlightenment, see García Garrosa, "Translation in Enlightenment Spain."

24. Martín-Valdepeñas Yagüe and Jaffe, *María Lorenza de los Ríos*, 100, 113–14. The reports are summarized by the Countess of Montijo in the minutes of the junta's meetings, and the censor also summarized the reports. Martín Valdepeñas Yagüe and Jaffe, *María Lorenza de los Ríos*, 389–93, 394–96.

25. There were a number of married couples in the Sociedad Económica and the Junta de Damas; 80 percent of the women members held aristocratic titles, as opposed to 10 percent of the male members, Martín-Valdepeñas Yagüe, "Relaciones de parentesco," 20–21, 25–26, 34.

26. Martín-Valdepeñas Yagüe and Jaffe, *María Lorenza de los Ríos*, 348, 116–17.

27. "Noticia de la vida y obras del conde de Rumford, traducida del francés, y presentada a la Sociedad Patriótica de Madrid por la marquesa de Fuerte-Híjar," in Martín-Valdepeñas Yagüe and Jaffe, *María Lorenza de los Ríos*, 351–60; see Jaffe, "'Noticia de la vida y obras del Conde de Rumford'"; Demerson, "La distribución de sopas económicas"; Martín-Valdepeñas Yagüe and Jaffe, *María Lorenza de los Ríos*, 223–24.

28. Elena Serrano has studied the scientific contributions of the Junta de Damas as a learned society in "Chemistry in the City."

29. On Enlightenment ideas about charity in Spain, see Serrano Jerez, "Chemistry in the City," 144–45; Lewis, "Actos de Caridad," and "Practicing Social Activism: The Spaces of Women's Charity" in this volume; Jaffe, "'Noticia de la vida y obras del Conde de Rumford.'"

30. Martín-Valdepeñas Yagüe and Jaffe, *María Lorenza de los Ríos*, 112–13.

31. "Informe sobre el establecimiento de un asilo de criadas," Martín-Valdepeñas Yagüe and Jaffe, *María Lorenza de los Ríos*, 366–74.

32. Martín-Valdepeñas Yagüe and Jaffe, *María Lorenza de los Ríos*, 374–82.

33. Martín-Valdepeñas Yagüe and Jaffe, *María Lorenza de los Ríos*, 384–85.

34. Martín-Valdepeñas Yagüe and Jaffe, *María Lorenza de los Ríos*, 399–400.

35. Martín-Valdepeñas Yagüe and Jaffe, *María Lorenza de los Ríos*, 404–13.

36. Martín-Valdepeñas Yagüe and Jaffe, *María Lorenza de los Ríos*, 404, 401–4.

37. Martín-Valdepeñas Yagüe and Jaffe, *María Lorenza de los Ríos*, 413–16.

38. Martín-Valdepeñas Yagüe and Jaffe, *María Lorenza de los Ríos*, 417–23.

39. Martín-Valdepeñas Yagüe and Jaffe, *María Lorenza de los Ríos*, 170–72.

40. Martín-Valdepeñas Yagüe and Jaffe, *María Lorenza de los Ríos*, 177.

41. Martín-Valdepeñas Yagüe and Jaffe, *María Lorenza de los Ríos*, 103–7, 255–59, 410–11, 429.

María Tomasa Palafox, Marquise of Villafranca, 1780–1835

A Life in Times of Crisis

GLORIA ESPIGADO TOCINO

María Tomasa Palafox y Portocarrero's life can be pictured as a hinge spanning the complicated transition from the eighteenth to the nineteenth century in Spain and in Europe as a whole. The well-known and crucial changes that occurred at the turn of the century transformed a feudal society into a liberal one. This was a turbulent process, and during her lifetime it brought revolutions, wars, and coups d'état in Spain that put her in mortal danger, along with the rest of Spain's population. However, she and her family were not simply mute witnesses to these events but took a leading role in them, thanks to their aristocratic rank and connections. Her childhood was shaped by the influence of her mother, the Countess of Montijo, a leading figure in Spanish Enlightenment culture; her youth, by marriage into the highest echelon of the aristocracy, the Álvarez de Toledo family, which made her Duchess of Medina Sidonia. In her mature years—after she was widowed and remarried—she reverted to her maiden name and traveled around Spain and Italy, where she eventually died. (See fig. 10.)

In her life span of a little over half a century, besides amply fulfilling her reproductive duty to bear offspring to carry on the family name, and managing the affairs of her aristocratic household, she was extensively involved in public life as a member and eventually president of the Junta de Damas de Honor y Mérito of the Real Sociedad Económica Matritense de Amigos del País.[1] Prior to that, the vicissitudes of the Peninsular War resulted in her becoming president of the Sociedad de Señoras de Fernando VII (Society of Ladies for Fernando VII), founded in Cádiz while the city was being besieged by Napoleon's troops in 1811.[2] Her life was thus devoted both to the service of her own family's affairs and to wider issues, to private and public matters; it is impossi-

FIG. 10. The Marquise of Villafranca (Agustín Esteve), ca. 1800. Hispanic Society of America.

ble to differentiate between the spheres of interest, involvement, and agency in which she acted and was constructed as an individual. Individual and collective issues were intimately interwoven, following chains of meaning that help us to understand a crucial period in Spain's history. This path through a reading of gender reconstructs the contribution of a femininity committed to its historical moment, contemplated in discourse and in representations generated since the period of the Enlightenment, and reacted to by our protagonist during times of change. Hers was an act of feminine appropriation that took the form of social maternity poured into philanthropy and reserving for itself a space for public, patriotic service, making the best of the new political discourse leading to liberalism.

Raised under Her Mother's Wing

Tomasa Palafox was born in Madrid on March 8, 1780, nine years before the French Revolution shook the foundations on which the aristocracy rested. She was the daughter of Felipe Palafox y Croy de Habré (1739–1790), who died when she was just ten years old, and María Francisca de Sales Portocarrero, the Countess of Montijo (1754–1808). Her childhood, like that of her five siblings, matched her social condition and, above all, the intellectual and philanthropic concerns of one of the most notable figures of the Spanish Enlightenment, her own mother.[3]

The salon her mother hosted brought the crème de la crème of Madrid cultural and political life to their home. Tomasita, as she was known in the family, must have shared the drawing room with famous writers who visited the countess, such as Jovellanos, Cabarrús, Meléndez Valdés, and Vargas Ponce; well-known artists such as Bayeu, Vicente López, Agustín Esteve, and Goya; and leading politicians such as Mariano Luis de Urquijo or Manuel Godoy.[4] She became friends with some of them, later appointing José Vargas Ponce, for example, to catalog her library, and seeking advice in her most worrisome political moments from Jovellanos. It is possible that, like her mother, she was educated at the Visitación convent in Madrid, at a school known as Las Salesas. Young women of her class received an excellent education there, but it is clear that her most powerful formative influence came from within the home.[5]

According to the *Journal* of Lady Holland, who traveled to Spain with her husband at the beginning of the century, Tomasa was "[v]ery like her mother in figure and person. Extremely clever, but not quite so cheerful."[6] This comment can only be seen as an immense compliment to a daughter who followed in her mother's footsteps in her intense philanthropic work and who showed great admiration for her, going so far as to collect all of the written texts—reports, letters, *memorias*, and so forth—her mother produced while leading the Junta de Damas in Madrid.[7] The likeness between mother and daughter can also be seen in a family portrait attributed by most critics to Esteve that immortalizes the countess surrounded by her daughters, with the older girls standing, flanked by the little ones, who are seated. (See fig. 7.) Tomasa, the closest to her mother, is leaning over the embroidery her mother is doing, an example of her work as secretary of the Junta de Damas, a position she occupied for eighteen years. This image foreshadows where fate would lead her daughter.

The main rite of passage into adulthood for a young woman in her position was marriage.[8] On January 29, 1798, shortly before turning eighteen, she married Francisco de Borja Álvarez de Toledo (1763–1821), the Duke of Medina Sidonia and Marquis of Villafranca, and this last title would be her calling card in society. She was the next to last of her siblings to wed, since her mother had seen to it that her sisters had already married into important noble families. Hers was another advantageous match that not only preserved her position and fortune but increased them considerably. Her future husband was a second son who had gone into the military and reached the rank of colonel by 1795. When his firstborn brother, who had married the Duchess of Alba, died without children in 1796, Francisco inherited one of the greatest estates in the country, with possessions throughout Spain and Italy, which he shared with young Tomasa when she became his wife. The new duchess complied with social expectations by promptly becoming pregnant and producing an heir, whom they named Francisco, in 1799. Tomasa bore many sons and daughters. She gave birth at least ten times in total. However, only five of the infants reached adulthood: Teresa, Pedro, Tomasa, and the twins José and Ignacio.[9]

At almost the same time she became a mother, she joined the Junta de Damas on January 20, 1799.[10] From then on, she engaged in philanthropy as a socially conscious form of motherhood, as her peers had been doing since the organization was founded in 1787. Tomasa's life was divided relatively peacefully between managing her household and family and her duties at the Junta de Damas, as her mother's had been. On the personal side, she had developed an interest in painting that was rewarded by the prestige of being named an honorary member of the Real Academia de Bellas Artes de San Fernando in 1805.[11] A year earlier, Goya had immortalized her in a portrait now on display at the Museo Nacional del Prado in Madrid, showing her as a young wife in a fashionable Empire-style dress, holding a brush and a maulstick as she works on a portrait of her husband, whose image faces her in the painting.[12] This was a novel, original way of representing a wealthy couple with shared cultural interests.

But their happiness was not destined to last. There were worrying signs that uprisings and war were in the offing. The international political outlook had been tense ever since Napoleon proclaimed himself emperor of the French. The Spanish monarchy, under King Carlos IV, was undergoing turbulent times, with allies who were also powerful enemies. The War of the Pyrenees (War of the Convention, 1793–95) was over, as was the conflict with Portugal masterminded by Godoy, the king's ambitious favorite, and thousands of Spanish and French sailors had perished in the naval defeat at the Battle of Trafalgar (1805). Both Spain's monarchy and its empire, which stretched across the Atlantic, were seriously endangered.

The War Years and the Patriotic Cause

Tomasa's family, which was close to Prince Fernando's circle, engaged in the dangerous game of trying to lobby against the royal favorite, Godoy, and thus against the legitimate monarch. Her older brother, the Count of Teba, had already been banished from Court for seven years. Godoy took out his anger on the matriarch of the Palafox clan. The Countess of Montijo was sent into exile, which lasted until her death in Logroño in 1808. The firstborn and heir, the Count of Teba, was involved in a failed conspiracy against the monarchy, which led to his being tried after the conspiracy of El Escorial; he subsequently conspired against the monarchy again, this time successfully. The neighboring town of Aranjuez rose up against King Carlos IV and proclaimed Fernando king, leading to the removal of the despised Godoy and the abdication of Carlos IV. Tomasa and her husband supported the conspirators and had been banished after the first unsuccessful uprising; they now cast in their lot with the new monarch. This all occurred at a precarious point when the Spanish monarchy was being manipulated from abroad. Napoleon, the French emperor, had already decided that the Iberian Peninsula was essential to his interests in Europe and sent troops to occupy both Spain and Portugal, proclaiming his brother Joseph Bonaparte king of Spain. He was not expecting the patriotic resistance in Spain to the invasion, which led to a long war. Those in prominent positions were forced to come out in favor of one side or the other, putting their families and estates in jeopardy.

For Tomasa and her husband, there was a moment of hesitancy. The popular uprising on May 2, 1808, in Madrid, immortalized by Goya, was an unexpected and suicidal event. In fact, the marquis had joined the local authorities in begging for a cease-fire against the occupying French troops commanded by Murat.[13] When Joseph I arrived in the capital, the family was forced to make a decision. The victory over the French troops at Bailén on July 19 opened up the route to Andalusia, and the family left Madrid on July 24, 1808. Their arrival in Seville was celebrated with a solemn confirmation ceremony for their children.[14] However, they were dismayed by the chilly reception they received there, and ended up taking refuge on their lands in Murcia. Their decision led to major financial losses, since their estates and property in the French-occupied zone were seized and confiscated. They had been keeping a low profile, to no avail. Tomasa took the initiative and wrote to an old family friend, Jovellanos, a leading figure on the Junta Central (Patriotic Council) coordinating the resistance to the French that was scattered throughout the regions: "I would like you to advise me what we should do, since it is no longer enough to mind one's own business, the public and the entire nation must be satisfied" (yo deseo que V. me aconseje qué debamos hacer, pues ahora no basta cumplir uno consigo mismo, es necesario que el público y toda la nación quede satisfecha).[15]

Her communication was doubtless intended to erase any suspicion that her husband might have colluded with the French by demonstrating conclusive proof of their support for the patriotic cause. And indeed, Jovellanos replied that they should declare their stance unequivocally and get involved with the army, which sorely needed leadership for the resistance. Tomasa herself took over the patriotic job of fundraising for the troops from the capital city of Murcia, contributing a major donation.[16] The amounts received were published next to donors' names in the press in Murcia, which publicized her noble initiative. This act portrayed her in the patriotic act of leading a campaign to save the nation and signaled a possible way for women to participate. Meanwhile, her husband was appointed military governor of Murcia, and in late 1809 was named by popular vote to head the local Junta de Murcia (Murcia Patriotic Council). This launched his political career, which would later lead him to become a congressman for Murcia on the national assembly at the Cádiz Cortes.[17]

As the French troops advanced in early 1810, occupying the south of Spain, the family was forced to flee. They had already lost two children in the midst of all this: a newborn girl and their youngest, who was just two. On the way to Alicante, accompanying the retreat of the Junta de Murcia, Tomasa boldly changed her initial plan to take refuge in Mallorca and instead chartered a boat to take her and her family to Cádiz, which was heroically withstanding the French siege and being defended by the allied British fleet.[18] In the teeming, lively Andalusian city, which had been revitalized by political debates in the press and the political, legal, and social writings that flourished during the war, she met up with old friends who were also refugees.[19] The Junta Central was eventually replaced by a Regency Council. The setbacks in the war led to the formation of the Cádiz Cortes, the national assembly that would take the political pulse of the nation.

It was clear that patriotism was also a women's issue. The city welcomed famous heroines like the defenders of Zaragoza—the Countess of Bureta and Agustina de Aragón—as well as Ángela de Tellería, a brave woman from the Basque country.[20] It also allowed female authors to publish political screeds and newspaper articles of various types, such as Carmen Silva or Manuela López de Ulloa, to name just two examples. This was also a time when women showed their unequivocal support for the cause of King Fernando VII, for whom they made major sacrifices. The patriotic mobilization of women against Napoleon seen in other parts of Europe also reached Spain.[21] There was a proposal floating around to create a Sociedad de Señoras to support Fernando VII, and after a failed attempt to found it in Seville in 1809,[22] it finally materialized in Cádiz, which was dauntlessly withstanding the siege. In the summer of 1811, when the Anglo-Spanish forces suffered a series of defeats, the call by some patriots finally bore fruit and, that October, the Sociedad de Señoras de Fernando VII (Society of Ladies for Fernando VII) was founded, with Tomasa as president.[23] The society was the result of joint, coordinated action by famous women who, like Tomasa, were members of the Madrid Junta de Damas, and ladies from the Cádiz elite who also joined. The example was set by their main advocates, the Marquise of Villafranca and the Marquise of Casa-Rábago, who requested and successfully obtained permission from the Regency Council to found the society. Their previous experience as partners who had shared with her charitable activities in the capital would be adapted to the new demands posed by times of war. The next month, they held an opening ceremony in the city's Women's Hospital (Hospital de Mujeres de Cádiz), with a speech by the new organization's president that had an immediate public impact.[24]

Tomasa presented herself as the symbolic mother of the soldiers, undertaking the patriotic job of raising funds to cover their equipment and clothing. At this point she was pregnant again, with twins this time, and her bulging figure could not have made a clearer connection the two faces of motherhood, private and public. She was very aware that she was writing a women's version of a decisive chapter in patriotic service that would require recognition from the nation's representatives. The statutes were passed formalizing this new space for female civic relations and social contact.[25] The Ladies' Society credentials were endorsed by the experience some members had gained in their earlier work at the Junta de Damas in Madrid, namely Tomasa herself and the secretary, Loreto Figueroa y Montalvo, born in Cádiz.[26]

Like modern-day Penelopes, they had promised to make soldiers' uniforms "in workshops" in their own homes. The image was reassuring, presenting their work modestly so as not to arouse suspicion. But anyone who looks at the details of the fundraising, garment manufacture, purchases, contracts, and management involved in what they produced, all of which can be found in the archives of the City of Cádiz, will get an idea of the magnitude of this endeavor.[27] A whole battalion of soldiers, made up of some 850 men, was completely outfitted, and others followed. To mark the initial solemn handover of materials to the first recipients, the Guadix Regiment, there was a civic and religious ceremony at the location where the Ladies' Society had been founded, the Women's Hospital. The first batch was delivered in the spring of 1812, and flags were blessed and speeches were made that portrayed them as true Cornelias, celebrating them as the nation's motherly benefactors.[28] This opened up a path for demonstrating a female civilian role in the new liberal political order that promulgated the constitution, approved by the Cortes (National Congress) that same year. It was a gesture that until recently was not appreciated as an act of feminine involvement in the political transformation of the nation. However, we have now reclaimed it as such in our studies, despite the evident lack of feminine citizenship equivalent to masculine citizenship in the new constitutional order.

In search of new ways to expand their work, the ladies sought out their colleagues and friends on the other side of the Atlantic. They published an appeal to compatriots in Spanish America in the press and garnered a response.[29] From Havana, Veracruz, Guatemala, and Campeche, like-minded women mobilized, accompanying their generosity with speeches that recorded the patriotism behind their deeds.[30] In late 1812, a boat arrived from Havana bearing a major donation. Funds were also sent from neighboring locations and, once the siege of the city was lifted and part of Spain was liberated, it emerged that there had been contributions from other cities in Spain, which had also founded similar societies. The example had born fruit and been imitated around the country.

Once the siege of Cádiz was lifted and the war shifted in favor of the allies, the urgency of the ladies' work lessened. King Joseph I fled Madrid in March

1813, so it was possible to return home. The end of the war was near. Tomasa went back to Madrid with her family in September 1813. It was time to say goodbye to her companions in Cádiz, although she promised that she would continue the work they had begun. Indeed, she remained in contact with them and launched a branch of the Ladies' Society in Madrid to continue fund-raising, which was not entirely well received by some of the authorities, who believed it was no longer necessary.[31] However, the women continued their work and considered the possibility of building a monument to the Duke of Wellington in recognition of British help. Their persistence was rewarded by a request to clothe the troops scheduled to receive King Fernando VII when he returned from exile. A thanksgiving service was also held in Cádiz to celebrate their work at the Ladies' Society. It included a list of the names of all the ladies and things they had achieved.[32] It was necessary to create a lasting written re-cord of this major female patriotic initiative that would be engraved in memory and be republished in future societies.[33]

At this point the time had come to dissolve the Ladies' Society; this was decreed by King Fernando VII in the spring of 1815, with the acknowledgment that they could wear a distinctive commemorative armband whenever they donned formal or ceremonial dress. Certificates were also issued to all the group's participants. Tomasa's contained a dual listing, since hers recognized her activity both in Cádiz and in Madrid.[34]

President of the Junta de Damas

After the war ended, there was a period of reckoning as the resentful king took out his fury on Francophiles and liberals alike. The time had come to purge the leadership and replace Madrid's former Junta de Damas with ladies who had served Fernando's cause well.[35] Tomasa and her husband were rewarded for their loyal service. The marquis rose up the military ladder and was awarded a medal. The marquise was named vice president of the Junta de Damas in Madrid in 1816 and subsequently became president there, a position she held from 1817 to 1823.[36] This was a return to her origins that palpably demonstrated the contiguous ties that united both feminine corporations, the one in Cádiz and the one in Madrid.

During that time, Tomasa had to deal with bitter family setbacks. In 1816, her first child, Francisco, a frail youth to whom she was very close, died. Another infant was stillborn the following year, and finally, her youngest child, Pepita, was born in 1818. Her husband died in 1821. From then on, the widowed Marquise of Villafranca managed the household affairs and arranged her children's marriages single-handedly. Her eldest son, Pedro, made a crucial match in 1822 with Joaquina de Silva, daughter of the Marquis of Santa Cruz.

Running the Junta de Damas was something she was well equipped to handle. Her own mother had been the best of teachers in that regard. But Tomasa had to deal with new and weighty challenges to the association's hard-won philanthropic work, taking on responsibility for the survival of orphans by taking charge of the Inclusa children's home, the education of working-class girls, running the Colegio de Niñas de la Paz, rehabilitating fallen women, and overseeing work done in the women's prisons and the Sala de Reservadas, as well as launching new institutions that were essential to the nation's economic and social progress. She felt perfectly up to the challenge because, as she put it: "women are not devoid of understanding, reason, education, and even more importantly, humane sentiments that promote the general good of society" (no está negado a las mujeres el entendimiento, la razón, la instrucción, y lo que es más aún, los sentimientos de humanidad a favor del bien general de la sociedad).[37]

Her work as president is summarized in the four reports she prepared to give an account of her management to her companions and the general public; the first three of these were published. From these, it is clear that the endemic problem the junta faced was chronic underfunding.[38] Its income was supposed to be guaranteed by public contributions from charitable works and tax revenue, but these regularly failed to materialize, leaving the establishments Tomasa ran in serious difficulties. Attempts to come up with alternative funding sources via raffles, lotteries, and even charity bullfights did not yield the desired result.[39] Only during the Trienio Liberal (1820–23), a generous gesture on the part of the armed volunteer corps created by Madrid's City Council after the adoption of the Cádiz Constitution of 1812 brought relief to the Junta de Damas' perpetually empty coffers.[40] In fact, the president, who got on well with the mayor but was very critical of the government, gives us a glimpse of serious tensions with the new authorities, who were starting to hold a very different idea of how public philanthropy should work.[41] From then on, the Junta de Damas' work was undermined and the women were eventually relieved of their mission by government agencies.[42] While the General Law of Beneficence that was passed in 1822 was not completely implemented until 1836 due to the fall of the constitutional regime, it was a sign of what was to come. In subsequent years, there was a struggle that was eventually resolved by the state taking over the work that for years had been carried out by women.

But before that happened, the Marquise of Villafranca worked tenaciously as head of the principal institutions under her care: the Inclusa and the Colegio de Niñas de la Paz. Her main goal at the Inclusa was to bring down the high death rate among the abandoned, vulnerable children they took in. Even though her reports show unusual success in this endeavor, it is doubtful, given the means at her disposal, whether they managed to lower the high mortality rate. It is clear, however, that everything possible was done to alter that cruel reality. Tomasa herself took the step of requesting information from ambassadors and famous people living abroad about successful methods that had been employed with good results in different countries.[43] In terms of day-to-day life, they tried to improve the sanitation conditions and nutrition of the children under their care. They also improved the well-being of wet nurses, and supervision of their work, since on occasion they had been caught breaking the rules and committing fraud. To do this, the ladies considered adopting a system used in orphanages in France for properly identifying boys and girls.

Under Tomasa's presidency, a determined attempt was made to care for girls from the Inclusa by arranging for them to be educated at the Colegio de Niñas de la Paz.[44] She made this clear in the first report, acknowledging that the priority given to preventing the greatest number of children from dying had unjustly relegated the attention given to the "fate of girls."[45] The mission to educate them "in religion and the tasks appropriate to their sex" was aimed at making them useful to society and financially self-sufficient, so they could handle an uncertain future. Once educated, the girls could go on to serve at the orphanage itself or in private homes, or they might win dowries to marry "honest tradesmen."[46] The goal was to offer these girls an honorable path that spared them from worse evils. The elitist viewpoint underlying this intervention on behalf of society's most vulnerable members is clear.

This elitism was so strong that, broadening the girls' horizons, it raised the possibility of opening a new school for girls "for whom mixing with the lower classes would be most harmful" (cuyo roce con la de las clases bajas sería sumamente perjudicial), intended for daughters of families struggling to meet the cost of their education.[47] The new school required the application of a revolutionary teaching method that made it possible to educate a greater number of girls in less time. An early French method was rejected in a report by the Marquise of Espeja.[48] Then Tomasa took it upon herself to ask the Sociedad de Amigos del País de Cádiz (Society of Friends of the Country of Cádiz), which had recently named her an honorary member.[49] Knowing that this organization used the Lancasterian method (also known as the Mutual method) in its schools, she was interested in its advantages; it consisted of training specific talented students who were then used as teachers for the rest. Tomasa herself was convinced of the power of the method, since she had placed her sons in the only male school in Madrid that used it, sponsored by the Matritense. At last, the feminine Lancasterian School opened in 1820, with many pupils signed up, following the new method that used blackboards and slates to read and write.[50] The results over the first year were satisfactory, so the ladies of the junta, encouraged by their work, requested to be able to supervise all schools devoted to girls' education from then on. The Marquise of Villafranca, who knew that opening a Normal School to train female teachers in this method would be very effective, went so far as to ask the Cortes to open a pair of schools for boys and girls where the theoretical knowledge gained at the Normal School could be taught. This request was made several decades before the establishment of the first professional teacher-training school for women in Madrid in 1838, which was only legally required in Spain thanks to the Moyano Law of 1857. However, the authorities' neglect caused the Normal School to go under after only one year.[51]

Besides the Inclusa and the Colegio de Niñas de la Paz, there were other establishments that required the attention of the Junta de Damas. The jurisdiction over some of them was in dispute, such as the Escuela de Flores Artificiales (Artificial Flower School) or the Noviciado de las Hermanas de la Caridad (Novitiate of the Sisters of Charity of Saint Vicent de Paul) that functioned in the Inclusa. Meanwhile there was the work the junta was still doing in the women's prisons and the Sala de Reservadas for both prisoners and "fallen" women. As well as managing the Junta de Damas, Tomasa was involved with other educational institutions, such as the Real Escuela de Dibujo y Adorno (Royal School for Drawing and Decoration) opened by King Fernando VII in the spring of 1819, which she was involved with in her role as honorary member of the Royal Fine Arts Academy of San Fernando.[52] This school was intended to allow the daughters of honest craftsmen to learn a trade that would help boost the nation's economy.

It is absolutely clear that the Marquise of Villafranca used her writing skills to make herself understood and respected, to interact with people and to manage and handle all the functions she took on. Her speeches, reports, and letters amply attest to her abilities, exercised over a long period. However, she wrote barely anything of a literary nature. An *Elogio a la Reina Isabel de Braganza* (Eulogy to Queen Isabel de Braganza), composed in 1819 in response to the queen's death, reveals this facet. Although this was a more personal kind of writing, it was very constrained by the conventions for this type of document, which were highly codified in terms of the resources employed to praise the figure of a king or a queen. Tomasa was clearly an avid reader, and she possessed a very interesting library. This can be glimpsed in the fact that around 1819 she had a tricky moment with the Inquisition, which accused her of owning the book *Venida del Mesía en Gloria y Majestad* (The Coming of the Messiah in Glory and Majesty) by Manuel Lacunza, even though it was not yet on the list of banned volumes.[53] This awkwardness was removed in 1824 when she obtained a papal bull to read books prohibited by the Inquisition.[54]

Later Years: Putting Her House in Order

The death of her husband seems to have triggered a new phase in Tomasa's life. Six months after the funeral, she resigned from the Junta de Damas, but her resignation was not accepted. Her change of mood can be seen in the terseness of the report she wrote that year. Once again, she had to deal with family affairs, which were strained by the clash between the legitimate heirs (herself and her children) and the new legislation on disentailment of estates, recently passed by the liberal government on October 11, 1820. This new set of circumstances brought her considerable anxiety and went on for years, draining large amounts of her energy. She resigned irrevocably from the Junta de Damas in 1823.[55]

The following year, she got married in Naples to José Álvarez de Toledo Dubois, a relative of her husband's. He was a bachelor the same age as herself, forty-four years old, an army officer who had a diplomatic career as an ambassador in Europe. This led Tomasa to travel and change her signature to "Tomasa de Palafox." However, she never stopped demanding the honors she felt she deserved. In 1827, she started lobbying to be awarded the greatest honor the monarchy could bestow on ladies of her rank, the Real Orden de Damas Nobles de la Reina María Luisa (Royal Order of Noble Ladies of Queen Maria Luisa), which was granted in 1831. She received it in Naples, where her husband was stationed. Naples and the neighboring countryside would become her home in her later years. "The old lady," as the servants called her, suffered from migraines and entertained herself by painting in those years. She had a reputation for bad temper. The news from Spain was not exactly encouraging. The death of King Fernando VII had unleashed a battle over the succession that her family was involved in, since her older son had embraced the Carlist cause. She never saw the end of that fratricidal civil war, since she died in the commune of San Giorgio a Cremano (Naples) on October 14, 1835.

Her life, modeled on her mother's example, was spent in the service that ladies of her class had undertaken to provide since 1787. However, the tumultuous, volatile, and risky times she lived through made for a very different environment than the one her mother had faced. Tomasa did not shrink from the challenges raised by the new times. She firmly believed that women of her class could play a role, and she even helped create new spaces of agency linked to a new patriotic vocabulary that was emerging with the liberal state. Intelligent and hardworking, she handled both her public and her private business with ease while simultaneously fulfilling her duties as a wife and mother. Her figure can do no less than reflect the profile of a femininity in evolution under the exigencies of political and social changes brought by the new society. Her actions demonstrate her intelligence, dedication, and versatility to face the historical challenges posed by the new outlines of a nation under construction.

NOTES

Essay translated by Catherine Jagoe.

This work was carried out under the research project I+D, "Espacios de conocimiento, cultura y agencia femeninas en el mundo Moderno y Contemporáneo (siglos XV–XX), Ministerio de Ciencia Innovación y Universidades: PGC2018-097445-B-C21.

1. Espigado Tocino, "En la estela de las Luces."
2. Espigado Tocino, "La Marquesa de Villafranca."
3. Demerson, *María Francisca de Sales Portocarrero.*

4. Demerson, *María Francisca de Sales Portocarrero,* 110.

5. Franco Rubio, "Una vida poco convencional en la España de las Luces."

6. Holland, *The Spanish Journal,* 194.

7. Espigado Tocino, "La Marquesa de Villafranca," 320.

8. López-Cordón Cortezo, "Definición social y estrategias matrimoniales," 37–58.

9. Espigado Tocino, "La Marquesa de Villafranca," 318–22.

10. ADMS, Legajo 4840/14.

11. ADMS, Legajo 4840/12.

12. Prado Museum inventory no. MNP, P002448.

13. AHN, Consejos, Legajo 5512/7.

14. Espigado Tocino, "La Marquesa de Villafranca," 325.

15. ADMS, Legajo 6313, 2a carta, f. 1–v., November and December 1808.

16. *Correo de Murcia* 98 (December 29, 1808): 390–92.

17. Fraser, *La Maldita Guerra de España,* 372–80.

18. ADMS, Legajo 4303/3, Documento 13.

19. Cantos Casenave, Durán López, and Romero Ferrer, *La Guerra de Pluma.*

20. Fernández García, *Mujeres en la Guerra de la Independencia.*

21. Maierhofer, Roesch, and Bland, *Women Against Napoleon.*

22. Espigado Tocino, "La Marquesa de Villafranca," 331.

23. Coronel, *Discurso que hizo;* L. M. P. "A las damas de Cádiz, una gaditana," *El Redactor General,* August 9, 1811.

24. [Villafranca], *En la apertura de la Sociedad Patriótica.*

25. *Estatutos de la Sociedad de Señoras.*

26. Martín-Valdepeñas Yagüe, "Ilustrados, afrancesados y liberales," 355.

27. AHMC, Caja 5699.

28. Cos, *Sermón que en la bendición de banderas.*

29. *El Conciso,* January 4, 1812.

30. Espigado Tocino, "La Marquesa de Villafranca," 334–35.

31. *Diario de Madrid,* April 1 and 9, 1814.

32. Lazo de la Vega, *Discurso que en la solemne acción de gracias.*

33. Salaverri Baro, "La Junta de Damas como modelo de acción social de género."

34. ADMS, Legajo 4840/4.

35. Martín-Valdepeñas Yagüe, "Afrancesadas y patriotas."

36. Espigado Tocino, "En la estela de las Luces."

37. Villafranca, *Memoria instructiva,* 1820, 14.

38. Villafranca, *Memoria expositiva.*

39. Villafranca, *Memoria instructiva,* 1819.

40. *Suplemento a la Miscelánea de Comercio, Artes y Literatura,* April 15, 1820, 2–3.

41. ADMS, Legajo 4840/1, Documento 37.

42. Campos Díez, "La Junta de Damas de Honor y Mérito," 633.

43. Villafranca, *Memoria instructiva,* 1820.

44. Maceiras Rey, "Las niñas abandonadas."

45. Villafranca, *Memoria instructiva*, 1819.

46. Villafranca, *Memoria expositiva*, 10.

47. Villafranca, *Memoria instructiva*, 1819; *Suplemento de la Crónica Científica y Literaria* 202: 3.

48. ADMS, Legajo 4840/1, Documento 23.

49. Martín-Valdepeñas Yagüe, "El eco del saber," 102; Espigado Tocino, "En la estela de las Luces," 262.

50. *El Censor*, July 27, 1821, 229.

51. ADMS, Legajo 4840/1, Documento 37.

52. *Real Cédula de S.M. y señores del Consejo.*

53. ADMS, Legajo 6314/13.

54. ADMS, Legajo 235/5, Documento 1.

55. Espigado Tocino, "En la estela de las Luces," 266.

Veiled Biographies

The Other Women of the Junta de Damas

ELISA MARTÍN-VALDEPEÑAS YAGÜE

The founding group of the Junta de Damas de Honor y Mérito was composed of sixteen women. To the two women previously admitted by the Sociedad Económica on an honorary basis, the rest were added after the king authorized the creation of the new women's institution. All of the women were part of a group chosen from damas of the nobility, the state, and the military who frequented royal circles and were, therefore, very close to the monarchy.

Thanks to the interest that some of the founding women of the Junta de Damas have sparked in historians, there are excellent studies of their life stories available. Scholars have coincided in highlighting the uniqueness of these women within the cultural landscape of the Spanish eighteenth century. This is the case, for example, of the first two members, María Isidra Quintina de Guzmán y de la Cerda, the "Doctora de Alcalá," and María Josefa Alfonso-Pimental, the Countess-Duchess of Benavente, the first president of the institution.[1] The same situation has occurred with the Countess of Montijo, María Francisca de Sales Portocarrero—the indefatigable secretary of the junta—and María del Rosario Cepeda—her substitute from 1805 on.[2] Biographical sketches of Rita de Barrenechea, the Countess of Carpio, whose literary works have been the topic of editions in recent years, have also been written.[3] The life of Petra de Torres y Feloaga, the Marquise of Valdeolmos, is only superficially known thanks to the obituary that the Countess of Montijo dedicated to her friend after her passing.[4]

I propose to raise the visibility of some of the more obscure women of the Junta de Damas, thereby rescuing them from oblivion. They were elite women of the Spanish Enlightenment—united by their work in the Junta de Damas—who wanted to contribute their energy to the objectives that King Carlos III proposed upon creating that feminine institution. Through this public platform emblematic of the Enlightenment, "the ladies could feel and

"

show themselves to be participants in the country's reform."[5] Our analysis of the recruitment of the members shows that, although elitism predominated, the women's connections transcended the ties of family, friendship, or place of origin. Despite the difficulty posed by attempting to piece together the lives of women of the past, the following short biographical sketches of the lesser-known women of the Junta de Damas reveal a group of diverse personalities—cosmopolitan women, occasional writers, enliveners of Spanish cultural life—who proposed, united together, to improve, as far as they were able, the condition of the lives of women and children from the most disadvantaged levels of eighteenth-century Madrid society, and by extension, Spanish society of the eighteenth century.

The Women of the Junta de Damas (1787–1823)

At the end of 1787, the junta consisted of thirty members, among whom were three members of the royal family who headed the list of the chosen group: the Princess of Asturias, María Luisa de Parma, and the Infantas María Ana Victoria de Braganza and María Josefa de Borbón; also Josefa Amar y Borbón, whose *Discurso en defensa del talento de las mujeres* played an essential role in the controversy surrounding the admission of women to the Real Sociedad; and Francisca María Dávila y Carrillo de Albornoz, Countess of Torrepalma, who was the second president of the Junta de Damas.[6]

Despite the initial success, during the following years entries continued at a declining rate—with an average of three annual admissions, even though there were years without new members joining—until reaching one hundred members around 1823.[7] The elimination of the maximum limit of fifty members—established in the provisional statutes of 1788 but superseded by the definitive statutes in 1794—did not significantly increase recruitment.

The aristocratic status of a considerable percentage of the damas, which stands at approximately 67 percent—excluding the women from the royal family, who were included in the catalog as honorary members—demonstrates the profoundly elitist character of the institution.[8] More than twenty members were awarded the Real Orden de Damas Nobles de la Reina María Luisa, a noble order for women created in 1792 to reward noblewomen who had distinguished themselves through their service or their virtue.[9]

New members were attracted in different ways; of great importance was the recruitment of relatives and of those with ties to the same place of origin or of friendship, which favored restricting the selection of candidates to Madrid's most select circles. Kinship between the members established the interest of mothers and daughters united in a common cause. Younger women, who wanted to accompany and assist their mothers, joined the first generation. The most active damas of the junta were very aware that, in order to be successful in the arduous tasks that they were taking on as time went by, they needed to strengthen themselves as a group. The more members there were, the better the association would operate. Enlistment was opened to the closest female relatives such as sisters, cousins, and daughters-in-law.

The best-known cases were those of the Countess-Duchess of Benavente and the Countess of Montijo, two of the association's very active women. The daughters of the first woman, Josefa Manuela and Joaquina Téllez-Girón, Marquise of Camarasa and Marquise of Santa Cruz, respectively, joined the Junta de Damas in 1805, while her daughter-in-law, Francisca Beaufort, married to the Countess-Duchess of Benavente's eldest son, Francisco de Borja Téllez-Girón, heir to the Duke of Osuna, had joined a year earlier. Later, in 1814, the youngest daughter of the family, Manuela Isidra, Duchess of Abrantes, was admitted.

María Francisca de Sales Portocarrero, Countess of Montijo, added two of her daughters to the institution: the Marquise of Villafranca, María Tomasa Palafox, and the Countess of Villamonte, María Benita de los Dolores Palafox. The first, admitted in 1799, successfully continued her mother's legacy, serving as president of the Junta de Damas between 1818 and 1823. Her sister, who joined in 1804, helped her with this task, performing the duties of secretary during the same time. The latter was related through her husband to María de la Concepción Belvis de Moncada, Marquise of Ariza, one of the founding ladies. The other two daughters of the Countess of Montijo, although they were not part of the Madrid women's group, nonetheless followed in the footsteps of their mother in other similar institutions. María Ramona, Countess of Contamina, was president of the Junta de Señoras de la Real Casa Cuna de Granada (Royal Foundling Home of Granada) at the end of 1815—a women's association created in 1811 to manage the orphanage of Granada—while María Gabriela, Marquise of Lazán, was president of the Sociedad Patriótica de Señoras de Granada in 1813.[10]

Additional instances of the founders' recruitment of family members have been discovered. The "Doctora de Alcalá" was accompanied by her mother,

María Isidra de la Cerda, Duchess of Nájera, in 1787. The Countess of Benalúa, Francisca de Paula Cañas y Portocarrero, enjoyed the presence of her sister María Josefa, Viscountess of Valoria. Francisca, sister of María del Rosario Cepeda, joined in 1798. María Ana Pontejos, Marquise of Pontejos, witnessed her daughter, María Vicenta Moñino y Pontejos, Countess of Floridablanca, join in 1814. María Vicenta served as president of the Junta de Damas between 1860 and 1867. The Countess of Ofalia, María de los Dolores Salabert y Torres, joined in 1821 and was president from 1824 to 1825; perhaps she joined thanks to the precedent of her mother, Petra de Torres y Feloaga, Marquise of Valdeolmos, one of the founding members.

María Josefa Díez de la Cortina, the author of one of the tributes to the queen, joined in 1796. Her mother, Beatriz Montiel, must have found the work of the women of the junta to be important because she too joined three years later. María de la Concepción de Valenzuela, Marquise of Sonora, and her daughter, María Josefa de Gálvez, Countess of Castroterreño, joined in 1789 and 1795, respectively. The Countess O'Reilly, María Rosa de las Casas y Aragorri, became affiliated in 1787, while her daughter Rosa O'Reilly did so in 1801. María Paz Girón y Moctezuma, Marquise of Altamira, was admitted in 1788, and her daughter, María de la Paz Rodríguez de Albuerne Girón-Moctezuma, joined in 1814. María de la Piedad Roca de Togores y Valcárcel joined in 1816, while her mother-in-law Francisca de Paula Benavides Fernández de Velasco, Duchess of Frías, had done so in 1807. The niece of Ana Rodríguez de Carasa—who had joined in 1792 and who performed important tasks during the years of the Peninsular War—Mercedes de Santa Cruz y Montalvo, Countess of Merlin, was admitted in 1811. The Countess of Villalobos, María Josefa Contreras y Vargas, joined in 1793, and her daughter-in-law, María Angustias Fernández de Córdoba, Marquise of Cerralbo, in 1820.

Other family relationships are more difficult to determine. Given the substantial intermarriage within the Spanish aristocracy, the existence of indirect family ties among many members cannot be discounted. For example, the second president, Francisca María Dávila y Carrillo de Albornoz, Countess of Torrepalma, was admitted as a member in 1787, a few days after her cousin, María del Rosario Jácome y Ricardos. In 1799, her great-niece, María del Carmen Ponce de León y Carvajal, Countess of Trastámara, joined.

While the women's proselytism through family relationships was important, so too were the ties of compatriotism and friendship. In addition to the women's relationships with certain circles of power in Madrid, such as the court, the government, and the judiciary—some were wives or daughters of members of the Consejo de Castilla or ministers of the King—their common geographical origin must be stressed. María Lorenza de los Ríos, Marquise of Fuerte-Híjar, who joined in 1788, was able to act as a connection between the women from Cádiz and those from Valladolid. María del Rosario Cepeda, her sister Francisca, Ana Rodríguez de Carasa, the Marquise of Fuerte-Híjar, and Loreto Figueroa, admitted in 1803, were close in age and from families from the mercantile or administrative circles of Cádiz. The connection to Valladolid—a city in which a Junta de Damas was also sponsored by the Sociedad Económica de Amigos del País de Valladolid—was established through the Marquise of Fuerte-Híjar; the Viscountess of Valoria, one of the founders of the Madrid association and president of that of Valladolid; Rafaela de San Cristóbal, who joined the Junta de Damas of Madrid in 1787; the Viscountess of Palazuelos, admitted in 1788; and María Josefa Burriel, who joined in 1790.[11] Cuban origin can be traced in the Countess O'Reilly, in María Josefa Veitia, a member since 1787, and the Countess of Merlin.

During the Peninsular War, the flight of many members from French-occupied Madrid forced the recruitment of women from the elite, Francophile class. The task of recruitment was likely carried out by Ana Rodríguez de Carasa, the wife of Gonzalo O'Farrill, the Minister of War to King Joseph Bonaparte. The six women admitted between 1811 and 1812 share this connection.[12]

There were also solicitations to join on one's own initiative or on the recommendation of a third party. A French woman, Mademoiselle le Masson le Goft, sent a letter at the end of 1788 in which she sought the "honor" of joining the women's association.[13] In September of 1788, María del Carmen de Betancourt y Molina, the sister of the famous Spanish engineer Agustín de Betancourt, was admitted based on the proposal of the Countess of Montijo, who learned of her excellent qualities from speaking with José de Betancourt, another brother. In February of 1790, Andrea de Varo Gil, a resident of Aguilar de la Frontera (Córdoba), was accepted after sending a letter in which she recounted her activities in support of the production of worsted wool in that town.[14]

✦ ✦ ✦

Some Sketches of Forgotten Women

The exuberant personality of some women of the Junta de Damas has helped to obscure those who also participated substantially in the activities of the association. One must not mistakenly think that the Junta de Damas was the work of only a few leading figures from Madrid's high nobility, determined to perform enlightened acts of humanitarian content.[15]

The Junta de Damas was a collective venture in which many women contributed their ideas and their work. Aligned on a second tier behind those who held leadership positions, they participated as guardians or supervisors of the Escuelas Patrióticas, the Inclusa, the Colegio de Niñas de la Paz, the Montepío de Hilazas, and the rest of the schools. A review of the minutes of the weekly sessions reveals the presence of many women who met together regularly. Their life stories, veiled, hidden, and relegated to remaining among the shadows, reveal a large number of women with diverse but interesting personalities who deserve to be rescued from obscurity.

Some were occasional writers, virtually unknown, whose written production is limited to their work for the Junta de Damas in speeches, tributes, statements, and reports. Others are known for their literary works or as translators. Fortunately, some were immortalized by the paintbrushes of the best Spanish artists of the eighteenth century, such as Francisco de Goya or Agustín Esteve. They were enlightened, committed, and inspiring "women of action" who, through education and charitable work, wanted to contribute "with their intelligence, with their hands, and with their wealth" (con sus luces, con sus manos, y sus caudales) to public happiness.[16]

The second president of the Junta de Damas (1790–1801), Francisca María Dávila Carrillo de Albornoz, Countess of Torrepalma and of Truillas—or "Trullás," as it is written in some documents—was a cosmopolitan woman and well-connected in the Bourbon court. (See fig. 4.) For more than thirteen years, she resided in various European capitals, frequenting the most select court circles. Francisca María had joined the Junta de Honor y Mérito on December 7, 1787, two months after its founding. She was the author of the first tribute to Queen María Luisa de Parma, published in 1794. Thanks to her direct access to the queen, she obtained numerous orders for the junta's textile schools in order to make wardrobes for the Casa Real (Royal Palace) servants.[17] She also belonged to the Real Asociación de Caridad de Señoras, which carried out its work in women's prisons.

Francisca María was born in Velez-Málaga (Málaga) on August 21, 1733, the daughter of the Counts of Valhermoso and niece of the first Duke of Montemar, a very prestigious military figure during the reign of Felipe V.[18] At nineteen years old, on May 15, 1753, she married Alonso Verdugo y Castilla, Count of Torrepalma. This writer and diplomat from Granada frequented Madrid's intellectual circles of the first half of the eighteenth century. In 1754 he was appointed minister plenipotentiary of Spain in Vienna, and in 1760, transferred to Turin as ambassador, where he died in 1767. In this city, Francisca María met the prolific French writer Jeanne-Marie Le Prince de Beaumont, who dedicated to her *Le Magasin des pauvres, artisans, domestiques et gens de la campagne*, published in Lyon in 1768.[19]

After her return to Spain, thanks to her good connections in the Bourbon Court, Francisca María held various palatine positions.[20] In 1794, she was awarded the sash of the Real Orden de Damas Nobles de la Reina María Luisa.[21]

The Dowager Countess of Torrepalma was married secretly, with dispensation for kinship from the Pope, to her cousin, the prestigious lieutenant general Antonio Ricardos Carrillo de Albornoz, on August 24, 1776, in the Palace of the Real Sitio de San Ildefonso (Segovia). After his death on March 13, 1794, Francisca María obtained, in perpetuity, the earldom of Truillas in memory of the celebrated victory of the Spanish troops, commanded by her husband, during the War of the Pyrenees (War of the Convention, 1793–95) against the French revolutionaries.[22] After losing the king's favor in 1805 because of her closeness to the opposition groups allied to the Prince of Asturias, the future King Fernando VII, she was exiled to Calatayud (Zaragoza), where she died on January 24, 1808.[23]

María del Rosario Cepeda y Mayo was one of the founding members of the Junta de Damas, in which she carried out important work for more than twenty-five years. (See fig. 11.) She accepted without hesitation the invitation made by the Sociedad Económica Matritense to become a part of the first group. Like many of her colleagues in the Junta de Damas, her profile is of an enlightened woman, an enthusiast of cultural life more than a great intellectual figure, although her culture and talent cannot be disregarded.[24]

María del Rosario was born in Cádiz on January 10, 1756. She was appointed honorary town dignitary of Cádiz in 1768 for her precocious talent after demonstrating her knowledge in a public examination attended by city authorities. To the astonishment of those in attendance, she was able to solve

FIG. 11. María del Rosario Cepeda y Mayo, 1855. Ayuntamiento de Cádiz. Museo de las Cortes.

the most complex mathematical problems and to successfully translate as many texts as were presented to her to Latin, Greek, and French. Her young age—she was only twelve years old—did not hinder her from delivering a public plea in favor of education for the female sex, "daring to claim that it was inappropriate that a rational being such as a woman was to receive an education only in domestic tasks."[25]

On November 20, 1774, she was married in Cádiz to the military officer Pedro Fernández de Gorostiza, with whom she had three children. She moved to Mexico, where her husband served as the governor of the city of Veracruz between 1789 and 1794. During those years, thanks to her friendship with the Viceroy of Nueva España (Mexico), the Count of Revillagigedo, she frequented the most distinguished circles of the Mexican capital. Following the death of her husband on November 8, 1794, María del Rosario and her children returned to Spain, settling again in Madrid.[26]

María del Rosario then resumed her duties with the Junta de Damas, over the years acquiring great prominence in the women's association. Until her transfer to Mexico, she had been responsible for supervising the work of the

Escuela Patriótica de San Ginés. Due to her interest in the development of national industry, a very enlightened issue, she had proposed to her colleagues that the silk attire they wore be made with fabric manufactured in Spain.[27] In 1797 she was appointed censor, vice president between 1798 and 1799, vice secretary between 1798 and 1805, and principal secretary from 1806 until 1813. She was also the author of the 1797 tribute to the queen, which was published.

During the Peninsular War, she remained in Madrid because her children served on the French-supporting side.[28] Her sons' escape to France after the defeat of the Napoleonic armies in Spain caused her to fall ill, for she could not bear, as a good "patriot," that her sons had enlisted to serve "the flags of the intruder" (en las banderas del intruso), according to the official report examining her loyalty during the war (expediente de depuración).[29] María del Rosario died in Madrid on August 2, 1815.

María de la Concepción de Valenzuela y Fuentes, Dowager Marquise of Sonora, was a part of what Demerson called the "principal quartet" of the Junta de Damas. (See fig. 13.)[30] She was born in Madrid around 1750, the daughter of the Count of Puebla de los Valles. On November 1, 1775, she married José de Gálvez, secretary of Indias (the ministry in charge of the Spanish empire's overseas territories) of King Carlos III, with whom she had a daughter.[31] María de la Concepción passed away in Madrid on April 14, 1811.[32] Francisco Saavedra remarked in his *Memorias* that, during the time he held a post in this ministry, he tried to get along with "la Señora" (the Lady),[33] the minister's wife, to whom was attributed a strong personality. José de Gálvez died in Aranjuez on June 17, 1787, beginning the decline of one of the most powerful families of eighteenth-century Spain.[34]

The Marquise of Sonora was admitted as a member of the Junta de Damas on December 12, 1789, performing noteworthy leadership positions in the twenty-two years that she belonged to the institution. She was vice president from 1800 until 1802 and from 1807 until her death. She was also the supervisor of the Inclusa, together with the Countess of Montijo, a position that she held continuously from the time when the Junta de Damas took charge of this establishment until her death. At the same time, she performed important work in the Real Asociación de Caridad de Señoras.[35]

In 1795 she published her tribute to the queen. For the physical education committee of the Junta de Damas, the Marquise of Sonora took charge of composing a report about "children's physical education during lactation and teething" (la educación física de los niños en todo el tiempo de la lactación y dentición), which was received positively by the censor of the Sociedad Económica.[36]

During the Peninsular War, María de la Concepción demonstrated her leadership ability when she had to assume direction of the Junta de Damas in the absence of the president, the Countess-Duchess of Benavente, who had escaped from Madrid at the end of 1808. Despite her disagreements with those supporting the French, on several occasions she visited Francisco de Cabarrús, Joseph Bonaparte's minister of finance, so that he might grant aid to the Inclusa since the seizure of funds and the loss of income as a result of the war had caused a dire situation. Her work heading the orphanage was immense: she collected donations, inspected the establishment, managed the rents of the Inclusa's buildings, and struggled with employees and suppliers who constantly complained about the lack of payment.[37]

Following in the footsteps of her mother, the Marquise of Sonora, and perhaps to help her with her duties, on October 9, 1795, María Josefa de Gálvez y Valenzuela joined the Junta de Damas, in which she held the positions of vice-censor in 1808 and secretary from 1814 until 1817. (See fig. 14.) Her cousin, the poet Rosa María de Gálvez, dedicated a poem to her, "La Beneficencia," after María Josefa published the tribute to the queen in 1801.[38] Like her mother, María Josefa also belonged to the Real Asociación de Caridad de Señoras.

María Josefa was born in Madrid on November 13, 1776.[39] On December 1, 1792, she married Prudencio de Guadalfajara, Count of Castroterreño, with whom she had several children, none of whom survived infancy.[40] On May 29, 1817, she died in Madrid after "much and prolonged suffering" (mucho y dilatado padecer).[41]

The Countess of Castroterreño was in all respects a "patriot" during the Peninsular War. She remained in Madrid, even though her husband, a lieutenant general of the army, had joined the patriotic faction.[42] He was on the verge of suffering death by hanging for aiding the enemies of the French. María Josefa herself related her bitter experience by requesting in writing in 1816 that she be bestowed the sash of the Real Orden de Damas Nobles de la Reina María Luisa as a public acknowledgment of the distinctions incurred during the past warfare, and it was granted to her. She blamed the French for having suffered "harsh treatment that her loyalty drew from the intruding government" (malos tratamientos que su fidelidad la atrajo de parte del Gobierno intruso), which imprisoned her for more than seven months in a Madrid convent.[43] Released from captivity, she tried to alleviate the fate of Madrid's hungry in 1811, collaborating with the Junta de Beneficencia by taking charge of the subscriptions in support of the establishment created to provide food for the poor.[44]

When the Marquise of Villafranca founded the Sociedad Patriótica de Señoras in Madrid, in imitation of the women's association that emerged in Cádiz, María Josefa joined as secretary in 1813. Then, she wrote a speech urging the women of Madrid to join the association in order to collaborate in the manufacture of uniforms for the Spanish Army.[45]

Ana Josefa Rodríguez de Carasa y Prichardo was born in Cádiz on May 1, 1763.[46] (See fig. 12.) A woman of expansive culture, with a great interest in charity, she became a member of the Junta de Damas in 1790, where she held various positions, such as deputy secretary in 1797, censor in 1811, and supervisor of the Inclusa the same year.

FIG. 12. Ana Carassa de O'Farrill (lithography of A. Delorieux), 1817. Authors' collection.

Ana was married for the first time on September 8, 1777, in Cádiz to the merchant Pedro Manuel Sáenz de Santa María, with whom she had a son, Pedro Miguel. After being widowed, she was married on March 22, 1788, in Cádiz as well, to Gonzalo O'Farrill, a military man of great prestige, and who would later play a great role in Spain during the Peninsular War as Joseph Bonaparte's minister of war. She accompanied her husband to his military and diplomatic postings through Europe, returning to Madrid in February of 1808 in the entourage of the former Queen of Etruria (Tuscany, Italy), María Luisa de Borbón, on the eve of the French invasion.[47]

Various testimonies coincide in noting that Gonzalo O'Farrill's constant distance from the Court was due to the bad influence of his wife: "His wife has hurt him by her indiscretion and violent speeches in favor of Jacobinism."[48] Around 1800 in Paris, both had frequented a type of club of Spanish revolutionaries. Ana's strong personality and her capacity for political influence were emphasized by her contemporaries.[49]

From the beginning of the Peninsular War, Ana Rodríguez de Carasa was one of the most active members of the Junta de Damas. By virtue of her proximity to the Josephine government, she managed to make the association survive despite the circumstances in which it was involved during the difficult times of French-occupied Madrid. King Joseph Bonaparte showed himself to be very interested in their work and supported the Inclusa. Ana served as supervisor of the Inclusa and carried out a policy of soliciting new members, recruited mostly among the Francophile elite.[50]

In 1813 she was exiled to France. She died in Paris on November 5, 1816. At her death, General O'Farrill wrote a vindicatory booklet in her memory in an effort to defend her from the harsh accusations to which she had been the subjected in various periodicals and pamphlets published during the war years.[51]

The authorization of the Junta de Damas by King Carlos III, conveniently publicized by the Madrid periodical press, produced a sensation of happiness among elite Spanish women. They felt very satisfied at having overcome the first barrier that until that moment had impeded women from committing themselves publicly to the principles of the Enlightenment. A young woman from Córdoba, Joaquina Domínguez Aguayo, later Countess of Hust, expressed her gratitude for having been admitted to the institution. She wishes a promising future for the Junta's "worthy Heroines" (beneméritas Heroínas) for "animated by the same spirit, the noble women who have joined it following the example of its excellent President together with the graces, wit, and liveliness that belong to Spanish ladies, will not have a lesser role in promoting and perfecting the happiness of this monarchy and the glorious memory of the incomparable reign of the great Carlos III than that of the wise and vigilant male patriots, to whose Society [the Junta de Damas] is united."[52]

As the years passed, she could feel satisfied that her desires had become reality. The first corporation of the "fair sex" (bello sexo) had met the expectations that had been created, thanks to the efforts of its members. These women, forgotten and silenced, hidden behind brilliant personalities, performed quiet work and were pioneers in exercising their rights—the few that women of the time had—despite the terrible circumstances in which they lived. They contributed to the common effort with their scarce means, with a sense of responsibility and the consciousness that their role should not be limited to remaining idle at a time when the country needed them. They were branded as frivolous by some of their contemporaries who focused only on the aristocratic aspect of the institution and did not delve into the work they were doing. Nevertheless, discreet and prudent, they believed that their vocation of service to others and that their work together made sense: they dedicated their efforts to improve, as much as was possible, the life of society's most disadvantaged.

NOTES

Essay translated by Kathleen Fueger.

Research for this essay was carried out within the project I+D: "Espacios de conocimiento, cultura y agencia femeninas en el mundo Moderno y Contemporáneo (siglos XV–XX)" (PGC2018-097445-B-C21), part of the collective project "Género, cultura y subjetividad: más allá de las políticas del conocimiento (siglos XV–XX)," financed by Spain's Ministerio de Ciencia, Innovación y Universidades (MICINN).

1. Vázquez Madruga, *María Isidra Quintina de Guzmán*; Fernández Quintanilla, "Una española ilustrada"; Yebes, *La condesa-duquesa de Benavente*; Fernández Quintanilla, *La IX Duquesa de Osuna.*

2. Demerson, *María Francisca de Sales Portocarrero*; Azcárate Ristori, *Una niña regidora honoraria.*

3. García Garrosa, "En los inicios de la comedia neoclásica"; Urzainqui Miqueleiz, *"Catalin" de Rita Barrenechea.*

4. Montijo, *Elogio de la Señora Doña Petra de Torres Feloaga.*

5. Bolufer Peruga, *Mujeres e Ilustración*, 371.

6. *Memorial literario*, T. VIII, XXXII, August 1786: 400–430. On Josefa Amar, see López-Cordón Cortezo, *Condición femenina y razón ilustrada*.

7. The most complete study of the catalog of members of the Junta de Damas (1786–1839) is Bezos del Amo, "La Junta de Damas de Honor y Mérito." Lists of the members have been published in Demerson, "Catálogo de las Socias de Honor y Mérito," and Smith, *The Emerging Female Citizen*, 136–39.

8. The small number of women of the middles classes in the institution can by explained by the thorough examination by the damas of all candidates and by the lack of incentives for women, the majority of whom lived confined to the domestic sphere. Although the ideal of the bourgeois women, the *ángel del hogar* (angel in the house) would not take root in Spain until the second third of the nineteenth century, during the Enlightenment the model of a Christian woman, wife, and mother, confined to the family circle, still existed, along with the assumption of her intellectual and physical inferiority to men.

9. Among those honored were the Countess-Duchess of Benavente; the Duchess of Almodóvar; the Countesses of Montealegre, Montijo, Torrepalma, Benalúa, O'Reilly, Montarco, Torrejón, Villalobos, Castroterreño, Castelflorido, and Nieulant; and the Marquises of Llano, Ariza, Villafranca. Regarding this award, see Ceballos-Escalera y Gila, *La Real Orden de Damas Nobles de la Reina María Luisa*, and Molas Ribalta, "Las primeras damas de la Orden de María Luisa."

10. María Gabriela Palafox drafted a petition in 1799 to join the Junta de Damas of Madrid that was never taken up. ARCM, Instituciones Antecesoras, Fondo Junta de Damas de Honor y Mérito, Expediente 8375/5.

11. Martín-Valdepeñas Yagüe and Jaffe, *María Lorenza de los Ríos*, 38, 111–12.

12. Martín-Valdepeñas Yagüe, "Ilustrados, afrancesados y liberales," 348.

13. Demerson, *María Francisca de Sales Portocarrero*, 140.

14. Martín-Valdepeñas Yagüe, "Ilustrados, afrancesados y liberales," 304.

15. Paula de Demerson asserted the importance of the "quartet formed by Osuna-Montijo-Truillas-Sonora," which has helped to accentuate the protagonism of a few women. Nevertheless, while a great deal is known about the lives of the first two women, that is not the case with the last two. Demerson, *María Francisca de Sales Portocarrero*, 244.

16. *Memorial literario*, T. VIII, XXXII, August 1786: 427.

17. Martín-Valdepeñas Yagüe, "La reina María Luisa de Parma," 753.

18. Martín-Valdepeñas Yagüe, "El retrato de la condesa de Truillas," 74–76.

19. Le Prince de Beaumont, *Le Magasin des pauvres*, 8; Montoya, "Marie Leprince de Beaumont," 24.

20. AGP, Personal, Caja 1037, Expediente 19 and 20.

21. *Mercurio de España*, April 1794: 416; August 1794: 474.

22. *Mercurio de España*, March 1794: 352–53; April 1794: 421–22.

23. AGP, Personal, Caja 16839, Expediente 8.

24. *Memorial literario*, T. V, June 1785: 154.

25. Azcárate Ristori, *Una niña regidora honoraria*, 40.

26. Azcárate Ristori, *Una niña regidora honoraria,* 101.

27. Demerson, *María Francisca de Sales Portocarrero,* 154.

28. Francisco Javier de Gorostiza was an infantry colonel in the Army of José I, and Pedro Ángel held the position of assistant to the Council of State. The youngest, Manuel Eduardo, reached the rank of infantry captain. He is known for his literary and journalistic activities. After the Liberal Triennium (Trienio Liberal, 1820–23), he left Spain for Mexico, where he became an activist for independence, reaching the position of minister of the new Republic of Mexico. López Tabar, *Los famosos traidores,* 80.

29. Martín-Valdepeñas Yagüe, "Afrancesadas y patriotas," 362.

30. Demerson, *María Francisca de Sales Portocarrero,* 244.

31. AHDM, Parroquia de San Martín, Libro 27, *Matrimonios (1771–1777):* 370–370v.

32. AHDM, Parroquia de San Martín, Libro 28, *Defunciones (1809–1812):* 69.

33. Moreno Alonso, *Memorias inéditas de un ministro ilustrado,* 145.

34. Regarding the powerful Gálvez clan, see Hernández González, *El círculo de los Gálvez.* It includes a biographical sketch of María de la Concepción Valenzuela and her daughter, María Josefa de Gálvez, and a review of the activities of each of them in the Junta de Damas (99–135). On the women of the Gálvez clan, in addition to the previous work, see also Santos Arrebola, "Las mujeres en la familia de los Gálvez."

35. On the Real Asociación de Caridad de Señoras, see Serrano Jerez, "Sex and prisons."

36. ARSEM, Expediente 146/11.

37. Martín-Valdepeñas Yagüe, "Afrancesadas y patriotas," 360–62.

38. Lewis, "'A su reina benéfica,'" 700.

39. AHDM, Parroquia de Santa Cruz, Libro 29, *Bautismos (1769–1784):* 219v.

40. AHDM, Parroquia de San Martín, Libro 31, *Matrimonios (1792–1801):* 22.

41. AHN, Estado, Legajo 7562, Expediente 16.

42. *Gaceta de Madrid* 93 (August 5, 1817): 827–28.

43. AHN, Estado, Legajo 7562, Expediente 16.

44. *Gaceta de Madrid* 327 (November 23, 1811): 1354.

45. Martín-Valdepeñas Yagüe, "Afrancesadas y patriotas," 364–65.

46. Martín-Valdepeñas Yagüe, "Ilustración, jacobinismo y afrancesamiento."

47. During her stay in Berlin in 1799, she met Louisa Catherine Johnson Adams, wife of the future sixth president of the United States, John Quincy Adams. Heffron, *Louisa Catherine,* 131.

48. Holland, *The Spanish Journal,* 159.

49. *El Duende de los cafés* 68 (November 8, 1813): 305.

50. Martín-Valdepeñas Yagüe, "Afrancesadas y patriotas," 354.

51. O'Farrill, *A D. Pedro Miguel Sáenz de Santa María.*

52. "animadas de un mismo espíritu las Nobles, que han entrado en ella poniendo a ejemplo de su Excelentísima Presidenta, en movimiento aquellas gracias, ingenio y viveza, que son tan propias de las Damas de España, no tendremos menos parte en promover y perfeccionar la felicidad de esta Monarquía y la gloriosa memoria del Reinado incomparable del gran Carlos 3º que la que tienen los sabios y celosos Patriotas, a cuya Sociedad está unida." ARCM, Instituciones Antecesoras, Fondo Junta de Damas de Honor y Mérito, Expediente 8482/7.

III

The Junta de Damas' Contributions to Enlightenment Projects

Helping by Teaching

The Junta's Role in Women's Education

JOSEFINA MÉNDEZ VÁZQUEZ

The Junta de Damas de Honor y Mérito, Spain's first lay organization for women, was created by a royal order on August 27, 1787. Reflecting the Enlightenment mentality of the time, its founding mission was to educate working-class women in order to include them in the reform plans of enlightened despot King Carlos III, whose goals included increasing production in the textile industry, improving the quality of textiles so they could compete with those produced abroad, and adjusting the balance of trade, which had been affected by large-scale imports of yarn and cloth. In order to achieve this, all active members of the population were needed, and therefore it was vital to incorporate qualified female workers into the textile industry.

However, the Junta de Damas transcended governmental objectives and, in addition to teaching women a trade, set out to provide them comprehensive training by incorporating elementary education into their curriculum.[1] This goal meant that the Junta de Damas created its own model for female education that diverged from the type of free schooling for the lower social strata prescribed by the monarchy.

In the last third of the eighteenth century, for women to enter the textile workforce fully, they needed to overcome a long-standing obstacle: the social stigma attached to many textile manufacturing jobs, which were considered degrading, especially if performed by women. Legislation such as the real cédula (royal decree) of September 2, 1784, authorized all women in the kingdom to work in yarn manufacture, as well as other arts appropriate to the decorum and strengths of their sex. Rulings like these were all promulgated to liberate female workers from the stigma associated with certain jobs.

✦ ✦ ✦

The Junta de Damas Takes Over Four Patriotic Schools Threatened with Closure

The Escuelas Patrióticas were set up in 1776, when the Real Sociedad Económica Matritense de Amigos del País publicly announced the founding of four free schools for women and girls in the parishes of San Ginés, San Sebastián, San Martín, and San Andrés, after which the schools were named. The first three schools taught pupils how to spin linen, hemp, and cotton while San Andrés taught exclusively wool spinning.

These Patriotic Schools were set up, among other reasons, to provide women with the qualifications needed to perform professional textile work, and to cover the gap created by the trade organizations' refusal to train women, which had been in effect since the preceding century.

When the Junta de Damas was created, it was charged with organizing and running the Patriotic Schools sponsored by the Matritense, subject to its oversight. For the preceding eleven years, the schools had been run directly by members of the Industry Commission (Clase de Industria), but thanks to unreliable funding and poor management, by 1787 the institutions were on the verge of closing.

With the new lady members on board, the leadership of the Matritense saw an opportunity to try and save the schools from disaster and the dishonor of failure by transferring the running of the schools to the Junta de Damas. As Fernández Quintanilla put it: "Closing the centers was unthinkable, since it involved a lot more than mere financial disaster; it would showcase the failure of the whole reformist ideology on which the Society prided itself."[2] The members were not about to accept that responsibility. They saw it as a good option because, if the debacle did finally occur, it could be attributed to the members of the Junta de Damas.

There were three stages in the evolution of the four Patriotic Schools. At first, from 1776 to 1787, they were run directly by members of the Matritense, which yielded poor results due to haphazard funding, the type of teaching, and the low number of pupils. Students were taught how to make yarn in order to be able to manufacture high-quality cloth that could compete with foreign textiles, which had cornered the national market. But they did not succeed.[3] "With that notion of the one-subject school specializing exclusively in yarn making, the Patriotic Schools were making the same mistake as the one-track trade technical schools; of which, although this was not spelled out, they were becoming the successors. It was clear that work focusing on a single branch of the textile industry was not productive, and that there was a need to broaden instruction to other skills, as the Junta de Damas realized when it took over the schools."[4]

In the second phase under the Junta de Damas, from 1787 to 1808, even though funding of the schools remained precarious, they started seeing positive results thanks to the effective changes they made. During this period, the schools met the goals for which they had been founded, and there was a major increase in the number of pupils.

In the third phase, which lasted from 1808 until the schools were ultimately closed in 1812–13, political instability caused by the war and the country's economic difficulties made it impossible to keep the schools running. As a result, after a dogged struggle to save them, the women were obliged to shut them down.

FIG. 13. María de la Concepción Valenzuela y Fuentes, Marquise of Sonora, ca. 1790. Photo from authors' collection.

Solutions Adopted by the Junta de Damas to Save the Schools

When the socias were assigned a set of schools in danger of imminent closure, they set about investigating the reasons for the situation and seeking solutions. They began by examining the area of operation, taking note of all they observed, and reading the records they requested from the Matritense. They immediately realized that the teaching staff needed to be replaced, since one of the mistakes the society frequently made was to keep employing people who were incapable of or unsuited to their tasks; the schools had stopped functioning in terms of promoting the textile industry, nor were they helping to address the poverty of the young women being trained there.

Another flaw the women discovered was that training was being offered only in one subject; for example, teaching pupils only to spin, at a point when artisanal yarn production had stalled in Spain, as it was being overtaken by factory-produced yarns. They decided, therefore, that the immediate solution was to diversify the subjects taught and thus the goods produced, since experience had demonstrated that a woman could not earn her living by spinning alone. This was the main reason why the number of pupils had dropped considerably, in comparison to the early years. So they argued for modifying the syllabus based on a new teaching method, replacing the activities offered with others that were more appropriate to the real needs of the market. In other words, they did a market research study.

As for the market value of handmade yarns, the Junta de Damas was clear on their utility at that point: "At a time when machines are replacing manual labor everywhere, when each machine can do the work of many hands, who will pay a living wage to a woman who, with nothing other than her own effort and a spinning wheel, spins in a month what a machine can turn out in a day?" (En un tiempo en que las máquinas suplen por todas partes las manos haciendo cada una de aquellas por muchas de estas, ¿quién pagaría un jornal suficiente para vivir, a la que sin otro auxilio que el de su trabajo y un torno, elaborara en un mes lo que una máquina en un día?)[5] The damas were not the only ones aware of the low value placed on female spinners in the labor market; girls and their families knew this too, since they refused the spinning wheels they were awarded as prizes and offered to exchange them for a sum of money that was less than the actual value of the spinning wheel.

On the other hand, the warehouse at the Montepío de Hilazas was full of yarn produced in the schools which could not easily be sold since they were of low quality and shoddily made. Or, in the best-case scenario, even when they were more expertly made, the production costs were so high because of the waste inherent in the learning process and the cost of materials, and because pupils were overpaid for spinning to motivate them to attend school, that the sale price needed in order to break even was so high that it could not compete with factory-made yarn. Aware of the situation, the junta tried to contribute in their own way to improving the small-scale manufacturing system in the country, and getting these jobs allotted mostly to women.

Continuing their innovations, in terms of the schools' internal regime, the Junta de Damas abolished the cap on the number of pupils. When a school reached the maximum number of pupils, an assistant would be hired after taking the same exam as the teachers. If candidates performed equally well on the exam, an ex-pupil would always be chosen over an outsider, because the former was trained in the school's method and the supervisor knew her character, thus avoiding much of the friction they had seen with incoming teachers. The assistants had become necessary not just because of the growing numbers of pupils in the schools but because the new teaching system meant that girls were separated into different rooms or floors of the building. Another modification introduced by the socias was to lower the age at which girls could enter the school, setting the range at four to twelve years, and to stop admitting adult pupils.[6]

In 1794, the damas managed to get the Matritense to end cotton spinning in the schools[7] while continuing to teach linen and wool. They added sewing to the curriculum, since this would allow their graduates to obtain work as dressmakers in wealthy households, where they could live comfortably, or open many doors to positions as ladies' maids. Either way, by learning needlework they would always be able to find a reliable way of feeding and clothing themselves.

Just as yarn spinning led to significant losses for the schools, sewing brought in income. Due to the schedule, there were times when the pupils were necessarily idle; the supervisors dealt with this by accepting needlework on consignment from private clients and stores so that the girls always had work to do.

To deal with the problem of absenteeism, the women proposed, among other measures, ending the custom of paying the girls a fixed sum regardless of whether the yarn they spun was good or bad; they saw this as a negative practice that encouraged greed instead of stimulating learning. It also meant that the pupils were paid more than the value of their work, and when their training ended, they refused to work for less money in the factories or for private clients.

In order to solve this problem, the damas came up with a new system for evaluating the quantity and quality of yarn a girl could spin in a month with average effort, and paid only those who surpassed that minimum quota of yarn. They hoped this would encourage their pupils to apply themselves, since their work would be fairly remunerated.[8]

Educational Systems at the Patriotic Schools under the Junta de Damas

In order to save the schools from failing and to boost their yarn production from its all-time low, the solution was to diversify the syllabus and thus the goods produced. In order to do this, the junta decided it was essential to come up with an overall plan of studies for the four Patriotic Schools.[9] This plan divided the curriculum into three classes or grades.[10] In the first, pupils would learn *hilar* (to spin raw textiles into yarn), *aspar* (to reel yarn onto a winding frame to make skeins), *devanar* (to wind yarn onto a spool or cone to make a ball or bobbin), to twist or "ply" yarn, make girdles, knit, and read. In the second, they would be taught to comb, card, sew fine linens Spanish- and French-style, write, and do arithmetic.[11] In the third grade they were trained in weaving, ribbon making, canvas fabrics, table linens, and *cotonías* (sailcloth with piping). This method was followed in all the schools except San Andrés, where they used the wool they spun to learn to make serge, girdles, and garters. The supervisor decided when a student was ready to move from one class to the next.

It is worth stressing how important it was that this plan included teaching basic literacy in the Patriotic Schools. The Junta de Damas was concerned about their students' illiteracy; from that point on, the schools would teach pupils to read and write, along with basic elementary education. This curriculum began in 1792 at the San Martín school with only a few pupils and was then extended to all the schools.

In winter, lesson times were from 8:00 to noon in the morning and from 1:00 p.m. until sunset. In summer, they ran from 7:00 to noon and then from 3:00 p.m. until sunset. The schedule was adapted to the hours of light, in an attempt to maximize natural light in order to avoid the expense of oil for lamps.

Spinning with a wheel was a laborious operation that was taught in the Patriotic Schools. Its use required precise and complicated training, since it was operated by using a foot treadle and both hands simultaneously, and the spinner had to be extremely careful not to break or knot the fiber. She also had to keep the diameter of the yarn consistent and make sure it was not mixed with straw or other impurities, which would make the yarn uneven.[12]

Use of the spinning wheel in these schools represented a real innovation, since in Spain spinning had traditionally been done with a distaff. With a wheel, you could spin more and better in less time, although it had its drawbacks: the wheel was very noisy and, if not skillfully used, could destroy the fiber. Many adult spinners came to the Patriotic Schools in the early years in order to learn to use the spinning wheel properly.

The other disadvantage of spinning wheels was that they were expensive to buy, if imported from abroad, and repairs were costly.[13] To prevent serious malfunctions, the pupils were taught how to set up and adjust the wheel and how each of the parts functioned. In their exams, they had to demonstrate that they had mastered this material before being tested on spinning. With the arrival of textile machinery, the spinning wheel would become obsolete.

SUPERVISORS AND TEACHERS

In the first meeting of the Junta de Damas, on October 5, 1787, eight supervisors were appointed for the four Patriotic Schools, one per school and one substitute. This shows that they were ready and willing to start work at the schools immediately.

The most direct link between the Real Sociedad and the Patriotic Schools was through the supervisors. Each one was a member of the society commissioned by the Junta de Damas to direct and manage her assigned school. They were to visit frequently in order to make sure the rules were being followed, to encourage the teachers and pupils to work hard, to observe the teaching, and to correct any problems that might arise. The supervisor was to convey to the Junta de Damas any new developments or events relevant to the proper functioning of the school. At the end of the academic year, she was to present a list of expenses and income.

Likewise, she had to decide whether each of the students could move up to the following level and whether to nominate them as candidates for the award examination. She was in charge of admitting new pupils, who needed a report from their parish priest, and she was to create a registration card for each one listing her name, her parents' names, and her home address. This card was submitted to the teacher, who could not admit any pupils without this requirement. The teacher had to enter this data into the Admissions Book later.

The supervisors were required to keep a record of attendance at the schools, so they collected a list signed by each teacher every day, stating who had attended and whether they had been present the whole day. These lists were taken into account when prizes were being awarded.

It was also the supervisor's job to explain to the teacher how to fill out the School Book. This book contained instructions on the running of the school, as well as an inventory of equipment, raw material for textile manufacture, and the yarns spun by the girls. The supervisor also presented an overview of the school accounts and the girls' progress at the first board meeting every month.

Another of the supervisors' missions was controlling school expenditure; they had to be present when the raw materials and equipment required for classes were delivered, with a receipt, to the teacher, and they had to make sure that both the custodian and the school had enough raw material, spinning wheels, and equipment that lessons never had to be interrupted.

The supervisor also had to make sure that the custodian received the yarn spun by the girls punctually, with a note listing the weight and any wastage that might have occurred. It was natural that, during combing, spinning, and other procedures, some of the raw fiber was discarded. The supervisor had to have calculated how much was a normal loss, in order to catch anyone fraudulently pocketing fiber, if she noted any irregularity. Basically, she was in charge of the use and management of the raw material supplied.

The teacher and the supervisor were key to the running of the school. The teacher had to be an expert in the skills she was explaining, and know how to read, write, and do arithmetic since her skills and knowledge were rigorously tested by the Examinations Board. Reports were drawn up about teachers' and assistants' lives and conduct, as well as that of their husbands. They could be married, although being single or a widow was considered the ideal state. Assistantships were preferentially granted to pupils who were over fifteen years of age.

The teachers had to live in their schoolhouse, keeping it clean and tidy; each of them was expected to model cleanliness and to insure that their pupils were well-behaved and neatly dressed at school. Likewise, their treatment of the students was to be neither strict nor very kind, so that they would not be disrespectful or hate her. The teachers' salary was five *reales* a day. During school hours, the teacher was to remain on-site, devoted to her pupils.[14]

The teacher taught the girls how to prepare and spin the raw fibers. She trained them to generate an even thickness of yarn, since uneven yarn could not be used. For linen and hemp, she taught them the best way to process and comb the fibers so as to extract the tow from the bundle without wasting any, and then to spin and bleach it. For wool, the students learned to untangle, card, spin, and weave; and so on with other types of materials. In short, they were taught all the techniques necessary to make raw fiber into fabrics.

EXAMS AND PRIZES

To motivate learning by the students, prizes were awarded annually. The award ceremony was held at the General Meeting, which was open to the public and attended by well-known figures from the worlds of politics, literature, business, aristocracy, and the church. Since the prizes were announced in the *Gaceta de Madrid*, the official government newspaper, and awarded in a solemn public ceremony before a large crowd, they became an important way of publicizing what went on in the schools, as well as motivating the students to work harder.

There were three sets of prizes: first came the third class, then the second class, and lastly the top class. They involved a sum of money, from 20 to 150 *reales*, depending on the category, and a spinning wheel. Award candidates were named by the supervisors after they had listened to the teachers' reports.

The examining board, which functioned like a civil service exam, was governed by the statutes and was made up of two supervisors of the junta and various male members of the Matritense: two members of the Industry Commission, two from the Arts and Trade Commission, and two more from the Agriculture Commission; the director, the censor,[15] and the secretary. Candidates took tests that involved spinning with a wheel for a number of hours, sewing, embroidery, and other work as well as reading, writing, and arithmetic. The exam was held in one of the schools, generally in San Ginés for linen and cotton and San Andrés for woolen yarns.

Every four years, there was a reward for the dedication and work of assistants who were former school pupils, in the shape of a prize given to the longest serving. Teachers, meanwhile, were paid a quarter of the value of the prizes awarded to their pupils.[16] And given their meager salary of five *reales* a day, they were awarded a bonus of 320 *reales* a year before the annual prizes were given out. This bonus was awarded both to thank them for their work that year and to encourage them to apply themselves to their teaching.

Dowries were another type of prize used to encourage learning among the students at the schools. Bearing in mind that it was normal practice for many girls from poor or middle-income families to go into service in order to save up for their dowries, the prospect of winning one was a powerful encouragement to attend the schools.

Dowries were bestowed on pupils who had no unexcused absences and who had passed and been awarded prizes in the five subjects of reading, writing and arithmetic, Christian doctrine, sewing, yarn-making and embroidery.[17] This was another innovation introduced by the Junta de Damas, since dowries were no longer awarded by lottery or when funds permitted, or by donation, as in the past, but were now regulated in terms of how often they were awarded, what the amount was, and what the requirements were for winning one.

Two dowries of 1,100 *reales* were awarded per year, which was a small fortune in comparison with the paltry sums for the annual prizes. But only two schools were eligible at a time; the following year two others, and so on. Dowries were also awarded to assistants of the teachers.

In essence, the dowries functioned as promissory notes; in other words, a document was awarded to the winner, which she could present in exchange for cash along with her marriage certificate or proof of having become a nun. If she married, the husband received the money. Normally a long time passed, even years, between receiving the award and cashing it. This often led to complaints.

Thanks to the social role of dowries in terms of entering a convent or as an aid to a future marriage and incentive for the husband, whose economic burden was lightened, dowries transcended the private sphere and became part of the charitable grants network. Having dowries as prizes really motivated students at the schools to attend and work hard.

Other Schools Run by the Junta de Damas

In the period 1787–1820, besides the four Patriotic Schools, the Junta de Damas ran other popular feminine schools: the Embroidery School, the Lace-making School, the Society Education School, the Retiro School, the Queen's Flower School, the Colegio de Niñas de la Paz, and the Lancasterian School.

FIG. 14. María Josefa de Gálvez
y Valenzuela, Countess of
Castroterreño (Agustín Esteve),
ca. 1800. Fine Arts Museums of
San Francisco. Gift of Mr. and
Mrs. Chauncey McCormick.

These were all schools that specialized in teaching a particular subject or covering other charity education areas.

The Embroidery School (Escuela de Bordados) was approved by royal order on June 9, 1786. However, it did not open until almost three years later, since an appropriate location could not be found. It taught all kinds of embroidery with silk and metal threads, as well as embroidery on plain and quilted fabrics. The complete training course lasted four years.

To encourage learning and completing the course, pupils' daily earnings doubled every year, starting with the second. At the end of four years, they were qualified to be embroiderers in a workshop. And if they wanted to stay at the school, they could become skilled assistants, and were paid the true value of each piece they completed. Thus it was a school that offered employment to its graduates.[18]

The Embroidery School workshop also had the notable honor of having the king and queen as clients: "The many examples of all kinds of embroidery performed at the school are a good example of the reputation it has gained among the public, not to mention how flattering it is that this patriotic institution is honored by your majesties sending their outfits here to be embroidered" (Que las muchas obras de toda clase de bordados que se han ejecutado en la escuela manifiestan bien la aceptación que merece al público, sin contar con lo lisonjero que debe ser a este Cuerpo Patriótico la protección con que la honran vuestras majestades mandando bordar en ella sus vestidos).[19] Likewise, in 1793 Queen María Luisa de Parma donated a grant of 6,000 *reales* to the Countess of Torrepalma to be divided among the girls at the Embroidery School.[20]

The Colegio de Educación de la Sociedad was inaugurated on September 1, 1790. It was really a multidisciplinary institution, with a pedagogic mission that was broader than the Patriotic Schools', and aimed to admit both well-to-do and poor girls. The supervisor, the Countess of Torrepalma, was the driving force behind the school, and thanks to her, it thrived. It was supported by 1,500 *reales* a year from the Fondo General de Expolios y Vacantes (General Seizures and Vacancies Fund).[21]

There were three types of pupil at this school: day-girls, whose education was free, half-boarders, and boarders; the latter lived at the school and paid a fee. The school taught two types of needlework: white needlework and decorative needlework in colors, with two different teachers. The items produced by the students were kept to fund the school.

A male professor with an official teaching qualification taught the girls reading, writing, and arithmetic as well as refined manners and modesty.[22] He taught the boarders while his assistant taught the day-girls. A chaplain gave them lessons in Christian doctrine. They also learned hairstyling with a hairdresser; three dummies on pedestals were bought for them to practice on, since this skill was very valuable in employment as a lady's maid.

This school aimed to educate the perfect housewife, both as mistress of the house and as maid to a wealthy family. This yielded two benefits: working-class girls could easily find employment when they finished their training, and upper-class women would not have to hire maids who were ignorant, slovenly, and useless at many types of needlework.

The Lacemaking School (Escuela de Blondas), which taught only lacework, was sponsored by the Real Junta de Comercio y Moneda (Royal Board of Commerce and Money), which asked the Junta de Damas to take charge; the women accepted on condition that they could run it along the same lines as the Patriotic Schools. It was located in the Real Casa del Hospicio (the Madrid Workhouse) on June 21, 1790.[23]

The school functioned smoothly for two years, until it ran into problems when the teacher, Agustina Castilla, asked for sixty girls from the workhouse to be admitted and the council approved only thirty. Because of this clash, the teacher resigned and the school remained closed until November 1794, when it reopened with another teacher. This new phase was a short one, since the school closed down in the summer of 1796 for lack of funding.

The Retiro School, located in the entrance at the set of buildings of the Buen Retiro Palace, was set up on May 6, 1796; pupils were taught knitting, Spanish- and French-style needlework, basic literacy, and Christian doctrine. During the years it was open, attendance was very regular.

This school had an unusual privilege in that the teaching position was not filled by civil service examination but by direct nomination on the part of the Junta de Damas, which always appointed the most senior of the four teachers at the Patriotic Schools, unless she was not ideal or turned down the position. This unusual practice was established as a form of internal promotion among the teachers as merit recognition and an incentive for performing their work well since this position was the best paid.[24]

The Queen's Flower School, approved by royal order on December 13, 1796, under the patronage of Queen María Luisa de Parma, was founded on January 9, 1797. In order to be admitted, the pupils, aged twelve to fifteen, had to present their academic record. It was an elite school and as such had only a few, select pupils.

The purpose of this school was to teach girls how to make artificial flowers to meet the queen's decoration needs, since approximately 75 percent of the school's products were destined to be used by the sovereign. The rate of production and the queen's rate of consumption were high; for example, in the first six months of 1799, pupils made 713 bouquets, of which 550 were for the queen.

Another of its goals was to prevent large-scale importation of artificial flowers at Court. The Junta de Damas sought to avoid this expense when it suggested, in May 1793, including artificial flower-making in the curriculum at the San Andrés School. The Matritense responded to the proposal as follows: "Such work, being too delicate, should not be mixed with other types that are less so, and thus it demands a school of its own that the Society wishes to establish with the help of the Junta de Damas" (Que dicha elaboración, por ser demasiado delicada, no se debe mezclar con otras que no lo son tanto, y por eso exigen una escuela aparte que la Sociedad piensa establecer con las luces de la Junta de Señoras).[25]

The Colegio de Niñas de la Paz was an institution for foundling girls created by the Duchess of Feria in the late seventeenth century. It was designed for girls from the Inclusa orphanage aged seven and older who had not been adopted. On November 4, 1802, the Countess of Truillas took over as headmistress.[26] But, like other educational centers run by the Junta de Damas, there was no fixed budget, and funding was needed to keep up with costs. In order to raise funds, on March 9, 1805, the Countess of Truillas launched a subscription for benefactors to be able to contribute to the upkeep of the institution.[27]

Under the leadership of the Junta de Damas, pupils at the Colegio de Niñas de la Paz learned needlework, reading, and writing. On September 20, 1818, three two-ounce silver medals were awarded to girls who had won them in various examinations: one for knitting, one for needlework, and the third for reading and writing.[28]

Three years later, the Junta de Damas sought to add drawing to the school's curriculum. The junta put out a call for volunteer instructors among the members of the Sociedad Económica Matritense since they could not afford a teacher's salary. When no volunteer came forward, they decided to ask the government to fund the position since they felt that drawing was a very useful skill for girls.[29]

The Lancasterian School, or Mutual Teaching School, was the last educational institution founded in the period we are examining and was inaugurated by the Junta de Damas in 1819. It was based on Joseph Lancaster's method,[30] which was very much in vogue at the time. In order to reduce the cost of buying books and notebooks, educational novelties such as syllabification tables and blackboards were introduced. "A year after it was opened, there were 164 girls attending the Lancasterian School. It was still running when the Moyano Education Law was passed in 1857."[31]

End of the Educational Work of the Enlightenment Period

The economic downturn in 1808 made it very difficult for the Junta de Damas to obtain the raw materials necessary for the schools and to market the goods produced in them. These adverse circumstances were exacerbated by the meager and irregular funding they had been receiving, and the chaos generated by the war, which even their good financial management could not overcome. When all avenues for keeping the schools open had been exhausted, in February 1811, the junta made the painful decision to propose shutting the schools down temporarily.[32] This proposal was not accepted by the Matritense.

The dire situation got worse in 1812. As the war dragged on, sowing hunger, disease, and death, it was detrimental to the schools that still remained open. In June 1812, after several months with almost no funding, the situation became untenable. The junta therefore made the decision to close the Embroidery School, the Flower-making School, and the Patriotic Schools of San Luis (previously San Ginés) and San Andrés.

San Sebastián, San Martín, and the Society Education School continued in operation until May 5, 1813, when they closed because they could not pay their debts, which included the salaries of the teaching staff and the rent for the buildings. After the war ended, the Patriotic Schools never reopened.[33]

The members of the Junta de Damas had adopted enlightened, Spanish discourse and innovative ideas that came from Europe. And they affiliated themselves with the reformist politics of the government, particularly with all that concerned improving the condition of women. Nevertheless, despite having driven social and work-related changes in the situation of women at the end of the old regime, they have been overlooked by history.

The Junta de Damas was impelled to break through inertia and confront centuries-old gender prejudices to open their way in an environment in which women's abilities to carry out activities with responsibility and talent were strongly questioned, including within the very heart of the Madrid Economic Society. However, their work was recognized not only by manufacturers, who consulted them on certain innovations in textile techniques, but also by citizens who brought them their dilemmas; and their presence was required by institutions at educational events such as exams and the awarding of prizes. They were recognized as well by the Crown, which counted on the Damas to contribute to the solving of government problems such as reducing the costly importation of clothing, the excesses of luxury, the increase in extreme feminine poverty, and especially, to take charge of the education of young girls and young women from the most disadvantaged strata of society.

Unlike factory schools and schools run by private teachers, in which the female students acquired only the simple practice of textile skills, in the classrooms run by the Junta de Damas instruction was regulated and structured by a curriculum divided by grade or level, that included, besides handiwork, reading, writing, and arithmetic calculation. The acquired qualification had to be earned by examination; and, in addition, passing these tests constituted a new requirement to award the prized dowries. All of these constituted significant novelties in the school organization established by the Junta de Damas.

Therefore, the schools led by the Junta de Damas achieved an educational mission of the first order, which was to be pioneers of regulated feminine professional training. At the same time, they represented a parcel of public space governed by an association of women in the vanguard whose knowledge, organizational ability, and generous commitment successfully carried out these objectives: that poor and marginalized young women could enter the textile labor market with a specific qualification to work autonomously, at home, or as a skilled worker in the shop of a dressmaker, seamstress, or tailor, or in a factory, and earn their living. And the basic cultural education they received equipped them to integrate themselves into the beginnings of a new stage in the long road toward the social visibility of women and their labor.

NOTES

Essay translated by Catherine Jagoe.

1. "Primeras Letras" was the basic literacy of the time.

2. Fernández Quintanilla, "La Junta de Damas de Honor y Mérito," 71.

3. Reading and writing were not taught, and the pupils were illiterate.

4. Méndez Vázquez, *Formación profesional de las mujeres*, 240.

5. ARSEM, Expediente 133/14; see Martín-Valdepeñas Yagüe and Jaffe, *María Lorenza de los Ríos*, 382–83.

6. ARSEM, Expediente 118/2.

7. ARSEM, Expediente 133/14.

8. ARSEM, Expediente 120/2.

9. ARSEM, Expediente 120/2.

10. Its length did not coincide with an academic year.

11. This last requirement was needed in order to produce fabrics.

12. Imbille and Sarralde, "Informe sobre la utilidad del torno," 207.

13. In order to obtain the spinning wheels at a more economical price, the society contracted with an official spinning-wheel maker who made excellent wheels at a more reasonable price.

14. *Instrucción para las escuelas patrióticas.*

15. The censor was one of the five officials who ran the Matritense and held the most important position after the director. He had to make rulings in procedural matters and ensured that the society's statutes were observed and that every member complied with his obligations. He also had to audit the treasurer's accounts.

16. ARSEM, Expediente 120/2.

17. ARSEM, Expediente 202/19.

18. ARSEM, Expediente 94/14.

19. ARSEM, Expediente 87/15.

20. Martín-Valdepeñas Yagüe, "La reina María Luisa de Parma," 753.

21. ARSEM, Expediente 131/7.

22. This would be a teacher with an official certification from the College of Primary Education (El Colegio Académico del Noble Arte de Primeras Letras), overseen directly by the Council of Castile. It was the official institution that educated and certified primary school teachers at the time.

23. ARSEM, Expediente 120/2.

24. Minutes of meeting. March 7, 1796. ARSEM, Libro A/56/4.

25. ARSEM, Expediente 125/20.

26. ARSEM, Expediente 194/6.

27. ARSEM, Expediente 194/6.

28. ARSEM, Expediente 262/19.

29. ARSEM, Expediente 292/16.

30. This consisted of using exceptional pupils who were trained as assistant teachers and called monitors, who would help teach their classmates. This system allowed a single teacher to attend to many students at once, in order to create more primary education schools for the less fortunate with the least possible expense.

31. Martín-Valdepeñas Yagüe, "El eco del saber," 102.

32. ARSEM, Expediente 212/19.

33. See Martín-Valdepeñas Yagüe, "Ilustrados, afrancesados y liberales," 351.

Practicing Social Activism

The Spaces of Women's Charity

ELIZABETH FRANKLIN LEWIS

The Royal Economic Society of Madrid and Gendered Spaces of Enlightenment

Madrid in the eighteenth century was a place of new, more open spaces where people gathered, interacted, and exchanged ideas. There were newly constructed public streets, parks, and buildings—from the redesigned Paseo del Prado, and the Royal Retiro park that was opened to the public in summer and fall, to newly constructed palaces and private homes that appeared throughout the city. Gatherings among the cultural and intellectual elite at salon-style tertulias were hosted in private homes, frequently by women, including María Josefa Alfonso Pimentel y Téllez-Girón (Countess-Duchess of Benavente and Duchess of Osuna), María del Pilar Teresa Cayetana de Silva y Álvarez de Toledo (Duchess of Alba), María Francisca de Sales Portocarrero y Zúñiga (Countess of Montijo), and María Lorenza de los Ríos y Loyo (Marquise of Fuerte-Híjar).[1] People also gathered at the meetings of the newly formed institutions of learning and debate, such as the Real Academia Española (founded in 1713 and first housed in the palace of the Marquis of Villena) or the Real Sociedad Económica Matritense de Amigos del País, which met at Madrid's town hall, the Casa de la Villa.[2] These were some of the many spaces of "sociability" in eighteenth-century Spain, a term that referred to the polite interaction among elites considered a hallmark of "civilized" cultures.

In Spain, as occurred throughout Enlightenment Europe, these new spaces of sociability brought together private individuals in the public sphere. Jürgen Habermas famously studied the emergence during the eighteenth century of a bourgeois public sphere in *The Structural Transformation of the Public Sphere.*[3] For Habermas, the public sphere, which encompassed literary and artistic production as well as politics, was intimately tied to the private domain of the family. Speaking of the interconnectedness of the public and the private, Habermas points to the architecture of bourgeois homes where public and private coexisted: "the line between private and public sphere extended right through the home. The privatized individuals stepped out of the intimacy of their living rooms and into the public sphere of the salon, but the one was strictly complementary to the other."[4] While Habermas did not study women's participation in the public sphere much beyond their roles as readers, feminist scholars such as Joan Landes and Dena Goodman have pointed out eighteenth-century French women's important roles in the public sphere, especially in the context of the salon.[5] Speaking of women's presence in both public and private spaces, James Van Horn Melton speaks of the ambiguity of their participation: "The belief that civil society depended on women as a moral and civilizing force rested on notions of sexual difference that could justify banishing them from the political arena. But in sanctioning women's activities as readers, writers, and sociable beings, it also gave them tools and venues for challenging that exclusion."[6] In Spain, women were readers, writers, and sociable beings too. Increasingly, Spanish women were not only found in public spaces of interaction and exchange, but their presence was even considered proof of societal progress "to the point that women were used as both positive and negative symbols of cultural civilization and the new values of capitalist commerce."[7] Nonetheless, even in the eyes of the most ardent male supporters of women's intellectual abilities and advocates of their physical presence in spaces of enlightened sociability and intellectual exchange, women's place was still primarily in the home, and limited to their domestic roles as wives and mothers.[8]

At the heart of the hotly debated controversy over women's admission as members of the Real Sociedad Económica Matritense was the question of their participation in these public spaces of enlightened sociability. For many *ilustrados* (enlightened men) a woman's place should be limited to the protective domestic space of her home, outside of which she posed a moral danger. This became the basis of arguments against the acceptance of women into the Madrid Economic Society. Even when the controversy over admission of women to the Economic Society was resolved with the creation of the separate all-female Junta de Damas de Honor y Mérito, new questions arose. What public role could intelligent women play in the shaping of society, and were the spaces where they could acceptably act and speak? In the first two decades after its creation, the Junta de Damas pursued charitable projects and social activism. The socias (members) of the junta themselves chose to leave their comfortable and exclusive domestic settings to traverse the streets and *barrios* of Madrid in order to work with poor women and children; they used a language of sentimentality and domesticity to describe the spaces where they worked.

The Junta de Damas was established in 1787 by royal order of King Carlos III after much debate over female membership in the all-male Economic Society of Madrid. Their membership was formed by upstanding aristocratic or wealthy women—countesses, duchesses, and a few untitled wealthy women— many of them wives, daughters, or sisters of the male members of the Madrid Economic Society. One opponent to women's presence in the Economic Society was member Francisco Cabarrús, a naturalized Spanish citizen born in France. For Cabarrús, a woman's place, especially for an aristocratic woman, was in purely domestic spaces. Outside of these spaces, says Cabarrús, women represent a real threat to morality—their own, and the men's with whom they come in contact: "I am not ignorant of the sophisticated and pleasant names with which they attempt to masquerade among us adultery, corruption, vulgarity and the abandonment of all decency" (no ignoro los nombres cultos y agradables con que procuran disfrazarse entre nosotros el adulterio, la corrupción, la grosería y el abandono de toda decencia).[9] Mónica Bolufer points out the echoes here of Jean-Jacques Rousseau, exhibited in the fear of women's damaging social influence when not controlled.[10] Like Rousseau's praise of his domestic angel Sophie in *Émile ou De l'éducation* (1762), Cabarrús also goes on to praise his idea of the model lady, *madrileñas* (ladies of Madrid):

> [P]erhaps fashion and its supporters will prevail over nature, which subjected women to modesty and reserve; [...] Madrid does not lack illustrious examples of these virtues. I have seen so many times, and with such veneration! such enthusiasm! a lady who after distributing all the hours of her day between religion and Nature, was at night surrounded by her mother, her siblings, her husband and her tender young children (often nursing one of them herself): On her face shone an innocent happiness, the prize and companion of virtue. [...] Do we propose that this woman, and others like her, abandon this true dignity for the pleasure of coming to our assemblies?[11]

Women are at the center of Cabarrús's idealized notion of the private domestic sphere, and to think of removing them from this space is to take away their dignity.

Josefa Amar y Borbón, herself already a member of the Economic Society of Zaragoza, opposed these views with her own arguments about where women could and should interact with men. In her *Discurso en defensa del talento de las mujeres* in 1786, Amar explains the problem that idealized feminine domestic space posed for real women, since: "Women know they cannot aspire to any employment or public position, and that their imagination cannot extend beyond the walls of a house or a convent" (Saben ellas que no pueden aspirar a ningún empleo o recompensa pública; que sus ideas no tienen más extensión que las paredes de una casa o de un Convento).[12] Later Amar describes the society's refusal to accept women into their ranks in spatial terms:

> And none is greater than the new dividing wall between them and the sanctuary that people intend to erect today; and what we are talking about here is more than a sanctuary or a dividing wall. It is the Madrid Economic Society, which is reluctant to admit women into its illustrious assembly. Perhaps it is those who call themselves the Friends of the Nation who will be able to keep them out? Perhaps women are spies, scattered around the kingdom and telling outsiders about the work being done for their benefit? Or are the matters discussed in the Economic Societies so mysterious and intricate that only men can understand them?[13]

The Economic Society was a figurative wall constructed to divide men and women, an obstacle preventing qualified women from recognition for their abilities. The sarcasm with which Amar describes overreaction to women's presence in the Economic Society is certainly in response to Cabarrús's charges of moral corruption. Amar's use of the term "friends of the country" (amigos del país) to refer both to the Madrid Economic Society itself (Real Sociedad Económica Matritense de Amigos del País) and more specifically to Cabarrús, who had claimed that women cannot be "friends of the country, when they are not even friends of their own homes, and can they be good citizens if they defy their obligations as mothers and wives?" (amigas del País las que no lo son de sus casas? ¿y buenas ciudadanas las que desdeñan las obligaciones de madre y esposa?).[14] Amar y Borbón maintains that women can leave their homes, they can mix with men in the public spaces of the Economic Society, and that they have important and unique contributions to make as dedicated female citizens, *amigas del país* (women friends of the country). One area where she thought women could make an important contribution was in the textile industry, which she knew was a pet project of the Madrid Economic Society.[15] Josefa Amar y Borbón would later be an honorary member the newly formed Junta de Damas, a group that would build upon Amar's call for women's active participation in the economic and cultural improvement of Spain in the public spaces of work and education.

Enacting Social Change from Behind the Enlightenment's Dividing Walls: Madrid's Patriotic Schools for Girls

While women were not admitted as members to the Madrid Economic Society, as Amar and others had wished, the women of the newly formed Junta de Damas were able to achieve some of the influence and recognition that Amar hoped for in her essay in defense of women, despite the "dividing wall" that she argued against. Many of the elite women who formed the membership of the junta were already recognized cultural and intellectual leaders in their own right, including women like the Countess of Montijo, the Countess-Duchess of Benavente, and the Marquise of Fuerte-Híjar who organized and hosted the aforementioned tertulias in their homes. (See map, p. 207, A and E.) Now, as members of the newly formed Junta de Damas, these women left their refined and protected homes, traveling across Madrid to gather for their meetings, and worked directly with poor women and children at the various locations of their projects across the city. On October 5, 1787, the Junta de Damas held its first assembly in the same public space where the Economic Society met: Madrid's city hall, the Casa de la Villa (see map, p. 207, 1), where the women thereafter met on Friday afternoons.[16] Paula de Demerson—in her study of the junta's long-time secretary, the Countess of Montijo—emphasizes the active participation of the almost fifty members.[17] In addition to attendance at official meetings, each woman of the junta also took a leadership role in one of the projects sponsored by the group, and she traveled to the various locations across the city to oversee the operations of these charitable works.

Their first project, assigned to them by the Economic Society, was the running of the trade schools for young girls—the Escuelas Patrióticas. Established in 1776 following ideas set out first by economist Bernardo Ward in 1750 and later presented to the Madrid Economic Society in a *memoria* by founding member Pedro de Campomanes,[18] the society sought through these schools to develop a more vibrant textile industry in Spain that utilized the po-

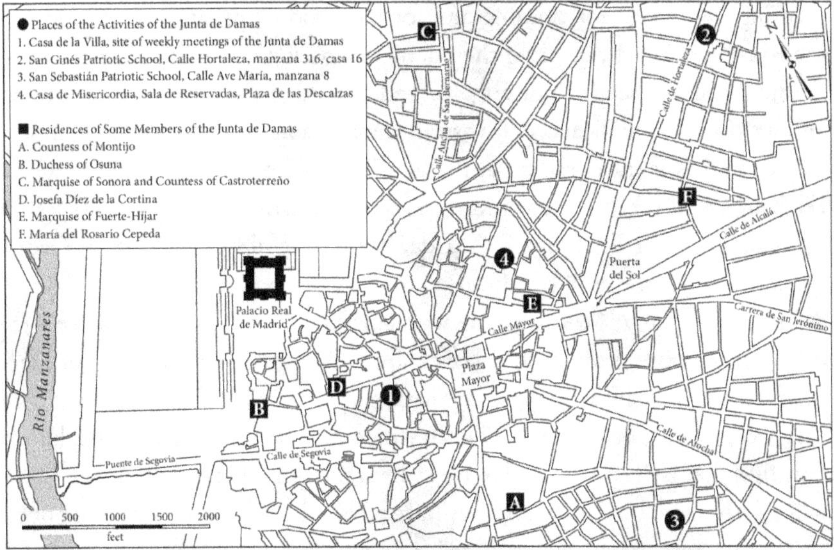

The places, activities, and residences of the women of the Junta de Damas (Map of Madrid by Tomás López, 1800). David Rumsey Map Collection. Stanford University. Art design by Mary Lee Eggart.

tential workforce found in working-class women, while at the same time it reduced poverty and idleness.[19] Amar y Borbón had mentioned the textile trade in her "Defence" as an issue about which women had special expertise. Rebecca Haidt studies the interplay among different classes of women around textiles and clothing, especially as observed in the multiple images of working-class traditional Spanish *majas* and upper-middle-class, French-influenced *petimetras* as representatives of working and bourgeois women.[20] While the interaction between the elite women of the Junta de Damas and their charges at the Patriotic Schools was quite different from the visual and theatrical representations of relations between *majas* and *petimetras*, both the fictional texts that Haidt studies and the historical descriptions of the work of the junta found in newspapers and official reports reveal that eighteenth-century women of diverse classes interacted in public spaces.

Each of the four schools assigned to the junta—San Ginés, San Sebastián (see map, p. 207, 2 and 3), San Andrés, and San Martín—served working-class neighborhoods in Madrid. Members of the junta served as curadoras—two per school. Their duties included frequent visits to the schools themselves; interviewing, hiring, and supervising instructors; overseeing expenses; implementing new plans for training and for the production and distribution of their products; and reporting their activities back to the junta and the Economic Society. The girls not only learned a trade, they learned some reading and writing as well. María del Rosario Cepeda, one of the original members of the junta, was the curadora of the San Ginés school,[21] located on the Calle Hortaleza and serving the working-class neighborhoods of Barquillo, Santa Bárbara, and San Ildefonso.[22] Cepeda, herself a child prodigy from Cádiz, spoke of the importance of education to the working-class girls in her *Elogio de la Reina* of 1797: "Those young women, with the education they have received, have more pride in themselves, are not content to hastily accept marriage without consideration and calculation of its domestic convenience, where they would likely be in a state of uselessness, and abandoned; their husbands now find themselves obligated to treat them with more respect, their children will benefit from the education they have received, and in sum they will not be at risk to resort to begging or disorder, and we must consider them as one of the supports of public happiness" (aquellas jóvenes con la educación que han recibido se estiman más a sí mismas, no se acomodan a colocarse en matrimonio sin muchos miramientos, y cálculos de conveniencia doméstica, de que prescindirían en el estado de inútiles, y abandonadas; sus maridos se ven obligados a tratarlas con mayor estimación; sus hijos participarán por necesidad de la educación que ellas recibieron; y en suma aquellas mismas mujeres, que estaban en riesgo de incurrir en la mendicidad, o en el desorden, nos vemos precisados a considerarlas como uno de los apoyos de la felicidad pública).[23]

Like Cabarrús, Cepeda also describes an idealized conception of women's central influence on the happiness and success of domestic life, but unlike Cabarrús, Cepeda argues that education is the key to both private and public happiness. Cepeda's description of the benefits of her work with these working-class girls stresses the values of an enlightened reformist agenda as she thought it applied to women. Cepeda and her fellow socias of the junta argued that education provided these young girls a brighter economic future and more autonomy over their own destiny, giving them the choice of a suitable marriage. In addition, education also gave women power and influence in the family, and their husbands were obliged to treat them with respect. Women's influence in their families in turn would reduce social disorder, increase productivity, and ultimately these educated women would become the basis of public happiness.

These *elogios* were an expected annual duty that fell to one member of the junta each year. They were presented at the Madrid Economic Society's public awards ceremony and subsequently published, typically by one of two principal Madrid printing houses, Ibarra or Sancha.[24] The essays were delivered in praise of Queen María Luisa, who was a generous benefactor of the junta's charitable projects. Although each *elogio* followed a predictable formula in its praise of the queen, these essays also take advantage of the public venues where they were presented to tout the efforts and successes of the Junta de Damas.[25] The Countess of Torrepalma also spoke of the Escuelas Patrióticas in her *Elogio* of 1794, highlighting the contrasting spaces that the women of the junta (and the girls of the escuelas) negotiated. On the one hand, there was the queen in her Royal Palace, an elegant and modern building that had been recently reconstructed after a fire destroyed the former residence of King Felipe V, and on the other hand are the schools, which were located across the city, often in simple houses located in the working-class neighborhoods they served. Torrepalma paints an image of Queen María Luisa as a domestic angel[26] in Rousseauian terms: "Let us follow Luisa to her palace, where we see her surrounded by her loving children; let us examine the care with which she oversees their education" (Sigamos a Luisa a su Palacio, veámosla rodeada de sus amables Hijos, examinamos el cuidado con que vela sobre su educación).[27] Later Torrepalma addresses the girls of the escuelas:

> Join me you innocent creatures, in the happy knowledge that your Queen reaches out from the heights of her throne to find you in your schools, she learns of your progress and dresses in the fruits of your labors, she spreads news about your advancements, and she extends her generosity and her protection and support. [. . .] When you reflect upon the kindness of her majesty who has been able to level out the immense distance between the Throne to your poor room, so that she may learn your name, your achievements, your conduct and the results of your work, who wouldn't lift her hands and prayers to Heaven to beseech God to rain blessing on your benefactor and mother![28]

Newspapers like the *Gaceta de Madrid* reported on the public appearances of women from the junta and their work, for example a notice on April 14, 1789, reporting on a public celebration of the Economic Society in which women from the junta presented the handiwork of their young pupils, after which, "The Society and everyone present applauded the notable effort and care put into these lessons" (la Sociedad y todos los que se hallaban presentes aplaudieron el notorio esmero y cuidado que emplean en estas enseñanzas).[29]

Another announcement in this same newspaper advertised a vacancy in the teaching staff of the school of embroidery. The junta invited "the teachers who wish to take a qualifying exam will present themselves [. . .] at the home of Doña María del Rosario Cepeda" (Los maestros o maestras que quieran sujetarse al examen se presentarán [. . .] en casa de la Sra. Doña María del Rosario Cepeda).[30] In this case, Cepeda opened her private residence as a public space to conduct the business of the junta in its endeavors to improve the education of the girls of the Escuelas Patrióticas. (See map, p. 207, F.)

Crossing Gendered Spaces of Contamination: The Real Asociación de Caridad de Señoras and Women's Prisons

One of the arguments against the admission of women into the Madrid Economic Society had been that, outside of their protected and controlled domestic spaces, they posed a moral threat to themselves and others. However, members of the Junta de Damas did not shy away from leaving the protection of their fine homes. They traveled about the city to interact in the few spaces sanctioned by the Economic Society for their work—the Casa de la Villa for their meetings, and the Patriotic Schools for their work educating young girls. But they also took on special projects where they entered spaces of moral and physical contamination. In February of 1788, just a few months after the formation of the junta, several members (notably led by the junta's secretary, the Countess of Montijo herself) banded together to extend aid to female prisoners in Madrid, at the behest of Father Pedro Portillo. Although a separate organization, these women, who called themselves the Real Asociación de Caridad de Señoras, were closely tied to the Junta de Damas as most were members of both organizations, and both groups were united in their aims to alleviate suffering and to encourage education, work, and morality. The female inmates that they assisted in three jails in Madrid—the Cárcel de la Corte, the Cárcel de Villa, and the Galera prison—were jailed for crimes such as prostitution, theft, or infanticide. They were housed in male prisons in separate holding cells that were filthy and full of sickness, hunger, and misery.[31]

An announcement of the new project, titled "Instituto piadoso" (Pious institute), appeared in June 1788 in the *Memorial literario* newspaper: "It has as its purpose to make the fallen women found in prisons useful, to inspire fear of God and love of work; to console these women in their imprisonment, and teach them tasks proper to their sex, among them those that would be most useful for them to support themselves once they regain their freedom. [. . .] For this purpose the ladies of this organization visit the prisons every Sunday and on holidays, spending all afternoon on these holy and useful activities, and offering their charity to serve these poor prisoners in their greatest afflictions" (Tiene por objeto el hacer útiles las mujeres perdidas qué se hallan en las Cárceles, y en la Galera, el inspirarlas el temor de Dios, y el amor al trabajo; el consolarlas en sus prisiones, y el enseñarlas aquellas labores propias de su sexo, y entre ellas las que sean más útiles para que puedan ganar con que vivir en recobrando su libertad. [. . .] Para esto, las Señoras asociadas asisten todos los Domingos y fiestas enteras a las prisiones, emplean toda la tarde en estos sanos ejercicios, y extienden su caridad hasta servir a las pobres presas en sus mayores aflicciones).[32]

The Countess of Montijo was one of the vocal proponents of this new project. She and a group of nine other women, assisted by Father Portillo, gained the support of King Carlos III's chief minister, the Count of Floridablanca, for their plan to work with the female prisoners.[33] An article in *Semanario de Agricultura y Artes* describes the reaction of the ladies upon a visit to the prison, contrasting the misery found there—the dirty and poorly clad inmates piled into a cold, smelly room—to the comfort that the ladies of the Asociación de Caridad de Señoras brought to them:

> although the first sight of that mansion of misery caused them horror, their charity did not waiver, but rather continuing their visits, they came to gain the confidence of the prisoners and convince them to improve their ways. They conversed familiarly with the inmates, in order to inspire in them a love of virtue and of honest work; they taught them to read; and seeing that the origin of their disgrace was idleness and misery, the ladies had them learn various labors that could occupy them for their own usefulness. In this way their ingenious virtue and perseverance changed the face of that abode of stench, converting it into a house of good customs, cleanliness, decency and love of work.[34]

The asociación brought order, cleanliness, and decency to what had been a place of disorder and disease—a "mansion of misery" (mansión de la miseria) and "abode of stench" (morada de la hediondez).

Two poems by male authors in praise of the asociación emphasize the Enlightenment values it promoted. A "Canción heroica," dedicated to the ladies of the junta and the asociación, praises the trades that they taught the incarcerated women. The author speaks of the prison as a sort of purgatory, from which, with the help of the ladies from the junta, the female inmates are able to redeem themselves: "The house known as the *Galera* / Destiny of delinquent women / [...] That was once, like Hell / the perpetual home of the impenitent / Is now a Purgatory of good souls" (La Casa conocida por Galera, / Destino de mujeres delincuentes, / [...] Donde, como el Infierno, siempre era / Continua habitacion de impenitentes, / Ya es como Purgatorio de almas buenas).[35] This author describes the domesticating effects that learning a useful trade has on these women, as a metamorphosis that turns the "lazy and terrible / [...] desperate and irascible" (holgazanas y terribles / [...] desesperadas e irascibles)[36] into honorable hard-working women who "will be loved by their country / and can teach their female neighbors / so they may avoid ruin" (Estarán en su Patria muy queridas, / Y podrán, enseñando á su vecina, / Conmutar en su bien la anterior ruina).[37] The second poem is an ode dedicated to the asociación for its creation of a Sala de Reservadas, a room reserved for unmarried pregnant women. The author, Joseph de la Olmeda y León, speaks of the innocent children saved by this action, future "citizens" whose lives are now protected.[38]

Junta and asociación members also spoke publicly and privately of their activities in the women's prisons. In December of 1799, member Josefa Díez de la Cortina, in her publicly delivered *Elogio*, praises the queen's support of all of the junta's endeavors—the schools, the Montepío de Hilazas (which helped graduates of the schools obtain production materials), the Inclusa, the prisons, and the Sala de Reservadas. Díez de la Cortina describes the prisons after receiving the "powerful protection" of the queen: "the prisons of the capital saw the merciful light of charity enter their dark and melancholy enclosures; the unhappy prisoners sentenced for their disorder heard the consoling voice of compassion; their idle hands found the opportunity and the means to be useful, and their wayward hearts motivation to change" (las cárceles de la capital vieron entrar en sus oscuros y melancólicos recintos la luz piadosa de la caridad; las infelices conducidas a los encierros por sus desórdenes oyeron la voz consoladora de la compasión; sus manos ociosas hallaron ocasión y medios para utilizarse, y sus corazones extraviados tiempo y motivos para corregirse).[39] The queen had paid for furnishing the three rooms reserved for expectant mothers—one for mothers from distinguished families, a second for "honorable" women able to pay for their pension, and a third for poor women.[40]

The Marquise of Fuerte-Híjar, in a letter to the Marquis of Almenara dated March 31, 1811, spoke candidly of their work with expectant mothers. In it, she requests assistance for a new home for poor expectant mothers, whom she calls "mis pobres *reservadas*" (my poor *reservadas*). She asks for a room "big or small, or even medium sized," in the Casa de Misericordia (see map, p. 207, 4), a hospital established in the sixteenth century near the Descalzas Reales Monastery. She begs him to help her find the space she needs, as she dramatically describes recent notice of fifteen pregnant girls, "whose parents will slit their throats, forgetting that they did the same when they were young" (si lo saben sus padres, las degüellan, sin acordarse que ellos, en sus tiempos, hicieron otro tanto).[41]

From *Mansión de la Miseria* to a Home of Hope: The Inclusa Orphanage

The Madrid Inclusa was an orphanage whose origins dated to 1567. Most of the children in the Inclusa were *expósitos:* "illegitimate" births, who not only brought shame to their families, but until 1794 were not even recognized as citizens by the state.[42] Joan Sherwood describes the original Inclusa building and neighborhood, located just off the Puerta del Sol at the center of the city, an easy-to-find location for both desperate mothers and the wet nurses employed to feed the infants: "It was four or five stories high, of brick. [...] The windows were barred with iron grille work and embellished with small balconies, and the roof was of red tile. [...] The doorway opened into an open courtyard, with a well or fountain where infants were often surreptitiously left."[43] Its administration had changed hands over the years and, by the end of the eighteenth century, it was being directed by Gonzalo José Vilches (member of the Consejo de Castilla) and administered by three priests. Conditions in the Inclusa were terrible, and in 1789 the Countess of Montijo addressed the junta to advocate that they take over operations: "The sad and miserable fortune of almost all of the homes for illegitimate children in the kingdom, where statistically more than three-fourths of the children perish for lack of care and assistance, is something that needs immediate attention by the Junta, which can employ its care, fulfilling its obligations to religion and the state" (La triste y miserable suerte de casi todas las casas de niños expósitos del reino, en donde por cálculos seguros perecen anualmente más de las tres cuartas partes de los que entran, es un objeto que merece la primera atención de la Junta, y en que puede emplear sus cuidados con lo que debe a la Religión y a la patria).[44]

She goes on to say that, although it would seem that the Economic Society should handle this, she believes the women of the junta to be better suited to the project: "That compassion, that natural affection for children, a certain patience, the pleasure that we take in holding them, caring for them, all of this seems to be telling us that children are the duty we women have been assigned and we should take care of them, and that while men with their intelligence and talents govern Republics [. . .] we are given the sweet care of those innocent creatures, formed from their beginning for us, and who will someday be the instrument of public happiness" (Aquella compasión, aquel natural cariño y agrado para los niños, una cierta paciencia, el gusto mismo que tenemos en acariciarlos, en cuidarlos, todo parece decirnos que los niños son la porción que se nos ha confiado; que a nosotras toca su cuidado, y que, mientras los hombres con sus luces y talentos cultivados gobiernan las Repúblicas [. . .] nos dejan a nosotras el dulce cuidado de aquellas inocentes criaturas cuyo corazón, formado desde su principio por nosotras, ha de ser algún día el instrumento de la pública felicidad).[45]

Although she saw women's motherly role as a natural fit with the supervision of the Inclusa, she and her fellow members also approached the problems of the orphanage very methodically, first requesting to inspect the facilities and examine the books, and later forming a plan for the supervision and management of its operations, which it finally took over in 1799.[46]

In 1801, the junta moved operations of the orphanage to a new building on the Calle del Soldado—today the Calle Barbieri in the Chueca neighborhood—and Calle Libertad. (See Fig. 15.)[47] In the coming years, the junta also implemented new hygiene practices, more staff and doctors to care for often very sick infants, and better feeding practices, which drastically lowered mortality rates.[48] In 1803, the Duchess of Osuna, president of the junta, spoke of their successes in the Inclusa in her annual report, as she had done in prior years:

The Inclusa this past year has undergone such progress and obtained such considerable assistance that we must double down on our hopes to see it in that state to which the Junta aspires. [. . .] Because of the knowledge that the Junta has acquired and continues to acquire daily on important topics, its tireless work and efforts, and the honor and selflessness that has gained public admiration, who knows if someday they might put all of the *expósitos* in the kingdom under our care? And who is capable of calculating the service that can be given to religion, the state and humanity in these circumstances?[49]

A new building and equipment, better trained staff, the care of doctors and surgeons, and the implementation of the latest scientific and nutritional knowledge of the time, all were attempts to lower the abysmal mortality rate of the infants.[50] María Josefa de Gálvez y Valenzuela, the Countess of Castroterreño (see map, p. 207, C),[51] spoke of these improvements in her *Elogio* of the queen delivered in 1801: "Ninety-six percent of the infants died before the pity of the Queen put them in the maternal care of the Junta. This horrible mortality rate was progressively lowered due to the improvements made: in the last month the rate has lowered to 42 percent" (Noventa y seis niños por ciento morían antes de que la piedad de la Reina los pusiese al cuidado maternal de la Junta: esta mortandad horrible fue progresivamente cediendo a las nuevas mejoras: en el mes último bajó a cuarenta y dos).[52] Castroterreño goes on to say that, for the children of the Inclusa, what had been a "place of negligence and filth" would now be a "beloved house."[53]

The Countess of Castroterreño's cousin, dramatist María Rosa de Gálvez, wrote a poem praising the women of the junta and Castroterreño for their

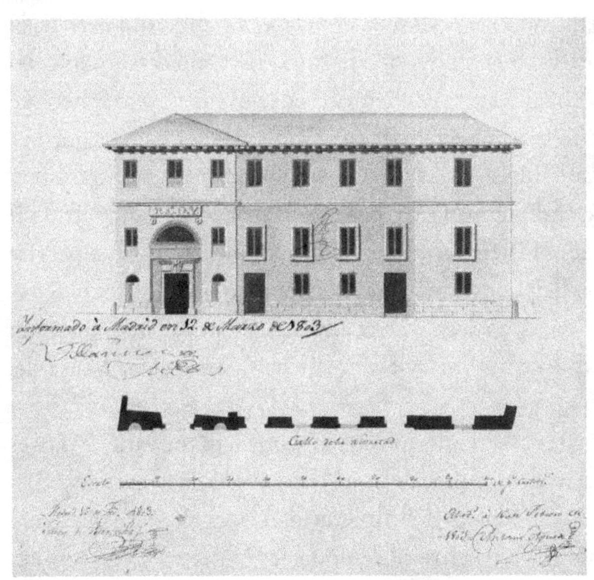

FIG. 15. Real Casa de la Inclusa at Libertad Street, 1803. Ayuntamiento de Madrid. Archivo Histórico de la Villa de Madrid.

efforts in the Inclusa. Similar to the description of the Galera prison by the writer in the *Semanario de agricultura y artes* as a "mansión de la miseria" is Gálvez's description of the Inclusa before the women of the junta took charge as a "mansion where defenseless and unfortunate children wail; / there horrible evils oppress them with misery" (mansión adonde gimen / los desvalidos niños desgraciados; / allí con la miseria los oprimen).[54] Gálvez later calls the Inclusa an "infeliz albergue" (unhappy shelter). But the misery of the past has been rectified, and Gálvez describes the Inclusa now as a happier place where the women of the Junta de Damas triumph in their practice of charity and social activism—"There my sex triumphs" (Allí triunfa mi sexo), Gálvez exclaims.[55]

Public Domestic Spaces for Women's Social Activism

Since the publication of Jürgen Habermas's *The Structural Transformation of the Public Sphere*, scholars have disagreed over the extent to which women were included or excluded from his notion of the transition from feudalism to liberalism through the bourgeois exchange of ideas and the creation of public opinion. In the Spanish context, Mónica Bolufer maintains that we cannot make a clear distinction between public and private realms, and neither can public and private be divided by gender, but rather that we must view these spaces with nuance: "It is more appropriate to understand these distinct spaces of sociability, in different ways for each one, as between public and private, in the social realm."[56] Clearly the women of the Junta de Damas were not deterred by the results of the debate over their presence in the public sphere. In their organization and in the projects that they took on—either assigned to them or that they pursued themselves—they sought out information, advocated for the economic and political support that they needed, and left their homes to go to the places of their social activism to implement and supervise the improvements that they hoped to achieve. They also brought their activism into their private homes, as seen in the advertisement for instructors in the Escuelas Patrióticas asked to interview at the private home of María del Rosario Cepeda.

In another context, Rebecca Haidt shows that women of the various classes in Madrid were as interwoven in their lives as the textiles they exchanged— their comings and goings as well as their migrations from the provinces and between *barrios* (neighborhoods) crossed boundaries of decency. In a similar way, the women of the Junta de Damas de Honor y Mérito were not afraid to leave their homes, crisscrossing Madrid to interact with poor women, children, and female convicts and expanding the boundaries of acceptable spaces for women beyond their private residences. The language of sentimentality and domesticity, but also of Enlightenment patriotism, that they used to describe their work in these places where they interacted communicated real improvements created in the lives of women and children and represented an expansion of these elite women's gendered domestic role. Instead of restricting women behind a "wall of division," the women of the Junta de Damas expanded opportunities for both working-class and wealthy women of the late Enlightenment period, transforming the former "mansions of misery" of orphanages and prisons into places of education, health, and reform—the spaces of the "triumph" of their sex.

NOTES

1. Fernández Quintanilla, *La mujer ilustrada*, 29–43.

2. Aguilar Piñal, *Madrid en tiempos del "mejor alcalde"*; see vol. 1, *El nuevo Madrid*, 133–89; vol. 3, *La económica matritense*, 287–341; and vol. 4, *Cultura académica*, 177–230.

3. First published in 1962; English translation in 1989.

4. Habermas, *The Structural Transformation*, 45.

5. Landes, *Women and the Public Sphere*; Goodman, *The Republic of Letters*.

6. Melton, *The Rise of the Public*, 15.

7. Bolufer Peruga, "Del Salón a la asamblea," 132. This and all translations from Spanish are my own.

8. Pérez Cantó and Mó Romero, "Las mujeres en los espacios," 45.

9. *Memorial literario*, T. VIII, XXIX, May 1786: 74–85 (quote on 79–80).

10. Bolufer Peruga, "Mujeres y hombres," 159.

11. "¿acaso la moda y sus partidarios prevalecerán contra la voz de la naturaleza, que sujetó a las mujeres a la modestia y al pudor; [. . .] Madrid no carece de ejemplos ilustres de estas virtudes. He visto varias veces, ¡y con qué veneración! ¡con qué entusiasmo! una Señora, que después de distribuir todas las horas del día entre la religión y la naturaleza, estaba por la noche rodeada de su madre, de sus hermanos, de su marido y de sus hijos aun tiernos, criando por sí misma al uno de ellos: en su semblante reinaba la inocente alegría, premio y compañera de la virtud. [. . .] ¿Acaso propondremos a esta y a las demás Señoras de su especie abandonar esta verdadera dignidad por el gusto de venir a nuestras asambleas?" *Memorial literario*, T. VIII, XXIX, May 1786: 80.

12. Amar y Borbón, "Discourse in Defence of the Talents," 99.

13. "Ninguno mayor, que el nuevo santuario o muro de división que se intenta formar en el día; más que santuario o muro de división es del que hablamos. Este es la Sociedad económica de Madrid la cual duda admitir mujeres en su ilustre Asamblea. ¿Por ventura los que se llaman amigos del país, podrán alejarlas? ¿Son acaso algunas espías esparcidas por el Reino, que puedan dar noticia a los extraños de cuanto se trabaje por su bien? ¿O son tan misteriosos, e intrincados los asuntos que se tratan en las Sociedades económicas que no puedan entenderlos sino los hombres?" Amar y Borbón, "Discourse in Defence of the Talents," 105–6.

14. *Memorial literario*, T. VIII, XXIX, May 1786: 81.

15. Amar y Borbón, "Discourse in Defence of the Talents," 111. See also Smith, *The Emerging Female Citizen*, 74–107.

16. Demerson, *María Francisca de Sales Portocarrero*, 138.

17. Demerson, *María Francisca de Sales Portocarrero*, 141.

18. Ward, *Obra pía*, 137–41; Rodríguez de Campomanes, "Memoria sobre el establecimiento."

19. Palma García, "Las Escuelas Patrióticas," 37.

20. Haidt, *Women, work and clothing*.

21. Demerson, *María Francisca de Sales Portocarrero*, 139.

22. Palma García, "Las Escuelas Patrióticas," 43.

23. Cepeda y Mayo, *Elogio*, 14.

24. Fernández Quintanilla, *La mujer ilustrada*, 125.

25. For an analysis of the *elogios* and the language of sensibility and sentimentality in them, see Lewis, "'A su reina benéfica.'"

26. This is something with which her many harsh critics might have disagreed; see Calvo Maturana, *María Luisa de Parma*, for more on Queen María Luisa and her critics.

27. *Junta General*, 42.

28. "Uníos a mi inocentes criaturas, que tenéis la felicidad de que vuestra Reina extienda su vista desde lo alto de su Trono para buscaros en vuestras escuelas, que se informe de vuestros progresos, que se vista de vuestras labores, que publique vuestros adelantamientos, que extienda hasta vosotras sus liberalidades, y en fin, que os ofrezca su protección y su amparo. [...] ¡la que cuando reflexione, que la bondad de S. M. ha sabido allanar a inmensa distancia que hay desde el Trono hasta su pobre habitación, para informarse de su nombre, de su aprovechamiento, de su conducta y de lo que le produce su trabajo, no levantará sus manos y sus votos al cielo, para impetrar que derrame sus bendiciones sobre su bienhechora y su madre!" *Junta General*, 43–44.

29. *Gaceta de Madrid* 30 (April 14, 1789): 266.

30. *Gaceta de Madrid* 78 (September 26, 1788): 627.

31. Demerson, *María Francisca de Sales Portocarrero*, 183.

32. *Memorial literario*, T. XIV, LXIII, June 1788, Part I: 236–37.

33. Fernández Quintanilla, *La mujer ilustrada*, 97; Demerson, *María Francisca de Sales Portocarrero*, 184.

34. "aunque les causó horror la primera vista de aquella mansión de miseria, no por eso desmayó su caridad, sino que continuando sus visitas llegaron a ganar la confianza de las presas, y que estas mejorasen de costumbres. Conversaban familiarmente con ellas a fin de inspirarles el amor a la virtud y al honesto trabajo; las enseñaban a leer; y viendo que el origen de su des-

gracia había sido la ociosidad y la miseria, las hacían aprender varias labores en que pudiesen ocuparse para su utilidad. Así hizo su ingeniosa virtud y constancia que variase de semblante aquella morada de la hediondez, de los vicios y de la desesperación, convirtiéndola en una casa de buenas costumbres, aseo, decencia y amor al trabajo." *Semanario de agricultura y artes dirigido a los párrocos*, vol. 11, no. 284 (June 10, 1802): 356–57, in Larriba and Dufour, eds., *El Semanario de Agricultura y Artes*, 170.

35. D. F. X. M., *Canción heroica*, VI.

36. D. F. X. M., *Canción heroica*, VII.

37. D. F. X. M., *Canción heroica*, IX.

38. Olmeda y León, *Oda en elogio de las señoras*, 5.

39. Díez de la Cortina, *Elogio*, 21–22.

40. Fernández Quintanilla, *La mujer ilustrada*, 99; Demerson, *María Francisca de Sales Portocarrero*, 193.

41. Martín-Valdepeñas Yagüe and Jaffe, *María Lorenza de los Ríos*, 403–4.

42. Bartolomé Martínez, "La crianza y educación de los expósitos," 58.

43. Sherwood, *Poverty in Eighteenth-Century Spain*, 8–9.

44. Quoted in Demerson, *María Francisca de Sales Portocarrero*, 206.

45. Quoted in Demerson, *María Francisca de Sales Portocarrero*, 206.

46. Demerson, *María Francisca de Sales Portocarrero*, 208–13; see also Serrano Jerez, "Bookkeeping for Caring," for an analysis of the significance of a new bookkeeping system established by the Junta de Damas for the Inclusa.

47. Sherwood, *Poverty in Eighteenth-Century Spain*, 195; AHVM, Sección Secretaría, Expediente 1–57–21.

48. Sherwood, *Poverty in Eighteenth-Century Spain*, 195; Fernández Quintanilla, *La mujer ilustrada*, 94–95.

49. "La Inclusa en este año ha experimentado tales ventajas, y logrado tan considerables auxilios, que debe redoblar ciertamente nuestras esperanzas de llegar a verla en aquel estado a que la Junta aspira. [. . .] ¿Quién sabe si el convencimiento general de la instrucción que esta Junta ha adquirido y adquiere diariamente sobre objeto tan interesante, si el de su desvelo y esmeros, y el de aquel honor y desinterés que tanto nos recomiendan en la estimación pública, podrán algún día bajo la inmediata dirección y dependencia de esta Junta a todos los expósitos del reino? ¿y quién es capaz de calcular ahora los servicios que podremos tener la dicha de hacer a la religión, al estado, y a la humanidad en tales circunstancias?" ARSEM, Expediente 176/9.

50. Martín-Valdepeñas Yagüe, "El eco del saber," 104–5.

51. María Josefa de Gálvez's family palace is the location of the present-day Spanish Ministry of Justice.

52. Castroterreño, *Elogio*, 34–35.

53. Castroterreño, *Elogio*, 36.

54. Gálvez, "La Beneficencia," 11.

55. Gálvez, "La Beneficencia," 13.

56. Bolufer Peruga, "Del salón a la asamblea," 144.

Networks of Enlightenment

Women Writers and the Republic of Letters

CATHERINE M. JAFFE

A Collective Identity in the Republic of Letters

Among the strategies deliberately employed by the women of the Junta de Damas to contribute to the public good was the power of the pen. The literary production of the Junta de Damas can be considered as a case of collective, feminine authorship that contributed to pragmatic reform in Enlightenment Spain. Through their writing, produced as individuals and collectively in jointly authored reports, the women of the junta participated in the Republic of Letters—described by Carol Pal as "a transnational, multi-confessional commonwealth of the learned"—that contributed to the circulation of Enlightenment ideas and knowledge.[1] Together they constructed a feminine authorial identity that was enlightened, pragmatic, and secular and that can be traced through their literary networks of contacts with other individuals and institutions. Although in eighteenth-century society these women's traditional identities fixed them within their family roles primarily as daughters, sisters, wives, and mothers, the body of written work they produced as members of the Junta de Damas created a corporate identity manifested as a network of literary relations through which they engaged in the free exchange of ideas that characterized the Republic of Letters. They based their authority as writers on their practical experience with the management of institutions of social welfare. In their official accounts of their activities, their collective identity often permitted the junta's members to dispense with the topoi of humility characteristic of women writers.[2]

Feminist criticism has questioned the accepted understanding of the Republic of Letters in the seventeenth and eighteenth centuries. Dena Goodman analyzes the importance of new practices of sociability to the literary world during the French Enlightenment.[3] Anne Goldgar points out that, while membership in learned societies was concrete, the Republic of Letters "only existed in the minds of its members." The members of the Republic of Letters considered themselves a community of equals without distinctions of nationality, ideology, or rank (although in practice these ideals were not always observed). Like Goodman, Goldgar emphasizes the importance of sociability in this imagined community.[4] Theresa Ann Smith describes how the Junta de Damas created a network through their work with institutions of social welfare that extended throughout Spain and even abroad, and Elisa Martín-Valdepeñas Yagüe mentions their literary connections with women in other countries and details the "echoes of knowledge" emanating from the Junta de Damas.[5]

Claiming identity as a writer is a type of "self-fashioning," observes Susan Dalton, who studies how women of the eighteenth century fashioned their identity through correspondence, blurring divisions between private and public spheres and participating in the public sphere described by Jürgen Habermas that met to freely exchange ideas and to debate matters of public concern.[6] Pal contends that our conception of the centers and peripheries of the Enlightenment must adapt to encompass the networks of influence and circulation of ideas formed by literary women.[7] To analyze how the Junta de Damas operated within a network of literary relations formed by Spain's economic societies at the end of the eighteenth century, which through publication and correspondence participated in a European context, we will examine four categories of their writing: series of discourses accepting admission to the junta, praising the queen or other women, and writing for the commissions on education and morality; annual extracts or summaries of the work of the Junta; translations or creative works written by members of the Junta de Damas; and works dedicated by outside writers to the Junta de Damas itself.[8] Finally, we suggest how network theory, developed in the social sciences, can be used to analyze how these female literary relationships functioned and to show how the junta's literary network helped to circulate Enlightenment thought and knowledge of Enlightenment reforms.

Discourses of Admission, Eulogies, and the Commission on Education

The discourses published by the Countess-Duchess of Benavente and by María Isidra de Guzmán in 1786 accepting honorary admission to the Sociedad Económica carried a clear performative intent and full knowledge of the polemic surrounding their admission. Their discourses were read publicly at a meeting of the Sociedad Económica and later printed. In the paratexts of the title pages (see table 1), the women authors proudly claimed their affiliation to the Real Sociedad Económica Matritense, and in María Isidra's case, to the University of Alcalá, from which she held a degree, and other learned societies of which she was a member, such as the Real Academia Española and the Basque economic society.[9] The title page of Josefa Amar's letter accepting membership into the newly formed Junta de Damas in 1787 mentions both the Real Sociedad Económica Matritense and the Junta de Damas.[10] Josefa Amar declares her willingness to participate because of her "truly patriotic heart" (un corazón verdaderamente patriótico); she lauds the male members of the Sociedad Económica for being willing to "give up part of their authority" (se despoja de una parte de su autoridad) and praises the other members of the Junta de Damas, who "gladly offer themselves to work for the good of the country" (se ofrecen gustosas a trabajar por el bien de la Patria).[11] Benavente, Guzmán, and Amar were self-consciously fashioning their authorial identity based on their patriotic zeal and their alliance to the elite and respected Sociedad Económica of Madrid and other enlightened institutions.

The eulogies (elogios) produced between 1789 and 1819 are the best-known publications of the Junta de Damas. Imitating the male society, each year a member of the junta wrote a discourse praising the queen or other women who were important patrons and delivered it in a public meeting. Of the ten extant eulogies, seven, produced between 1794 and 1801, are dedicated to Queen María Luisa de Parma.[12] Three eulogies are necrological: two dedicated to deceased royal patrons and one to a former member of the Junta de Damas. In the paratexts of the title pages, eight eulogies mention the author's affiliation with the Junta de Damas and eight mention the Real Sociedad Económica Matritense, foregrounding their association with these institutions. (See table 2 and fig. 16).

The eulogies are formulaic, but the authors nevertheless try to lend a personal eloquence to their imaginary, ideal portrait of the queen and the other women they honored, while expressing Enlightenment values of women's education, happiness, utility, and well-being. The Duchess of Almodóvar praised the "natural grandeur, that consists of true spiritual qualities of the heart" (grandeza natural, que consiste en las cualidades reales del espíritu y del corazón) of the deceased Infanta Ana María Victoria, acknowledging that "merit

TABLE I. Paratexts of the Discourses of Admission

YEAR & PUBLISHER	TITLE	WRITTEN BY	ADDRESSED TO
1786 Madrid, Sancha and *Memorial literario*	*Oración gratulatoria del género eucarístico*	Exc. Sra. Doña María Isidra Quintina de Guzmán y de la Cerda —Doctora en Filosofía y Letras Humanas, Consiliaria Perpetua, Examinadora de cursantes en Filosofía, y Cathedrática honoraria de Filosofía moderna en la Real Universidad de Alcalá —Socia de la Real Academia Española —Honoraria y literata Real Sociedad Bascongada de los Amigos del País	la Real Sociedad de Amigos del País de esta Corte: «Señores»
1786 Madrid, Sancha and *Memorial literario*	*Discurso*	Condesa Duquesa de Benavente, Marquesa de Peñafiel, etc.	la Real Sociedad Económica de Madrid: «Señores»
1787 Madrid, Sancha and *Memorial literario*	*Oración gratulatoria*	Sra. Doña Josefa Amar y Borbón —elegida Socia de Honor y Mérito de la Junta de Damas	la Junta de Señoras de la Real Sociedad Económica de Madrid: «Señoras»

is not always the inseparable companion of high rank" (el mérito no siempre es compañero inseparable de la elevación).[13] The Countess of Torrepalma in 1794 eulogized Queen María Luisa of Parma's example of promoting education and social welfare, and exhorts the Junta de Damas: "let your hearts fill with joy when you provide for honest artisans useful and hard-working companions who owe their progress and education to this beneficent body" (vuestros cora-

TABLE 2. Paratexts of the Eulogies

	YEAR	EULOGY OF	REFERENCE TO THE JUNTA DE SEÑORAS DE HONOR Y MÉRITO	REFERENCE TO THE REAL SOCIEDAD ECONÓMICA DE MADRID	WRITTEN BY
1	1789	Serenísima Señora María Ana Victoria [de Braganza] Infanta de Portugal, Esposa del Serenísimo Señor Infante Don Gabriel	«Socia de . . .»	yes	Exc. Sra. Duquesa de Almodóvar
2	1794	Reyna Nuestra Señora [María Luisa de Parma]	«Presidenta de . . .»	yes	Exc. Sra. Condesa de Torrepalma
3	1795	Reyna N. S. [María Luisa de Parma]	«Socia de honor y mérito de la Junta de Señoras»	yes	Exc. Sra. Marquesa de Ariza
4	1796	Reyna N. S. [María Luisa de Parma]	no	no	Exc. Sra. Marquesa de Sonora
5	1797	Sra. Dña. Petra de Torres Feloaga, Marquesa de Valdeolmos y de la Torrecilla	«Secretaría de . . .»	yes	Exc. Sra. Condesa del Montijo
6	1797	la Reyna N.S. [María Luisa de Parma]	«Socia de Honor y Mérito de la Junta de Señoras»	«Real Sociedad»	Sra. Doña María del Rosario Cepeda y Gorostiza
7	1798	la Reyna N.S. [María Luisa de Parma]	no	yes	Sra. Marquesa de Fuerte-Híjar
8	1799	la Reyna N.S. [María Luisa de Parma]	«Socia de Honor y Mérito de la RSEM»	yes	Sra. Doña Josepha Díez de la Cortina
9	1801	la Reyna N.S. [María Luisa de Parma]	«Socia de Honor y Mérito de la RSEM»	yes	Exc. Sra. Condesa de Castroterreño
10	1819	Reina Nuestra Señora Doña María Isabel de Braganza	«Junta de Sras. de esta Corte»	no	Exc. Sra. Marquesa de Villafranca

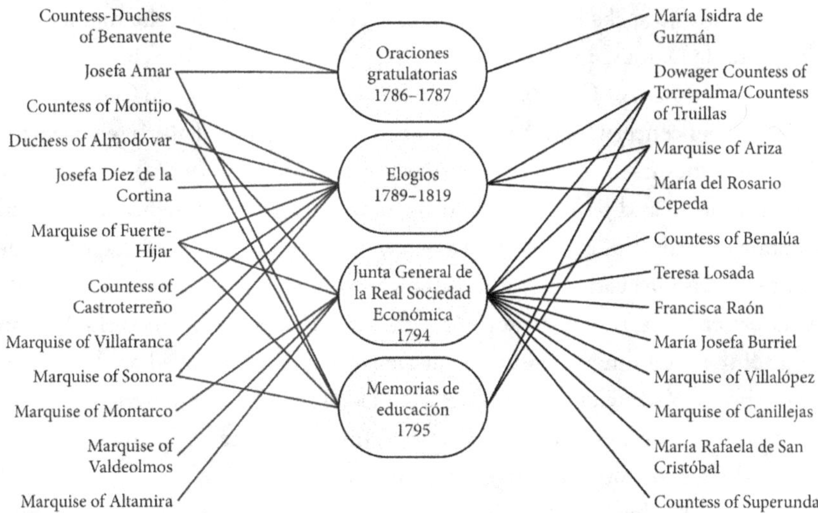

FIG. 16. Literary networks of the Junta de Damas: discourses of admission, eulogies, general meeting, and memorandums on education, 1786–1801. Art design by Mary Lee Eggart.

zones se llenen de júbilo cuando procureis unas compañeras útiles y laboriosas para los honrados artesanos, que deben sus adelantamientos e instrucción a este benéfico cuerpo).[14]

The Marquise of Ariza praised Queen María Luisa's care for her daughters' education, for the queen "extends and perpetuates the happiness of all nations" (es quien extiende y perpetúa la felicidad de los pueblos).[15] María del Rosario de Cepeda praises the Queen's support of the schools run by the Junta de Damas: "those young women with an education will have greater self-esteem. [...] their husbands will be obliged to treat them with greater respect" (aquellas jóvenes con la educación que han recibido se estiman más a sí mismas. [...] sus maridos se ven obligados a tratarlas con mayor estimación).[16] The junta's praise of Queen María Luisa as model mother and spouse stood in sharp contrast to the sharp criticism and slander directed at her later in her reign.[17]

In 1797, the Countess of Montijo dedicated a heartfelt eulogy to the deceased Marquise of Valdeolmos, Petra de Torres y Feloaga. Montijo praises her as a friend, a mother who dedicated herself to her children's education, and, as the consummation of her enlightened spirit, a tireless worker in the Junta de Damas. In this eulogy, published together with a beautiful engraving of her friend, Montijo seeks to project a more accessible model for the members of the Junta de Damas, and by extension, for other women of her class.

The Countess of Castroterreño dedicated her 1801 eulogy to Queen María Luisa's beneficence, which she exalts as the highest virtue of all: "a fertile virtue that multiplies itself infinitely, offering an unending variety of points of view for admiration and praise. [...] you know that I speak of beneficence" (virtud fecunda que, multiplicándose infinitamente, ofrece una variedad inagotable de puntos de vista a la admiración y a las alabanzas. [...] bien conocéis que hablo de la beneficencia).[18] Castroterreño's eloquent discourse defends the human value of the foundling (*expósito*)—"an innocent victim sacrificed on the altar of a false honor" (una víctima inocente inmolada sobre las aras sangrientas de un falso honor)—and even cites statistics on how the Junta de Damas has managed to lower the mortality rate at the Inclusa.[19]

The final eulogy of 1819 shows a stylistic change with an increased sentimentality typical of the period's gender ideology, which emphasized complementary gender roles and women's "natural" domestic role as "angel in the house." The Marquise of Villafranca speaks of the deceased Queen María Isabel de Braganza's reception in Madrid as an "angel of peace" (ángel de la paz), and praises her "sweet, untiring, meek, and celestial charity" (caridad dulce, incansable, mansa y celeste). The queen showed by example how to practice "true charity" (la verdadera caridad) with the orphans of the Inclusa, "humbling herself to dress and bathe these innocent creatures" (humillándose hasta vestir y lavar estas inocentes criaturas), thereby showing that "maternal functions are our essential attribute" (las funciones maternales entran esencialmente en el número de nuestras atribuciones).[20] As Mónica Bolufer observes, the eulogies, performed in public and published in elegant editions, served as propaganda justifying the monarchy's power and representing the queen as an enlightened absolutist.[21] These ideal portraits of the queen and other patrons served as a mediating image of the Junta de Damas' claim to the public sphere.[22]

In 1794, the president of the Junta de Damas, the Countess of Truillas, as stipulated in the recently approved *Statutes*, proposed the formation of two commissions to study the issues of physical and moral education for women.[23] The commission on moral education, led by the Countess of Montijo, was the most active and quickly produced its reports, which were presented the following year in meetings of the Junta de Damas. Unfortunately the commissions' reports themselves have not been preserved, but the censor wrote a summary in 1801 of the seven memorandums submitted for approval for publication—which never occurred—to the Real Sociedad Económica.[24]

Josefa Amar sent from Zaragoza her memorandum on moral education for young women about to marry; the Marquise of Fuerte-Híjar wrote memorandums about the importance of women's education to the state and about the corrupting influence of luxury and fashion; the Countess of Montijo wrote about the education that should be given to women regarding the civil constitution and public business; the Countess of Truillas wrote about religious education for women; the Marquise of Ariza described the importance of domestic economy; the Marquise of Sonora wrote about children's physical education before they are weaned and while they are teething. The censor's summary shows the strong interest of the Junta de Damas in theoretical issues regarding the appropriate education for women. These texts were an exercise in corporate writing and followed specific themes suggested by the Marquise of Ariza, with the participation some of the most active members of the Junta. (See fig. 16.) As reflected in the report of the censor, the *memorias* represent a collective and organized response by the junta to a contemporary polemical topic.

Reporting the Junta's Work

In their purely official writings, the women of the Junta de Damas record their administration of various institutions of social welfare in Madrid, such as the Patriotic Schools, the Inclusa, and the women's prison, the Galera. The summaries (*memorias*) of the presidents were published beginning in 1818. They were propagandistic writings that communicated the junta's accomplishments and activities. The "instructive accounts of the business of the Junta" (memorias instructivas de los negocios de la Junta) and "extracts of works" (extractos de tareas), were rather homogeneous but chronicle the work of the feminine association. The presidents' summaries began to be written after the approval of the junta's definitive statutes in 1794, although the secretary's extracts of work began in 1789, soon after the junta's founding.

Management reports (*memorias*) were produced annually, and biannually in some cases, such as the *Memorias expositivas* of the Countess of Ofalia (1825) and of the Duchess of Alagón (1827).[25] They were read aloud to the Junta de Damas, and then the author would read the report to the Sociedad Económica. They were intended for internal consumption, at least until 1817.

The president would elaborate upon the junta's successes and failures, congratulate the women for their dedication, and recount the obstacles they faced.[26] Practically the entire manuscript series of *memorias* is complete from 1796 on, except for the years 1809 and 1814. After 1818, the series, mostly published, is more irregular. The Duchess of Gor published some reports on the Inclusa and the Colegio de Nuestra Señora de la Paz between 1829 and 1840. The *memorias* are preserved, with a few missing years, until 1840.

The work extracts (*extractos de tareas*) were produced annually or semi-annually. They had greater public projection since they were read at public prize ceremonies held by the Real Sociedad Económica. Public officials and representatives from different political, cultural, and scientific institutions attended these general meetings, at which the Junta de Damas would present a summary of their work during a specific period of time.[27] The texts recount in an orderly fashion the accomplishments of each of the establishments of education and social welfare run by the Junta de Damas. The preserved records of the series run from 1789 to 1807. The publication *General Meeting of the Royal Madrid Economic Society, held in City Hall on Saturday, January 25, 1794* (*Junta General de la Real Sociedad Económica de Madrid, celebrada en las Casas de Ayuntamiento el sábado 25 de enero de 1794*) shows the context of production and dissemination of the works of the Junta de Damas. This was the only time that the entire record of one of the Sociedad Económica's public award ceremonies in which the Junta de Damas participated was published. Through this publication, which records the names of all the women who submitted written reports, we can trace the extent of the literary network of the Junta de Damas, and the different individuals, authorities, and collectives from Madrid who were invited. This publication includes the first eulogy to Queen María Luisa of Parma by Countess of Torrepalma. (See fig. 16.)[28]

Translations and Creative Works

The literary network of the Junta de Damas was extended by translations that connected its members to writers abroad and enabled the circulation of Enlightenment ideas. Josefa Amar established her scholarly credentials with a translation of Francisco Javier Lampillas's *Ensayo histórico-apologético de la literatura Española* (1782).[29] In 1774, when the Countess of Montijo was twenty years old, she published a translation of Nicolás Le Tourneux's *Instrucciones*

Christianas sobre el sacramento del matrimonio y sobre las ceremonias con que la iglesia lo administra (Christian instructions on the sacrament of matrimony and the ceremonies whereby the church administers it), thereby becoming enmeshed in the controversy over Jansenism in Spain. The Marquise of Espeja published two scholarly translations: from Italian, Francesco María Zanotti's *Compendio de la filosofía moral* (1785); and from French, Étienne Bonnot de Condillac's *La lengua de los cálculos* (1805). The Marquise of Fuerte-Híjar published a translation in 1802 of an article from a French scientific journal on the life and works of Count Rumford, in support of the Sociedad Económica's project to build soup kitchens to feed the poor. The title page states that the work is presented to the "Patriotic Society of Madrid," that Fuerte-Híjar is the translator and a "member of honor and merit" (Sociedad Patriótica de Madrid, Socia de Honor y Mérito). In a footnote, Fuerte-Híjar praises the Royal Madrid Society's extending of honorary membership to Rumford, thus claiming a collegial equality of interest between the Madrid Society and other learned societies of which Rumford was a member.[30] Petra Pedregal de Hervás participated in nationalistic discourse in defense of Spain's heroic past with her 1828 translation of *Pelayo, restaurador de la Monarquía española* (Pelayo, Restorer of the Spanish Monarchy), a historical novel written in French in 1818 by Mme de Rome.[31]

The junta's literary network was also enhanced by their creative works that were published or, in the case of dramatic works, performed in private tertulias. Josefa Amar's 1786 discourse defending women's admission to the Real Sociedad Económica is today considered a key text of Spanish feminist literature. Amar also wrote the only original book on women's education published in Spain in the eighteenth century: *Discurso sobre la educación física y moral de las mujeres* (1790; Discourse on the physical and moral education of women), where on the title page she proclaims that she is a "Member of merit of the Royal Aragonese Society, and of the Junta de Damas united to the Royal Madrid Society" (Socia de Mérito de la Real Sociedad Aragonesa, y de la Junta de Damas unida a la Real Sociedad de Madrid). Rita de Barrenechea, Marquise of la Solana and Countess of Carpio, published two original dramatic works: *Catalin* (1783) and *La aya* (1780; The Governess), both of which take as themes women's role in society and education.[32] The Marquise of Fuerte-Híjar wrote two plays that address women's role in marriage and the predicaments of educated women, *El Eugenio* and *La sabia indiscreta*. She also published an original

Ode in 1816 regarding the death of the Marquise of Villafranca's son.[33] Later in the century, the Cuban creole Countess of Merlin published several original works in French that were quickly translated into Spanish. Among the most notable dealing with the situation of women are her autobiography, published in Spanish in Philadelphia in 1838, and *Viaje a la Habana* (1844, Voyage to Havana), that criticized the institution of slavery.[34]

Dedications

The literary network of the Junta de Damas was extended paratextually by the many works dedicated to them individually or to the group as a whole. When María Isidra de Guzmán was granted a degree at the University of Alcalá in 1785 and when María del Rosario Cepeda passed a public examination in Cádiz in 1768, several publications celebrated the events, making the young women relatively famous.[35] Fernando de Gillemán of the Royal Academy of History published his Spanish translation of the Countess of Genlis's *Las Veladas de la Quinta* (Soirées at the Country House) in 1788, dedicating it to the "Señoras" of the Junta de Damas: "I dedicate these novels with the greatest affection and admiration to the respectable Society of Ladies united to the Madrid Society, as representatives of the entire body of ladies of the kingdom" (Dedico estas novelas con el mayor afecto y veneración a la respetable Sociedad de Señoras unidas a la Sociedad Matritense, como representantes de todo el cuerpo de señoras del reino).[36] In 1794, Juan Andrés published a treatise on the education of the deaf—of particular interest to the Real Sociedad Económica—dedicated to Isabel Parreño, Marquise of Llano, asserting the preeminence of the Spanish in this field.[37]

Reflecting the high public profile of the Junta de Damas, two published poems expressed admiration for the junta's work with women in the Galera and the Sala de Reservadas. In "Canción heroica en honor de las señoras socias económicas matritenses, y señoras asociadas, para la enseñanza de las infelices de la galera, y de las dos cárceles de Villa y Corte" (Heroic Song in Honor of the Ladies of the Madrid Economic Society, and Related Ladies, for Teaching the Unhappy Women in the Two Prisons of Madrid), published around 1788, the anonymous poet declares: "Madrid is a good witness / Let Madrid say it / Seeing how its excellent members / Work ingeniously and tirelessly / For the good of the people" (Buen testigo es Madrid, Madrid lo diga / Registrando sus

Socias excelentes / Trabajar con ingenio y con fatiga / Por el común provecho de las gentes).[38] In 1797, Joseph de la Olmeda published a poem in a similar vein, *Oda en elogio de las señoras de la Asociación, por el nuevo establecimiento reservado* (Ode in Praise of the Ladies of the Association, for the New Reserved Establishment). And in 1804 the famous female playwright María Rosa de Gálvez published a poem dedicated to the Countess of Castroterreño's work in the Junta de Damas, "La Beneficencia."

The works and experiences of the Junta de Damas echoed throughout other publications. In 1803, Santiago García, the physician in the Inclusa, sent a revised version of his 1794 treatise on caring for abandoned infants to the Junta de Damas for their review before its republication in 1805.[39] Vicente del Seixo dedicated his book on education and marriage, *Instrucción moral christiana, política y civil* (1790), to the Countess of Villalobos. María Loreto Figueroa, a member of the Junta de Damas, published a speech delivered by the Marquise of Villafranca in Cádiz in 1812, adding a prologue in which she urged the women of Seville to imitate the women of Cádiz by forming a junta to take on the task of clothing soldiers resisting the French invasion.[40]

There were personal dedications as well that reflected the literary networks of the socias of the Junta de Damas. Teresa González dedicated her book on astronomy to the Duchess of Osuna in 1788; Francisco Javier de Oviedo dedicated his work on public credit to Osuna; and Ramón Fernández sent her his manual on surgery with a dedication acknowledging her devotion to the arts and sciences and to the public good.[41] And in 1798, Inés Joyes dedicated to Osuna her "Apología de las mujeres en carta original de la traductora a sus hijas" (Defense of women in an original letter written by the translator for her daughters): "Inés Joyes, her most attentive and admiring servant, offers this small demonstration of her regard" (Ofrece esta leve demostración de obsequioso afecto su más atenta y apasionada servidora, Inés Joyes). This essay, appended to Joyes's translation of Samuel Johnson's *Rasselas*, is one of the most significant female-authored works defending women published in eighteenth-century Spain.[42] Saturio Ximénez de Berdoces dedicated his treatise on the refinement of hemp to the Marquise of Fuerte-Híjar, remarking on her "desire to promote economic knowledge that could help the nation."[43] The poet Nicasio Álvarez Cienfuegos dedicated his play, *La condesa de Castilla* (Countess of Castile), to the Marquise of Fuerte-Híjar, and wrote a poem, "La escuela del sepulcro" consoling her for the death of her friend, the Marquise of las Mercedes.[44]

When the Marquise of Fuerte-Híjar published her *Ode* in 1816 dedicated to the Marquise of Villafranca, she joined a network of writers of poems and other publications dedicated to Villafranca and her son, the Duke of Fernandina. This young man's illness, treatment, and death at age sixteen were chronicled by his doctor, Ignacio Jaúregui, who reported that the young duke requested that he be given a simple funeral and the savings donated to the children of the Inclusa. With her poem responding to this solemn event, Fuerte-Híjar links herself to a wide literary network comprising the Duke of Frías, Juan Nicasio Gallego, the anonymous author "B," Leandro Fernández de Moratín, Francisco Sánchez Barbero, Francisco Javier Vales Asenjo, and the doctor Jaúregui.[45]

Women's Literary Networks in the Republic of Letters

Networks are often loosely invoked as metaphors for literary relations, and applying the network theory used in social sciences to literary associations and coteries has helped scholars to produce a more complete understanding of how knowledge travels and circulates through society. In particular, it has shed light on overlooked networks of women writers and their contributions to the dissemination of Enlightenment thought.[46] Network theory describes nodes and edges, or the individuals and the links established between them. Tables 1 and 2 detail the paratexts of the discourses of admission and the eulogies written by members of the Junta de Damas. A network "is a set of relationships between objects or entities. We normally refer to the objects of entities as 'nodes' in the network and their relationships as 'edges' or 'ties.'" Network theorists analyze the "betweenness centrality"—"how central a particular node is to the network's organization, and how important it is in connecting other people." Important nodes have high betweenness centrality and connect many others throughout the network. Prestige or influence is measured through high "eigenvector centrality," meaning that such a node is adjacent to a node that in turn influences many other nodes.[47]

In a chronologically limited but telling sample of the literary network created by the Junta de Damas' collective writing, figure 16 shows the relation of authors to four sets of writings discussed above: the discourses of admission, the eulogies, the memorandums on education, and the activity reports summarized in the *Junta General* of 1794. The Countess of Montijo, the Countess of

Truillas, the Marquise of Fuerte-Híjar, and the Marquise of Ariza each have three edges that connect them to works produced by all the other women. They are the most important nodes of the network formed between 1786 and 1801 and have a high betweenness centrality. The Countess-Duchess of Benavente, María Isidra de Guzmán, and Josefa Amar can be said to have a high eigenvector centrality showing their prestige and influence, because they are chronologically first in a link to all other members and writings. Networks shift and evolve through time, and an analysis of the writings of the Junta de Damas through the early decades of the nineteenth century would show further relationships formed by corporate writing.

Network theorists also point to the importance of weak links in the wide diffusion of information. People form strong ties with others of their same profession, family, or associations, and therefore information only circulates within a restricted group. But weak ties formed with acquaintances seen less often are much more productive in spreading news outside the restricted group.[48] When the members of the Junta de Damas published their writings or presented them in public gatherings, they passed their information along to a much wider audience via weak links of contacts from other groups and associations. Although the Junta de Damas comprised privileged women, they were not all from same social background. Through their work together over the years, they formed relationships of equality with each other based on merit and shared work, as the *Statutes* they wrote prove. The literary network they created allowed them to diffuse their knowledge and experience to a wider audience than the limited circulation of their writings would suggest.

The debate over their admission to the Real Sociedad Económica Matritense echoed throughout Europe. The women's connections with economic societies in other parts of Spain—Zaragoza, Valladolid, the Basque country, Cádiz, Osuna, Ávila, and Seville—and their correspondence and contacts abroad disseminated their expertise in education, artisanal skills for women, and new manufacturing methods for textiles.[49] The Junta de Damas participated in scientific experiments—measuring the air in jails and experimenting with infant feeding—that were eventually published and circulated abroad, without necessarily acknowledging the contribution of the Junta de Damas.[50] They collaborated with medical experiments with smallpox vaccination beginning in 1802. In 1819, the Junta de Damas wrote to Spanish ambassadors in Europe, requesting that they send information on the practices in foundling hospitals in the cities that they visited. In the *Memoria* of 1820, the Marquise of Villafranca mentioned a letter written to the Junta de Damas by Sophie Dorothea of Württemberg, the mother of the Russian czar, Alexander I, asking for information about how they ran the Inclusa. The Junta de Damas managed its self-promotion astutely, and the press in Madrid regularly reported on its activities.[51]

The Republic of Letters, according to Carol Pal, is a diffuse, imagined entity with varied horizontal and transparent strata composed of groups dedicated to intellectual activities infused with Enlightenment values. Between these strata were vertical connections through which people and ideas could circulate to influence more groups.[52] The Junta de Damas was one such metaphorical strata of the Republic of Letters, a network of women practicing Enlightenment ideas that connected vertically to different strata through their writing and personal contacts. Acknowledging their corporate identity as authors allows us to re-center their role in Enlightenment reform, women's history, and the history of feminism.

NOTES

An earlier version of this essay was presented at the Congreso Internacional: "Redes y escritoras en la esfera cultural de la primera edad Moderna (siglos XV–SVIII)," organized by the project BIESES–Bibliografía de Escritoras Españolas, held in Madrid in November 2019: "Un espacio femenino para la creación cultural en el Madrid del siglo XVIII: la Junta de Damas de Honor y Mérito."

1. Pal, *The Republic of Women*, 1.

2. On topoi of modesty for women writers, see Bolufer Peruga in *Mujeres e ilustración*, 299–339; López-Cordón Cortezo, "La fortuna de escribir." On women writers and public identity, see Álvarez Barrientos, *Los hombres de letras*, 51; Lewis, "Women as Public Intellectuals."

3. Goodman, *The Republic of Letters*.

4. Goldgar, *Impolite Learning*, 2–3.

5. Smith, *The Emerging Female Citizen*, 171–77; Martín-Valdepeñas Yagüe, "El eco del saber."

6. Dalton, *Engendering the Republic of Letters*.

7. Pal, *The Republic of Women*, 4–6.

8. Regarding the published texts of the Junta de Damas, see Catalina García, *Datos bibliográficos*; Demerson, Demerson, and Aguilar Piñal, *Las Sociedades Económicas en el siglo XVIII*.

9. Guzmán y de la Cerda, *Oración del género eucarístico*.

10. Amar y Borbón, *Oración Gratulatoria*; see also the analysis of these paratexts in Martín-Valdepeñas Yagüe and Jaffe, "Un espacio femenino."

11. Amar y Borbón, *Oración gratulatoria*, 4, 6–7.

12. On the eulogies dedicated to Queen María Luisa de Parma, see also Calvo Maturana, *María Luisa de Parma*, 58–72; Lewis, "'A su reina benéfica.'"

13. Almodóvar, *Elogio*, viii, iv. The text has been modernized. All translations in this essay are the author's.

14. *Junta General*, 46.

15. Ariza, *Elogio*, xiii.

16. Cepeda y Mayo, *Elogio*, 14.

17. See Calvo Maturana, "Eva y la pérdida del Paraíso Imperial," and *María Luisa de Parma*; Lewis, "'A su reina benéfica.'"

18. Castroterreño, *Elogio*, 6–7.

19. Castroterreño, *Elogio*, 24, 34–35. Despite Castroterreño's optimism, however, Sherwood claims that the overall mortality rate at the Inclusa fluctuated with economic conditions, rose to 100 percent at one point during the war, and did not improve measurably until antiseptics were introduced in the late nineteenth century. *Poverty in Eighteenth-Century Spain*, 205. See also Lewis, "Practicing Social Activism," in this volume.

20. Villafranca, *Elogio*, 8, 11, and 13.

21. Bolufer Peruga, *Mujeres e ilustración*, 372.

22. For studies of the eulogies, see Lewis, "'A su reina benéfica'"; Martín-Valdepeñas Yagüe, "La reina María Luisa de Parma"; Martín-Valdepeñas Yagüe and Jaffe, *María Lorenza de los Ríos*, 115–18, 217–18.

23. Titles VII and VIII of *Statutes* of 1794. See appendix.

24. ARSEM, Expediente 146/11. For accounts of the process of the commissions on education, see Demerson, *María Francisca de Sales Portocarrero*, 169–81; Negrín Fajardo, *Educación popular*, 140–49; Smith, *The Emerging Female Citizen*, 149–57; Martín-Valdepeñas Yagüe and Jaffe, *María Lorenza de los Ríos*, 113–15.

25. Ofalia, *Memoria expositiva*; Alagón, *Memoria expositiva*.

26. Article IX of Title IV of the *Statutes* of 1794 specified the required items that should be contained in the president's annual reports.

27. Article VIII of Title VI of the *Statutes* of 1794 explained that one of the secretary's functions was to compose these reports.

28. See Martín-Valdepeñas Yagüe and Jaffe, "Un espacio femenino."

29. See Elizabeth Lewis's analysis of this translation in "Women as Public Intellectuals."

30. Martín-Valdepeñas Yagüe and Jaffe, *María Lorenza de los Ríos*, 360. For a study of the context of this publication, see Jaffe, "'Noticia de la vida y obras del Conde de Rumford.'"

31. For a study of this translation, see Martínez Ojeda, "*Don Pélage*."

32. For editions and studies of these works, see Urzainqui Miqueleiz, "*Catalín*" de Rita Barrenechea; García Garrosa, "En los inicios de la comedia neoclásica"; also see Altonaga, "The Basque Enlightenment," 87–90.

33. A recent critical edition of these works is in Martín-Valdepeñas and Jaffe, *María Lorenza de los Ríos*, 265–344.

34. See Méndez Ródenas, *Gender and Nationalism*; López-Cordón Cortezo, "Vida y ficción"; Martín-Valdepeñas Yagüe, "La condesa de Merlin."

35. See Delgado, *Por el magisterio en artes liberales*; E.A.J.D.A., *Aparato, ceremonias, y solemnidades*; Cepeda y Mayo, *Relación de los exercicios literarios*, and *Copia, y recolección de los papeles*.

36. Demerson, *María Francisca de Sales Portocarrero*, 171; Gillemán, "Prólogo," 5.

37. Andrés y Morell, *Carta del Abate Don Juan Andrés*.

38. D.F.X.M., *Canción heroica*, III.

39. García, *Breve instrucción* and *Instituciones*; see Martín-Valdepeñas Yagüe, "El eco del saber," 104.

40. Figueroa y Montalvo, *Señoras, Las de Cádiz han establecido una Junta*.

41. See Martín-Valdepeñas Yagüe, "El eco del saber," 110; González, *El estado del cielo*; Oviedo, *Memoria*; Fernández, *Principios*.

42. Joyes, *El Príncipe de Abisinia*. For a study and edition of this work, see Bolufer Peruga, *La vida y la escritura en el siglo XVIII*. An English translation may be found in Barker, *In Defence of Women*, 141–55.

43. Ximénez de Berdoces, *Tratado*, iii.

44. Álvarez de Cienfuegos, *Obras poéticas*, vol. 2: 109–10, and vol. 1: 175–88.

45. For an analysis of this literary event, see Martín-Valdepeñas Yagüe and Jaffe, *María Lorenza de los Ríos*, 227–33.

46. See Ahnert and Ahnert, "Protestant Letter Networks"; Bergstrom, "Literary Coteries"; Bourke, "Female Involvement"; Jacob, "The Mental Landscape."

47. Ahnert, "Maps versus Networks," 131–37; see also Borgatti, "Centrality and Network Flow," 61.

48. See Ahnert, "Maps versus Networks," 146; Granovetter, "The Strength of Weak Ties."

49. Smith, *The Emerging Female Citizen*, 171–77.

50. Serrano Jerez, "Chemistry in the City," 142–59, and "Science for Women."

51. See Martín-Valdepeñas Yagüe, "El eco del saber," 99–108.

52. Pal, *The Republic of Women*, 12.

Representing the Feminine Ideal

Portraits of the Members of the Junta de Damas

ÁLVARO MOLINA

The establishment of the Junta de Damas de Honor y Mérito in 1787 helped to shape a feminine ideal in which the moral virtues that had given meaning to women's experiences in the domestic sphere would fuel the patriotic actions they were called to perform in their new life in society. This intimate relationship between the private and the public legitimized the role that was reserved for these women as emerging citizens within the Real Sociedad Económica Matritense de Amigos del País, granting them a hitherto unprecedented visibility and ability to contribute to the happiness of the nation.[1] Among the reasons that led Charles III to support the creation of this women's group intended to address "the best means of promoting virtue, effort, and industry in their gender" (los mejores medios de promover la virtud, la aplicación y la industria en su sexo) was the clear intention that the future members considered "worthy of this honorable distinction" (acreedoras a esta honrosa distinción) would carry out "together the means of promoting good education" (unidas los medios de fomentar la buena educación) and "improving customs with their example and their writings" (mejorar las costumbres con su ejemplo y sus escritos).[2] In this way, the members became exemplary models of conduct for other women, a role that also would affect the manner in which their personal images were portrayed and exhibited.

The first consideration that must be taken into account in assessing the portraits of the members of the Junta de Damas is the difference in the ways this artistic practice remembered each of the genders during the Enlightenment. Whereas the portraits of men had preferably fulfilled a commemorative function intended to instill in their equals the desire to imitate the portrayed man's noble actions and admire his achievements in public life, the portraits of women had normally had a more intimate and personal purpose reserved for the private domestic sphere. They extolled the qualities that defined the portrayed woman as a good mother and wife, happy and content in Enlightenment terms to be in charge of the family and the upkeep of the home.[3] When, on the contrary, portraits of women represented those who had distinguished themselves in an outstanding way, more complex and subtle techniques were involved. This occurred especially in the case of those women who had demonstrated qualities that were exceptional for their gender, but which could not conflict with the virtues and values already set forth that the natural order—according to the discourse of traditional patriarchy—reserved for them.[4] The portraits that are preserved and known of some of the members of the Junta de Damas in the first years of their distribution—the time frame to which this study is limited—did not follow a single strategy in the conceptualization of the image of their subjects or in the circulation of their portrayals, which allows us to include the diverse solutions that were implemented to showcase the multifaceted identity of each of the women in distinct aspects of their lives and beyond the everyday nature of family life. Consequently, we analyze a selection of cases that recollects the context of the distinct purposes, practices, and situations that motivated the creation and circulation of these works from a public perspective as well as their reception by those who had the opportunity to contemplate them. This approach obliges us to bypass other typologies, such as the miniature, that had a more reserved and personal use.

The Activity of the Junta de Damas: Institutional and Familiar Portraits

One of the obstacles that prevents the determination of a unified image of the Junta de Damas members through the portrait—both conceptually as well as formally and compositionally—is the absence of an institutional gallery like those that other entities such as the royal academies promoted during the same time.[5] In the case of the Sociedades Económicas de Amigos del País, we still do not have a study of the collections that were inspired by portraits of distinguished members, despite attempts having been made. One of the earliest examples comes from the Sociedad Bascongada de los Amigos del País, when in 1773 the creation of a gallery of this type was approved. The project materialized in the so-called "sala de patriotas" (hall of patriots) located in the Seminario de Bergara, where the plan had been to display the portraits of the deceased members alongside a bust of Charles III presiding over the room.[6] The decision to locate the room in the seminary rather than in one of the *casas de juntas* (assembly houses) was due to the custom of displaying the image of protectors and benefactors of schools, seminaries, and teaching centers for the student body. Manuel de Aguirre recommended it be done this way when in 1785 he offered ideas about the establishment of a patriotic seminary under the direction of the Real Sociedad Económica Aragonesa de Amigos del País, explaining that the portrait of the first protector, "accompanied by those of the Director, Censor, and Secretary that govern the Society when the formation of the seminary takes place" (acompañado de los del Director, Censor y Secretario que rijan la Sociedad en el tiempo en que se verifique la formación del Seminario), and including the portrait of the member who presided over the Junta de Comisión del Seminario Patriótico Aragonés, ought to hang "in the most distinguished place in the *sala noble y de recibimiento.*"[7]

Although it is unknown if the members of the Matritense proposed the creation of a similar gallery, there does currently exist an emblematic example of the institutional, symbolic, and educational value of this type of portrait. This is the portrait that the *amigos* of Madrid requested that the artist Agustín Esteve paint of the Countess of Truillas, Francisca María Dávila Carrillo de Albornoz, when she served as the president of the Junta de Damas. (See fig. 4.)[8] Although the work has been studied in depth recently, it bears mentioning that its execution was absolutely exceptional because of its uniqueness: no other scenes that allude to the activities carried out by guild members on a daily basis are known; nor are there similar examples of portraits dedicated to a male society member as a public recognition and remembrance of his actions.

The full-length painting was commissioned in early 1797 to be displayed on the principal wall of the Hall of Student Rooms of the Colegio de Educación de la Sociedad. One of the organization's most ambitious initiatives, among others, this was spearheaded by the countess, who took charge of composing its internal operating regulations. In the portrait, she appears decorated with the sash of the Real Orden de Damas Nobles de la Reina María Luisa, indicating with her right hand an oval frame with the painted emblem of the Real Sociedad Económica Matritense de Amigos del País and its motto, "Helping by teaching" (Socorre enseñando). Her left hand rests in an affectionate attitude on the shoulder of a girl who seems to have caught her attention by tugging on her skirt, perhaps to proudly show her a sample of embroidery for which she has earned the third-place prize in the contest that the Escuela de Modas convened every year. On the floor, and in the foreground, other fabric samples are piled up, among which is a note announcing a second prize, awarded on this occasion to the best example of sewing, as well as the sign on which the Madrid ladies' dedication of the painting can be read.[9] The painting was debuted publicly in a solemn ceremony on April 5 on the occasion of that year's examinations. A great number of male and female members attended, and the ceremony provoked "lively feelings of tenderness and rejoicing" among those present because, "on one hand, the virtuous actions of the person to whom that tribute of recognition and gratitude was offered was presented to them; and on the other hand, they witnessed the enlightened thinking and generosity of the Real Sociedad, which in recognizing and justly appreciating the benefits that its members provide to it, knows how to fittingly reward them by erecting monuments that might perpetuate their memory in the centuries to come."[10]

The composition designed by Esteve, somewhat contrived if one considers the pose of the principal figure reacting to the girl and holding the emblem, is nevertheless perfectly appropriate for the purpose for which it had been painted, since it not only provided a way to preserve the memory of the countess for future female students of the institute, but also encouraged them to fully engage themselves in learning distinct needlework skills, an effort that might be rewarded with prizes from the institution. The countess's personal attention towards the small girl helps, in addition, to convey the virtues belonging to the female gender, an indisputable guarantee of her ability to contribute to public happiness and to the common good as the president of the Junta de Damas. Thus, in efforts like those carried out at the Escuela de Modas and other establishments, the members of the group ended up modeling a civic motherhood for the social body that justified their action in the public sphere. This reasoning was ably employed by members such as María Francisca de Sales Portocarrero, Countess of Montijo, who as secretary had to oversee numerous requests to expand the leadership initiatives of the Junta de Damas; for example, it petitioned King Carlos IV for the management of the Inclusa based on "the natural maternal inclinations" of their gender, which allowed them to care for better than anyone else all of "those who, through wicked practices, misery, and an inhumane brutality denied them the consolation of their own mothers" (aquellos a quienes la perversidad de costumbres, la miseria, y una inhumana barbarie privó de los consuelos de sus propias madres).[11]

The conceptualization of motherhood as a civic virtue that responded to personal success in family life turned out to be an effective representational strategy in portraiture, as can be seen in the group scene that the Countess of Montijo herself commissioned of Agustín Esteve. (See fig. 7.)[12] The composition must have been an absolute novelty in the artistic landscape of the time. In the first place, we must remember that, in the Spanish pictorial tradition, the group portrait had scarcely been circulated. Francisco de Goya was, as in so many other things, an exception and in the 1780s painted the family of Infante (Prince) don Luis in Arenas de San Pedro (1783), a scene similar to the genre of English conversation pieces; the family of the Duke of Fernán Núñez in their domains in Córdoba (1786), who shows the double paternal role (natural and collective) in the governance of his estates; and, finally, the portrait of the Dukes of Osuna surrounded by their children (1787), a quintessential image of the modern vision of the family as conceived by enlightened thinkers.[13] The fact that the Countess of Montijo directed that she be painted accompanied exclusively by her daughters was a clear declaration of her intentions and is proof of the awareness that the members of the Junta de Damas had come to have of themselves as women at the close of the century.

The work, life-sized like the previous ones, reflects a seemingly everyday moment in the subject's family life. The dimensions of the painting invite the viewer to consider the importance that the client wanted to give to the work in order to exhibit it in a prominent location of her Madrid palace in spite of its being a somewhat intimate scene. We must recall that the countess welcomed in her home one of the era's most recognized gatherings, which her daughters attended from their childhood as part of their formation for society life; as a result, the painting gained an enormous relevance in the impression that its protagonist wanted to give of herself in those years when she had already been widowed.[14] María Francisca occupies the center of the composition and is seated in front of an embroidery frame next to her daughter María Tomasa, the future Marquise of Villafranca. To her left, her youngest daughter, María Benita de los Dolores, the future Countess of Villamonte, is seated with a book and seems to interrupt the reading that livens up the evening in order to pose for the painter. Behind the countess are her older daughters, María Ramona, the Countess of Contamina, and María Gabriela, the Marquise of Lazán, who is resting her hand on her sister's shoulder.[15]

Reading and needlework reflect the role the countess personally assumes in the education of her daughters, for it is a way to exhibit the acquisition of intellectual abilities and the moral values of domesticity and work that enlightened thought and Christian tradition advocated.[16] Regarding the practice of embroidery specifically, this skill was considered one that every woman should learn during her upbringing through childhood, and set an example of in maturity as well, as the Countess of Montijo seems to embody here by following exactly the advice that Josefa Amar y Borbón gave about the issue: "mothers should seek to give a good example in this matter, sometimes working in their daughters' presence, because the lady who knows how to do it will know how to pass it to her daughters as well as to others because of the good example that they receive" (procuren las madres dar buen ejemplo en esta materia, trabajando algunas veces en presencia de sus hijas [porque] la señora que sepa hacerlo, sabrá mandarlo a sus criadas; y a las demás gentes por el buen ejemplo que reciben de esto).[17]

Aside from the countess's maternal responsibilities for the education of her daughters, the painting brings to mind her impact as a citizen and the activities she carries out in the public sphere. The practice of embroidery represented in the work alludes to the activities that the Junta de Damas performed in the Patriotic Schools such as in the Escuela de Modas, whose purpose it was that girls learn a trade based on "tasks appropriate to their gender" (las labores propias de su sexo), which might be, in Campomanes's opinion, "embroidery, many types of knitting and crocheting, some styles of tailoring, and various other things" (el bordado, muchos géneros de tejidos, algunos ramos de sastrería, y otras varias cosas), for women were "more willing, and had a greater facility to learn them, than men" (mayor disposición que los hombres, y más facilidad para aprenderlas).[18] Finally, the countess also wears across her breast the sash of the Real Orden de Damas Nobles de la Reina María Luisa, an honor granted to many ladies of the aristocracy and whose insignia they wore in their portraits whenever they had the opportunity to do so, whether or not they were members of the Junta de Damas. For most of them this was a class distinction that, as also happened in the men's orders, conferred a higher social status; it is for this reason that they were normally portrayed in paintings separated from any reference to the charitable or philanthropic works for which they had been rewarded.[19]

Models of Imitation and Virtue: Engraved Portraits and the Public Sphere

The impact of the Junta de Damas on the periodical press was continuous, beginning even before the organization's establishment, when debates taking place in the Real Sociedad Económica Matritense regarding the admission of women were made known to the public. Since its creation in 1787, news of which would be given from the outset, the press routinely communicated all types of references to the junta's activity, from prayers, commemorations or reports prepared by its members to charity acts, award presentations, subscriptions, or open houses that were celebrated regularly in order to make the public aware of the organization's progress.[20] This intense journalistic activity was not accompanied, however, by similar activity in the field of engraving, as there are scarcely any examples of the circulation of prints with the members' portraits to make the public aware of the merit of their efforts and to be remembered for posterity. This situation was part of a broader predicament since the exclusion of women was systematic in the production of galleries of distinguished figures who were painted throughout the modern age. This exclusion responded to the patriarchal logic of history itself, in whose account women were included only as an exception, an extreme that continued in the eighteenth century.[21] Among those exceptions, belonging to the royalty was one of the most usual ones; an example of this is the painting *Memorias de las reinas católicas* (1761) by the Augustinian friar Father Enrique Flórez, the first to form a collection of portraits of a Spanish feminine collective to accompany the corresponding biographies.[22]

In the early years of the Junta de Damas, the production of single-sheet portraits of women was also very limited. Likenesses of well-known women such as actresses and singers were in high demand and dominated the market, as demonstrated by many examples we encounter during the last years of the century.[23] One of the few members whose portrait circulated was María Isidra Quintina de Guzmán y de la Cerda when she earned a degree in philosophy and letters from the University of Alcalá in 1785, that is, two years before the Junta de Damas was founded. (See fig. 2.)[24] Her extraordinary achievement led to her joining the Real Academia Española and the Sociedad Bascongada almost immediately and, shortly thereafter, to her becoming the first member of the Matritense, together with the Countess-Duchess of Benavente. Her portrait, engraved by José Giraldo, presents the young doctor dressed in an academic cape and mortarboard with an oval medallion that rests on a plinth, alongside a writing set and stacked books, symbols that normally identified the male writer. The bottom of the painting includes a description explaining María Isidra's achievement that warrants the fame and recognition afforded by the portrait.[25] No press notice announcing the sale of the engraving has been located, suggesting that the print was commissioned by María Isidra's father, the Marquis of Montealegre and Count of Oñate, or by another closely related person who could distribute the print among friends, family members, and acquaintances. Although there is no documentation that confirms this hypothesis, it was a common practice at the time.

This same situation occurs, in fact, with the portrait of Isabel Parreño Arce, the Marquise of Llano (fig. 17), whom Manuel Salvador Carmona engraved in 1792, reproducing an original that Anton Raphael Mengs had painted when the model was eighteen years old, dressed as a *maja* on the occasion of a *baile de máscaras* (masquerade).[26] In this case, the portrait formed part of a series of reproductions that Salvador Carmona had begun to engrave from Mengs's paintings from several years earlier, so it is possible that the merit of the original painting's artist is preferred over that of the painting's subject herself.

FIG. 17. Isabel Parreño Arce, Marquise of Llano (Anton Raphael Mengs, engraved by Manuel Salvador Carmona), 1792. Ministerio de Cultura y Deporte. Biblioteca Nacional de España.

Although we do not know in this case the reasons why this commission was fulfilled, there is a notice that the Marquis of Llano committed to acquiring 250 prints for a price of 24 *reales* each and to relinquishing the ownership of the plate to the engraver, who also seems to have not put the print on sale after the run of the initial copies.[27]

Two years later a subscription began to the *Galería de mujeres fuertes*, a work of Pierre Le Moyne published in 1647 and translated to Spanish more than a century later. The advertisement included in the *Gaceta de Madrid* explains that "the work is composed of four volumes in eight issues and comes embellished with twenty fine engravings by one of the best masters of this court. [. . .] The price of each paper volume will be ten *reales* for each volume in paper and thirteen *reales* for each hardcover volume" (se compone la obra de cuatro tomos en 8°, y va adornada con 20 láminas finas grabadas por uno de los mejores profesores de esta corte. [. . .] El precio de cada tomo en papel será de 10 reales y en buena pasta 13).[28] The project assembled twenty biographies of women, accompanied by their corresponding portraits, classifying these heroic female models as Jews, Romans, Barbarians, and Christians. The author had dedicated the original work to Anne of Austria as regent of France during the minority of Louis XIV, adding an allegorical portrait in the frontispiece.

Anticipating that the book could be reissued or translated, Le Moyne had requested "that a heroine who would give it her name, lend it authority, and be adorned with virtue, discretion, strength, and spirit" (que se pusiera al frente de la obra una heroína que llenase su nombre, le diese autoridad, y estuviese adornada de virtud, discreción, fortaleza y espíritu) be put in charge,[29] the reason for which the promotor of the Spanish translation dedicated the work to the Countess-Duchess of Benavente. Everything seems to indicate that the decision to include the portrait on the frontispiece was made once the subscription started since its preparation delayed the sale of the work until the beginning of 1795 (see fig. 6), being a publicity strategy to attract clientele, since it was a portrait "on which Don Francisco de Goya and Don Fernando Selma have gone to great effort" (en el cual se han esmerado Don Francisco de Goya y Don Fernando Selma).[30] The bust of the duchess is placed into a simple frameless medallion with a neutral background, and over her chest she wears the sash of the Real Orden de Damas Nobles de la Reina María Luisa. Her attire is the French revolutionary fashion, shown in the use of ribbons and scarves like the one she uses to gather her hair, which many Spanish noblewomen had adopted at the time as an expression of solidarity toward the aftermath of the Reign of Terror. In other words, the Countess-Duchess of Benavente presents herself to be a contemporary model of the *mujer fuerte* as an example of virtue for the women of her time.[31] As with the print of the Marquis of Llano, in this case the portrait was financed by the Duke of Osuna, who retained several unbound examples for his private use.[32]

The only portrait we have found of a member of the Junta de Damas engraved as a tribute to her membership in the organization was that of Petra de Torres y Feloaga, the Marquise of Valdeolmos and of Torrecilla, which was published after her death to adorn the publication of the *Elogio* that her friend the Countess of Montijo dedicated to her and that was published in the Sancha Printing House in 1797. (See fig. 8.)[33] The half-length portrait of the marquise is an oval medallion similar to that of the Countess-Duchess of Benavente although in this case it is adorned with simple lines that form a frame and serve to accommodate the curved shape of the signatures of the artist and the engraver, while the portrayed subject is identified in the inscription below. Although we have not found documentation about the order for the painting, it is probable that in this case it was likewise the husband of the deceased who financed the expense of drawing the portrait and beginning the print. Neither can we discount the possibility that it was the author of the tribute who assumed the cost because of the affectionate ties that bound her to the deceased, as can be appreciated from reading the text. This was a practice that the Count of Campomanes had already suggested several years earlier when he gave a series of "remarks for the orderly composition of academic accolades" (observaciones para la composición ordenada de los elogios académicos) made for deceased members, a discourse he presented to the Real Sociedad Económica Matritense on September 24, 1776. The author proposed, among other measures, to accompany these publications with a print, and thus, "if it is retained well, the physiognomic description can be made, and if some friend would like to request that a portrait be made, one mustn't refuse that it be made at their expense" (si se retiene bien, se puede hacer la descripción fisionómica, si algún amigo quisiera mandar grabar su retrato, no debe rehusarse se haga a su costa).[34]

Whatever the case may be, both the accolade as well as the portrait itself were enormously original. We have been unable to find a similar one dedicated to another member during these years. Even the tributes dedicated to the queen, María Luisa, as the patroness and protector of the junta's projects were not accompanied, as far as we know, by any engraved portrait. In this way, the Marquise of Valdeolmos became one of the first members who, apart from being portrayed, embodied the collection of feminine virtues normally attributed to the sovereign,[35] unequivocal proof of these women's triumph in recognizing themselves as citizens and patriots.

From the Palace to the Academy:
The Circulation of the Portrait beyond the *Salón*

Portraiture in this period was substantially more complex and diverse than what is typically thought to be the case today, especially if we consider how the era's social networks between individuals and the multiple institutions that were a part of their daily lives were formed, which also influenced the manner in which these types of objects were circulated. In this sense, the creation of the Junta de Damas allowed its members to establish new relationships with entities such as the Real Academia de Bellas Artes de San Fernando, which since 1790 invited them to attend the public awards ceremonies as recent members of the Real Sociedad Económica Matritense. Despite the new status through which they were recognized collectively, the Junta de Damas was not, however, a determining factor to be able to participate in the artistic life of the institution, given that there were many woman admitted as academics from different ranks practically from its foundation.[36]

One of the most interesting cases of this subject is the entry of María Tomasa Palafox y Portocarrero as an academician of merit in 1805. On July 25 of that same year, the Marquis of Espeja, vice protector of the Academy, had convened a regular meeting in order to "show two little oil squares of a crucifix and the Holy family that the Honorable Lady Marquise of Villafranca had copied from some originals by Alonso Cano, and so that the Academy might show her the appreciation that her laudable effort in the study of painting merits by including her in this Royal Society (se viesen en ella dos cuadritos al óleo de un crucifijo y una Sacra familia copiados por la Excma. Sra. Marquesa de Villafranca de unos originales de Alonso Cano, y pudiese la Academia manifestar a esta Sra. el aprecio que la merece su loable aplicación al estudio de la pintura incorporándola a este Real Cuerpo). Once the works were examined and the pertinent vote was taken—in which the candidate earned twenty-six votes of support of a total of twenty-eight—the applicant was named "academician of merit in painting with respect to the dispensation of evidence in the Royal Order of February 27, 1785, for distinguished persons who for pleasure alone are occupied in the noble arts" (*académica de mérito* en la pintura respecto de estar dispensadas las pruebas en la Real Orden de 27 de febrero de 1785 para las personas de calidad que solo por gusto se ocupan en las Nobles Artes).[37]

The two works with religious themes—fully adapted to the types of subjects that were expected of a painting enthusiast and that express the Christian and family values of the good wife and mother—were exhibited a few days later in the halls of the academy. During that time the halls were customarily opened to the public for a couple of weeks to exhibit both the organization's art and antiquities collection as well as the most recent works created by its members. That year attendance must have been high since visitors could also view the works awarded prizes at the competition that the academy convened every three years to honor the most outstanding students in the three noble arts and in engraving. As was announced in the *Gaceta de Madrid* at the end of the same month, the public was able to gain entry to "the rooms of the main hall of the Academy house from the 1st to the 14th of August (excluding days of holy obligation), in the mornings from 10 to 12, and in the afternoons from 5 to 7" (las salas del cuarto principal de la casa de la Academia desde el día 1º hasta el 14 de agosto [excepto los de fiesta de precepto], por la mañana de 10 a 12, y por la tarde de 5 a 7).[38] Apart from the works painted by the Marquise of Villafranca, visitors could see almost one hundred more paintings. Among them were pieces by other noblewomen such as Marcela de la Valencia, the daughter of the Count of Valencia, who joined as an academician of merit at the same time as María Tomasa, and Mariana Waldstein, the Marquise of Santa Cruz, who enjoyed honorary academic status and the title of honorary director from 1782.[39] Of all the works exhibited by women in the summer of 1805, those of the Marquise of Villafranca must have stood out if we consider their formal characteristics: on one hand, they were medium-sized paintings, not miniatures like those of most of her companions; on the other hand, the two works were painted in oil, a technique that required greater skill in comparison with pastels, pencil, or gouache.[40]

These two characteristics are what María Tomasa Palafox y Portocarrero demonstrates in the full-length portrait that Francisco de Goya had made a year earlier and that she opportunely submitted to the 1805 exposition, for it confirmed the validity of the academician-of-merit title that the lady had recently acquired. The model is seen seated upon a luxurious armchair uphol-stered in crimson silk damask and supports her feet on a pillow covered in the same fabric.[41] With her left hand she holds the maulstick and with the right, a brush; the palette rests on a side table with other tools. In front of the aris-tocratic lady represented as an artist is a life-sized canvas with her husband's image, which she seems to paint in frontal or three-quarter view; that is, she demonstrates that she knows how to make excellent portraits. At the same time, she directs her gaze away from the painting, possibly toward the real subject of the portrait, who remains beyond the field of vision, like another spectator who glances back at her. The work synthesizes several key ideas re-garding the multifaceted image that the enlightened woman wanted to project of herself at the close of the eighteenth century and that many members of the Junta de Damas embodied when they were portrayed. In this instance, the model is not simply a woman painter but a great Spanish lady who manifests her social refinement through the meticulous setting of the room where she paints and the luxuriousness of her outfit. The practice of painting is not only the expression of a pastime but also a form of demonstrating her good taste and intellectual status.[42] Finally, but no less importantly, the painting's play of glances alludes to the Enlightenment's modern conception of marriage, based on relationships of affection, love, and felicity in which every marital relation-ship should be established in accordance with the new dictates of the period, and that the couple also expressed in other portraits in which they posed to-gether. (See fig. 10.)[43]

The portrait of the Marquise of Villafranca was accompanied in the exhi-bition by that of another member of the junta: the Marquise of Espeja, wife of the vice protector of the academy, painted by Antonio Poza. If the former expressed her refined education through her mastery of portraiture, the lat-ter emphasized her intellectual impact in her capacity as a translator. At a compositional level, the work is more conventional: the model poses seated in the foreground next to a desk and dressed in the latest fashion in the Im-perial court style similar to that of Palafox. In the background to the left, a view of a landscape opens, and the rest of the room is covered with drapery as an element of aristocratic distinction, which was outdated in portraiture at the beginning of the new century. Her literary activity, unusual in portraits of women, is brought to life through the practice of translation; she shows the spectator two of her works, whose titles are written on the spines of each book:

FIG. 18. Josefa Mónica Alvarado y Lezo, Marquise of Espeja (Antonio Poza), 1805. Ministerio de Cultura y Deporte. Instituto del Patrimonio Cultural de España. Casa Moreno. Archivo de Arte Español (1893–1953).

the first, on which she rests her left arm, is the *Compendio de la Filosofía Moral* by Francesco Maria Zanotti, published in Spanish in 1785; the second, which she holds on her lap, is *La Lengua de los Cálculos* by Abbot Condillac, a work that the marquise had finished the same year, 1805, in which her portrait was painted and exhibited in the halls of the academy.

This publication was dedicated to the Prince of Peace, Manuel de Godoy, as the recognized protector of the sciences, a circumstance that is noted at the same time in the sheet of paper that protrudes from the table (fig. 18).[44] Although the peculiarities of this commission are not known, it is evident that its exhibition responded to a clear strategy to gain visibility since the sale of the translation had been announced scarcely a month before the painting was exhibited.[45] Thus, just as Goya portrays María Tomasa Palafox creating an oil painting as an expression of her artistic mastery upon entering the Academy of San Fernando, Poza shows the intellectual aspect of the Marquise of Espeja by foregrounding one of her works. Her merit resides not only in her mastery of foreign languages, but also in her ability to engage Spanish culture in different European schools of thought. We must not forget that the Marquise of Espeja took interest in the philosophical essay, pedagogy, and ethics—that is, topics that concerned any thinker of the time and that conferred on the translator the possibility of expressing her own ideas by adding to her reading of the original text, since she was able to include those modifications that she deemed appropriate in order to guide the reader in the interpretation of the content.[46]

The intellectual dimension that prevails in the portraits of the Marquises of Villafranca and Espeja was customary for those women who desired to display their refined education, as the second generation of members of the Junta de Damas who would take the reins of the institution in the early decades of the nineteenth century liked to do. A good example with which to conclude is that of María Joaquina Téllez-Girón, the daughter of the Duke and Duchess of Osuna. In this full-length portrait painted by Agustín Esteve in 1798, the young lady is shown accompanied by a globe where she studies geography, an indication of the breadth of subjects that her education entailed. Some years later, when she was already the Marquise of Santa Cruz, Francisco de Goya painted another portrait, in which she appears sensually reclined like a classical muse and posing with a lyre-shaped guitar, an expression of her fondness for music, a pleasure shared by her sister, Manuela Isidra, who was likewise painted by Goya in 1816 with a musical score in her hands.[47]

With the Peninsular War concluded, portraiture of women did not undergo new representational strategies, despite the Junta de Damas continuing to broaden its efforts. The stagnation of the ideals of the Enlightenment—exacerbated by the return to absolutism during the reign of King Fernando VII—also influenced the manner of being portrayed: thus, neither the members of the Junta de Damas nor other distinguished ladies of the Court seemed to be interested any longer in defending their intellectual position or their civic inclinations in the public sphere. On the contrary, these aspects gradually dwindled in favor of the values that the Romantic ideal of *ángel del hogar* (the angel in the house) would embody beginning in the 1830s.

NOTES

Essay translated by Kathleen Fueger.

1. Smith, *The Emerging Female Citizen*, 106.

2. Quoted by Fernández Quintanilla, *La mujer ilustrada*, 69. Other objectives of the Junta de Damas were to "reduce extravagance [. . .] and replace foreign adornments or those merely

whimsical with domestic kinds" (cortar el lujo [. . .] y sustituir para sus adornos los géneros nacionales a los Extranjeros, y de puro capricho). To achieve these objectives, Count Floridablanca, secretary of state, sent the Junta de Damas the *Discurso sobre el lujo de las señoras y proyecto de un traje nacional* (*Discourse on Women's Luxury and Project for a National Dress*) so that they could offer a prize to whoever designed a model of a national dress made of fabrics made in Spain. (See Martín-Valdepeñas Yagüe, "Women's Associationism and the Pursuit of Public Happiness," in this volume.)

3. Duncan, "Happy Mothers," 7. This ideal of maternity, widely disseminated throughout all of Europe in the works of philosophers such as Rousseau, was conditioned in Spain by the importance of other values stemming from Catholic morality. This singularity also distinguishes the representation of the familial role of Spanish women in their portraits as compared with women from other countries, a question which exceeds the object of this study.

4. Sheriff, *The Exceptional Woman*, 2.

5. See as an example the gallery that began to develop informally since the middle of the century at the Academia de Bellas Artes de San Fernando (Royal Academy of Fine Arts of San Fernando). Alonso Cabezas, "Una galería de retratos," 195. About the gallery of directors of Real Academia Española, see Quintana Bermúdez de la Puente, "La galería de retratos de los directores."

6. Blanco Mozo, *Orígenes y desarrollo de la Ilustración vasca en Madrid*, 235–36.

7. "The *noble reception* hall" (emphasis in the original). Aguirre, *Sistema de sociedades patrióticas*, 57–58.

8. Collection of the Real e Ilustre Junta de Damas de Honor y Mérito, Madrid.

9. Martín-Valdepeñas Yagüe, "El retrato de la condesa de Truillas," 71–73.

10. "vivos sentimientos de ternura y júbilo; porque de un lado se les representaban las acciones virtuosas de la persona a quien se ofrecía aquel tributo de reconocimiento, y gratitud, y del otro la ilustración, y generosidad de la Real Sociedad, que conociendo, y apreciando justamente los beneficios, que la proporcionan sus individuos sabe también corresponder a ellos dignamente, erigiendo monumentos que perpetúen su memoria en los siglos venideros." Quoted, along with other descriptions of the ceremony, by Martín-Valdepeñas Yagüe, "El retrato de la condesa de Truillas," 77.

11. Quoted by Fernández Quintanilla, *La mujer ilustrada*, 151; Bolufer Peruga, *Mujeres e Ilustración*, 376.

12. Collection of the Duke of Peñaranda.

13. Preserved, respectively, in the Fondazione Magnani-Rocca, the collection of the Dukes of Fernán Núñez, and Museo del Prado, inventory no. P000739. Molina, *Mujeres y hombres*, 227–39.

14. Demerson, *María Francisca de Sales Portocarrero*, 74, 101–23; Fernández Quintanilla, *La mujer ilustrada*, 39–40. The work has been dated between 1795 and 1797, when María Gabriela married. This would explain why she posed standing next to her sister since by then both would be married to other members of the Spanish nobility, another personal success for the countess, who settled advantageous marriages for all of her children. Soria, *Agustín Esteve y Goya*, 56–57.

15. Molina, *Mujeres y hombres*, 259–64.

16. It must not be forgotten that the countess herself received a strong education with the women religious of the Convent of the Visitation, which included learning living foreign languages. From this stage a beautiful portrait of her in student attire painted by Andrés de la Calleja in 1765 is preserved (Fundación Casa de Alba). Demerson, *María Francisca de Sales Portocarrero*, 43.

17. Amar y Borbón, *Discurso sobre la educación física*, 160–62.

18. Campomanes, *Discursos sobre la educación popular de los artesanos*, 237.

19. An example is Concepción de Belvis de Moncada y Pizarro, the Marquise of Ariza, who was portrayed by Agustín Esteve in 1796 (Collection of the Duke of Infantado). Dressed in an evening gown, her fondness for music as the main element of social distinction and refinement prevails in the painting.

20. Martín-Valdepeñas Yagüe, "El eco del saber," 106–8.

21. Fraisse, *Musa de la razón*, 27; Bolufer Peruga, "Galerías de 'mujeres ilustres,'" 183.

22. Molina, "De mujer fuerte a ciudadana," 80–88. Nor did they take the opportunity to add any feminine portrait, in spite of their original proposal, to the collection *Retratos de españoles ilustres con un breve epítome de sus vidas* that began to be sold by subscription in 1791. Molina, "Retratos de españoles ilustres," 49.

23. Several portraits housed in the BNE serve as an example, such as those of María Lavedant (IH/4706/2), Rita Luna (IH/5132/1), and María Antonia Vallejo y Fernández, alias "La Caramba" (IH/9563/1) or Mariana Márquez (IH/5437).

24. BNE, IH/4222/1.

25. There exists another portrait of the young woman, painted by Joaquín Inza the same year and commissioned by the university itself (Collection of the Universidad Complutense de Madrid), which also constitutes an early example of the feminine institutional portrait. Molina, *Mujeres y hombres*, 244–47.

26. BNE, IH/6959/1.

27. Carrete Parrondo, *El grabado a buril*, 163.

28. *Gaceta de Madrid* 56 (July 15, 1794): 843.

29. Le Moyne, *Galería de las mujeres fuertes*, iv–v.

30. *Diario de Madrid* 7 (January 7, 1795): 26. BNE, IH/298/1.

31. Schulz, "Goya's Portraits," 279; Molina, "De mujer fuerte a ciudadana," 98–100.

32. Albarrán Martín, *El desafío del blanco*, 40.

33. BNE, IH/9316/1. Montijo, *Elogio de la Señora Doña Petra de Torres Feloaga*.

34. Campomanes, "Observaciones," 59.

35. Lewis, "'A su reina benéfica,'" 700.

36. Smith, *The Emerging Female Citizen*, 50–73.

37. Minutes of meeting, July 25, 1805, 189, ARABSF, Legajo 3–87. The scene relating to *The Sacred Family in the Carpenter's Workshop* (Inv. 0181) is preserved in the museum's collection. For other female members, see the list of "Señoras Académicas" (ARABSF, Legajo 1–40–4), whose records have recently been transcribed and studied by Pérez Martín in "Ilustres e ilustradas," 623–87.

38. *Gaceta de Madrid* 61 (July 30, 1805): 655–56.

39. Other participants in the exhibit included María Maciá, Francisca Sabatier, and María Ignacia de Tejada, who, although they were never admitted as academicians, regularly sent their works to the exhibitions. Navarrete Martínez, *La Academia de Bellas Artes de San Fernando y la pintura*, 300, 468–69.

40. Greer, *La carrera de obstáculos*, 106; Smith, *The Emerging Female Citizen*, 62.

41. MNP, P002448.

42. Its practice was recommended by Josefa Amar y Borbón in 1790, who deemed it "a very honest exercise" (ejercicio muy honesto) for women. Among its characteristics, she notes "the attributes of what the artist is trying to portray, which become like the soul of the painting and which distinguishes the great geniuses from the middling ones" (la propiedad de lo que intenta representarse, que viene a ser como el alma de la pintura, que distingue los grandes genios de los medianos). In this way she defended a woman artist with knowledge of composition, that is, with ingenuity and inventiveness. Amar y Borbón, *Discurso sobre la educación física*, 192.

43. Molina, *Mujeres y hombres*, 252–56. A good example is the portrait painted by Agustín Esteve around 1800 (Hispanic Society of America, New York), in which the scene of the young couple with their first-born son exemplifies the ideal family of the Enlightenment. (See fig. 10.)

44. Rose-de Viejo, "Ni Goya, ni Esteve, sino Poza," 43–44. The author adds a black-and-white reproduction of the work, which is currently missing.

45. The work was for sale "in Francés's bookstore, in front of the steps of San Felipe, for 24 *reales* for a hardcover and 20 for a paperback" (en la librería de Francés, frente a las gradas de San Felipe, a 24 reales en pasta y 20 en rústica). *Gaceta de Madrid* 53 (July 2, 1805): 572.

46. Bolufer Peruga, "Traducción y creación," 140.

47. The three mentioned works are preserved in the MNP (P002581, P007070, and P007713).

Epilogue

The Junta de Damas, the Enlightenment, and Feminism

CATHERINE M. JAFFE AND
ELISA MARTÍN-VALDEPEÑAS YAGÜE

We must never forget that the Enlightenment is an event, or a set of events and complex processes, that is located at a certain point in the development of European societies. As such, it includes elements of social transformation, types of political institution, forms of knowledge, projects of rationalizations of knowledge and practices, technological mutations that are very difficult to sum up in a word, even if many of these phenomena remain important today. The one I have pointed out and that seems to me to have been at the basis of an entire form of philosophical reflection concerns only the mode of reflective relation to the present.
—MICHEL FOUCAULT, "What Is Enlightenment?" 1984

Becoming an Enlightened man was a process that began with an education, was consolidated with personal promotion, and culminated in intellectual recognition. It was not an easy road, but it was full of encouragement, and it was travelled in company. Becoming an Enlightened woman was a decision made on less firm ground: it was an exercise in surmounting deficiencies and misgivings, a test of liberty that yielded satisfactions, and was an end in itself.
—MARÍA VICTORIA LÓPEZ-CORDÓN CORTEZO, "Situating Women," 2018

What was the contribution of the Junta de Damas of the Real Sociedad Económica Matritense to the Enlightenment and to the history of feminism in Spain and beyond? As the previous essays have suggested, the work and example of the Junta de Damas must be assessed within a discrete historical and cultural moment: the transition from the end of the old regime to nineteenth-century liberalism. The socias of the Junta de Damas represented a range of political ideologies, and their vision of society was conditioned by their rank and privilege. But they nevertheless participated in the circulation of enlightened ideals regarding women's role in the progress of society, the importance of women's education, and in new, enlightened practices of charity, and so contributed to the evolving understanding of gender roles in Spain. The discourses surrounding the founding of the Junta de Damas in 1787 and the junta's activities during the first decades of its existence that are chronicled in this book, such as the pedagogical innovations they made in their professional schools for women, described by Josefina Méndez, manifested qualities of Enlightenment such as those Foucault describes: "elements of social transformation, types of political institution, forms of knowledge, projects of rationalizations of knowledge and practices, technological mutations."[1]

At the end of the eighteenth century, only decades before the political and social turbulence of the Peninsular War and its aftermath, the women of the Junta de Damas provided a model for how educated women could form an association—one that has endured to this day—to contribute to the betterment of society by using their reason, intelligence, and feminine experience to enter the public sphere of secular charity. They participated in the creation of public opinion by openly debating, in an orderly fashion, ideas, rationales, processes, and innovations regarding the welfare and education of poor women and children, and by recording and publishing their debates and reports. They were closely aligned to the monarchy, they did not envision a society based on social equality, and their reforms in education and the care of orphans and infants were later subsumed into the institutions and ideologies of nineteenth-century moderate and progressive liberalisms, as Mónica Burguera discusses in her essay in this volume. However, they set an example of rational, hands-on leadership and drew on up-to-date knowledge of science, hygiene, and pedagogical theory to carry out their reforms. They circulated this knowledge and their practical experience through public debates and strategic publications and reports. In Spain, they modeled women's participation in secular economic societies with the goal to improve society apart from traditional charitable institutions of the Catholic Church, thus providing an example for women to practice their utility to their society outside their traditional family duties.

In this way, the Junta de Damas claimed an unprecedented role for women in the public sphere in late-Enlightenment Spain. James Melton describes this conceptual space, theorized by Jürgen Habermas, as "a sphere of sociability and discussion distinct from the realm of state power." Melton points out that women were crucial to the public sphere's "practices and institutions":

"Legitimizing their participation were Enlightenment notions of sociability that considered the mingling of the sexes as crucial to the progress of society."[2] During the eighteenth century, women participated in the public sphere by writing, reading, publishing, attending the theater, hosting salons, and participating in practices of mixed sociability. Karen O'Brien has argued that a key tenet of Enlightenment thought was the idea of the progress of society and of history as a "civilising process," and therefore a society's progress and modernity could be judged by the status of its women.[3] Elizabeth Lewis has shown in her essay how the socias of the Junta de Damas carried out their charitable works by physically moving between private and public spaces as they circulated throughout the city, complicating the supposed division between the domestic and the public spheres.

This book began by citing Josefa Amar's claim for women's right to an education because of the equality of reason between men and women and with Mary Wollstonecraft's observation that, for a society to progress, both women and men must be educated to seek virtue. The Junta de Damas' example of women's exercise of public virtue—using their talents and intelligence to provide for the welfare and education of poor women and children, and so help them to become useful and productive members of society—contributes to the wider European and American Enlightenments by showing how women as a group participated in the public sphere to promote the progress of society outside their domestic space. The efforts of the Junta de Damas, and the opposition its members faced as they claimed a role in the public sphere, attracted notice outside of Spain. The Russian ambassador to Spain, Stepán Stepánovich Zinóviev, wrote in a report to his government about the novelty of women joining Madrid's Economic Society and their effort to replace imported textiles with those manufactured in Spain. He observed that these women's aspirations to enact reform were so novel in Spain that "[t]he public made fun of them, saying that their efforts were nothing but frivolous and a 'pure bagatelle'" (Le public se moque des dames, on dit que cela n'est qu'une chose frivole et de pure bagatelle).[4] The Junta de Damas firmly and consistently rejected criticism that belittled their work. These attitudes persisted even as late as the mid-twentieth century, when a historian concluded that the Junta's "activity—aside from benevolence—was much on the same level as fashionable interest in milking at Versailles."[5] Certainly the evidence of the dedication and the sacrifices made during the desperate war years by the women of the Junta de Damas, like the Marquise of Fuerte-Híjar, belie such a patronizing assessment of the women's work and their motivations.

A salient aspect of the Junta de Damas' contribution to the Enlightenment is that they formed a secular feminine association and acted through it. As María Victoria López-Cordón rightly pointed out, an Enlightened woman had to find her own way, and it was often a lonely road: "Feminine voices that were consistent with Enlightened ideology were never numerous in Spain or anywhere else. Although rhetorically Enlightenment ideology was directed at women, its arguments were devised by a public formed by men, and for this reason, rather than asserting unrealizable goals, Enlightened women displayed what was their greatest conquest: the ability to express themselves as subjects."[6] The *Statutes* of the Junta de Damas are a clear indication of the ability of women to "express themselves as subjects," to rationally discuss goals and ideas, assign tasks, and measure and report the results of their activities. The junta's continued assertions of their equality with and independence from the male Sociedad Económica, described by Elisa Martín-Valdepeñas Yagüe in her essay, prove that they were well aware that their status had to be constantly defended. They persisted despite many attempts to check their agency.

The Junta de Damas as an event or phenomenon of the Enlightenment both modeled and reflected subtle changes in society regarding women's status and abilities that point to the junta's modernity. In their essays, Mónica Bolufer and María Victoria López-Cordón analyze the remarkable intellectual polemic regarding the rational equality of men and women and masculine and feminine gender roles that erupted upon the founding of the Junta de Damas and that echoed around Spain and in the European press. The creation of the Junta de Damas also provoked a linguistic polemic in Spain, as Pedro Álvarez de Miranda has shown, when the feminine form "presidenta" of the word "presidente" was used to refer to the first president of the Junta de Damas, the Duchess of Osuna. Álvarez de Miranda attributes the polemic to the "social novelty presented by the accession of women to positions, activities or functions that until then had been reserved for men." He points out the modernity of this debate, for today there are still linguistic disputes over the feminine form of words for traditionally masculine professions like judge (juez/jueza), doctor (médico/médica), or lawyer (abogado/abogada).[7] Letters protesting this "ungrammatical" innovation of "presidenta" for the leader of the Junta de

Damas were quickly published in the periodical press in 1787, only to be countered by others defending it. Álvarez de Miranda notes that the feminine form "presidenta" had in fact been in use since the mid-fifteenth century. While earlier it had tended to be associated with a symbolic or mythological creature or woman, as the centuries progressed it began to appear more frequently, most often referring to the wife of a man who held the role of president rather than to a woman who held that position herself.

The Enlightened writer Tomás de Iriarte, a friend of the Duchess of Osuna, joined this linguistic dispute by publishing a letter in the press defending the use of "presidenta," arguing that usage and not merely grammatical rules should determine acceptability. Iriarte even left a series of notes, now held in the archive of the Real Academia Española (Royal Academy of Spain), documenting the use of "presidenta" to refer to a woman who held such a leadership role in her own right. Álvarez de Miranda observes that this grammatical polemic might not have arisen if "presidenta" had not been used to refer to the leader of this unusual and prominent female society. He suggests that the unusually rapid adoption by the Real Academia's dictionary—between the third edition of 1791 and the fourth edition of 1803—of the feminine form "presidenta" to signify "[t]he wife of the president; or the woman who is in command of and presides in some community" (la muger del presidente; o la que manda y preside en alguna comunidad) may have been encouraged in part by the polemic over the founding of the Junta de Damas and by evolving social roles that were reflected in changes in linguistic usage.[8]

Álvarez de Miranda also shows that, besides generating the neologism "sociabilidad" (sociability) to signify a human virtue, the word "sociedad," little used before 1700, gained in importance and accrued new resonances throughout the eighteenth century.[9] Early in the century it held both an abstract meaning of "behavior, coexistence, human commerce" (trato, convivencia, comercio humano) and referred to a concrete reality—influenced by the founding in 1662 of the Royal Society in Britain—of "a group or company of individuals for the advancement of the faculties and sciences" (la junta o compañía de varios sugetos para el adelantamiento de las facultades y ciencias).[10] Citing the historian José Antonio Maravall, Álvarez de Miranda points out that "socio" even gains, by the end of the eighteenth century, a political value like that of "citizen" (ciudadano).[11] When the members of the Junta de Damas claimed the title of "socias," then, they also were fashioning themselves as modern citizens.

The Junta de Damas, the discourses and polemics associated with it, its *Statutes,* and the concrete evidence of the reforms the members attempted to carry out represented a society in transition to modernity, one in which each subject would reflect on his or her own place in history and its relation to the past and to the future. Mulling over Immanuel Kant's famous 1784 essay "Was ist Aufklärung?" Foucault suggests that we think of modernity as an "attitude" rather than a historical period: "A mode of relating to contemporary reality; a voluntary choice made by certain people; in the end, a way of thinking and feeling; a way, too, of acting and behaving that at one and the same time marks a relation of belonging and presents itself as a task." Modernity, Foucault writes, is a "consciousness of the discontinuity of time: a break with tradition, a feeling of novelty."[12]

Spain's Junta de Damas, like other eighteenth-century economic societies, took as its raison d'être this sense of living in a new era that for its *socias* meant breaking with traditional feminine roles and reforming institutions to address the problems of the present and thereby bring about a better future for marginalized women and children. This does not mean that they were all revolutionaries, nor that they all supported the political and social changes introduced following the Cortes de Cádiz and the end of the old regime, as Paloma Fernández-Quintanilla has shown in her essay regarding the Duchess of Osuna. Yet within their time and moment in history, they collectively carried out an innovation in women's role in the public sphere that pointed to modernity. The Countess of Montijo, Gloria Franco explains in her essay, challenged the limitations of women's traditional role to help to lead the reform projects of the Junta de Damas. During the crisis of the Peninsular War, women were forced into new roles of public action. Afterwards, as Gloria Espigado has shown in her essay, when Montijo's daughter, the Marquise of Villafranca, founded the Sociedad de Señoras de Fernando VII, the women's earlier experience as members of the Junta de Damas favored their collective entrance into the public sphere.

Most eighteenth-century women were not sufficiently educated to follow the "philosophical life" that Foucault says is required for the critique of our consciousness and the analysis of our limits that is the condition for Enlightenment, although neither were most men of that period either. Foucault insists, though, that what is necessary is to distinguish between "universal" and "arbitrary constraints": "to transform the critique conducted in the form of necessary limitation into a practical critique that takes the form of a possible transgression."[13] The women of the Junta de Damas recognized the "arbitrary constraints" placed on women's action and agency, and they insisted on overcoming them through their association and activities. In this way, they were transgressive.

All this does not mean that they were able to change the status of women in their society, however. For example, one of the precursors of Spanish feminism, Concepción Arenal (1820–1893), who was very interested in women's education, the eradication of poverty, and prison reform, refers to the Junta de Damas in her book *La beneficencia, la filantropía y la caridad* (1861, Beneficence, Philanthropy, and Charity). Arenal praises the anonymous actions of the aristocratic women who contributed to improving the lives of other women, and their effort to reform the institutions in their charge:

> Do you see that great lady, beautiful, perfumed, brilliant, adored, proud? The dressing table, the salon, the carriage, the theater; this is her life [. . .]. So reasons mistakenly the person who sees her: but that woman dedicates many hours and entire days caring for motherless children, and thanks to her attentions and those of her friends, the mortality of the children in the Inclusa has been vastly reduced. She goes in a carriage to aid the miserable! Certainly. but in the end, for men, and probably for God, it is better to do good in a carriage, than to do nothing on foot.[14]

Perhaps the Junta de Damas was not able to change the status of women in society to the extent of acquisition of political rights, but the junta did make manifest that women should improve the conditions of their lives, access education, and be supported and protected when they found themselves abandoned.

Carla Hesse cautions that, in Kant's view, "women [and servants] were not perceived to be either capable of self-governance or of reasoning about general rather than particular interests." Hesse states that, during the liberal era following the Enlightenment, women had to struggle to be granted "recognition of their capacity to make independent judgements (independent, especially, of their priests) and the capacity to represent something larger than their own sex."[15] The Junta de Damas proved that women could reason about the general interest, but their example was limited by powerful ideologies of gender that also grew out of the Enlightenment, partly as a response to women's newly assertive role. Jean-Jacques Rousseau's model of complementary gender roles, expressed in his treatise on education, *Émile* (1762), and widely known in Spain despite the prohibition of all his works by the Inquisition in 1764, rationalized the confinement of women to the domestic sphere and influenced gender roles during the transition from the eighteenth to the nineteenth century.[16] The Enlightenment's legacy for women in Spain and elsewhere was in many ways ambiguous, as Mónica Bolufer has shown.[17] The Enlightenment did not posit women's independent agency; it acknowledged women's right to an education but left the appropriate scope of women's instruction undecided; and it likewise left unresolved many questions regarding gender roles, particularly whether such roles were natural and immutable, or constructed and subject to change.

Foucault questioned whether we will ever truly fulfill the Enlightenment project, "whether we will ever reach mature adulthood."[18] The women of the Junta de Damas were certainly aware of the arbitrary limitations imposed on their agency and capacity to act as adults in the public sphere. Nevertheless they persevered in asserting their rationality, pragmatism, capacity for action, and independence. In this way they transgressed the gender roles of their day and pushed at the limits placed on women at the time that relegated them to dependent roles as wives, mothers, and daughters. The Junta de Damas wrote and published their *Statutes*, held orderly meetings, kept minutes, gave reports, ran charitable institutions, studied and reported on topics of interest, wrote and published reports and summaries of their activities. As individuals, they also wrote, translated, and published works that circulated in the Republic of Letters and identified them as members of the Junta de Damas, as described in Jaffe's essay "Networks of Enlightenment," and they commissioned portraits that represented them as enlightened women, as Álvaro Molina discusses in "Representing the Feminine Ideal."

Modern feminism is "the demand, first made at the very end of the [eighteenth] century, for equal civil and political rights for women," according to Karen O'Brien.[19] This was not the platform of the Junta de Damas, who chose to actively engage in the public sphere of enlightened charity under the cloak of a traditional role of "civic motherhood."[20] However, Bolufer points to the "profound and ambiguous footprint that the Enlightenment left in all of these debates and in the very origins of modern feminism."[21] O'Brien insists that Enlightenment discourses provided the essential foundation for the development of modern feminism: "Enlightenment philosophical and historical enquiries created a framework and a language for understanding the gendered structures of society without which nineteenth-century feminism would not have been possible."[22] Family relationships were the basis for feminine identity at the turn of the eighteenth century, but the women of the Junta de Damas also claimed a secular, corporate identity as agents of public utility that transcended their traditional roles. Their self-fashioning as an association of enlightened civic mothers was a deliberate attempt to use an acceptable feminine role as a pragmatic vehicle to access the public sphere. For this reason, they stand as a vital example of Enlightenment women's independent agency at the dawn of modern feminism.

NOTES

1. Foucault, "What Is Enlightenment?" 43.

2. Melton, *The Rise of the Public*, 14, 202–5.

3. O'Brien, *Women and Enlightenment*, 1–2.

4. Tratchevsky, "L'Espagne à l'époque de la Révolution française," 4. Zinoviev was ambassador in Madrid between 1774 and 1792. Sarrailh, *La España ilustrada*, 258.

5. Shafer, *The Economic Societies in the Spanish World*, 71.

6. López-Cordón Cortezo, "Situating Women," 37.

7. We thank Pedro Álvarez de Miranda and David T. Gies for their comments and help with this issue. Álvarez de Miranda, "*La presidenta o la presidente?*" 805.

8. Quoted in Álvarez de Miranda, "*La presidenta o la presidente?*" 822.

9. Álvarez de Miranda, *Palabras e ideas*, 373–78.

10. Álvarez de Miranda, *Palabras e ideas*, 351–52, 359.

11. Álvarez de Miranda, *Palabras e ideas*, 367.

12. Foucault, "What Is Enlightenment?" 39.

13. Foucault, "What Is Enlightenment?" 45.

14. "Veis aquella gran señora, hermosa, perfumada, brillante, adorada, orgullosa? El tocador, el salón, el coche, el teatro; esta es su vida [. . .]. Así discurre el que la ve, y se equivoca: aquella mujer dedica muchos ratos, días enteros a cuidar de los niños que no tienen madre, y gracias a sus cuidados y los de sus amigas, la mortandad de los niños de la Inclusa ha disminuido de una manera increíble. ¡Va en coche a auxiliar a los miserables! Cierto. Pero al cabo, para los hombres, y probablemente para Dios, vale más hacer bien en coche, que no hacer nada a pie." Arenal de García Carrasco, *La beneficencia, la filantropía y la caridad*, 70. On Arenal and the charity of the Junta de Damas, see Lewis, "La caridad de una mujer," 198–201; Caballé Masforroll, *Concepción Arenal*; Romeo Mateo, "Concepción Arenal"; Bieder, "Women Authors," 139–46.

15. Hesse, *The Other Enlightenment*, xiv–xv.

16. Bolufer Peruga, *Mujeres e Ilustración*, 74–75.

17. Bolufer Peruga, *Mujeres e Ilustración*, 399, and "New Inflections."

18. Foucault, "What Is Enlightenment?" 49.

19. O'Brien, *Women and Enlightenment*, 2.

20. Bolufer Peruga, *Mujeres e Ilustración*, 341–88; Smith, *The Emerging Female Citizen*, 149–52; and Lewis, "Women and 'Civic Motherhood,'" among others, use this term to describe the identity assumed by the Junta de Damas.

21. Bolufer Peruga, "New Inflections," 49.

22. O'Brien, *Women and Enlightenment*, 2.

Appendix

Statutes of the Junta de Socias de Honor y Mérito of the Real Sociedad Económica de Madrid, 1794

"Helping by teaching" (*Socorre enseñando*)

Imprenta de Sancha [Madrid], 1794

TITLE I

Of the Junta and Its Individual Members in General

I.

The Junta de Socias de Honor y Mérito of the Sociedad Económica de Madrid will be comprised of an undetermined number of members.

II.

Its purpose is to establish and spread good education, improve manners through its example and enlightenment, introduce the love of work, and foment industry.

III.

Members must have a good education and good conduct, with proven instruction in the objectives of the Junta.

IV.

Those seeking admission must submit their request to the Junta through the Secretary.

V.

Once admission is granted by the Junta, and confirmed by the Sociedad, the new member,[1] will be sent a certificate of admission, a copy of these Statutes, and those of the Sociedad.

VI.

From this time on, she may attend sessions of the Junta, and those of the Sociedad, as she wishes.

VII.

She may also propose any useful thought either orally or in writing.

VIII.

Those who are absent[2] will execute the experiments the Junta requests of them and communicate their reports to the Junta.

IX.

The reports that the Socias want to present or send to the Junta, will be published separately or in the Sociedad's collection, either in entirety or in extract, to be determined.

X.

Each Socia will contribute one hundred and sixty reales de vellón per year.

XI.

No Socia will solicit certification of services rendered to the Sociedad to obtain any outside prize, for the esteem of her fellow Socias and of the public shall be her sole compensation.

TITLE II

On the Sessions

I.

The Junta will usually meet every Friday.

II.

In January, February, March, October, November, and December, the meetings will begin at 5 P.M.; they will begin at 6 P.M. during the other months, and at all times they will last two hours.

III.

The order of seating will be according to the arrival of the Socias, placing the President at the head of the table, the Censor[3] and the Secretary at either side of her at the table, and the Vice President at the head of the right-hand bench.

IV.

The meeting will begin with the reading and ratification of the minutes of the preceding meeting, which will be drafted and presented in case any notes or corrections should be made.

V.

Once the minutes are ratified, any orders, reports, or other papers which the Junta must address will be read aloud; and their disposition will be decided upon in the same order they are presented, or they will be examined directly.

VI.

Every Socia will read, and then will leave in the Secretary's office the paper she has written; with the understanding that no discourse or project will be printed, adopted, or executed, until two assigned Socias read it and express their judgment, listening first to the Socia who wrote it.

VII.

The Junta will not attack another's opinion, leaving every Socia the liberty to reflect on matters of opinion while maintaining modesty and order.

VIII.

Always when one or more Socias contradicts any judgment or proposal, the opinion or will of the Junta shall be determined by voting.

IX.

The proposal and the counter-proposal to be voted upon shall be written down with all possible exactness, and they will be read three times, and each Socia will adhere precisely to each one, unless she herself proposes or follows a different vote.[4]

X.

Voting shall be done in public, except in the two cases of the admission of Socias and the election of officers, when the votes shall be counted in private.

XI.

No proposition shall be resolved unless a simple majority of the Socias present at the meeting vote in favor of it.

XII.

The minutes will specify the principle reasons for which every resolution voted upon was supported or contradicted.

XIII.

Any Socia may demand that her own particular vote be inserted in the resolution; but she must submit her request in writing and signed, explaining the reasons behind it, and recognizing the reasoning of others who have had a different or contrary opinion.

XIV.

In no session shall the resolution of another session be revoked or reformed, unless new reasons are presented that clearly contradict the initial reasons, and that are qualified as such by the vote of two-thirds of the Socias in attendance.

XV.

No Socia may interrupt the speech of another.

XVI.

When a Socia has a personal interest in the matter under discussion, she will allow the Junta to deliberate.

XVII.

The application that anyone presents with a proposal to be a Socia, will be read in the first meeting after its reception by the Junta; and the voting will be deferred until the next meeting, under the unalterable rule that those who did not attend the meeting when the application was first read will not have a vote.

XVIII.

If any extraordinary or urgent matter should arise, the President may call to her home the Censor, the Secretary, and the six most senior Socias who attended the latest meeting, with the obligation to make a report in writing at the next meeting of the matter and its resolution.

TITLE III

On Offices and Elections

I.

There shall always be a President, a Censor, and a Secretary with their respective substitutes, who shall be elected by a free vote of the Junta.

II.

Elections will be preceded by a formal convocation of all the Socias who have a vote.

III.

Any Socia who has not attended twelve sessions in the entire year shall not have an active or a passive vote[5] in the elections of the Junta nor of the Sociedad.

IV.

During the election each Socia will be given a list of the names of those eligible to vote, excluding her own; all will choose, according to their will, putting their votes secretly in the urn.

V.

The President will count the ballots collected, and finding as many votes as there are eligible voters present, she will read them aloud one by one, and the Secretary will record them; the Socia will be elected who at the first count has received more than half of the votes; but if no one obtains this plurality, the second count will proceed by sortition (casting lots), and only those two who have received the greatest number of votes will be entered, and in the case of a tie luck will decide the outcome.

VI.

The voting lists will always include as a general rule the Socias who have finished their term of office, because they can be reelected.

TITLE IV

About the President

I.

It is the President's duty to begin and end the meetings, to maintain order in them, distribute charges and commissions, and indicate the direction that business should take.

II.

Whenever the President names a commission regarding the Schools, some of the Curadoras (supervisors or guardians) should always be included.

III.

It is also her duty to encourage the work of the Junta, for which reason she is considered a member of all the commissions.

IV.

She will ensure that all resolutions are carried out exactly.

V.

She will not permit that the Junta's harmoniousness be disturbed by talkative personalities in the meetings but rather she will impose silence which will be observed as inviolable.

VI.

When any affair has been sufficiently discussed, she will summarize the case and establish the propositions for voting.

VII.

She will always be the last to vote in public; and in the case of the votes of the Junta dividing into two equal parts, her vote will be the tiebreaker.

VIII.

She will attend the sessions strictly at the assigned time, or she will excuse herself ahead of time in writing.

IX.

In the meeting before the elections, she will present an instructive report in which she explains the state of the affairs of the Junta at the time of her accepting office: the projects, undertakings, and operations that have been executed that year, and the state in which she is leaving everything, so that a fair idea can be formed of how much has been done, or remains to do.

X.

In the absences and illness of the President, all her rights and obligations will fall on the Vice President; and in the absence of both of them, the most senior Socia will preside, excluding the Censor and the Secretary because of their tasks.

XI.

The Presidency shall last one year.

TITLE V

About the Censor

I.

It is the responsibility of the Censor to ensure the observance of the Statutes and resolutions of the Junta, and that each Socia carries out her offices and commissions.

II.

She will also have a book in which she notes all the commissions that are conferred in the Juntas, and she will point out any oversight or transgression that she observes.

III.

During the meeting she will record the resolutions as notes that will then be used to write the minutes.

IV.

Purely procedural matters may not be resolved without hearing her ruling, which is strictly limited to whether they conform or disagree with the Statutes.

V.

In no case is she to give advice, but she must oppose and submit a complaint against any decision that directly or indirectly is contrary to the Statutes.

VI.

She is never to vote on a matter in which she has issued a ruling.

VII.

As the Socias finish attending twelve meetings [of the year in session], she will record them on a list, which should agree with another that the Secretary shall present in the meeting previous to the elections, announcing those who are allowed to vote.

VIII.

The duration of this task shall be a year.

TITLE VI

About the Secretary

I.

It shall be the obligation of the Secretary to give an account to the Junta of everything that occurs, and to read herself the orders and papers, and also the reports and memorandums of the Socias who are not present.

II.

She should write up the minutes, and send them ratified by the Junta for confirmation by the Sociedad, and later ensure that they are copied in the official books of minutes together with any clarifications or considerations that were offered.

III.

She will be the person through whom the will of the Junta is expressed; for this purpose she will follow the correspondence with the Ministry and the Tribunals, and with all the institutions and persons inside and outside the Sociedad.

IV.

When writing officially, she will begin writing everything that is said, and finish with her signature, having included exactly in the papers a literal copy of the resolutions to which she refers.

V.

The certificates of admission of new Socias issued by the Secretary's office of the Sociedad will be delivered to the new Socias by the Secretary.

VI.

She may of course remit written warnings, reminders, and other corresponding charges to carry out the business agreed upon in the meeting, without waiting for ratification of the minutes.

VII.

She will bring a record of the attendance of each Socia at the Junta's sessions, and according to it she will present in the meeting before an election the list of those who should have a vote in it.

VIII.

Before the public sessions of the Sociedad, she will present to the Junta an accurate, reasoned account of the work completed or agreed upon by the Socias since the last annual public session, which, once approved by the Junta, will be sent to the Sociedad to be read.

IX.

In this annual report on the Junta's activities she will honor deceased Socias, to whom no special eulogy was granted.

X.

She will not give any other certifications than those that were specifically agreed upon, read, and approved by the Junta.

XI.

She will be careful to send those papers to the Secretary's office until there are enough to be archived.

XII.

Each semester she will present a signed account of the costs incurred by her office, which will be paid from the funds of the Sociedad.

XIII.

In her absences and illnesses her Substitute will take her place; and in case of the Substitute's absence the Socia appointed by whoever presides over the Junta, the minutes having always to be signed by the Socia who acted as secretary; but the Secretary herself will carry out the orders or charges that result from them.

XIV.

If any Socia asks to borrow a report or document, the Secretary will give it to her in exchange for a receipt.

XV.

The office of Secretary will last three years.

TITLE VII

Of the Commissions in General

I.

Commissions or assignments of the Junta are understood generally to be everything that should be done in its name, and to which the entire membership cannot attend, or which by its nature requires that it be carried out by one or by a few people.

II.

If some members were named to any deputation or commission, even one to be carried out verbally, they will bring their results in writing, and the most senior one will read it, and then will have it copied into the minutes, and kept in the Secretary's office by the Secretary.

III.

The principal commissions are those that address what is the constant observance or purview of the Junta's objectives, that is, those whose object is education in general, practical teaching in the Schools, and rendering necessary public aid, consistent with the fomenting of popular industry.

TITLE VIII

On the Education Commissions

I.

There will be two permanent commissions whose object will be the education of women; the first shall be occupied with moral education, and the other with respect to physical education.

II.

All the members will sign up for one of the two commissions, according to her own choice.

TITLE IX

On the Schools

I.

Each of the Sociedad's Schools will be in the charge of a member as Supervisor (Socia Curadora); and in her absence or illness, it will be necessary to name an interim supervisor.

II.

In each School there will be a Teacher and an Assistant well instructed in their respective tasks.

III.

Those who wish to be Teachers will present a memorandum to the Junta, and they will undergo a public exam, but they will not be admitted to it unless confidential reports have been made regarding their good conduct.

IV.

The exams will be made in front of the Junta with the assistance of the Oficials of the Sociedad's, and two individuals from each of the Commissions of Agriculture, Industry, and Trades.

V.

The Teachers shall be chosen based solely on their greater ability exhibited in the exam; and in the case of equality of merit, preference will be given to those who have been Assistants.

VI.

The same formalities will be observed in the naming of Assistants as in naming Teachers, and in the case of equality of merit, former students of the School, no younger than 15 years of age, will be given preference.

VII.

The Teachers and Assistants will be subordinate to the respective Supervisors, under penalty of being excluded by the Junta.

VIII.

In each School a male reading and writing Teacher will be designated with the obligation to teach Christian Doctrine, named by the Junta and removable at the Junta's will.

IX.

The memorandums or reports that the Teachers and the Assistants make to the Junta at any time will come by the hand of their respective Supervisors, unless they are to complain about the same Supervisors; in this case they will be addressed specifically to the President, who will recognize it in the following session, acknowledging the right of the petitioners to present their complaint in person to the Junta, whenever a report has been hidden or suppressed.

X.

The expenses of the Schools shall be paid by the Sociedad in the form agreed upon between the Junta and the Sociedad, but always in a uniform manner in all the Schools.

XI.

All the Supervisors shall give their account at the end of each academic year.

XII.

For each of the current Schools, and for those that shall be established in the future in Madrid and in towns in the province [of Madrid] in the charge of the Junta, there will be regulations approved by the Sociedad in which it is determined with all possible exactitude the different trades [that are to be taught] according to the curriculum of each school, such as spinning, weaving, sewing, embroidering, etc.; the plan of teaching; the prizes awarded to the most applied, and the system of economy and accounting.

XIII.

The Supervisors shall inform the Junta of any innovation that they judge to be convenient in their respective schools, with everything else that their zeal and their experience might dictate, to form in the schools virtuous citizens.

TITLE X

On the Observation of the Statutes

I.

No statute may be altered or repealed without proceeding according to the meeting of the Junta de Señoras formally convoked with that intent, and observing also the same formalities that were observed upon its approval.

II.

The Junta shall be very circumspect regarding the alteration or variation of their rules; and every member herself shall be scrupulous in adjusting herself exactly to what they lay out, and in completing her charges with no omission or distortion.

APPROVAL OF HIS MAJESTY

Excellent Ladies. The King has seen fit to approve the Statutes which the Junta de Señoras Socias de Honor y Mérito of the Real Sociedad Económica de Madrid has formed for its organization and governance, and has presented to your Excellencies. Which I communicate to you for your government and satisfaction, returning to you the referred to Statutes. God preserve your Excellencies for many years. Aranjuez, April 10, 1794. The Duke of the Alcudia. The Señoras Countess of Truillas, and Marquise of Ariza.

This is a copy of the original Statutes, that are held in the Secretary's office of the Junta de Señoras, that is in my charge, and that I certify.
Madrid, May 6, 1794.

The Countess of Montijo.

NOTES

Translated by Catherine M. Jaffe.

1. The members were called "Socias."
2. The members who cannot attend weekly meetings because they live outside Madrid.
3. The censor would be responsible for the observance of the statutes, the agreements, and the members' fulfillment of their duties. See Title V.
4. Particular vote.
5. Active vote means to vote, and passive vote, eligible to stand for election.

Bibliography

ARCHIVES AND MANUSCRIPT MATERIALS

ADMS. Archivo Ducal de Medina Sidonia, Sanlúcar de Barrameda, Cádiz.

Legajo 235/5, Documento 1. "Buleto honorífico a Doña María Tomasa Palafox." July 16, 1824.

Legajo 4303/3, Documento 13. "Contrata de fletamento convenido entre el capitán del bergantín español Santo Domingo de la Victoria y la Excma. Marquesa de Villafranca." Alicante, April 26, 1810.

Legajo 4840/1, Documento 23. "Carta de José María Celas Muñoz para que se apoye la escuela de sordomudos e información sobre el plan de educación para mujeres hecha a instancias de aquel profesor por la señora Marquesa de Espeja." March 10, 1818.

Legajo 4840/1, Documento 37. "Memoria de la Junta de Honor y Mérito." Madrid, February 8, 1822.

Legajo 4840/4. "Diploma acreditativo pertenencia a Junta de Damas Españolas de Fernando VII firmada en Madrid. Firmada por el Consejero de Estado Pedro Cevallos." July 13, 1816.

Legajo 4840/4. "Diploma acreditativo pertenencia a Junta de Damas Españolas de Fernando VII formada en Cádiz. Firmada por el Consejero de Estado Josef García de León y Pizarro." December 12, 1817.

Legajo 4840/12. "Título de académica de mérito de la Real Academia de San Fernando." July 25, 1805.

Legajo 4840/14. "Título de Socia de la Real Junta de Damas de Honor y Mérito de la Sociedad Económica de Madrid." January 20, 1799.

Legajo 6313, 2a. "Intercambio epistolar entre Jovellanos y la Marquesa de Villafranca." November and December 1808.

Legajo 6314/13. "Inquisición, libros prohibidos." January–April 1819.

AGP. Archivo General de Palacio, Madrid.

Personal. Caja 1037, Expediente 19. "Francisca María Dávila Carrillo de Albornoz, condesa viuda de Torrepalma." 1771.

Personal. Caja 1037, Expediente 20. "Francisca María Dávila Carrillo de Albornoz, condesa viuda de Torrepalma." 1771–83.

Personal. Caja 16839, Expediente 8. "Francisca María Dávila Carrillo de Albornoz, condesa de Torrepalma y Truillas." 1808.

AHDM. Archivo Histórico Diocesano de Madrid.
Parroquia de San Martín. Libro 27, *Matrimonios (1771–1777)*.
Parroquia de San Martín. Libro 28, *Defunciones (1809–1812)*.
Parroquia de Santa Cruz. Libro 29, *Bautismos (1769–1784)*.
Parroquia de San Martín. Libro 31, *Matrimonios (1792–1801)*.

AHMC. Archivo Histórico Municipal de Cádiz.
Caja 5699. "Memorial y expuesto de la Sociedad Patriótica de Señoras de Cádiz."

AHN. Archivo Histórico Nacional, Madrid.
Consejos. Legajo 5512/7. "Expediente formado con motivo del alboroto suscitado por el Paisanaje en Madrid contra las tropas francesas en la mañana del 2 de mayo de 1808." www.mcu.es/archivos/docs/MC/AHN_Nota_Guerra_Independencia.pdf.
Consejos. Legajo 11907. "Reales órdenes reservadas para la salida de varios sujetos de esta Corte; sobre reclusiones y otros puntos." 1805–6.
Estado. Legajo 3234, Expediente 30. "Expediente de publicación de la obra Ensayo Histórico Apologético del abate Lampillas traducida por Doña Josefa Amar y Borbón." 1782.
Estado. Legajo 7562, Expediente 16. "Expediente de Nombramiento de la Orden de Damas Nobles de la Reina María Luisa de María Josefa Gálvez Valenzuela, Condesa de Castroterreño." 1816.

AHNSG. Archivo del Hospital de Nuestra Señora de Gracia, Zaragoza.
Libro IV de Acuerdos.

AHPM. Archivo Histórico de Protocolos de Madrid.
Libro 19556. "Capitulaciones Matrimoniales de los marqueses de Peñafiel, firmadas en Madrid el 27 de diciembre de 1771 ante el notario Don Simón de Rozas y Negrete."

AHVM. Archivo Histórico de la Villa de Madrid.
Sección Secretaría. Expediente 1–57–21. "Licencia a las damas de Honor de la Caridad para reedificar la fachada de la Casa Real de la Inclusa." 1803. memoriademadrid.es.
Sección Secretaría. Expediente 2–371–13. "Socorros a la Casa Inclusa y Colegio de la Paz." 1813.
Sección Secretaría. Libro 242. *Libro de Acuerdos del Ayuntamiento (1812)*.

ARABSF. Archivo de la Real Academia de Bellas Artes de San Fernando. Madrid.
Legajo 1–40–4. "Señoras Académicas: Desde 1773 a 1821." 1773–1821.
Legajo 3–87. "Actas de Sesiones de la Real Academia de Bellas Artes de San Fernando." 1803–18.

ARCM. Archivo Regional de la Comunidad de Madrid.
Expediente 8375/5. "Comunicaciones emitidas y/o recibidas por la Junta de Damas de Honor y Mérito sobre diversos asuntos relacionados con el funcionamiento y administración de la Inclusa." 1799–1817.
Expediente 8482/7. "Correspondencia sobre admisión de Socias en la Junta de Damas de Honor y Mérito." 1787–99.
Expediente 8880/17. "Memorias del estado de los negocios de la Junta de Damas de Honor y Mérito, relativas a los establecimientos benéficos que están a su cargo, y de la situación de la Inclusa y Colegio de la Paz." 1797–1839.

ARSEA. Archivo de la Real Sociedad Económica Aragonesa, Zaragoza.
Actas.

ARSEM. Archivo de la Real Sociedad Económica Matritense de Amigos del País, Madrid.
Expediente 81/10. "Comisión sobre la admisión de señoras. Memoria sobre la admisión de Señoras en la Sociedad escrita por doña Josefa Amar." 1786.
Expediente 87/15. "Sobre el pago de la casa, Escuela de Bordados y algunos antecedentes sobre dicha Escuela." 1787–1801.
Expediente 93/8. "Papeles y expedientes pertenecientes a la Comisión que entiende en el reglamento de la Junta de Damas." 1787–88.
Expediente 93/10: "Nombramiento para Presidenta en la persona de la Condesa de Benavente, Duquesa de Osuna." 1786.
Expediente 94/14. "Sobre la Escuela de Bordados a cargo de José Nieto y su mujer María Rada." 1787–92.
Expediente 98/9. "Papeles sobre el uso los tejidos nacionales." 1788.
Expediente 98/16. "Expediente sobre un discurso sobre el lujo y creación de un traje nacional para las Damas compuesto de géneros del país." 1788.
Expediente 115/1. "Josefa Amar y Borbón, socia de Honor y Mérito, remite un ejemplar de su obra 'Discurso sobre la educación física y moral de las mujeres.'" 1790.
Expediente 117/17. "Extracto de las Tareas de la Junta de Señoras de honor y mérito en el primer semestre de 1790." 1790.
Expediente 118/2. "Copia del Reglamento de las escuelas patrióticas formado por la Junta de Damas y aprobado por la Sociedad." 1792.

Expediente 120/2. "Extracto de las tareas de la Sociedad en 1791. El Secretario de la clase de Agricultura (Güell) expone los trabajos hechos desde la última Junta General de Premios. Trabajos hechos en las escuelas del cargo de la Junta de Damas. Extracto de las tareas de la Junta." 1791.

Expediente 125/20. "Informaciones referentes a las dificultades presentes de la Escuela de San Andrés." 1792–94.

Expediente 131/7. "Relación de las tareas de la Real Sociedad a lo largo del año de 1793 en la clase de Agricultura, Industria y Artes y Oficios, Escuela de San Andrés, Bordados y juntas diversas." 1794.

Expediente 133/14. "La Marquesa de Fuerte-Híjar hace presente a la Sociedad las causas por las que convendría suprimir en las escuelas el ramo de hilazas de algodón por la costura y otras labores." 1794.

Expediente 138/3. "Estatutos de la Junta de Socias de Honor y Mérito de la Real Sociedad Económica de Madrid." 1794–95.

Expediente 146/11. "Se solicita publicar unas memorias escritas por la Junta de Damas de la Comisión de Física y Moral. Informe favorable del Censor (Guevara Vasconcelos) al respecto. Informes de: Amar y Borbón, Marquesa de Fuerte-Híjar, Marquesa de Montijo, Condesa de Truillas, Marquesa de Ariza, Marquesa de Sonora." 1796–1801.

Expediente 176/9. "Memoria que contiene los trabajos y ocupaciones de la Junta de Señoras del Honor y Mérito." 1803.

Expediente 194/6. "La Condesa de Trullás, de la Junta de Damas, remite a la Sociedad 24 ejemplares de la suscripción que se ha hecho para poder auxiliar al Colegio de Niñas de la Paz." 1805.

Expediente 202/19. "Expediente sobre la dote adjudicada a Marcela Zorrilla por haber ganado los 5 premios que previene el Reglamento de las escuelas patrióticas." 1807–8.

Expediente 205/9. "Memoria instructiva de los negocios de la Junta de Honor y Mérito, desde agosto de 1807 a agosto de 1808. Condesa de Benavente y Duquesa de Osuna." 1808.

Expediente 212/19. "La Junta de Damas de Honor y Mérito da cuenta del apurado estado de las escuelas patrióticas por falta de recursos y propone que se cierren temporalmente hasta que el Gobierno pueda dotarlas." 1811.

Expediente 262/19. "Sobre medallas de plata para premios a las niñas del Colegio de la Paz." 1818.

Expediente 292/16. "Moción de Sánchez sobre la enseñanza de principios de dibujo a las niñas expósitas del Colegio de la Paz." 1820–21.

Libro A/55. *Libro de Acuerdos de la Junta de Comisión, nombrada por la Real Sociedad Económica de Madrid para tratar del Reglamento de la de Señoras socias de Honor y Mérito (1787–1788).*

Libro A/56/4. *Copia de las Actas de la Junta de Señoras* (1795–1796).
Libro A/56/9. *Copia de las Actas de la Junta de Señoras* (1805–1808).
Libro A/56/10. *Copia de las Actas de la Junta de Señoras* (1809–1811).
Libro A/110/38. *Libro de actas de las Juntas de la Sociedad* (julio 1812–junio 1815).

PUBLISHED WORKS

Acereda Extremiana, Alberto. *La Marquesa de Fuerte Híjar, una dramaturga de la Ilustración (estudio y edición de La sabia indiscreta)*. Cádiz: Servicio de Publicaciones de la Universidad de Cádiz, 2000.

Adams, Christine. *Poverty, Charity and Motherhood: Maternal Societies in Nineteenth-Century France*. Champaign: University of Illinois Press, 2010.

Agnesi, Gaetana. *Instituzioni analitiche ad uso della gioventú italiana*. Milano: Nella Regia Ducal Corte, 1748.

Aguilar Piñal, Francisco. *Bibliografía de Autores españoles del siglo XVIII*. 10 vols. Madrid: Consejo Superior de Investigaciones Científicas, 1981–2001.

———. *Madrid en los tiempos del "mejor alcalde."* 4 vols. Sant Cugat del Vallés: Editorial Arpegio, 2016.

Aguirre, Manuel de. *Sistema de sociedades patrióticas, y de seminarios o casas públicas de educación*. Madrid: Imprenta de Joaquín Ibarra, 1785.

Ahnert, Ruth. "Maps versus Networks." In *News Networks in Early Modern Europe*, ed. Joad Raymond and Noah Moxham, 130–57. Leiden: Brill, 2016.

———, and Sebastian E. Ahnert. "Protestant Letter Networks in the Reign of Mary I: A Quantitative Approach." *ELH* 82, no. 1 (2015): 1–33.

Alagón, Duchess of [María del Pilar Fernández de Híjar Silva y Palafox]. *Memoria expositiva de la situación de la Inclusa y Colegio de niñas de la Paz, en seis de mayo del mil ochocientos veinte y siete: Presentada a la Real Junta de Señoras por su presidenta la Excma. Señora Duquesa de Alagón*. Madrid: Imprenta de Don Eusebio Álvarez, 1827.

Albarrán Martín, Virginia. *El desafío del blanco: Goya y Esteve, retratistas de la casa de Osuna*. Madrid: Museo del Prado, 2017.

Almodóvar, Duchess of [María Joaquina de los Desamparados de Montserrat Acuña]. *Elogio de la serenísima señora Doña María Ana Victoria, Infanta de Portugal, esposa del serenísimo Señor Infante Don Gabriel formado por la Excelentísima Señora Duquesa de Almodóvar; leído en la Junta General que celebró la Real Sociedad Económica de Madrid el sábado 28 de marzo de 1789; publicado de acuerdo y a expensas de la misma sociedad*. Madrid: Imprenta de Antonio de Sancha, Madrid, 1789.

Alonso Cabezas, María Victoria. "Una galería de retratos en la Real Academia de Bellas Artes de San Fernando (1754–1833)." *Archivo Español de Arte* 366 (2019): 191–202.

Altonaga, Bakarne. "The Basque Enlightenment: New Visions of Gender in the Crisis of the Old Regime." In *A New History of Iberian Feminisms*, ed. Bermúdez and Johnson, 82–90.

Álvarez Barrientos, Joaquín. "Eutrapelia y control de la distinción: el proyecto de traje nacional de 1788." In *Para Emilio Palacios Fernández*, ed. Álvarez Barrientos and Herrera Navarro, 465–83.

———. *Los hombres de letras en la España del siglo XVIII: Apóstoles y arribistas*. Madrid: Editorial Castalia, 2006.

———, and Jerónimo Herrera Navarro, eds. *Para Emilio Palacios Fernández: 26 estudios sobre el siglo XVIII español*. Madrid: Fundación Universitaria Española–Real Sociedad Bascongada de los Amigos del País, 2011

Álvarez de Cienfuegos, Nicasio. *Obras poéticas*. 2 vols. Madrid: Imprenta Real, 1816.

Álvarez de Miranda, Pedro. "Las inquietudes lingüísticas de Cienfuegos: Noticia de los papeles del autor conservados en la Real Academia Española." *Cuadernos Dieciochistas* 10 (2009): 87–110.

———. "¿Una niña en la Academia? El caso de María del Rosario Cepeda y su orgulloso padre." *Boletín de la Real Academia Española* 82 (2002): 39–45.

———. *Palabras e ideas: el léxico de la Ilustración temprana en España (1680–1760)*. Madrid: Real Academia Española, 1992.

———. "*La presidenta o la presidente?* Una polémica de 1787." In *Corcillum: Estudios de traducción, lingüística y filología dedicados a Valentín García Yebra*, ed. Rosario Consuelo González García and Pollux Hernúñez, 805–23. Madrid: Arco Libros, 2006.

Amar y Borbón, Josefa. "Discourse in Defence of the Talents of Women, and their Aptitude for Government and Other Positions in which Men are Employed." In *In Defence of Women*, trans. Barker, 97–112.

———. *Discurso sobre la educación física y moral de las mujeres*. Madrid: Imprenta de Don Benito Cano, 1790.

———. *Discurso sobre la educación física y moral de las mujeres*, ed. María Victoria López-Cordón Cortezo. Madrid: Editorial Cátedra, 1994.

———. *Oración Gratulatoria que la Señora Doña Josefa Amar y Borbón, elegida socia de honor y mérito dirigió a la Junta de Señoras de la Real Sociedad Económica de Madrid*. Madrid: Imprenta de Antonio de Sancha, 1787.

———. "Prólogo de la traductora." In Lampillas, *Ensayo histórico-apologético de la literatura Española*.

Amo Lobo, José Ignacio del, Manuel Barrio Prada, and Fernando Regueras Grande. *El Hospital de la Piedad de Benavente, 500 años*. Benavente: Centro de Estudios Benaventanos Ledo del Pozo, 2018.

Andrés y Morell, Juan. *Carta del Abate Don Juan Andrés sobre el origen y las vicisitudes del arte de enseñar a hablar a los mudos sordos*. Madrid: Sancha, 1794.

————. *Origen, progresos, y estado actual de toda la literatura.* 6 vols. Madrid: Imprenta de Antonio de Sancha, 1784–1805.

Andreu Miralles, Xavier. *El descubrimiento de España: Mito romántico e identidad nacional.* Barcelona: Taurus, 2016.

Añón Feliú, Carmen. *El Capricho de la Alameda de Osuna.* Madrid: Fundación Caja Madrid, 2001.

Appolis, Emile. *Les Jansénistes Espagnols.* Bordeaux: Sobodi, 1966.

[Aranda, Countess of (Luisa María Padilla Manrique y Acuña)]. *Nobleza virtuosa.* Zaragoza: Juan de Lanaja y Quartanet, 1637.

Arenal de García Carrasco, María de la Concepción. *La beneficencia, la filantropía y la caridad: Memoria premiada por la Real Academia de Ciencias, morales y políticas, en el concurso de 1860.* Madrid: Imprenta del Colegio de sordomudos y ciegos, 1861.

Arias de Saavedra Alías, Inmaculada. "Las Sociedades Económicas de Amigos del País y la mujer." In *Homenaje a la profesora María Dolores Tortosa Linde,* ed. Remedios Morales Raya, 46–91. Granada: Universidad de Granada, 2003.

Ariza, Marquise of [María de la Concepción Belvis de Moncada y Pizarro]. *Elogio de la Reyna N.S. formado por la Marquesa de Ariza; leído en la Junta Pública de Distribución de Premios, celebrada por la Real Sociedad Económica de Madrid en 22 de enero de 1795.* Madrid: Imprenta de Sancha, 1795.

Astigarraga Goenaga, Jesús. "Connecting with the Enlightenment: European Political Economy in Eighteenth-Century Spain." In *The Routledge Companion to the Hispanic Enlightenment,* ed. Lewis, Bolufer Peruga, and Jaffe, 99–111.

————. "Economic Societies and the Politicisation of the Spanish Enlightenment." In *The Spanish Enlightenment Revisited,* ed. Astigarraga, 63–81.

————. *Los ilustrados vascos: Ideas, instituciones y reformas económicas en España.* Barcelona: Editorial Crítica, 2003.

————, ed. *The Spanish Enlightenment Revisited.* Oxford, UK: Voltaire Foundation, 2015.

————, María Victoria López-Cordón Cortezo, and José María Urkia Etxabe, eds. *Ilustración, Ilustraciones.* Azcoitia: Real Sociedad Bascongada de los Amigos del País, 2009.

Atienza Hernández, Ignacio. *Aristocracia, poder y riqueza en la España moderna: La casa de Osuna, siglos XV–XVI.* Madrid: Siglo XXI, 1987.

Azcárate Ristori, Isabel de. *Una niña regidora honoraria de la ciudad de Cádiz.* Cádiz: Quorum Libros, 2000.

Badinter, Elisabeth, ed. *Paroles d'hommes (1790–1793): Condorcet, Prudhomme, Guyomar.* Paris: POL, 1989.

[Bandiera, Giovanni Niccolo]. *Trattato degli studi delle Donne in due parti diviso: Opera D'un Accademico Intronato.* Venezia: Francesco Pitteri, 1740.

Barker, Joanna M., trans. *In Defence of Women*. Cambridge, UK: Modern Humanities Research Association, 2018.

Barry, Jonathan, and Colin Jones. "Introduction." In *Medicine and Charity Before the Welfare State*, ed. Barry and Jones, 9–15.

———, eds. *Medicine and Charity Before the Welfare State*. London: Routledge, 1991.

Bartolomé Martínez, Bernabé. "La crianza y educación de los expósitos en España entre la Ilustración y el Romanticismo (1790–1835)." *Historia de la educación: Revista interuniversitaria* 10 (1991): 33–62.

Beer, Jeremy. *The Philanthropic Revolution: An Alternative History of American Charity*. Philadelphia: University of Pennsylvania Press, 2015.

Benavente, Countess-Duchess of [María Josefa Alfonso Pimentel Téllez-Girón]. *Discurso que la Excma. Sra. Condesa, Duquesa de Benavente, Marquesa de Peñafiel [...] hizo a la Real Sociedad Económica de Madrid, el día de su recepción 22 de Julio de 1786*. Madrid: Imprenta de Sancha, 1786.

Bergstrom, Carson. "Literary Coteries, Network Theory and the Literary and Philosophical Society of Manchester." *ANQ: A Quarterly Journal of Short Articles, Notes and Reviews* 26, no. 3 (2013): 180–88.

Bermúdez, Silvia, and Roberta Johnson, eds. *A New History of Iberian Feminisms*. Toronto: University of Toronto Press, 2018.

Bezos del Amo, Nuria. "La Junta de Damas de Honor y Mérito y su índice de autoridades." Master's thesis, Universidad Complutense de Madrid, 2013. eprints.ucm.es/23771/.

Bieder, Maryellen. "Women Authors in the Romantic Tradition (1841–1884) and Early Feminist Thought (1861–1893)." In *A New History of Iberian Feminisms*, ed. Bermúdez and Johnson, 128–46.

Blanchard, Jean-Baptiste. *Escuela de costumbres, o Reflexiones morales e históricas sobre las máximas de la sabiduría*. 4 vols. Madrid: Imprenta de Blas Román-Imprenta de Pedro Marín, 1786.

Blanco Mozo, Juan Luis. *Orígenes y desarrollo de la Ilustración vasca en Madrid (1713–1793). De la Congregación de San Ignacio a la Sociedad Bascongada de Amigos del País*. Madrid: Real Sociedad Bascongada de Amigos del País, 2011.

Bolufer Peruga, Mónica. "Del salón a la asamblea: sociabilidad, espacio público y ámbito privado (siglos XVII–XVIII)." *Saitabi* 56 (2006): 121–48.

———. "The Enlightenment in Spain: Classic and New Historiographic Perspectives." In *The Routledge Companion to the Hispanic Enlightenment*, ed. Lewis, Bolufer Peruga, and Jaffe, 3–16.

———. "Galerías de 'mujeres ilustres' o el sinuoso camino de la excepción a la norma cotidiana (siglos XV–XVIII)." *Hispania* 60–61, no. 204 (2000): 181–224.

———. *Mujeres e Ilustración: La construcción de la feminidad en la España del siglo XVIII*. Valencia: Institució Alfons el Magnànim, 1998.

———. "Mujeres y hombres en los espacios del reformismo ilustrado: debates y estrategias." *HMiC: història moderna i contemporània* 1 (2003): 155–70.

———. "Neither Male, nor Female: Rational Equality in the Spanish Enlightenment." In *Women, Gender and Enlightenment,* ed. Taylor and Knott, 389–409.

———. "New Inflections of a Long Polemic: The Debate Between the Sexes in Enlightenment Spain." In *A New History of Iberian Feminisms,* ed. Bermúdez and Johnson, 38–49.

———. "Traducción, cultura y política en el mundo hispánico del siglo XVIII: Reescribir las *Lettres d'une Péruvienne* de Françoise de Graffigny." *Studia histórica, Historia Moderna* 36 (2014): 293–325.

———. "Traducción y creación en la actividad intelectual de las ilustradas españolas: el ejemplo de Inés Joyes y Blake." In *Frasquita Larrea y Aherán,* ed. Pascua Sánchez and Espigado Tocino, 137–55.

———. *La vida y la escritura en el siglo XVIII: Inés Joyes: Apología de las mujeres.* Valencia: Publicacions de la Universitat de València, 2008.

———, and Mónica Burguera López, eds. "Género y modernidad en España: de la Ilustración al liberalismo." *Ayer* 78 (2010): 13–168.

Bonells, Jaime. *Perjuicios que acarrean al género humano y al Estado las madres que rehusan criar a sus hijos.* Madrid: Imprenta de Miguel Escribano, 1786.

Borgatti, Stephen P. "Centrality and Network Flow." *Social Networks* 27 (2005): 55–71.

Bosch, Alberto. *El centenario: apuntes para la historia de la Sociedad Económica Matritense.* Madrid: Imprenta y Fundición de Manuel Tello, 1875.

Bourke, Evan. "Female Involvement, Membership and Centrality: A Social Network Analysis of the Hartlib Circle." *Literature Compass* 14, no. 4 (2017): 1–17.

Boyde, Henry. *Several Voyages to Barbary: Containing an Historical and Geographical Account of the Country.* London: Oliver Payne, 1736.

[Brucourt, Charles François Oliver Rosette]. *Ensayo sobre la educación de la nobleza. Lo escribió el caballero *** y trasladó al castellano Don Bernardo María de la Calzada.* Madrid: Imprenta Real, 1792.

Burdiel Bueno, Isabel. *Isabel II: Una biografía.* Madrid: Taurus, 2010.

———. "Myths of Failure, Myths of Success: New Perspectives on Nineteenth-Century Spanish Liberalism." *Journal of Modern History* 70 (1998): 892–912.

Burguera López, Mónica. "Coronado a la sombra de Avellaneda: La reelaboración (política) de la feminidad liberal en España entre la igualdad y la diferencia (1837–1868)." *Espacio, tiempo y forma* 29 (2017): 93–127.

———. *Las damas del liberalismo respetable: Los imaginarios sociales del feminismo liberal en España (1834–1850).* Madrid: Cátedra, 2012.

———. "Mujeres y revolución liberal en perspectiva: Esfera pública y ciudadanía femenina en la primera mitad del siglo XIX en España." In *Cuando todo era posible:*

Liberalismo y antiliberalismo en España e Hispanoamérica, 1780–1842, ed. Encarnación García Monerris, Ivana Frasquet Miguel, and Carmen García Monerris, 257–96. Madrid: Sílex, 2016.

Butterwick, Richard, ed. *Peripheries of the Enlightenment*. Oxford, UK: Voltaire Foundation, 2008.

Caballé Masforroll, Anna. *Concepción Arenal: La caminante y su sombra*. Madrid: Taurus, 2018.

Calderón España, María Consolación. "Presencia de la mujer en las Reales Sociedades Económicas de Amigos del País (1775–1808)." *Foro de Educación* 12 (2010): 185–231.

Callahan, William J. "Caridad, sociedad y economía." *Moneda y crédito* 146 (1978): 65–77.

Calvo Maturana, Antonio Juan. *Cuando manden los que obedecen: la clase política e intelectual de la España preliberal (1780–1808)*. Madrid: Marcial Pons, 2013.

———. "Eva y la pérdida del Paraíso Imperial: alegorías misóginas de María Luisa de Parma en el siglo XIX." *Reales Sitios* 167 (2006): 68–77.

———. *María Luisa de Parma, reina de España, esclava del mito*. Granada: Editorial Universidad de Granada, 2007.

Campomanes, Count of [Pedro Rodríguez de Campomanes]. *Discursos sobre la educación popular de los artesanos y su fomento*, ed. Gonzalo Anes. Oviedo: Grupo Editorial Asturiano, 1991.

———. "Observaciones para la composición ordenada de los Elogios Académicos: Escrito y presentado a la Real Sociedad por el Ilustrísimo Señor Don Pedro Rodríguez Campomanes en 24 de setiembre de 1776." In *Memorias de la Sociedad Económica*, vol. 2: 56–60. Madrid: Imprenta de Antonio Sancha, 1780.

Campos Díez, María Soledad. "La Junta de Damas de Honor y Mérito. Su vinculación con la Real Sociedad Económica Matritense de Amigos del País." *Anuario de Historia del Derecho Español* 84 (2014): 623–45.

Cantos Casenave, Marieta, Fernando Durán López, and Alberto Romero Ferrer, eds. *La Guerra de Pluma: Estudios sobre la prensa de Cádiz en el tiempo de las Cortes (1810–1814)*, vol. 1: *Imprentas, literatura y periodismo*. Cádiz: Servicio de Publicaciones de la Universidad de Cádiz, 2006.

Capel Martínez, Rosa María. "Las mujeres de la Matritense: un ejemplo de asociacionismo ilustrado." *Asparkía* 17 (2006): 19–38.

Carbón, Damián. *Libro del arte de las comadres o madrinas y regimiento de las preñadas y paridas y de los niños*. Mallorca: Hernando de Cansoles, impresor, 1541.

Carrete Parrondo, Juan. *El grabado a buril en la España Ilustrada: Manuel Salvador Carmona*. Madrid: Fábrica Nacional de Moneda y Timbre, 1989.

Casamayor, Faustino. *Años políticos e históricos de las cosas más particulares ocurridas en la imperial, augusta y siempre heroica ciudad de Zaragoza (1808–1809)*, ed. Pedro Rújula. Zaragoza: Editorial Comuniter-Institución Fernando el Católico, 2008.

[Casamayor y de la Coma, María Andrea.] *Tyrocinio arithmético: instrucción de las quatro reglas llanas, que saca a la luz Casandro Mamés de Lamarca, y Araioa, discípulo de las Escuelas Pías.* Zaragoza: Imprenta de Joseph Font, 1738.

Caso González, José Manuel. "*El Censor*, ¿periódico de Carlos III?" In *El Censor, obra periódica.* Edición facsímil. Oviedo: Publicaciones de la Universidad, 1989.

Castells Oliván, Irene, Gloria Espigado Tocino, and María Cruz Romeo Mateo, eds. *Heroínas y patriotas: Mujeres de 1808.* Madrid: Cátedra, 2009.

Castro Monsalve, Concepción de. "Orden público, política social y manufactura en el Madrid de Carlos III." In *Madrid en la época moderna: espacio, sociedad y cultura,* ed. Santos Madrazo Madrazo and Virgilio Pinto Crespo, 11–26. Madrid: Universidad Autónoma de Madrid-Casa de Velázquez, 1991.

Castroterreño, Countess of. [María Josefa de Gálvez y Valenzuela.] *Elogio de la Reyna Nuestra Señora formado por la Condesa de Castroterreño de la Real Sociedad Económica de Madrid: Leído en la Junta Pública de Distribución de Premios en 7 de febrero de 1801.* Madrid: Imprenta Real, 1801.

Catalina García, Juan. *Datos bibliográficos sobre la Sociedad Económica Matritense.* Madrid: Imprenta y fundición de M. Tello, 1877.

Cavallo, Sandra. *Charity and Power in Early Modern Italy: Benefactors and their Motives in Turin, 1541–1789.* Cambridge, UK: Cambridge University Press, 1995.

———. "The Motivations of Benefactors: An Overview of Approaches to the Study of Charity." In *Medicine and Charity Before the Welfare State,* ed. Barry and Jones, 34–42.

Cavanilles, Antonio José. *Observaciones sobre el artículo España de la Nueva Encyclopedia. Escritas en francés por el doctor D. Antonio Cavanilles, Presbítero. Y traducidas al castellano por Don Mariano Rivera.* Madrid: Imprenta Real, 1784.

Cavazza, Marta. "Between Modesty and Spectacle: Women and Science in Eighteenth-Century Italy." In *Italy's Eighteenth Century: Gender and Culture in the Age of the Grand Tour,* ed. Paula Findlen, Wendy Wassyng Roworth, and Catherine M. Sama, 275–302. Stanford, CA: Stanford University Press, 2009.

Ceballos-Escalera y Gila, Alfonso. *La Real Orden de Damas Nobles de la Reina María Luisa: fundada en 1792.* Madrid: Real Sociedad Económica Segoviana de Amigos del País, 1998.

Cepeda y Mayo, María del Rosario. *Elogio de la Reyna N.S. formado por señora Doña María del Rosario Cepeda y Gorostiza y leído en la junta pública de distribución de premios que celebró la Real Sociedad el sábado 15 de julio de 1797.* Madrid: Imprenta de Sancha, 1797.

[Cepeda y Mayo, María del Rosario]. *Copia, y recolección de los papeles, que en prosa, y verso han dirigido, algunos doctos ingenios de esta ciudad, en debido aplauso del desempeño que en sus actos literarios.* Cádiz: Imprenta Real de Marina, 1768.

———. *Relación de los ejercicios literarios.* Cádiz: D. Manuel Espinosa de los Monteros, Impresor Real de Marina, 1768.

Chadwick, Whitney. *Women, Art, and Society.* London: Thames & Hudson, 1990.

Chartier, Roger. *Les origines culturelles de la Révolution française.* Paris: Seuil, 1991.

Condillac, Étienne Bonnot de. *La lengua de los cálculos,* trans. Marquise of Espeja [Josefa Mónica Alvarado y Lezo]. Madrid: Imprenta de Ruiz, 1805.

Corona Baratech, Carlos. *Revolución y reacción en el reinado de Carlos IV.* Madrid: Rialp, 1957.

Corona Marzol, María Carmen. "La voz de las mujeres de la Guerra en los Sitios de Zaragoza. De la heroína mitificada a la amazona popular." *Tiempos de América: Revista de historia, cultura y territorio* 17 (2010): 141–70.

Coronel, Engracia. *Discurso que hizo a las Señoras de la Sociedad Patriótica del Señor don Fernando VII su fundadora el día de su establecimiento.* Cádiz: Imprenta de Gómez de Requena, 1811.

Cos, Manuel de. *Sermón que en la bendición de banderas del regimiento de Guadix celebrada en el Hospital de Enfermas de Nuestra Señora del Carmen de la ciudad de Cádiz el día 23 de abril de 1812 por la Sociedad de Señoras baxo el título de Fernando VII dixo el Dr. D [. . .] prebendado de la Santa Iglesia Catedral de la misma Ciudad, del Consejo de S.M., dase a la luz a expensas de la mencionada Sociedad.* Cádiz: Imprenta de Carreño, 1812.

D.F.X.M. *Canción heroica en honor de las señoras socias económicas matritenses y señoras asociadas, para la enseñanza de las infelices de la galera, y de las dos cárceles de Villa y Corte.* Madrid: n.p., [1788].

Dalton, Susan. *Engendering the Republic of Letters: Reconnecting Public and Private Spheres in Eighteenth-Century Europe.* Montreal: McGill-Queen's University Press, 2003.

Deacon, Philip. "Juan Meléndez Valdés en la Real Sociedad Económica Aragonesa, 1789–1791 (Con unos datos sobre Goya)." *Dieciocho: Hispanic Enlightenment* 18, no. 1 (1995): 7–25.

———. "Notes on Spain and Enlightenment: Concepts, Distinctions, Limitations." *Bulletin of Spanish Studies* (2018): 1–12. DOI: 10.1080/14753820.2018.1481652.

Delgado, Antonio José. *Por el magisterio en artes liberales que se confirió en la Real Universidad de Alcalá en 6 de junio de 1785 a la ilustrísima señora doña María Isidra de Guzmán y de la Cerda, hija dignísima de los excelentísimos señores marqueses de Montealegre, condes de Oñate, duques de Nájera, &c.* Madrid: Antonio Delgado, 1785.

Demerson, Jorge de. "Un canarien eclairé: D. Estanislao de Lugo (1753–1833)." In *Melanges à la memoire de Jean Sarrailh,* 311–29. París: Centre de Recherches Hispaniques, 1966.

Demerson, Paula de. "Catálogo de las Socias de Honor y Mérito de la Junta de Damas Matritense (1787–1811)." *Anales del Instituto de Estudios Madrileños* 7 (1971): 269–74.

———. "La distribución de sopas económicas por la Real Sociedad Matritense en 1803–1804." *Boletín de la Real Academia de la Historia* 164 (1969): 119–35.

———. "Las Escuelas Patrióticas entre 1787 y 1808." In *Las Reales Sociedades Económicas de Amigos del País y su obra*, 191–205. San Sebastián: CSIC, 1972.

———. *María Francisca de Sales Portocarrero (condesa del Montijo): Una figura de la Ilustración*. Madrid: Editora Nacional, 1975.

———. "La Real Inclusa de Madrid a finales del siglo XVIII." *Anales del Instituto de Estudios Madrileños* 8 (1972): 261–72.

———, Jorge de Demerson, and Francisco Aguilar Piñal. *Las Sociedades Económicas en el siglo XVIII: Guía del Investigador*. San Sebastián: Patronato José María Quadrado, CSIC, 1974.

Denina, Carlo. *Respuesta a la pregunta: ¿Qué se debe a la España? Discurso leído en la Academia de Berlín en la asamblea pública de 26 de Enero de 1786, día del Aniversario del Rey por el abate Denina, traducido por Don Manuel de Urqullu*. Cádiz: Imprenta de Manuel Ximénez Carreño, 1786.

Díaz Saiz, Mar. "D. Luis de los Ríos y Velasco. Un magistrado campurriano (1735–1786)." *Cuadernos de Campoo* 19 (2000). www.vacarizu.es/Cuadernos/Cuaderno_19.htm.

———. "Las estrategias familiares de los Ríos y Velasco en el siglo XVIII." In *De peñas al mar: Sociedad e instituciones en la Cantabria moderna*, ed. Tomás Manteón Movellán, 135–57. Santander: Ayuntamiento de Santander, 1999.

Díez de la Cortina, Josefa. *Elogio de la Reina Nuestra Señora*. Madrid: Imprenta de Pereyra, 1800.

Diggins, John Patrick. "The Oyster and the Pearl: The Problem of Contextualism in Intellectual History." *History and Theory* 23 (1984): 151–69.

Discurso sobre el lujo de las señoras y proyecto de un traje nacional. Madrid: Imprenta Real, 1788.

Dixon, Susan M. "Women in Arcadia." *Eighteenth-Century Studies* 32, no. 3 (1999): 371–90.

Dosse, François. *Le pari biographique: Écrire une vie*. Paris: La Découverte, 2005.

Duncan, Carol. "Happy Mothers and Other New Ideas in Eighteenth-Century French Art." *Art Bulletin* 55, no. 4 (1973): 570–83.

E.A.J.D.A. *Aparato, ceremonias y solemnidades que se ejecutaron en la entrada que hizo en la Real Universidad de Alcalá la Excelentísima Señora Doña María Isidra de Guzmán*. [Alcalá de Henares], n.p., 1785.

Egido López, Teófanes. *Carlos IV*. Madrid: Arlanza Ediciones, 2001.

Eiximenis, Francesc. *Llibre de les dones, 1387–1392*. [Incunabula edition. Barcelona: Joan Rosembach, 1495].

Elorza Domínguez, Antonio. *La ideología liberal de la Ilustración Española*. Madrid: Editorial Tecnos, 1970.

Espigado Tocino, Gloria. "En la estela de las Luces: La Marquesa de Villafranca, una ilustrada del siglo XIX." In *El siglo XVIII en femenino: Las mujeres en el siglo de las Luces,* ed. Manuel-Reyes García Hurtado, 251–75. Madrid: Editorial Síntesis, 2016.

———. "La Junta de Damas de Cádiz: entre la ruptura y la reproducción social." In *Frasquita Larrea y Aherán,* ed. Pascua Sánchez and Espigado Tocino, 243–66.

———. "La Marquesa de Villafranca y la Junta de Damas de Fernando VII." In *Heroínas y patriotas,* ed. Castells Oliván, Espigado Tocino, and Romeo Mateo, 317–42.

———. "Las mujeres en el nuevo orden político." In *Historia de las mujeres en España y América Latina,* ed. Morant Deusa, vol. 3: 27–60.

Espoz y Mina, Countess of [Juana María de Vega]. "Apuntes para la historia: Del tiempo que ocupé los destinos de aya de S.M. y A.R. y camarera mayor de palacio." In *Memorias.* Madrid: Tebas, 1977.

Estatutos de la Junta de Honor y Mérito de la Real Sociedad Económica de Madrid. Madrid: Imprenta de Sancha, 1794.

Estatutos de la Sociedad de Señoras establecida en esta ciudad de Cádiz bajo el título de Fernando VII. Cádiz: Imprenta Niel Hijo, 1812.

Eximeno, Antonio: *El espíritu de Maquiavelo.* Valencia: Imprenta de Benito Monfort, 1799.

———. *Institutiones Philosophicae et Mathematicae.* 2 vols. Madrid: Imprenta Real, 1796.

Ezquerra del Bayo, Joaquín, *Retratos de la familia Téllez-Girón: Novenos Duques de Osuna.* Madrid: Blass S.A., Tipográfica, 1934.

Fernández, Ramón. *Principios de cirugía en general.* Madrid: Benito Cano, 1788.

Fernández Almoguera, Adrián. "From the Private Cabinet to the Suburban Villa: Caprices and Fantasies in Eighteenth-Century Madrid." In *Fancy in Eighteenth-Century European Visual Culture,* ed. Melissa Percival and Muriel Adrien, 223–40. Oxford, UK: Voltaire Foundation, 2020.

Fernández García, Elena. *Mujeres en la Guerra de la Independencia.* Madrid: Editorial Sílex, 2009.

Fernández Quintanilla, Paloma. "Una española ilustrada: Doña María Isidra Quintina de Guzmán y de la Cerda." *Tiempo de historia* 60 (1979): 96–105.

———. *La IX Duquesa de Osuna: una ilustrada en la Corte de Carlos III.* Madrid: Editorial Doce Calles, 2017.

———. "La Junta de Damas de Honor y Mérito." *Historia 16* 54 (1980): 65–73.

———. *La mujer ilustrada en la España del siglo 18.* Madrid: Ministerio de Cultura, 1981.

Fernández Rodríguez, Pura, and Marie-Linda Ortega, eds. *La mujer de letras o la letra-herida: Discursos y representaciones sobre la mujer escritora en el siglo XIX.* Madrid: Consejo Superior de Investigaciones Científicas, 2008.

Figueroa y Montalvo, María Loreto de. *Señoras: Las de Cádiz han establecido una Junta.* Cádiz: n.p., 1812.

Findlen, Paula. "Translating the New Science: Women and the Circulation of Knowledge in Enlightenment Italy." *Configurations* 3, no. 2 (1995): 167–206.

Fitzpatrick, Martin, Peter Jones, Christa Knellwolf, and Iaian McCalman, eds. *The Enlightenment World.* London: Routledge, 2004.

Flórez, Enrique. *Memorias de las Reinas Católicas.* 2 vols. Madrid: Imprenta de Antonio Marín, 1761.

Forner, Juan Pablo. *Oración apologética por la España y su mérito literario: para que sirva de exornación al discurso leído por el abate Denina en la Academia de Ciencias de Berlín, respondiendo a la cuestión qué se debe a España? por Don Juan Pablo Forner.* Madrid: Imprenta Real, 1786.

Forniés Casals, José Francisco. *La política social y la ilustración aragonesa (1773–1812): la acción social de la Real Sociedad Económica Aragonesa de Amigos del País.* Zaragoza: Real Sociedad Ecónomica Aragonesa de Amigos del País, 1997.

Foucault, Michel. "What Is Enlightenment?" *The Foucault Reader: An Introduction to Foucault's Thought,* ed. Paul Rabinow, 32–50. London: Penguin Books, 1984.

Fraisse, Geneviève. *Musa de la razón: La democracia excluyente y la igualdad de los sexos.* Madrid: Cátedra, 1991.

———. "Poullain de la Barre ou le procés des prejugés." In *Corpus des Oeuvres de Philosophie en Langue Francaise,* vol. 1: 27–41. París: Fayard, 1985.

Franco Rubio, Gloria A. *El ámbito doméstico en el Antiguo Régimen: De puertas adentro.* Madrid: Editorial Síntesis, 2018.

———. "Captar súbditos y crear ciudadanos, doble objetivo de los 'Amigos del País' en el siglo XVIII." *Historia Social* 64 (2009): 3–23.

———. "El ejercicio del poder en la España del Siglo XVIII: Entre las prácticas culturales y las prácticas políticas." *Mélanges de la Casa de Velázquez* 35, no. 1 (2005): 51–77.

———. "María Francisca de Sales Portocarrero y Guzmán (1754–1808), VI Condesa de Montijo ¿una mujer peligrosa?" *Anejos de la Revista de Historiografía* 9 (2019): 127–50.

———. "Patronato regio y preocupación pedagógica en la España del siglo XVIII: el Real Monasterio de la Visitación de Madrid." *Espacio, tiempo y forma: Historia Moderna* 7 (1994): 227–44.

———. "El salón parcialmente iluminado: Prejuicios, contradicciones y tópicos sobre las mujeres en los espacios de sociabilidad de la España ilustrada." In *El antiguo Régimen: Una mirada a dos mundos: España y América,* compiled by María Inés Carzolio, Celia Fernández, and Cecilia Lagunas, 151–74. Buenos Aires: Prometeo, 2010.

———. "Una vida poco convencional en la España de las Luces: la Condesa de Montijo (1754–1808)." In *Para Emilio Palacios Fernández*, ed. Álvarez Barrientos and Herrera Navarro, 79–98.

Fraser, Ronald. *La Maldita Guerra de España: Historia Social de la Guerra de la Independencia (1808–1814)*. Barcelona: Editorial Crítica, 2006.

Froldi, Rinaldo. "Lirismo, sensibilidad y moralidad en la inspiración iluminista de las tragedias de Cienfuegos." *Cuadernos dieciochistas* 10 (2009): 59–73.

Fuente Galán, María del Prado de la. "Aportación al estudio de los sectores marginados de la población: pobreza, caridad y beneficencia en la España moderna." *Boletín de la Asociación de Demografía Histórica* 18, no. 1 (2000): 13–27.

Fuentes Aragonés, Juan Francisco, and Pilar Garí Aguilera. *Amazonas de la libertad: Mujeres liberales contra Fernando VII*. Madrid: Marcial Pons, 2015.

Gálvez, María Rosa de. "La beneficencia: oda a la Excma. Sra. Condesa de Castroterreño con motivo del discurso que pronunció en la Real Junta de Damas en Elogio de la Reina Nuestra Señora." In *Obras poéticas*, vol. 1: 9–13. Madrid: Imprenta Real, 1804.

García, Santiago. *Breve instrucción sobre el modo de conservar los niños expósitos: aprobada por el Real Tribunal del Protomedicato*. Madrid: Por Manuel González, 1795.

———. *Instituciones sobre la crianza física de los niños expósitos: obra interesante a toda madre celosa de la conservación de sus hijos*. Madrid: Imprenta de Vega y Compañía, 1805.

García Garrosa, María Jesús. "En los inicios de la comedia neoclásica: 'La aya,' de María Rita de Barrenechea (1750–1795): Estudio y edición." *Cuadernos de estudios del siglo XVIII* 14 (2004): 25–66.

———. "Translation in Enlightenment Spain." In *The Routledge Companion to the Hispanic Enlightenment*, ed. Lewis, Bolufer Peruga, and Jaffe, 258–70.

Garrioch, David. "Making a Better World: Enlightenment and Philanthropy." In *The Enlightenment World*, ed. Fitzpatrick, Jones, Knellwolf, and McCalman, 486–501.

Genlis, Countess of [Stéphanie-Félicité Du Crest]. *Las veladas de la quinta, o Novelas e historias sumamente útiles para que las madres de familia, á quienes las dedica la autora, puedan instruir a sus hijos, juntando la doctrina con el recreo*. 3 vols. Madrid: Imprenta de Manuel González, 1788.

Gies, David T., and Cynthia Wall, eds. *The Eighteenth Centuries: Global Networks of Enlightenment*. Charlottesville: University of Virginia Press, 2018.

Gil Novales, Alberto. *Diccionario bibliográfico de la Guerra de la Independencia*. 3 vols. Fundación Mapfre, 2010.

Gillemán, Fernando. "Prólogo del traductor." In *Las veladas de la Quinta*, by the Countess of Genlis [Stéphanie Félicité du Crest], trans. Fernando de Gillemán, 3–5. 1788. México: Casa de Cornelio C. Sébring, 1831.

Goldgar, Anne. *Impolite Learning: Conduct and Community in the Republic of Letters, 1680–1750*. New Haven, CT: Yale University Press, 1995.

González, Teresa. *El estado del cielo: para el año de 1788*. Madrid: Imprenta de Manuel Marín, [1788].

Goodman, Dena. *The Republic of Letters: A Cultural History of the French Enlightenment*. Ithaca, NY: Cornell University Press, 1994.

Gor, Duchess of [María del Carmen Chacón Carrillo de Albornoz]. *Memoria leída por la Presidenta de la Asociación para el socorro de las religiosas de esta corte, duquesa viuda de Gor, en la junta general celebrada el 15 de enero de 1844*. Madrid: Imprenta de Fuentenebro, 1844.

Granovetter, Mark S. "The Strength of Weak Ties." *American Journal of Sociology* 78, no. 6 (1973): 1360–80.

Graziosi, Elisabetta. "Arcadia femminile: Presenze e modeli." *Filologia e critica* 17 (1992): 321–58.

Greer, Germaine. *La carrera de obstáculos: Vida y obra de las pintoras antes de 1950*. Madrid: Bercimuel, 2005.

Guerra, François Xavier, et al., eds. *Los espacios públicos en Iberoamérica: ambigüedades y problemas: siglos XVIII–XIX*. México: Fondo de Cultura Económica, 1998.

Guzmán y de la Cerda, María Isidra Quintina. *Oración del género eucarístico que hizo a la Real Sociedad de Amigos del País de esta corte la Excelentísima Señora Doña María Isidra Guzmán y la Cerda, doctora en Filosofía y Letras Humanas [. . .] En el día 25 de Febrero del año de 1786 en que fue incorporada en esta Real Sociedad*. Madrid: Imprenta de Antonio de Sancha, 1786.

Habermas, Jürgen. *The Structural Transformation of the Public Sphere: An Inquiry into a Category of Bourgeois Society*. Trans. Thomas Burger, with Frederick Lawrence. Cambridge, MA: MIT Press, 1989.

Haidt, Rebecca. *Women, work and clothing in Eighteenth-Century Spain*. Oxford, UK: Voltaire Foundation, 2011.

Hamnett, Brian. *The Enlightenment in Iberia and in Ibero-America*. Cardiff: University of Wales Press, 2017.

Heffron, Margery M. *Louisa Catherine: The Other Mrs. Adams*. New Haven, CT: Yale University Press, 2014.

Hernández González, Manuel. *El círculo de los Gálvez. Formación, apogeo y ocaso de una élite de poder indiana*. Madrid: Ediciones Polifemo, 2019.

[Hernández y Pérez de Larrea, Juan Antonio]. "Prólogo." In Francesco Griselini, *Discurso sobre el problema de si corresponde a los Párrocos y Curas de las aldeas el instruir a los labradores en los buenos elementos de la economía campestre*, 3–6. Zaragoza: Imprenta de Blas de Miedes, 1784.

Herr, Richard. *España y la revolución del siglo XVIII*. Madrid: Aguilar Ediciones, 1964.

Hervás y Panduro, Lorenzo. *Historia de la vida del hombre*, vol. 1: *Concepción, Nacimiento, Infancia y Niñez del hombre*. Madrid: Imprenta de Aznar, 1789.

Hesse, Carla. *The Other Enlightenment: How French Women Became Modern*. Princeton, NJ: Princeton University Press, 2001.

Holland, Lady [Elizabeth Vassall Holland]. *The Spanish Journal of Elizabeth, Lady Holland*, ed. The Earl of Ilchester. London: Longmans, Green and Co., 1910.

Homero. *La Ilíada de Homero, traducida del griego en verso endecasílabo castellano por D. Ignacio García Malo*. Madrid: Imprenta de Pantaleón Aznar, 1788.

Imbille, Luis, and Miguel Sarralde. "Informe sobre la utilidad del torno de hilar con ambas manos a un tiempo, por los señores Imbille y Sarralde, leído en junta de 2 de marzo de 1779." In *Memorias de la Sociedad Económica*, vol. 3: 204–9. Madrid: Imprenta de Antonio de Sancha, 1787.

Instrucción para las escuelas patrióticas. Madrid: Imprenta de D. Antonio de Sancha, 1776.

Iverson, John, and Marie-Pascale Pieretti. "'Toutes personnes [. . .] seront admises à concourir'": la participation des femmes aux concours académiques." *Dix-Huitième Siècle* 36 (2004): 313–32.

Jacob, Margaret. "The Mental Landscape of the Public Sphere." *Eighteenth-Century Studies* 28, no. 1 (1994): 95–113.

Jacob, Margaret C., and Dorothée Sturkenboom. "A Woman's Scientific Society in the West: The Late Eighteenth-Century Assimilation of Science." *Isis* 94, no. 2 (2003): 217–52.

Jaffe, Catherine M. "'Noticia de la vida y obras del conde de Rumford' (1802) by María Lorenza de los Ríos, Marquesa de Fuerte-Híjar: Authorizing a Space for Female Charity." *Studies in Eighteenth-Century Culture* 38 (2009): 91–115.

———, and Elizabeth F. Lewis, eds. *Eve's Enlightenment. Women's Experience in Spain and Spanish America, 1726–1839*. Baton Rouge: Lousiana State University Press, 2009.

———, and Elisa Martín-Valdepeñas Yagüe. "Sociabilidad, filantropía y escritura: María Lorenza de los Ríos y Loyo, marquesa de Fuerte-Híjar (1761–1821)." In *Mujeres y culturas políticas en España (1808–1845)*, ed. Yetano Laguna, 83–124.

Jagoe, Catherine, Alda Blanco, and Cristina Enríquez de Salamanca, eds. *La mujer en los discursos de género: textos y contextos en el siglo XIX*. Barcelona: Icaria, 1998.

Jenofonte. *La Economía, y los medios de aumentar las Rentas Públicas de Athenas, dos tratados de Xenofonte*. Madrid: Imprenta de Benito Cano, 1786.

Jovellanos, Gaspar Melchor de. "Elogio a Carlos III." In *Poesía. Teatro. Prosa*. Madrid: Editorial Taurus, 1980.

Joyes, Inés. *El Príncipe de Abisinia: Novela traducida del inglés por Doña Inés Joyes y Blake. Va inserta a continuación una apología de las mujeres en carta original de la traductora a sus hijas*. Madrid: Imprenta de Sancha, 1798.

Junta General de la Real Sociedad Económica de Madrid, celebrada en las Casas de Ayuntamiento el sábado 25 de enero de 1794. Madrid: Imprenta de Sancha, 1794.

Kerber, Linda K. *Women of the Republic: Intellect and Ideology in Revolutionary America.* Chapel Hill: University of North Carolina Press, 1980.

Kitts, Sally Ann. *The Debate on the Nature, Role and Influence of Woman in Eighteenth-Century Spain.* Lewiston, NY: Edwin Mellen Press, 1995.

———. "The role of Holland House in the diffusion, exchange, and transformation of Spanish enlightened ideas, 1793–1845." In *The Routledge Companion to the Hispanic Enlightenment,* ed. Lewis, Bolufer Peruga, and Jaffe, 243–57.

———. "Spain and Habermas's Public Sphere: A Revisionist Perspective." In *The Configuration of the Spanish Public Sphere: From the Enlightenment to the Indignados,* ed. David Jiménez Torres and Leticia Villamediana González, 25–43. Oxford, UK: Berghahn Books, 2019.

Knott, Sarah, and Barbara Taylor, eds. *Women, Gender and Enlightenment.* London: Palgrave, 2005.

Knox, Vicesimus. *Liberal education, or a practical treatise on the methods of acquiring useful and polite learning.* London: Charles Dilly, 1781.

Koerner, Lisbet. "Women and Utility in Enlightenment Science." *Configurations* 3, no. 2 (1999): 233–54.

Kontler, László. "What Is the (Historians') Enlightenment Today?" *European Review of History* 13, no. 3 (2006): 357–71.

La Parra López, Emilio. *Manuel Godoy: La aventura del poder.* Barcelona: Editorial Tusquets, 2002.

Lambert, Marquise of [Anne-Thérèse de Marguenat de Courcelles]. *Obras de la Marquesa de Lambert traducidas del francés por Doña María Cayetana de la Cerda y Vera, Condesa de Lalaing.* Madrid: Oficina de D. Manuel Martín, 1781.

Lampillas, Francisco Javier. *Ensayo Histórico apologético de la literatura española contra las opiniones preocupadas de algunos escritores modernos italianos: Disertaciones del abate don Xavier Lampillas. Segunda edición corregida, enmendada, e ilustrada con notas, por la misma Traductora.* 7 vols. Madrid: Imprenta de don Pedro Marín, 1789.

———. *Ensayo histórico-apologético de la literatura Española contra las opiniones preocupadas de algunos Escritores modernos Italianos,* trans. Josefa Amar y Borbón. 6 vols. Zaragoza: Oficina de Blas Miedes, 1782–86.

———. *Respuesta del Señor Abate Don Xavier Lampillas a los cargos recopilados por el Señor Abate Tiraboschi en su carta al Señor Abate N. N. sobre el ensayo histórico apologético de la Literatura Española traducida del italiano por Doña Josefa Amar y Borbón.* Zaragoza: Blas de Miedes, 1786.

Landes, Joan B. *Women and the Public Sphere in the Age of the French Revolution.* Ithaca, NY: Cornell University Press. 1988.

Larriba, Elisabel. *Le public de la presse en Espagne à la fin du XVIIIe siècle (1781–1808)*. Paris: Honoré Champion, 1998.

———. *El público de la prensa en España a finales del siglo XVIII (1781–1808)*. Zaragoza: Prensas Universitarias de Zaragoza, 2013.

———, and Gerard Dufour, eds. *El Semanario de Agricultura y Artes Dirigido a los Párrocos (1797–1808)*. Valladolid: Ámbito, 1997.

Latassa y Ortín, Félix de. "Doña Josefa Amar, y Borbón." In *Biblioteca Nueva de los escritores aragoneses que florecieron desde el año de 1795 hasta el de 1802*, vol. 6: 231–35. Pamplona: Oficina de Joaquín de Domingo, 1802.

Lazo de la Vega, José María. *Discurso que en la solemne acción de gracias por la libertad de nuestro amado Soberano y su restitución al trono de las Españas celebrada por la real Sociedad de Señoras bajo la advocación de Fernando VII, pronunció en la Iglesia de EE. PP. Franciscanos Observantes de la ciudad de Cádiz en 28 de mayo de 1814, el P. Fr . . . ex Lector de Artes, Maestro de Teología en dicho convento y Examinador sinodal del Obispado de Sigüenza*. Cádiz: Imprenta Tormentaria, 1814.

Le Moyne, Pierre. *Galería de las mujeres fuertes*, vol. 1. Madrid: Oficina de Benito Cano, 1794.

Le Prince Beaumont, Jeanne-Marie. *Almacén de las señoritas adolescentes, o Diálogos de una sabia directora con sus nobles discípulas; para servir de continuación al almacén de los Niños*. 4 vols. Madrid: Imprenta y librería de Plácido Barco López, 1787.

———. *Almacén y biblioteca completa de los niños, o Diálogos de una sabia directora con sus discípulas de la primera distinción*. 4 vols. Madrid: Oficina de Manuel Martín, 1774–76.

———. *Biblioteca completa de educación, o Instrucciones para las señoras jóvenes en la edad de entrar ya en la sociedad, y poderse casar*. 6 vols. Madrid: Imprenta de don Manuel Martín, 1779–1780.

———. *Conversaciones familiares de doctrina cristiana entre gente del campo, artesanos criados y pobres*. 2 vols. Madrid: Oficina de don Manuel Martín, 1773.

———. *Le Magasin des pauvres, artisans, domestiques et des gens de la campagne: Première partie*. Lyon: Chez Pierre Bruyset-Ponthus, 1768.

Le Tourneaux, Nicolas. *Instrucciones cristianas sobre el sacramento del matrimonio y sobre las ceremonias con que la Iglesia le administra*, trans. Countess of Montijo [María Francisca de Portocarrero y Zúñiga]. Barcelona: Imprenta de Bernardo Pla, [1774].

Leckey, Colum. "Patriotism, Agronomy and the Peasant Question: The Free Economic Society in Eighteenth-Century Russia." In *The Rise of Economic Societies in the Eighteenth Century*, ed. Stapelbroek and Marjanen, 232–56.

Lehner, Ulrich. *The Catholic Enlightenment: The Forgotten History of a Global Movement*. Oxford, UK: Oxford University Press, 2016.

———, ed. *Women, Enlightenment and Catholicism: A Transnational Biographical History*. New York: Routledge, 2018.

Leveson, C. de. *Émile Chrétien ou de l'éducation*. Paris: Libraires Associés, 1784.

Levy, Darline Gay, Harriet Branson Applewhite, and Mary Durham Johnson. *Women in Revolutionary Paris, 1789–1795: Selected Documents Translated with Notes and Commentary*. Urbana: University of Illinois Press, 1979.

Lewis, Elizabeth Franklin. "'A su reina benéfica': representaciones de María Luisa de Parma." In *La época de Carlos IV (1788–1808): Actas del IV Congreso Internacional de la Sociedad Española de Estudios del Siglo XVIII*, ed. Elena de Lorenzo Álvarez, 697–706. Oviedo: Instituto Feijoo de Estudios del Siglo XVIII–Sociedad Española de Estudios del Siglo XVIII, 2009.

———. "Actos de caridad: Women's Charitable Work in Eighteenth-Century Spain." *Dieciocho: Hispanic Enlightenment* 31, no. 2 (2008): 267–82.

———. "La caridad de una mujer: modernización y ambivalencia sentimental en la escritura femenina decimonónica." *Anales de literatura española* 23 (2011): 185–204.

———. "Women and 'Civic Motherhood.'" In *A New History of Iberian Feminisms*, ed. Bermúdez and Johnson, 50–57.

———. "Women as Public Intellectuals during the Hispanic Enlightenment: The Case of Josefa Amar y Borbón's *Ensayo histórico-apologético de la literatura española*." In *The Routledge Companion to the Hispanic Enlightenment*, ed. Lewis, Bolufer Peruga, and Jaffe, 112–25.

———. *Women Writers in the Spanish Enlightenment: The Pursuit of Happiness*. Aldershot, UK: Ashgate, 2004.

———, Mónica Bolufer Peruga, and Catherine M. Jaffe. *The Routledge Companion to the Hispanic Enlightenment*. Abingdon, UK: Routledge, 2020.

Lindenmeyr, Adele. "Public Life, Private Virtues: Women in Russian Charity, 1762–1914." *Signs* 18, no. 3 (1993): 562–91.

López Barahona, Victoria. *Las trabajadoras en la sociedad madrileña del siglo XVIII*. Madrid: ACCI Ediciones, 2016.

López Tabar, Juan. *Los famosos traidores: Los afrancesados durante la crisis del Antiguo Régimen (1808–1833)*. Madrid: Biblioteca Nueva, 2001.

López-Cordón Cortezo, María Victoria. *Condición femenina y razón ilustrada: Josefa Amar y Borbón*. Zaragoza: Prensas Universitarias de Zaragoza, 2005.

———. "Definición social y estrategias matrimoniales en la España del siglo XVIII." In *Vínculos y sociabilidades en España e Iberoamérica: Siglos XVI–XX*, ed. Enrique Martínez Ruiz, 37–58. Madrid: Universidad Complutense de Madrid–Universidad de Zulia-Ediciones Puertollano, 2005.

———. "The Enlightenment and Its Interpreters." In *The Routledge Companion to the Hispanic Enlightenment*, ed. Lewis, Bolufer Peruga, and Jaffe, 203–17.

———. "La fortuna de escribir: Escritoras de los siglos XVII y XVIII." In *Historia de las mujeres en España y América Latina*, ed. Morant Deusa, vol. 2: 193–234.

———. "Josefa Amar y Borbón y sus escritos sobre educación." In *Famille et éducation en Espagne et en Amérique Latine*, ed. Jean-Louis Guereña, 509–23. Tours: Presses universitaires François Rabelais, 2002.

———. "Situating Women in the Society of the Old Regime: The Other Spanish Enlightenment." In *A New History of Iberian Feminisms*, ed. Bermúdez and Johnson, 25–37.

———. "La vida intelectual de las mujeres entre los siglos XVII y XX." In *Historiar la educación de las mujeres en tiempos de cambio (siglos XVII–XX)*, ed. Josefina Méndez Vázquez and Francisco Chacón Jiménez, 3–30. Granada: Editorial Comares, 2020.

———. "Vida y ficción en la escritura de una dama afrancesada: María Mercedes de Santa Cruz y Montalvo." In *Para Emilio Palacios*, ed. Álvarez Barrientos and Herrera Navarro, 113–35.

Maceiras Rey, Carmen. "Las niñas abandonadas: la Inclusa de Madrid y el Colegio de la Paz, (1807–1934)." PhD diss., Universidad Complutense de Madrid, 2018. eprints.ucm.es/48343/.

Madoz, Pascual. *Diccionario geográfico-estadístico-histórico de España y sus posesiones de Ultramar: Madrid*. Madrid: Agualarga, 1999. Partial reproduction of 1845–50 edition.

Maierhofer, Waltraud, Gertrud M. Roesch, and Caroline Bland. *Women Against Napoleon: Historical and Fictional Responses to his Rise and Legacy*. Frankfurt: Campus Verlag, 2007.

Martín Gaite, Carmen. *Usos amorosos del dieciocho en España*. Barcelona: Anagrama, 1987.

Martín-Gaite, Carmen. *Love Customs in Eighteenth-Century Spain*, trans. Maria G. Tomsich. Berkeley: University of California Press, 1991.

Martín Valverde, José María. *María del Rosario Fernández: La Tirana (1755–1803), Una actriz en la época de Carlos III*. Sevilla: Fundación José Manuel Lara, 2018.

Martínez Ojeda, Beatriz. "*Don Pélage ou le fondateur de la monarchie espagnole* (1818) de Mme de Rome y la traducción española de Doña Petra Pedregal de Hervás (1828)." In *La traducción humanístico-literaria y otras traducciones especializadas*, ed. Soledad Díaz Alarcón and Eva Parra-Membrives, 59–68. Berlin: Lit Verlag, 2016.

Martín-Valdepeñas Yagüe, Elisa. "Afrancesadas y patriotas: la Junta de Honor y Mérito de la Real Sociedad Económica Matritense de Amigos del País." In *Heroínas y patriotas*, ed. Castells Oliván, Espigado Tocino, and Romeo Mateo, 343–70.

———. "Beneficencia y mujeres en tiempos de guerra: la Junta de Honor y Mérito." *Torre de los Lujanes, Revista de la Real Sociedad Económica Matritense de Amigos del País* 67 (2010): 175–98.

———. "La condesa de Merlin: una criolla en la Guerra de la Independencia." In *Hacia 1812 desde el siglo ilustrado: actas del V Congreso Internacional de la Sociedad Española de Estudios del Siglo XVIII*, ed. Fernando Durán López, 1125–40. Madrid-Gijón: Sociedad Española de Estudios del Siglo XVIII–Trea, 2013.

———. "El eco del saber: La Junta de Honor y Mérito de la Real Sociedad Económica Matritense de Amigos del País y la ciencia en la Ilustración." *Historia Social* 82 (2015): 97–114.

———. "Ilustración, jacobinismo y afrancesamiento: Ana Rodríguez de Carasa (1763–1816)." *Cuadernos de estudios del siglo XVIII* 18 (2008): 33–80.

———. "Ilustrados, afrancesados y liberales: La Sociedad Económica Matritense de Amigos del País durante la Guerra de la Independencia (1808–1814)." PhD diss., Universidad Nacional de Educación a Distancia, 2015. e-spacio.uned.es/fez/view/tesisuned:GeoHis-Memartin.

———. "La reina María Luisa de Parma y la Junta de Damas de la Real Sociedad Económica Matritense de Amigos del País." In *La época de Carlos IV (1788–1808): Actas del IV Congreso Internacional de la Sociedad Española de Estudios del Siglo XVIII*, ed. Elena de Lorenzo Álvarez, 749–61. Oviedo: Instituto Feijoo de Estudios del Siglo XVIII–Sociedad Española de Estudios del Siglo XVIII, 2009.

———. "Relaciones de parentesco entre los miembros de la Sociedad Económica Matritense en el reinado de Fernando VIII (1808–1833)." *Espacio, Tiempo y Forma. Historia Contemporánea* 17 (2005): 13–43.

———. "El retrato de la condesa de Truillas de Agustín Esteve y Marqués (1797)." *Archivo Español de Arte* 361 (2018): 70–78.

———, and Catherine M. Jaffe. "Un espacio femenino para la creación cultural en el Madrid del siglo XVIII: la Junta de Damas de Honor y Mérito." In *Redes y escritoras españolas en la esfera cultural de la primera Edad Moderna*, ed. María Dolores Martos Pérez, 149–166. Madrid: Editorial Iberoamericana-Vervuert, Madrid, 2021.

———, and Catherine M. Jaffe. *María Lorenza de los Ríos, marquesa de Fuerte-Híjar: Vida y obra de una escritora del siglo de las Luces.* Madrid: Iberoamericana-Vervuert, 2019.

Masson de Morvilliers, Nicolas. "Espagne." In *Encyclopédie méthodique ou par ordre des matières: Géographie moderne*, vol. 1. París: Panckoucke, 1782.

Melton, James van Horn. *The Rise of the Public in Enlightenment Europe.* Cambridge, UK: Cambridge University Press, 2001.

Méndez Ródenas, Adriana. *Gender and Nationalism in Colonial Cuba: The Travels of Santa Cruz y Montalvo, Condesa de Merlin.* Nashville: Vanderbilt University Press, 1998.

Méndez Vázquez, Josefina. *Formación profesional de las mujeres en las escuelas de la Matritense: un proyecto político-económico en la España ilustrada.* Oviedo: Editorial Trabe, 2016.

———. "La Junta de Damas y las Escuelas Femeninas de Formación Profesional (1787–1811)." *Cuadernos de Estudios del siglo XVIII* 14 (2004): 113–38.

Mendigorría, Marqués de [Fernando Fernández de Córdova]. *Mis memorias íntimas,* vol. 1. Madrid: Establecimiento Tipográfico Sucesores de Rivadeneyra, 1886.

Miguélez, Manuel. *Jansenismo y regalismo en España.* Valladolid: Imprenta de Luis N. Gaviria, 1895.

Millán García-Varela, Jesús, and María Cruz Romeo Mateo. "Was the Liberal Revolution Important to Modern Spain? Political Cultures and Citizenship in Spanish History." *Social History* 29, no. 3 (2004): 284–300.

Molas Ribalta, Pere. "Las primeras damas de la Orden de María Luisa." *Trocadero* 12–13 (2001): 265–75.

Molina, Álvaro. "De mujer fuerte a ciudadana: Modelos heroicos femeninos a través del arte del grabado." In *El dominio de la realidad y la crisis del discurso: El nacimiento de la conciencia europea,* ed. Concepción Camarero Bullón and Juan Carlos Gómez Alonso, 77–111. Madrid: Ediciones Polifemo, 2017.

———. *Mujeres y hombres en la España ilustrada: Identidad, género y visualidad.* Madrid: Cátedra, 2013.

———. "Retratos de españoles ilustres con un epítome de sus vidas: Orígenes y gestación de una empresa Ilustrada." *Archivo Español de Arte* 353 (2016): 43–60.

———, and Jesusa Vega. *Vestir la identidad, construir la apariencia: La cuestión del traje en la España del siglo XVIII.* Madrid: Ayuntamiento de Madrid, 2005.

Montengón, Pedro. *Eudoxia, hija de Belisario.* Madrid: Casa de Sancha, 1793.

Montesino, Pablo. *Manual para los Maestros de Escuela de Párvulos publicado por la Sociedad encargada de propagar y mejorar la educación del pueblo.* Madrid: Imprenta Nacional, 1840.

Montijo, Countess of [María Francisca de Sales de Portocarrero y Zúñiga]. *Elogio de la Señora Doña Petra de Torres Feloaga, Marquesa de Valde-Olmos y de la Torrecilla, por la Excelentísima Señora Condesa del Montijo, leído en la junta de Señoras de honor y mérito, el día 27 de Junio de 1797.* Madrid: Imprenta de Sancha, 1797.

Montoya, Alicia C. "Marie Leprince de Beaumont (1711–1780): A popular religious pedagogue." In *Women, Enlightenment and Catholicism,* ed. Lehner, 22–34.

Morant Deusa, Isabel, ed. *Historia de las mujeres en España y América Latina.* Madrid: Editorial Cátedra, 2006.

Moreno Alonso, Manuel. *Memorias inéditas de un ministro ilustrado: Francisco Saavedra.* Sevilla: Editorial Castillejo, 1992.

Navarrete Martínez, Esperanza. *La Academia de Bellas Artes de San Fernando y la pintura en la primera mitad del siglo XIX.* Madrid: Fundación Universitaria Española, 1999.

Negrín Fajardo, Olegario. *Educación popular en la España de la segunda mitad del siglo XVIII.* Madrid: Universidad Nacional de Educación a Distancia, 1987.

————. *Ilustración y Educación: La Sociedad Económica Matritense*. Madrid: Editora Nacional, 1984.

Novísima Recopilación de las Leyes de España. 6 vols. Madrid: Imprenta Real, 1805–7.

Nussbaum, Felicity. *The Global Enlightenment*. Baltimore: Johns Hopkins University Press, 2003.

O'Brien, Karen. *Women and Enlightenment in Eighteenth-Century Britain*. Cambridge, UK: Cambridge University Press, 2009.

Ofalia, Countess of [María de los Dolores Salavert y Torres]. *Memoria expositiva de la situación de la Inclusa y Colegio de niñas de la Paz, en seis de mayo de mil ochocientos veinte y cinco: Presentada a la Real Junta de Señoras por su presidenta la Excma. Señora condesa de Ofalia*. Madrid: Imprenta que fue de García, 1825.

O'Farrill, Gonzalo. *A D. Pedro Miguel Sáenz de Santa María y Carassa: Carta de su padre político D. Gonzalo O-Farrill, Sobre la vida y buenos ejemplos de su Madre*. París: n.p., 1817.

Offen, Karen. *European Feminisms 1700–1950: A Political History*. Stanford, CA: Stanford University Press, 2000.

Olmeda y León, Joseph de la. *Oda en elogio de las señoras de la Asociación, por el nuevo establecimiento Reservado*. Madrid: Imprenta de Ramón Ruiz, 1797.

Ortega López, Margarita. "El Siglo XVIII." In *Las mujeres de Madrid como agentes de cambio social*, 3–55. Madrid: Instituto Universitario de Estudios de la Mujer, 1994.

Outram, Dorinda. *The Enlightenment*. 3rd ed. Cambridge, UK: Cambridge University Press, 2013.

Oviedo, Francisco Javier de. *Memoria sobre el crédito público: y medios de satisfacer la deuda general de España*. Sevilla: Imprenta de Bartolomé Caro Hernández, 1821.

Pagden, Anthony. *The Enlightenment and Why It Still Matters*. New York: Random House, 2013.

Pal, Carol. *The Republic of Women: Rethinking the Republic of Letters in the Seventeenth Century*. Cambridge, UK: Cambridge University Press, 2012.

Palau y Dulcet, Antonio. *Manual del librero hispanoamericano: bibliografía general española e hispano-americana desde la invención de la imprenta hasta nuestros tiempos*. 28 vols. Barcelona: Librería Palau, 1948–77.

Palma García, Dolores. "Las Escuelas Patrióticas creadas por la Sociedad Económica Matritense de Amigos del País en el siglo XVIII." *Cuadernos de Historia Moderna y Contemporánea* 5 (1984): 37–56.

Pascua Sánchez, María José de la, and Gloria Espigado Tocino, eds. *Frasquita Larrea y Aherán: Europeas y españolas entre la Ilustración y el Romanticismo (1750–1850)*. Cádiz: Universidad de Cádiz–Ayuntamiento de El Puerto de Santamaría, 2003.

Pérez Cantó, Pilar, and Esperanza Mó Romero. "Las mujeres en los espacios ilustrados madrileños." *Signos históricos* 7, no. 13 (2005): 43–69.

Pérez Hernández, María Isabel. *Correspondencia de la Duquesa de Osuna con Pepe-Hillo y Pedro Romero*. Madrid: Unión de Bibliófilos Taurinos, 2014.

Pérez Martín, María Ángeles. "Ilustres e ilustradas: Académicas de Bellas Artes en España (ss. XVIII–XIX)." PhD diss., Universitat de València, 2018.

Pérez Moreda, Vicente. "La Junta de Damas y las inclusas españolas." *Boletín de la Real Academia de la Historia* 208, no. 2 (2011): 13–34.

Pérez Núñez, Javier. "Del Ministerio del Interior al de la Gobernación: El gobernador civil de Madrid en tiempo del Estatuto Real (1834–1836)." *Anuario de Historia del Derecho Español* 77 (2007): 255–375.

Pérez Sarrión, Guillermo. "Casual poverty in the Spanish Enlightenment: Josefa Amar y Borbón and the Real Sociedad Económica Aragonesa de Amigos del País." *Dieciocho: Hispanic Enlightenment* 25, no. 2 (2003): 265–94.

Petrovich, Vesna Crnjanski. "Women and the Paris Academy of Sciences." *Eighteenth-Century Studies* 32, no. 3 (1999): 383–90.

Picó Pascual, Miguel Ángel. *El padre Antonio Eximeno Pujades*. Valencia: Alfons el Magnánim, 2003.

Pinches, Silvia. "Women as Objects and Agents of Charity in Eighteenth-Century Birmingham." In *Women and Urban Life in Eighteenth-Century England: "On the Town,"* ed. Rosemary Sweet and Penelope Lane, 65–85. Aldershot: Ashgate, 2003.

Piquer, Andrés. *Praxis médica: ad usum Scholae Valentinae*. Madrid: Apud Benedictum Cano, 1786.

Poovey Mary. *Making a Social Body: British Cultural Formation, 1830–1864*. Chicago: University of Chicago Press, 1995.

Portillo Valdés, José María. *Revolución de nación: orígenes de la cultura constitucional en España*. Madrid: BOE, 2009.

Poulain de la Barre, François. *De l'éducation des dames pour la conduite de l'esprit dans les sciences et dans les mœurs*. Paris: Chez Jean Du Puis, 1674.

———. *De l'excellence des hommes, contre l'égalité des sexes*. Paris: Chez Jean Du Puis, 1675.

Pumar Martínez, Carmen. *Don Antonio Amar y Borbón: último virrey del Nuevo Reino de Granada*. Borja: Centro de Estudios Borjanos, 1991.

Quintana Bermúdez de la Puente, Covadonga de. "La galería de retratos de los directores de la Real Academia Española en los documentos de su archivo: Los seis primeros retratos." *BILRAE* 12 (2019): 70–97.

Real cédula de S.M. y señores del Consejo, por la cual se aprueben los estatutos de la Real Junta de Damas creada para el gobierno de los estudios de dibujo y de adorno destinados a la enseñanza de la juventud de su sexo. Madrid: Imprenta Real, 1819.

Regueras Grande, Fernando. *Pimentel, fragmentos de una iconografía*. Benavente: Centro de Estudios Benaventanos Ledo del Pozo, 1998.

Remón Menéndez, Juan F. "The Alameda of the Duchess of Osuna: A Garden of Ideas." *Journal of Garden History* 13, no. 4 (1993): 224–40.

Respuesta a las objeciones que se han hecho contra el proyecto de un traje nacional para las damas. Madrid: Imprenta Real, 1788.

Richardson, Samuel. *Clara Harlowe: Novela traducida del inglés al francés por Mr. le Tourneur, siguiendo en todo la edición original revista por su autor Richardson, y del francés al castellano Don Joseph Marcos Gutiérrez.* Madrid: Imprenta de Fermín Villalpando, 1795.

Ríos Izquierdo, Pilar, and Ana Rueda Roncal. "Análisis de las normas jurídicas de la Junta de Damas de Honor y Mérito." *Torre de los Lujanes* 13 (1989): 151–61.

Rodríguez de Campomanes, Pedro. "Memoria sobre el establecimiento de escuelas patrióticas de hilados." In *Memorias de la Sociedad Económica*, vol. 2: 50–56. Madrid: Imprenta de Antonio Sancha, 1780.

Rome, Mme de [Marné de Morville]. *Pelayo, restaurador de la monarquía española,* trans. Petra Pedregal de Hervás. Madrid: Imprenta de Pedro Sanz, 1828.

Romeo Mateo, María Cruz. "Concepción Arenal: Reformar la sociedad desde los márgenes." In *Liberales eminentes,* ed. Manuel Pérez Ledesma and Isabel Burdiel Bueno, 213–44. Madrid: Marcial Pons, 2008.

———. "Destinos de mujer: esfera pública y políticos liberales." In *Historia de las mujeres en España y América Latina,* ed. Morant Deusa, vol. 3: 61–83.

———. "Juana María de la Vega, condesa de Espoz y Mina (1805–1872): Por amor al esposo, por amor a la patria." In *Liberales, agitadores y conspiradores: Biografías heterodoxas del siglo XIX,* ed. Isabel Burdiel Bueno and Manuel Pérez Ledesma, 209–38. Madrid: Espasa Calpe, 2000.

———, and María Sierra Alonso, eds. *Historia de las culturas políticas en España y América Latina. La España liberal 1833–1874,* vol. 2. Zaragoza: Marcial Pons-Prensas Universidad de Zaragoza, 2014.

Rose-de Viejo, Isidora. "Ni Goya, ni Esteve, sino Poza: el retrato de la XI[a] marquesa de Espeja y otras obras suyas." *Archivo Español de Arte* 337 (2012): 37–54.

Rueda Roncal, Ana, Pilar Ríos Izquierdo, and María Esperanza Zábalo Rojas. "Carlos III y la Junta de Damas." *Torre de los Lujanes* 12 (1989): 113–25.

Sáez Ordóñez, Pedro. "De la supresión de la mendicidad, y organización de las juntas de caridad." In *Memorias premiadas en 1850 por la Sociedad Económica Matritense, sobre la extinción de la Mendicidad, y el establecimiento de las Juntas de Caridad.* Madrid: Imprenta de Sordo-mudos, 1851.

Sagra, Ramón de la. *Discurso leído el día 2 de enero de 1842 en la apertura de la escuela dominical para artesanos, establecida en el Instituto Español.* Madrid: Compañía Tipográfica, 1842.

———. *Lecciones de Economía social.* Madrid: Imprenta de Ferrer y Compañía, 1840.

Salas Valdés, Mario de la. *Obelisco Histórico en honor de los heroicos defensores de Zaragoza en sus dos sitios (1808–1809)*. Zaragoza: Imprenta de M. Salas, 1908.

Salaverri Baro, Fátima. "La Junta de Damas como modelo de acción social de género: aproximación a su constitución en Cádiz a principios de siglo XIX." In *Mujeres e Investigación: Aportaciones interdisciplinares: VI Congreso Universitario Internacional "Investigación y Género,"* ed. Carmen García-Gil, Consuelo Flecha García, María Jesús Carrillo, Marina Núñez Gil, and Ana Guil Bozal, 367–646. Sevilla: Seminario Interdisciplinar de Estudios de las Mujeres de la Universidad de Sevilla, 2016.

San Narciso Martín, David. "Políticas desde las cámaras de Palacio: Las Camareras Mayores en la España liberal (1808–1868)." *Aportes* 96 (2018): 9–31.

Santos Arrebola, María Soledad. "Las mujeres en la familia de los Gálvez de Macharaviaya." In *Historia(s) de mujeres en homenaje a María Teresa López Beltrán*, vol. 2, ed. Pilar Pezzi Cristóbal, 245–56. Málaga: Perséfone-Ediciones Electrónicas de la AEHM-UMA, 2013.

Sarrailh, Jean. *La España ilustrada de la segunda mitad del siglo XVIII*. México: Fondo de Cultura Económica, 1979.

Saugnieux, Jöel. *Le jansénisme espagnol du XVIIIe siècle: ses composantes et ses sources*. Oviedo: Instituto Feijoo de estudios del siglo XVIII, 1975.

Schroeder, Anne L. "Going Public against the Academy in 1794: Mme de Genlis Speaks out on Gender Bias." *Eighteenth-Century Studies* 32, no. 3 (1999): 376–82.

Schulz, Andrew. "Goya's Portraits of the Duchess of Osuna: Fashioning Identity in Enlightenment Spain." In *Women, Art and the Politics of Identity in Eighteenth-Century Europe*, ed. Melissa Hyde and Jennifer Milam, 263–83. Aldershot: Ashgate, 2003.

Schurman, Anna Maria van. *Whether a Christian Woman Should Be Educated and Other Writings from Her Intellectual Circle*, ed. and trans. Joyce L. Irwin. Chicago: University of Chicago Press, 1998.

Scott, Joan Wallach. *The Fantasy of Feminist History*. Durham, NC: Duke University Press, 2011.

———. *Gender and the Politics of History*. New York: Columbia University Press, 1999.

Sebold, Russell P. "Hórrido yermo de inflamada arena: Cienfuegos y el dolor cósmico romántico." *Cuadernos Dieciochistas* 10 (2009): 75–85.

Seixo, Vicente del. *Discurso filosófico y económico político sobre la capacidad ó incapacidad natural de las mujeres para las ciencias y las artes*. Madrid: Imprenta de Repullés, 1801.

———. *Instrucción cristiana, política, y civil, sobre la cual se forma la felicidad de un matrimonio*. Madrid: Imprenta de Gerónimo Ortega e hijos de Ibarra, 1790.

Sempere y Guarinos, Juan. "Sociedad Económica de Madrid." In *Ensayo de una biblioteca española de los mejores escritores del reinado de Carlos III*, vol. 5: 178–218. Madrid: Imprenta Real, 1789.

Sepinwall, Alyssa Goldstein. "Robespierre, Old Regime Feminist? Gender, the Late Eighteenth Century and the French Revolution Revisited." *Journal of Modern History* 82 (2010): 1–29.

Serrano Jerez, Elena. "Bookkeeping for Caring: Notebooks, Parchment Slips and Enlightened Medical Arithmetic in Madrid's Foundling House." In *Working with Paper: Gendered Practices in the History of Knowledge*, ed. Carla Bittel, Elaine Leong, and Christine von Oertzen, 77–90. Pittsburgh: University of Pittsburgh Press, 2019.

———. "Chemistry in the City: The Scientific Role of Female Societies in Late Eighteenth-Century Madrid." *Ambix: Journal of the Society for the History of Alchemy and Chemistry* 60, no. 2 (2013): 139–59.

———. "Science for Women in the Spanish Enlightenment (1753–1808)." PhD diss., Universitat Autònoma de Barcelona, 2012. https://www.tdx.cat/handle/10803/284493#page=1.

———. "Sex and Prisons: Women and Spanish Penitentiary Reform, 1787–1808." *Journal for Eighteenth-Century Studies* 42, no. 4 (2019): 501–17.

———. *Women and Science in the Spanish Enlightenment: Making Useful Knowledge.* Pittsburg: University of Pittsburg Press, 2022.

Settala, Ludovico. *De ratione instituendae et gubernandae familiae.* Mediolani: Giovanni Battista Bidelli, 1626.

Shafer, Robert Jones. *The Economic Societies in the Spanish World, 1763–1821.* Syracuse: Syracuse University Press, 1958.

Sheriff, Mary. *The Exceptional Woman: Elisabeth Vigée-Lebrun and the Cultural Politics of Art.* Chicago: University of Chicago Press, 1996.

Sherwood, Joan. "El niño expósito: cifras de mortalidad de una inclusa del siglo XVIII." *Anales del Instituto de Estudios Madrileños* 18 (1981): 299–312.

———. *Poverty in Eighteenth-Century Spain: The Woman and Children of the Inclusa.* Toronto: University of Toronto Press, 1988.

Shubert, Adrian. *Espartero, el Pacificador.* Barcelona: Galaxia Gutenberg, 2018.

Siskin, Clifford, and William Warner, eds. *This Is Enlightenment.* Chicago: University of Chicago Press, 2010.

Smith, Theresa Ann. *The Emerging Female Citizen: Gender and Enlightenment in Spain.* Los Angeles: University of California Press, 2006.

Soria, Martín. *Agustín Esteve y Goya.* Valencia: Institución Alfonso el Magnánimo, 1957.

Stapelbroek, Koen, and Jani Marjanen, eds. *The Rise of Economic Societies in the Eighteenth Century: Patriotic Reform in Europe and North America.* New York: Palgrave Macmillan, 2012.

Steinbrügge, Lieselotte. *The Moral Sex: Women's Nature in the French Enlightenment.* Oxford, UK: Oxford University Press, 1995.

Stuurman, Siep. *François Poulain de la Barre and the Invention of Modern Equality.* Cambridge, MA: Harvard University Press, 2004.

Sullivan, Constance A. "Josefa Amar y Borbón and the Royal Aragonese Economic Society (with documents)." *Dieciocho: Hispanic Enlightenment* 15, no. 1–2 (1992): 95–148.

Taylor, Barbara. *Mary Wollstonecraft and the Feminist Imagination.* Cambridge, UK: Cambridge University Press, 2003.

Terral, Mary. "Gendered Spaces, Gendered Audiences: Inside and Outside the Paris Academy of Sciences." *Configurations* 3, no. 2 (1994): 207–32.

Thomas, Antoine Léonard. *Historia, ó Pintura del carácter, costumbres, y talento de las mugeres en los diferentes siglos.* Madrid: Oficina de Miguel Escribano, 1773.

Tito Livio. *Décadas de Tito Livio, Príncipe de la Historia Romana traducidas al castellano por Fr. Pedro de Vega, del orden de S. Jerónimo; corregidas y aumentadas posteriormente por Arnaldo Byrkman.* 3 vols. Madrid: Imprenta Real, 1793–94.

Tomsich, Maria Giovanna. *El jansenismo en España, Estudio sobre ideas religiosas en la segunda mitad del siglo XVIII.* Madrid: Siglo XXI, 1972.

Tratchevsky, Alexandre. "L'Espagne à l'époque de la Révolution française." *Revue Historique* 31 (May–August 1886): 1–55.

Trojani, Cécile Mary. *L'écriture de l'amitié dans l'Espagne des Lumières: la Real Sociedad Bascongada de los Amigos del País, d'après la source épistolaire.* Toulouse: Presses Universitaires du Mirail, 2004.

Urzainqui Miqueleiz, Inmaculada. *"Catalin" de Rita de Barrenechea y otras voces de mujeres en el siglo XVIII: Estudio introductorio de Inmaculada Urzainqui.* Vitoria: Editorial Ararteko, 2006.

Vázquez Madruga, María Jesús. *María Isidra Quintina de Guzmán y de la Cerda: La Doctora de Alcalá.* Alcalá de Henares: Ayuntamiento de Alcalá de Henares, 1999.

Veiga Alonso, Xosé Ramón. "Modelos de feminidad: Juana de Vega, condesa de Espoz y Mina, en la cultura política liberal progresista del siglo XIX." *Historia contemporánea* 56 (2018): 47–80.

Vicente, Marta V. *Debating Sex and Gender in Eighteenth-Century Spain.* Cambridge, UK: Cambridge University Press, 2017.

Vidal Galache, Florentina. "El impacto de la Ley General de Beneficencia de 1822 en Madrid." *Revista de la Facultad de Geografía e Historia* 1 (1987): 41–56.

———, and Benicia Vidal Galache. *Bordes y bastardos: una historia de la Inclusa de Madrid.* Madrid: Compañía Literaria, 1994.

Villafranca, Dowager Marquise of [María Tomasa Palafox y Portocarrero]. *Memoria expositiva de la situación de la Inclusa y Colegio de la Paz, en fin de diciembre de mil ochocientos veinte, presentada a la Real Junta de Señoras por su presidente la Excelentísima Señora.* Madrid: Imprenta del Censor, 1821.

Villafranca, Marquise of [María Tomasa Palafox y Portocarrero]. *Elogio a la reina nuestra señora Dª María Isabel de Braganza, leído en virtud del acuerdo de la Junta de Señoras de esta corte, por la Excma. Señora . . . Duquesa de Medinasidonia, en la sesión celebrada el día 17 de febrero de 1819, con superior permiso.* Madrid: Imprenta de Repullés, 1819.

———. *En la apertura de la Sociedad Patriótica, La Excelentísima Señora Marquesa de Villafranca, su Presidenta, dijo lo siguiente.* Cádiz: Imprenta de Josef Antonio Niel Hijo, 1811.

———. *Memoria instructiva de los negocios de la Real Junta de Señoras de Honor y Mérito, presentada por su presidenta la Excelentísima Señora . . . duquesa de Medinasidonia.* Madrid: Imprenta de Sancha, 1819.

———. *Memoria instructiva de los negocios de la Real Junta de Señoras de Honor y Mérito, presentada por su presidenta la Excelentísima Señora . . . Duquesa de Medinasidonia.* Madrid: Imprenta de Repullés, 1820.

Ward, Bernardo. *Obra pía y eficaz modo para remediar la miseria de la gente pobre de España.* Madrid: Imprenta de Marín, 1767.

Williams, Raymond. *Keywords: A Vocabulary of Culture and Society.* Rev. ed. New York: Oxford University Press, 1983.

Wollstonecraft, Mary. *Thoughts on the Education of Daughters: With Reflections on Female Conduct, in the More Important Duties of Life.* London: J. Johnson, 1787.

———. *Vindicación de los derechos de la mujer,* ed. Isabel Burdiel Bueno. Madrid: Editorial Cátedra, 1994.

———. *A Vindication of the Rights of Woman* and *A Vindication of the Rights of Man,* ed. Janet Todd. Oxford, UK: Oxford University Press, 1993.

———. *A Vindication of the Rights of Woman with Strictures on Political and Moral Subjects.* London: J. Johnson, 1792.

Woolf, Stuart. "The *Société de Charité Maternelle,* 1788–1815." In *Medicine and Charity Before the Welfare State,* ed. Barry and Jones, 63–70.

Ximénez de Berdoces, Saturio. *Tratado para afinar el cáñamo, y hacer de él el lino de mar, o de libretas.* Madrid: Imprenta de Sancha, 1793.

Yebes, Countess of. [Carmen Muñoz Roca-Tallada.] *La condesa-duquesa de Benavente: una vida en unas cartas.* Madrid: Editorial Espasa-Calpe, 1955.

Yetano Laguna, Ana, ed. *Mujeres y culturas políticas en España.* Barcelona: Universitat Autònoma de Barcelona, 2013.

Zanotti, Francesco Maria. *Compendio de la filosofía moral, escrito en lengua Italiana,* trans. Marquise of Espeja [Josefa Mónica Alvarado y Lezo]. Madrid: Imprenta de Joaquín Ibarra, 1785.

Contributors

MÓNICA BOLUFER PERUGA is professor of modern history at the University of Valencia and currently principal investigator of the project CIRGEN: Circulating Gender in the Global Enlightenment: Ideas, Networks, Agencies (ERC2017–Advanced Grant 787015). Her research interests include women's writing, discourses on gender, notions and practices of politeness, sensibility and the self, and travel narratives in the eighteenth century, in comparative and transnational perspective. She has published extensively on these issues in Spanish, English, and French, and recently coedited, with Elizabeth Lewis and Catherine Jaffe, *The Routledge Companion to the Hispanic Enlightenment* (2019).

MÓNICA BURGUERA LÓPEZ is associate professor of modern history at the National University of Distance Education, Spain. She holds a PhD in history and women's studies from the University of Michigan. She specializes in gender in political cultures and women's identity in the nineteenth century. She has published *Las damas del liberalismo respetable: los imaginarios sociales del feminismo liberal en España, 1834–1850* (2012). She is coeditor of *Historias de España contemporánea: Cambio social y giro lingüístico* (2008) and coordinator of *Género y modernidad en España: de la Ilustración al liberalismo* (2010).

GLORIA ESPIGADO TOCINO is professor of modern history at the University of Cádiz. She is a specialist in women's history and gender relations in the nineteenth century, concentrating on Spanish women's participation in the political cultures of that century, from liberalism, utopian socialism, republicanism, and anarchism. Her publications include *Aprender a leer y a escribir en el Cádiz del ochocientos* (1996) as well as the coordination of the collective volumes *Mujer y deseo: representaciones y prácticas de vida* (2004), *Heroínas y patriotas: Mujeres de 1808* (2009), and *La Constitución de Cádiz: Genealogía y desarrollo del sistema educativo liberal* (2013).

PALOMA FERNÁNDEZ QUINTANILLA holds a PhD in modern history from the Complutense University of Madrid. She has collaborated in periodicals such as *Historia 16, Cambio 16,* and *Tiempo de Historia.* She was a literary critic for the newspaper *ABC Cultural* and is the author of three monographs: *Mujeres ilustradas en la España del s. XVIII* (1981), *Mujeres de Madrid* (1984), and *La IX Duquesa de Osuna: Una ilustrada en la corte de Carlos III* (2017).

GLORIA FRANCO RUBIO is professor of modern history at the Complutense University of Madrid. Her research centers on the history of everyday life and women's history. Her books include *Cultura y mentalidad en la Edad Moderna* (1998) and *El ámbito doméstico en el Antiguo Régimen: De puertas adentro* (2018), and she coordinated the volumes *Las mujeres, entre la realidad y la ficción: Una mirada feminista a la literatura española* (2008), *Debates sobre la maternidad desde una perspectiva histórica (siglos XV–XX)* (2010), and *Herederas de Clío: Mujeres que han impulsado la Historia* (2014).

CATHERINE M. JAFFE is professor of Spanish literature at Texas State University. She works in modern Spanish and comparative literature, with a focus on eighteenth-century women writers and gender issues in the Enlightenment, translation, and quixotism. Her research has been supported by the National Endowment for the Humanities and the Madrid Institute for Advanced Study. She is coauthor of *María Lorenza de los Ríos, marquesa de Fuerte-Híjar: vida y obra de una escritora del siglo de las Luces* (2019). She coedited *Eve's Enlightenment: Women's Experience in Spain and Spanish America, 1726–1839* (2009) and *The Routledge Companion to the Hispanic Enlightenment* (2020).

ELIZABETH FRANKLIN LEWIS is professor of Spanish at the University of Mary Washington in Fredericksburg, Virginia. Her research specialty is eighteenth- and early nineteenth-century Spanish peninsular literature with a focus on gender. Lewis's book *Women Writers in the Spanish Eighteenth-Century: The Pursuit of Happiness* (2004) was one of the first monographs treating gender and Spanish eighteenth-century studies. She coedited *Eve's Enlightenment: Women's Experience in Spain and Spanish America, 1727–1839* (2009), an interdisciplinary exploration of the question of women and Enlightenment experience in the Hispanic context. She coedited the *Routledge Companion to Hispanic Enlightenment* (2019).

MARÍA VICTORIA LÓPEZ-CORDÓN CORTEZO is professor emerita of modern history at the Complutense University of Madrid. Among her numerous works focusing on women's history are *Condición femenina y razón ilustrada: Josefa Amar y Borbón* (2005), and critical editions of Josefa Amar y Borbón's *Discurso sobre la educación física y moral de las mujeres* (1994) and Madame de Staël's *Reflexiones sobre el proceso de la reina* (2009). She has recently collaborated on *A New History of Iberian Feminisms* (2018) and *The Routledge Companion to the Hispanic Enlightenment* (2020).

ELISA MARTÍN-VALDEPEÑAS YAGÜE holds a doctorate in modern history from the National University of Distance Education, Spain. Her current areas of research focus on the evolution of the phenomenon of eighteenth-century associationism and on the reconstruction of the biographies of eighteenth-century women, studying the collective and individual strategies for the creation and development of feminine consciousness and identity. She participated in an edition of the work of Abbé de Mably, *Derechos y deberes del ciudadano* (2010), and is coauthor of *María Lorenza de los Ríos, marquesa de Fuerte-Híjar: vida y obra de una escritora del Siglo de las Luces* (2019).

JOSEFINA MÉNDEZ VÁZQUEZ holds a PhD in history from the University of Murcia. She specializes in eighteenth-century studies in areas such as women's work and education, and matrimony and daily life in the modern period. She has published *Maternidad, familia y trabajo: De la invisibilidad histórica de las mujeres a la igualdad contemporánea* (2008) as well as *Formación profesional de las mujeres en las escuelas de la Matritense: un proyecto político-económico en la España ilustrada* (2016), and is coeditor of *Historiar la educación de las mujeres en tiempos de cambio (Siglos XVII–XX)* (2020).

ÁLVARO MOLINA is assistant professor of art history at the National University of Distance Education, Spain. He researches various issues of gender roles and identities in eighteenth-century Spanish visual culture. He is author of *Mujeres y hombres en la España ilustrada: Identidad, género y visualidad* (2013) and coauthor of *Vestir la identidad, construir la apariencia: La cuestión del traje en la España del Siglo XVIII* (2005), *Imágenes de la tradición clásica y cristiana: una aproximación desde la iconografía* (2018), and *La decoración ideada por François Grognard: para los apartamentos de la duquesa de Alba en el palacio de Buenavista* (2020).

Index

CPSIA information can be obtained
at www.ICGtesting.com
Printed in the USA
LVHW091041190322
713719LV00026B/85